TERROR & TRUTH

Davis W. Houck, General Editor

TERROR & TRUTH

CIVIL RIGHTS TOURISM AND THE MISSISSIPPI MOVEMENT

STEPHEN A. KING & ROGER DAVIS GATCHET

University Press of Mississippi / Jackson

The University Press of Mississippi is the scholarly publishing agency of
the Mississippi Institutions of Higher Learning: Alcorn State University,
Delta State University, Jackson State University, Mississippi State University,
Mississippi University for Women, Mississippi Valley State University,
University of Mississippi, and University of Southern Mississippi.

www.upress.state.ms.us

The University Press of Mississippi is a member
of the Association of University Presses.

Any discriminatory or derogatory language or hate speech regarding race,
ethnicity, religion, sex, gender, class, national origin, age, or disability
that has been retained or appears in elided form is in no way an
endorsement of the use of such language outside a scholarly context.

A section of the introduction and a version of chapter 5,
"Marking the Past: The Mississippi Freedom Trail and Signs of Racial Truth,"
were originally published as "Marking the Past: Civil Rights
Tourism and the Mississippi Freedom Trail," by Stephen A. King
and Roger Davis Gatchet, in *Southern Communication Journal*,
83.2 (2018): 103–18, doi: 10.1080/1041794X.2017.1404124.

Copyright © 2023 by University Press of Mississippi
All rights reserved

∞

Library of Congress Control Number: 2023019892

Hardback ISBN: 9781496846532
Trade paperback ISBN: 9781496846549
E-pub single ISBN: 9781496846570
E-pub institutional ISBN: 9781496846525
PDF single ISBN: 9781496846563
PDF institutional ISBN: 9781496846556

British Library Cataloging-in-Publication Data available

Dedicated to the Mississippi Movement and Its Descendants

The past that is not past reappears, always, to rupture the present.
—**CHRISTINA SHARPE,** *In the Wake: On Blackness and Being*

I think all these folks are stirring crap up. Every day, somebody's dragging up the race card. Somebody saying we have racial disparity here. If nobody would stir that damn pile of stuff up, it wouldn't stink.
—**JOHN W. WHITTEN III,** attorney, Sumner resident and son of one of the defense attorneys at the Emmett Till murder trial

To forget the Mississippi movement is to lose a precious part of the hope for change in this country.
—**VICTORIA J. GRAY,** field secretary for the Student Nonviolent Coordinating Committee and founding member of the Mississippi Freedom Democratic Party

[Emmett Till] was the first George Floyd.
—**PHILONISE FLOYD,** speaking after the verdict in the Derek Chauvin trial (CNN, April 21, 2021)

CONTENTS

ACKNOWLEDGMENTS xi

PREFACE xv

INTRODUCTION 3

CHAPTER ONE. From Movement to Memory: A Rhetorical History
of Civil Rights Tourism in Mississippi 31

CHAPTER TWO. Breaking Ground: Vernacular Efforts
in Mississippi Civil Rights Tourism 57

CHAPTER THREE. Remembering the Lynching of Emmett Till:
From Experiential to "Dark" Tourism 87

CHAPTER FOUR. Private Spaces, Public Memories:
Mississippi's Civil Rights Historic House Museums 117

CHAPTER FIVE. Marking the Past: The Mississippi Freedom Trail
and Signs of Racial Truth 139

CHAPTER SIX. "This Little Light of Mine": Truth Telling
at the Mississippi Civil Rights Museum 163

CONCLUSION 183

NOTES 203

BIBLIOGRAPHY 243

INDEX 269

ACKNOWLEDGMENTS

The authors wish to acknowledge and thank the following individuals who graciously shared their time and life stories for the oral history portion of this project. Their collective backgrounds, experiences, and wisdom provided valuable insights into the ground-level realities of Mississippi's efforts to promote its civil rights history: Katie Blount, Glen Cotton, Dr. John Dittmer, Dr. Rolando Herts, Emily Jones, Pamela Junior, Charles McLaurin, Danielle Morgan, Dr. Rickey Thigpen, Mayor Johnny B. Thomas, Charlene Thompson, Hezekiah Watkins, and Patrick Weems. Our email correspondence with Dr. Stacy White shed light on Mississippi's historical markers and the public work surrounding Fannie Lou Hamer in Ruleville. We thank Mackenzie Hine, Mychelle Huynh, and Kaitlin Brinker for their help with transcribing several of these interviews.

Our fieldwork benefited from the assistance of several other individuals who are part of the larger constellation of local and state organizations involved in civil rights tourism, especially Bobbie Bound, Bolivar County administrator Will Hooker, Mississippi state senator David L. Jordan, Georgia Sibley, Helen Sims, and Minnie White Watson. Brother Rogers and Kamel King provided invaluable information about the Parchman Penitentiary Mississippi Freedom Trail marker. We are also grateful to Dr. Dave Tell for his collegiality and encouragement, especially during this book's early stages. His book, *Remembering Emmett Till*, is a model exemplar of rhetorical and public memory scholarship.

We were fortunate to have Dr. Maegan Parker Brooks, a rhetorical scholar and noted Fannie Lou Hamer expert, as one of the book's reviewers. Her thorough feedback improved the quality of the manuscript tremendously, and her insight into Hamer memorialization in Ruleville was particularly helpful. We also thank a second (anonymous) reviewer who recommended useful sources and offered suggestions that led to a more nuanced critique of the state's tourism goals. In the end, this book is proof that the peer review process works.

The authors highlight the invaluable contributions of P. Renée Foster, instructor of marketing emerita at Delta State University, and Dr. Amanda Davis Gatchet, department coordinator and associate professor of communication at Montgomery County Community College. Both tirelessly read (and reread) numerous drafts of the book and offered astute feedback every step of the way. To say that they helped improve the manuscript would be an understatement. Foster also accompanied the authors on multiple trips into the field and shared numerous articles that appear in the book's references.

The authors would be remiss if they did not acknowledge the staff at the Museum of Mississippi History–Mississippi Civil Rights Museum, the Mississippi Department of Archives and History, Delta State University's Archives and Museums and the University of Mississippi Department of Archives and Special Collections. Other individuals we would like to thank include Dr. Daniel Grano, who provided a helpful critique of an early draft of chapter 3, and Dr. Trevor Parry-Giles for feedback on our analysis of the Amzie Moore House Museum and Interpretive Center. We also extend our appreciation to the National Communication Association's African American Communication and Culture Division (AACCD). We presented early drafts of several of the book's chapters at AACCD-sponsored panels at NCA conventions from 2017 to 2020. The postpresentation discussions were intellectually stimulating and very supportive.

A special note of appreciation goes to University Press of Mississippi director Craig Gill (as well as others), who enthusiastically supported this project from the very beginning. Other staff members at the press involved in the editing, production, and marketing of the book deserve recognition, especially Jackson Watson (assistant to the director), Steven B. Yates (associate director/marketing director), and Camille Hale, who did an amazing job copyediting the manuscript.

Stephen acknowledges the faculty in the Department of Communication at St. Edward's University: Drs. Billy Earnest, Teresita (Tere) Garza, Stephanie Martinez, Innes Mitchell, Lori Peterson, Nancy Reiter-Salisbury, Teri Varner, and Susan Whiteside. Dean Sharon Nell and the School of Arts and Humanities were also supportive of this project, including providing professional development funding to attend conferences and purchase materials. Stephen would also like to thank Renée, Lajara and his parents for their steadfast support and love.

Roger is deeply thankful for the support of Dr. Jen Bacon, Dr. Hyoejin Yoon, and the College of Arts and Humanities at West Chester University of Pennsylvania, who provided three Research and Creative Activity Grants that funded recording equipment, interview transcription, and most importantly, travel to Mississippi. Our fieldwork would not have been possible without their support. Roger also thanks Catherine Spaur in the Office of Research and Sponsored Programs and the Academic Affairs Division at West Chester University of Pennsylvania, whose Provost Research Grant funded additional transcription labor. Roger extends a heartfelt thanks to Dr. Joshua Gunn, Dr. Barry Brummett, and Dr. Martha Norkunas for their wisdom and mentorship, and to Amanda and Wesley for their enduring support throughout this project—especially during the long periods when he was traveling in Mississippi or sequestered in the basement office trying to meet a looming deadline.

Finally, both authors would like to acknowledge that while publishing norms require one of our names to appear before the other on the front cover, in reality, the book's authorship reflects a seamless collaboration that recognizes complete equity of spirit, diligence, and grace. While coauthoring can have its challenges, this book reflects what happens when it works as it should: both authors working in tandem with unity of vision to advance the seed of an idea that first took shape over eight years ago to the final book you are reading today.

PREFACE

With time, historical amnesia becomes untenable. The truth will come out, or in the case of the Mississippi Civil Rights Museum (MCRM)—the state's preeminent civil rights public memory and tourism site—gush out in blood and bullets, trees and nooses, prisons and torture. The suppressed screams of centuries of oppression and struggle for human rights. Civil rights. Medgar Evers gunned down by a white supremacist in his driveway in June 1963, his blood still visible in the stained concrete. Nearly a decade earlier, Reverend George W. Lee died in explosive gunfire, too, losing part of his face and his life at the hands of unidentified assassins on another dark night in Mississippi. Bullets and assassins. A Mississippi Freedom Trail (MFT) historical marker, dedicated in his honor, sits on a quiet street corner in Belzoni, the self-proclaimed "Catfish Capital of the World." Fannie Lou Hamer's savage beating and sexual assault in a Winona jail cell in 1963 partly inspired her brave and brilliant testimony of that horrific experience on national television during the 1964 Democratic National Convention. She survived but was never the same, and she died in poverty in 1977, her legacy resurrected in a memorial garden in her hometown of Ruleville, Mississippi. Many stayed in Mississippi and continued the fight—Aaron Henry, Amzie Moore, Unita Blackwell. Others, including T. R. M. Howard and Gus Courts, fled the state for their and their families' safety. And Emmett Till, who was not even part of the civil rights movement but became a civil rights martyr after his lynching left his body battered and unrecognizable, is now a cottage industry unto itself, with his face, body, and story drawing tourists from around the world to the Magnolia State.

This book is not about the civil rights movement. Rather, it is about the *memory* of the civil rights movement. But in chronicling how Mississippi is finally acknowledging, in a very real way, the state's role in systemic acts of unimaginable brutality—slavery and rape, torture and lynching, segregation and sharecropping, poverty and child exploitation—we *are* writing about the civil rights movement, too. Its past, its present, and its future. In contrast to the Lost Cause narrative that dominated Mississippi's and other southern states' population for decades with romanticized white supremacy nostalgia, the civil rights movement has been accurately described as the "won-cause" movement. Its hard-fought struggles for the vote, for participatory democracy, for education, and for much, much more, cannot be denied. And fifty years later, the movement's grandchildren, Black Lives Matter and countless other civil rights and nonprofit groups, are pursuing a similar line of justice, resulting in the removal and redesign of the Mississippi flag—the last state flag to publicly legitimatize the Confederacy, in 2020.

But spend any time in Mississippi (or anywhere in the United States for that matter) and the danger of believing the movement "won" is as debilitating as the postracial myth that claims racism and prejudice no longer exist in this country. The impact of the Black Codes that emerged in the post–Civil War South are still with us today. Even passive tourists who visit Mississippi's civil rights memory landscape, particularly in Jackson and the Delta region, will find vivid reminders that the struggle for social justice is not in the past. It is depressingly visible today. Poverty, illiteracy, de facto segregation, food deserts, voter suppression, education inequality, and a host of other social issues reverberate from the past through present-day practices and policies that continue to hold African Americans and other marginalized populations in what Isabel Wilkerson aptly called the country's enduring caste system. As she notes in *Caste: The Origins of Our Discontents*,

> We cannot fully understand the current upheavals or most any turning point in American history, without accounting for the human pyramid encrypted into us all. The caste system, and the attempts to defend, uphold, or abolish the hierarchy, underlay the American Civil War and the civil rights movement a century later and pervade the politics of twenty-first-century America. Just as DNA is the code of instructions for cell development, caste is the operating system for economic, political, and social interaction in the United States from the time of its gestation.[1]

Civil rights tourists examining Ku Klux Klan robes, burned crosses, and columns documenting the state's lynching victims at the MCRM; reading the tragic story and early death of Clyde Kennard (a young Black man who dared to seek admission to Mississippi Southern College, now the University of Southern Mississippi) on an MFT marker; or following the timeline of Emmett Till's lynching at the Emmett Till Historic Intrepid Center (ETHIC) are experiencing the collective memories of how the US caste system feverishly sought to defend itself through legal and extralegal means. At the same time, the story of the people, places, and events of the Mississippi Movement is proof that the caste system is not permanent. The Mississippi Movement was an organized challenge to that system. A caste insurrection. However one frames this movement for social justice, Mississippi's rendering of its past sins through the economic agency of civil rights tourism portends an optimistic future—a future where truth challenges silence and reveals a human story of resistance and resolve in the face of state power and violence. This Mississippi story—and more importantly, how we remember it—is the focus of this book.

TERROR & TRUTH

INTRODUCTION

He's been dead 30 years and I can't see why it can't stay dead.
—ROY BRYANT

An Encounter in Money

Money, Mississippi, is a small hamlet eleven miles north of Greenwood near the eastern edge of the Mississippi Delta. Over the past several decades, this "blip of a place," as one writer referred to it, has become one of the most visited sites by civil rights tourists in the state outside the capital city of Jackson.[1] Indeed, Money is the kind of place that hardly seems a place at all. At first glance, present-day Money would appear to be the unlikeliest of tourist destinations. The first time we came here in 2013, and again in 2016 and 2021, the place was deserted save for a lone freight train that passed by shortly after our arrival. There is little to speak of beyond the Riverside Baptist Church, a dormant volunteer fire station, and a closed, yet renovated, service station where the gas stopped flowing years ago. The buildings that once housed a handful of local businesses lining this short stretch of Leflore County Road 518 opposite the railroad tracks were long gone. There are no visitor centers, no museums, no souvenir shops.

And yet, like the thousands of visitors who had come before us and would most assuredly come after, our journey to Money was inspired by a desire to witness one of the most notorious sites on Mississippi's memory landscape, the entropic remains of the building where Roy and Carolyn Bryant operated Bryant's Grocery and Meat Market from 1953 to 1955. A recent edition of the *Mississippi Official Tour Guide* describes the site's historical significance in no uncertain terms: "The death of 14-year-old Emmett Till outside a grocery store in the Delta town of Money ignited a spark in the hearts of Americans— a spark that launched the civil rights movement."[2] Although the Mississippi Tourism Association's guide misleadingly suggests that Money was the site

Site of Bryant's Grocery and Meat Market in 2016. Photo by Roger Davis Gatchet.

of Till's murder (in truth, he was most likely lynched in a seed barn on the Milam Plantation miles away in neighboring Sunflower County), it is one of many voices that casts this desolate place as the undisputed birthplace of the modern civil rights movement.[3]

Up until the 1980s, the Bryant's Grocery building served as a grocery store under the management of other tenants. The Bryants closed shop in the wake of the trial in which Roy Bryant and his half-brother, J. W. Milam, were acquitted for Till's murder.[4] By 1988 "the store had begun its decline into ruin," and when we saw it during our second trip in 2016, it was little more than a crumbling, vine-covered shell surrounded by sagging plastic orange safety fencing, its front porch and roof long-since collapsed.[5] A loud drone of buzzing insects emanated from the inner side of its buckled walls, further amplifying the sense of decay that enveloped the structure and the rest of the town. As Dave Tell observes in his riveting study of Emmett Till commemoration in Mississippi, there is an inverse relationship between tourists' desire to visit this place and the building's condition—their interest only intensifies the further the building deteriorates. "The greater the ruin, the more urgent the memory," Tell writes.[6]

We made our visit at the end of one long, hot summer day in 2016 and were struck by the newly restored Ben Roy's, a neighboring service station that had fallen into disrepair when we saw it three years earlier. The structure had been recently restored thanks to a sizeable Mississippi Civil Rights Historical Sites Grant awarded by the Mississippi Department of Archives and History (MDAH) in 2011.[7] Ben Roy's is owned by Harry Tribble and Annette Morgan, who, along with their brother Martin Tribble, also own the Bryant's Grocery building. Their father, Ray Tribble, was a juror in the Till trial, giving them a keen interest in the development and commemorative use of both properties. The MDAH awarded the grant despite the fact that the long-defunct service station has no "civil rights history of its own," and now we found ourselves seeking refuge from the hot summer sun underneath the station's front portico, gazing through the large glass windows at an array of 1950s-era memorabilia and pondering the stark contrast between this building and the Bryant's Grocery building.[8]

As we sat taking fieldnotes and considering the site, a cyclist in racing wear on a state-of-the-art bike stopped to chat with us. "What are you doing here?" he asked, with an unmistakable air of suspicion. We described the purpose of our visit and this book project, adding that we felt it was important to uncover our collective past and how that shared history is remembered—so we can learn from it. A white man who lived nearby, the cyclist recounted a conversation with another tourist in this same spot regarding the potential use of county or state funds to restore the remains of the Bryant's building. Pointing to the MFT historical marker that sits between Ben Roy's and Bryant's (the first example of a sustained state-funded effort to promote Mississippi's civil rights history to tourists and a sign that would be vandalized less than a year later), he said that the state's involvement in promoting Till's memory was "like beating a dead horse."[9] He asserted that the story of this place "should be kept in the history books where it belongs." And with that, he got back on his bicycle and rode off.

Of the many spontaneous, unexpected encounters we experienced with both locals and other tourists while conducting fieldwork in Mississippi for this book, none captures its purpose more than this conversation in Money in 2016. Shockingly, the cyclist's assertions reflected a sentiment that appeared in a 1955 *Clarion-Ledger/Jackson Daily News* editorial published soon after the Till murder trial concluded. The paper declared, "It is best for all concerned that the Bryant-Milam case be forgotten as quickly as possible. It has received far more publicity than [it] should have been given."[10] Here in Money decades later, the local cyclist's position on Till's story—to limit access to it, to restrict it to the page of a history book—mirrors what once was the state of Mississippi's own official attitude toward promoting its civil rights history.

The cyclist's perspective, a call *against* civil rights tourism and the public commemoration of cultural heritage sites, was expressed at a conspicuous moment in the state's recent history. When we met him by chance that summer underneath the canopy of Ben Roy's, Mississippi was gaining momentum with what was becoming a burgeoning civil rights tourism industry—an industry that would soon be anchored in Jackson with the opening of the Museum of Mississippi History–Mississippi Civil Rights Museum (MMH-MCRM) the following year. In that context, his comments neatly distilled long-simmering anxieties over civil rights remembrance in a state that was, and is, making extraordinary progress in not only promoting, but *embracing* its civil rights history.

Given the well-developed heritage tourism infrastructure in the sister southern states of Alabama and Georgia, it may seem unthinkable that Mississippi would have long ignored the opportunity to feature its contributions to the civil rights movement as part of tourism in the state. But those contributions and opportunities were largely ignored by the state, especially in Money, which was devoid of interpretive signage until the MFT's inaugural marker was unveiled at the Bryant's Grocery building in 2011.

Rhetorical scholar David Zarefsky once wrote that "history and criticism are not identical, but they are overlapping circles."[11] Like other works of public memory, our book is situated in the overlap between history and criticism. As scholars of communication and rhetoric, our attention turns to how Mississippi *communicates* about its history through various memory-building practices, with a specific focus on tourist sites associated with the Mississippi Movement (and not, for example, plantation or slave tourism). From grassroots vernacular efforts to those implemented under the official umbrella of the state, we explore how the people, places, and events of the movement are represented here-and-now, especially where economic motives underlie promotion to tourists. *Terror and Truth* is a study of Mississippi's civil rights memorial landscape, a vast constellation of sites and experiences where the state's—and, by extension, the nation's—public and collective memories of the movement and its legacy are enshrined, constructed, and contested. Rather than strictly chronicle the lives of the activists that drove the Mississippi Movement, we consider instead the sites and artifacts marketed to heritage tourists in the Magnolia State. Subsequent chapters explore how these memory sites actively shape our interpretation of the past symbolically in the service of particular local, state, and national interests.

Broadly speaking, public memory sites refer to those spaces and structures where the past is evoked materially and mediated for public consumption through curated museum displays, monuments carved from granite, or the stories of fallen heroes emblazoned in historical markers, as well as films and other popular culture texts. These artifacts are comprised of what rhetorical theorist Michael Calvin McGee calls textual fragments, a constellation of rhetorical "scraps and pieces of evidence" that are not singular texts so much as "a dense reconstruction of all the bits of other discourses from which it was made."[12] A common thread running through this literature is the belief that the past has special significance to social actors in the present, a significance that goes beyond the human desire to chronicle our collective history for future generations. As communication scholar Bruce E. Gronbeck has argued, the past can be understood "as prologue for varied social dramas: political deliberation over future action, economic controversy over what indicators of supply affect what indexes of demand, myths of origin that ground the religious dogma and the collective identity of a people, and repository of the neuroses and psychoses that affect us individually and collectively."[13]

In contrast to traditional history, which draws on primary source documents (archival records, oral histories, and so forth) to chronicle the past, public memory examines how that history is re-presented for contemporary audiences. It is an act of translation, interpretation, and curation, whereby complex histories are distilled into accessible narratives that can take a dizzying array of forms depending on the medium through which they are presented, from a bronze statue to a one-hundred-word abstract cast onto a roadside marker to a more complex museum display, replete with captioned photographs, video or audio recordings, and interactive touch screens. In contrast to history, which is often associated with the pages of books, public memory is distinct for its *publicness*—it is always located somewhere, some *place*, and these "locations value and legitimate some views and voices, while ignoring or diminishing others."[14] By engaging visitors' senses and directing them, both physically and cognitively, through the places they inhabit, public memory sites "encode power and possibility."[15]

In the field of rhetorical studies, work in public memory often addresses sites' ideological character and the way they shape, promote, or challenge a society's values. For example, Kendall R. Phillips describes public memory as "fragmentary, mutable, and always fleeting," and Sara R. Kitsch observes that it is "necessarily partial"—characterizations that both reinforce why it is also a dynamic, and often contentious, site of struggle over meaning and power.[16] From this perspective, public memory is more about the present than simply remembering the distant past. As Carole Blair, Greg Dickinson, and Brian L. Ott argue, public memory sites are spaces where "groups tell their pasts to themselves and others as ways of understanding, valorizing, justifying, excusing, or subverting conditions or beliefs of their current moment."[17] Public memory is, simply put, a site of active struggle over what happened in the past and how—and more importantly, why—we remember it in the present.

As a public memory project, *Terror and Truth* examines how we communicate about the past and how that past is ultimately interwoven with the present and future. The collective fascination with civil rights history and how it is promoted for touristic consumption reveals contemporary anxieties regarding our current social, cultural, and political climate. Nowhere is this more evident, perhaps, than in ongoing conflicts over the removal of Confederate monuments from public spaces throughout the American South. Although less controversial, the *addition* of civil rights memorials in Mississippi and elsewhere parallels this shifting ground over who and what gets remembered. What does it look like when Mississippi, an impoverished and racially divided state with a long and troubling history marked by systemic racial oppression, lynching, and white supremacy, actively packages its civil rights history for tourists? Whose stories are told? And what perspectives are emphasized or marginalized in the telling of those stories? Most importantly, what can a close study of those stories and those sites teach us about the relationship between race, identity, and public memorialization and how they are reflected in national discourses about our collective past beyond Mississippi's borders?

As we will explore in the following pages, Mississippi has made tremendous, quantifiable progress in developing a civil rights tourism infrastructure and marketing it to visitors throughout the region and nation. Just over a decade ago, visitors searching for many of the state's most prominent civil rights sites, from the Bryant's Grocery building in Money to the Woolworth's location in downtown Jackson where Black Tougaloo College students were attacked during a sit-in at the store's lunch counter in 1963, would arrive (if they were able to find them, that is) only to discover nothing indicating the sites' historical significance. When noted Mississippi civil rights historian John Dittmer returned to the state with a group of university students to tour civil rights sites in the late 1990s, "there was just practically nothing" in terms of tourism infrastructure, he told us. "We had to invent our own way."[18] This previously unmarked terrain—save for the handful of local public memory sites created through grassroots efforts—has changed dramatically and now offers visitors a range of museums, historical markers, memorials, and interpretive centers to explore across the state, bringing some measure of balance to a memorial landscape previously strewn with only monuments to the Confederacy and white supremacy. Many of those monuments still exist, but they are now confronted by civil rights sites that offer an unvarnished look at the horrors inflicted on movement activists and the bravery, ingenuity, and perseverance of those involved in the freedom struggle. Although how that history is framed and the underlying economic motive driving it is problematic at times, one of the goals of civil rights tourism, to achieve social justice through truth telling, is a laudable one.

Skeptics who assume that the state of Mississippi would exploit memory to serve the goal of minimizing or denying the events that took place decades (and centuries) ago will be surprised to learn that truth telling is a significant rhetorical feature in how the state remembers its terrible past. Ironically, while elements of vernacular tourism certainly have engaged in truth telling for years, it actually *expanded* with the creation of major state-led memory projects, especially the MFT and the MMH-MCRM. This is not to say that Mississippi's civil rights tourism industry does not, in some measure, repurpose the state's wrenching civil rights memories for its own ideological purposes. It does, particularly in advancing both the myth that Mississippi is the "birthplace" of the civil rights movement and a progressive narrative that asserts that advances in racial justice and African American political power have been so extraordinary and so sweeping as to render Mississippi "racially healed," or close to it. For this and other reasons that will be explored in this book, Mississippi's civil rights tourism industry is not immune to criticism. Far from it. Nonetheless, this industry, both at the vernacular and official levels, is arguably one of the most powerful efforts in truth telling to date.

As part of this truth-telling narrative, Mississippi's civil rights story is narrated through vernacular and official memory sites that include museums, interpretive centers, roadside markers, and historic homes. Collectively, these various sites remember the Mississippi Movement and the courageous actions of local heroes and grassroots civil rights organizations who risked their lives to challenge the state's racist Jim Crow laws. As a spiritual force for expanding the American experiment in participatory democracy, well-known (Medgar Evers, Fannie Lou Hamer) and more obscure (Amzie Moore) leaders are portrayed asserting their Constitutional rights through a mixture of agitation tactics ranging from marches to demonstrations, sit-ins to strikes. Although some sites embrace truth telling more than others, this story also highlights in a very real way, certainly the most public admission to date, the lengths to which Mississippi would go to preserve its "southern way of life": church burnings and bombings, verbal and physical harassment, beatings and shootings, arrests and imprisonment, and the use of targeted assassinations to quell protest. The predominant narrative theme—Black resistance and white violence—is revealed across multiple sites that embody the appalling violence that engulfed the state and the nation. While not a member of the Mississippi Movement, the memory of Emmett Till's grotesque lynching is strategically deployed, alternatively, as argument for the state's birthplace claim, exemplar of white racism and terror, and justification for the pursuit of social justice, one of the goals of civil rights tourism.

Of course, all memory work is selective in nature, and Mississippi's reinterpretation of its civil rights heritage is no exception. Mississippi's civil rights story largely overlooks the most radical element of the civil rights movement: Black Power, with its philosophy of armed self-defense, rejection of the white ally, and a revolutionary impulse that casts off America's political and economic system—a system the mainstream civil rights movement sought to perfect. And consistent with the memory work of other local and national civil rights projects, the story of the Mississippi Movement, for the most part, subordinates the important role of women played in the movement, a rhetorical strategy scholars call the "Great Man" version of history. Moreover, in most cases, the memory of the Mississippi Movement story is rooted in the safe and distant past, where it avoids the uncomfortable truth that while Mississippi has changed many of its unimaginable ways in the last fifty years, the state (and the nation) still struggles to uphold basic civil and human rights for all its citizens.

The remainder of this introduction lays a foundation for exploring Mississippi's civil rights tourism industry. We offer a historical overview of civil rights tourism in the South and discuss the public memory context in which this industry is situated, its goals, and the characteristics and demographics of civil rights tourists. As we will see in the next section, our encounter in Money—and the counterargument of memory negation—reflects longstanding national efforts to marginalize African American memory building efforts, including the civil rights movement, and relegate it to private and nondominant spaces.

History of Civil Rights Tourism in the South

Until the early 1980s, most southern states did not consider the civil rights movement worthy of memorialization. And certainly, in the minds of many politicians and tourism officials, the movement was wholly inappropriate for the kind of nostalgic mythmaking associated with cultural tourism. Instead, southern states have historically (and enthusiastically) promoted the antithesis of civil and human rights—the institutions of slavery and the Civil War—through battlefields, cemeteries, Confederate statues, plantations, antebellum homes, and slave quarters. These efforts promoted the "southern way of life," casting slavery as a benign institution and the Civil War as a "war against the states," a product of northern aggression. To be sure, memory has been the lifeblood of many variants of southern mythmaking—the Old South, the New South, the Benighted South, the Lost Cause, and the Sunbelt South, to name a few.[19] Historically, tourism officials have exploited the myths of the Old South and the Lost Cause as a means to ground white supremacy and patriarchy as "natural" ways of seeing and acting in the world.

The construction of civil rights memorials was, in no small way, a "watershed event in the commemoration of American history" because African American history rarely occupied public spaces.[20] Instead, African American memory work occurred through a variety of texts including storytelling, sermons, or the renaming of buildings in segregated Black spaces, and it was mostly confined to private and marginalized public spaces.[21] By contrast, public acts of commemoration reflected the values of patriarchy and white supremacy: white men were remembered, and subaltern groups were kept invisible, forgotten.[22] "Civil rights memorials reflect a turning of the tide away from a version of history that underwrote white supremacy," writes cultural geographer Owen J. Dwyer, "toward one that celebrates its downfall." Indeed, "civil rights memorials offer a stunning rebuke to centuries of American public history."[23]

During the 1980s, a number of important organizational efforts and memorialization events served to re-remember the movement and activists, with considerable investment in reappropriating the image and legacy of Martin Luther King Jr. These included the creation of the Birmingham Civil Rights Museum Study Committee in 1981,[24] the passage of historic legislation in 1983 that turned Martin Luther King Jr.'s birthday into a federal holiday,[25] the publication of an Alabama travel guide, *Alabama's Black Heritage: A Tour of Historic Sites* in 1983,[26] the proliferation of renamed street signs to evoke the memory of King and other civil rights activists,[27] and the unveiling of the Civil Rights Memorial in Montgomery, Alabama in 1989.[28] While the construction of these memory sites (and the publication of related tourism brochures and other documents) provided an early foundation for what would later become a full-fledged tourism enterprise, at that time, civil rights tourism was still in its nascent stage throughout the country, lacking a basic material substructure.

While serving as a foundation for future civil rights memory work, this preoccupation with King has had consequences for not only how we remember the late civil rights leader but also how we remember the movement. First, through the nation's memory building practices, King has been transformed into a national mythic figure and, as a consequence, his radical critique of capitalism as well as his opposition to the Vietnam War have been silenced. "Public memory's Martin Luther King Jr. has been ideologically sanitized," writes Edward P. Morgan, "detached from his own politics and their more radical, or system-critical, implications."[29] Second, with almost exclusive focus on venerating King, other civil rights leaders have been virtually erased from the memory landscape including King's mentor, Bayard Rustin, Robert Moses, and other, more radical members of the movement, including Eldridge Cleaver, Bobby Seale, and Robert F. Williams. When asked, most US citizens can name King and Rosa Parks, but struggle when pressed to name other civil rights leaders and activists. Finally, this nearly exclusive focus on King, and to some degree Parks, has not only contributed to the nation's civil rights amnesia, but also obscured the grassroots organizing that was essential to the movement's success and essential to the Mississippi Movement's success. The focus on national leaders or the "Great Man" version of history has "obscured a movement built on the courageous and determined efforts of thousands upon thousands of everyday people—a revision of the past that removes the struggle for justice, and its potential continuity with today's world, from the realm of what 'the people' can do."[30] This is ironic because the MFT, as we will see in chapter 5, features four themes, including grassroots agitation and organizing.

Not surprisingly, the development of sites related to the civil rights movement was met with fierce opposition and beset by internal squabbling, financial difficulties, and bureaucratic red tape, among other obstacles. For example, the decision to recognize Martin Luther King Jr.'s birthday as a federal holiday in 1983 proved to be highly controversial. By 1988, only thirty-eight states officially observed it, with Louisiana celebrating the civil rights leader's birthday only every other year.[31] A handful of states, including Arizona, claimed "that it would be a drain on their treasuries if state employes [sic] are given paid vacations."[32] Noting that street names are an "important and contentious commemorative practice,"[33] Alderman observed that efforts to rename major thoroughfares after King (as opposed to less-traversed streets in marginalized, segregated areas) were met with hostility and protest by "business owners and operators, who cite the financial costs of changing their address and the social stigma, as they see it, of being associated with the black community."³⁴ In yet another example, Memphis's white community decried efforts to transform the Lorraine Motel (the site of King's assassination in 1968) into the National Civil Rights Museum (NCRM).³⁵ For white Memphians, according to then-NCRM executive director Juanita Moore, a national civil rights museum would be a counterproductive move: "White Memphians felt that you just tear it down and put a marker up and that would be it—and not try to keep dredging up the past—they wanted to let it die."³⁶

During the 1990s, civil rights tourism continued to develop as several southern states—including Georgia, Alabama, and Tennessee—promoted their respective civil rights histories. The King National Historic Site in Atlanta, Alabama's Birmingham Civil Rights District, and the NCRM in Memphis are just a few examples of this growing sector of cultural tourism.³⁷ A 1998 *Marketing News* article, "Black Tourism Power," claims that southern communities such as Memphis and Chattanooga began "spotlighting their black history" in 1989 in response to economic recession, the subsequent decline in tourism, and the belief that the "multibillion-dollar black tourism market" was a lucrative source of untapped revenue.³⁸ While the article does not mention Alabama, it was the first southern state to "aggressively market its civil rights past and African-American heritage for tourism purposes."³⁹ Ironically, a key figure in this new marketing scheme was then-governor George Wallace, the outspoken race-baiting segregationist who, by the 1980s, had transformed himself into a "racial liberal" with African American support as evidence of his racial-spiritual conversion.⁴⁰ Glenn T. Eskew argues that the impetus for such a move was rooted in an opportunity to rehabilitate the state's negative image by championing the contributions of its African American citizens.⁴¹ Beyond image management, it was the growing awareness that African American history and civil rights tourism were an untapped source of economic revenue that propelled increased interest in promoting the state's civil rights history.

By the 2000s, interest in promoting civil rights as a viable tourism opportunity intensified. As reported by the *New York Times* in 2004, a "surge of interest in the civil rights movement has dislodged lingering discomfort with the past, bringing new attention to the lunch counters, bus terminals and churches that were the movement's battlegrounds."⁴² A year later, the *Washington Post* had reached the same conclusion. "More and more," its reporter observed, "the tourism industry is awakening to the interest—and profitability—of African American history, from the concrete steps in Fredericksburg, where slaves were bought and sold, to the Black pioneer towns in the West to the scenes of the civil rights struggle in Alabama and Mississippi."⁴³ During the decade, tourism officials, city leaders, local entrepreneurs, and others moved quickly to transform civil rights spaces and events into museums, erect monuments and historical markers and build visitor centers and other structures to memorialize the movement. Moreover, to meet the increasing demands for civil rights tourists, at least four major travel guidebooks were published in the late 1990s and 2000s, with titles such as *Weary Feet, Rested Souls: A Guided History of the Civil Rights Movement* (1998) and *On the Road to Freedom: A Guided Tour of the Civil Rights Trail* (2008).[44]

While Alabama was one of the first southern states to recognize the promise of its own civil rights legacy and history as a potential space to expand its tourism market, Mississippi's official culture apparently believed such efforts would be counterproductive and reinforce long-standing negative perceptions of the state. As we will see in the next chapter, Mississippi's civil rights tourism industry developed gradually, with initial efforts occurring at both the grassroots level and in more official circles. However, it was not until 2011 and the unveiling of the first MFT marker at the site where Emmett Till whistled at Carolyn Bryant in Money, Mississippi, that the state started to actively incorporate civil rights tourism as part of its overall heritage tourism offerings. This brief historical overview of civil rights tourism in the US showcases how African American experiences and memories have moved into the public sphere in ways that seemed unimaginable in the late 1970s. However, this section has not addressed what is at stake when public memory sites in this growing industry attempt to recover Black spaces and re-present the stories of trauma and triumph associated with those spaces. We explore this fundamental issue of memory and power in the section that follows.

African American Identity and Public Memory

"Nothing is more fully agreed," Karen Fields writes, "than the certainty that memory fails."[45] As one of the authors in Geneviève Fabre and Robert O'Meally's important 1994 edited collection that developed out of a years-long seminar series at Harvard and the University of Mississippi, *History and Memory in African-American Culture,* Fields joins the other contributors in dismantling the history-memory dichotomy as they explore its relationship to race, identity, and culture. *History and Memory*, along with others comprising the rich body of scholarship on African American history and memory, informed both our fieldwork in Mississippi and the composition of *Terror and Truth*. Memory is always necessarily constructed, Fabre and O'Meally argue, "slanted by the teller's choice of words and by his or her sense of how to shape a tale. It is a created version of an event snatched from the chaos of the otherwise invisible world gone by."[46] Likewise, their observation (with a nod to Werner Sollors) that history "can imply motives of aggressively willful exclusion" certainly echoes the historical reluctance and refusal of Mississippi's official culture to invest in civil rights tourism.[47] Discussing one of the essays in the collection, O'Meally and Fabre assert that some US memory sites "inspire us to remember, to forget, and even to fabricate untrue stories in support of our familial and national myths of what we wish had happened, the way we wish we were."[48] Reading this, we are reminded of the countless monuments and memorials to the Confederacy that we encountered during our trips to Mississippi and the problematic Lost Cause narratives those sites continue to promote through their very presence on the state's memorial landscape.

Although monuments to the Confederacy continue to pervade the South, communities in Mississippi and other states are employing counterhegemonic memory practices that resist such discourses. Patricia G. Davis's book *Laying Claim* interrogates a litany of these sites, practices, and performances, revealing how they shape conceptions of southerness and its relationship with African American identity. Turning her attention to Civil War history and public memory specifically, Davis shows how artifacts that once "relegat[ed] black people to at best supporting roles and at worst dehumanized caricatures in the very time period that defines their identity as African Americans" now engage in "symbolic annihilation, or the lack of representation, of African American experiences."[49] Although she does not focus on Mississippi, Davis's work highlights why Mississippi's progress in expanding its civil rights tourism infrastructure after decades of inactivity and willful neglect is so significant, while also urging a critical awareness of how representation is articulated in southern states' contemporary public memory sites. Her observation that "stories about the past are really focused on the needs and power relations of the present" is somewhat of a mantra among public memory scholars, and it is supported in her book through careful analyses of Civil War battle reenactments, traditional brick-and-mortar museums, and cybermuseums that traverse digital spaces, particularly those that resist hegemonic memory practices through discourses of vernacular resistance.[50] "Memory is not something that exists," Davis astutely reminds us. "It is, rather, something we *do*, something we produce through social practices. We construct, maintain, represent, articulate, and contest memories."[51]

The active production of a memory infrastructure through touristic sites is fraught with challenges, particularly when memory workers—both vernacular and official—address Mississippi's history of lynching in historical markers, tourism advertisements, museum exhibits, and performances, a subject we address in greater detail in chapters 3 and 5. In *Beyond the Rope*, historian Karlos K. Hill demonstrates how "when lynched black bodies enter narrative discourse, they become a rhetorical instrument" and "a floating signifier that could be fashioned for varying rhetorical purposes."[52] The meanings attached to that signifier change depending on the context and the agents who deploy it. For example, in response to whites' dehumanizing portrayals of Blacks as animalistic rapists who deserved the "justice" dealt by lynch mobs, Hill shows how Black newspapers and activists in the early decades of the 1900s crafted counternarratives framing the victims as "hapless, dehumanized sufferers."[53] By emphasizing "black humanity in the face of white depravity" in this way, these narratives, collectively, were able to shift public perceptions of lynching and influence antilynching legislation.[54] Similarly, Leigh Raiford's work on the use of photographs in these early antilynching campaigns shows how they "reconceived the received narrative of black savagery as one of black vulnerability" and reframed "white victimization . . . as white terrorization."[55] We can see this narrative approach at work in the wake of Emmett Till's lynching in 1955, where Raiford notes how the publication of photographs of Till's corpse "renewed lynching as a powerful symbol of black vulnerability in the struggle for social justice" and inspired others to join the movement for civil rights.[56] Over time, this rhetoric of victimization transformed into what Hill calls more empowering *consoling narratives* that emphasized African Americans' heroic resistance, even when faced with certain death at the hand of white lynch mobs.[57] Once largely absent from Mississippi's memory landscape, visitors will now find both types of lynching narratives circulating in touristic discourses, including the MFT, historic houses, and displays throughout the MMH-MCRM.

In many ways, the vernacular and official sites that now comprise Mississippi's civil rights tourism industry can be read as a reaction to, and a corrective of, the representational practices that erase African American experiences from the state's memorial landscape. Davis identifies several of these practices in plantation tours and historic houses that refer to enslaved Africans as "servants" and actively omit their histories, instead focusing on the white families and slave owners who lived there—even in spaces "where the specter of slavery looms more insistently."[58] Many of the sites examined throughout this book confront whitewashed histories such as these with explicit accounts of Black agency in the struggle for civil rights. That the *state-funded* MMH-MCRM museums do this in such a critical and detailed fashion is a testament to the exhibits' curators, consultants, and designers as well as the state's willingness to not control those narratives. "The result," Susan Neiman observes, "is an honest portrait of a very complicated place that is indeed able to face up to its history—at least as long as it's inside a museum."[59] Although there is much to applaud in the growth of Mississippi's civil rights tourism industry, these public memory efforts (both in Mississippi and elsewhere) are not immune to critique.

The Civil Rights Movement in Public Memory

Despite the extensive scholarship on African American history and memory as well as civil rights movement history, work on civil rights memory has seen less scholarly interest and is primarily confined to cultural geographers. This is ironic given the fact that "some of the most heated battles in the arena of the black freedom struggle are not about resources or laws. Rather, many of today's conflicts revolve around *how* the civil rights movement should be remembered."[60] Civil rights memory scholarship has examined civil rights museums (e.g., the NCRM in Memphis, Tennessee), memorials (e.g., the Carrie A. Tuggle Memorial in Birmingham, Alabama, and the MLK Memorial in Washington, DC), historical markers (e.g., North Carolina highway markers), parks (e.g., Kelly Ingram Park in Birmingham, Alabama), renaming streets after Martin Luther King Jr., racial and gendered attitudes about the past, media representations of the movement, and civil rights tourism.[61]

While obviously supportive of antiracist memory places, civil rights memory scholars have been critical of the manner in which some civil rights memory workers have remembered the movement. For example, as noted earlier, Morgan and other critics decry the memory-building practices that illuminate national leaders over local, grassroots leaders and ordinary citizens (refocusing the public's attention on local heroes is a consistent theme across the sites in Mississippi civil rights tourism, as we will demonstrate throughout this book). Morgan's critique of the Great Man historical narrative also illuminates how the act of remembering has been gendered, revealing the sexism and patriarchy that existed within the movement. In his examination of the intersection of gender and race in the Mississippi Movement in 1964, Steve Estes notes that although the Student Nonviolent Coordinating Committee (SNCC) attempted to replace segregation with a new community based on love, respect, and integration, women in the movement paradoxically experienced both "liberation and discrimination."[62] Civil rights museums and memorials typically favor men—King, in particular—leaving the contributions of women, who played a significant role in directing, organizing, and staffing movement initiatives, underappreciated. Furthermore, when women are memorialized, they are often subordinated in diminutive form, "cast as local actors, whereas men are national and international ones."[63]

Morgan's critique also reveals other limitations of civil rights memory work, including its nearly exclusive focus on the past at the expense of creating an important space for conversations about contemporary racial injustice in the United States. As Dwyer argues in his critique of civil rights public memory sites, "most of the memorials and museums fail to make convincing connections to the present condition of racism in the United States. For instance, little or no mention is made of affirmative action or discriminatory loan policies."[64] The emphasis on the "safe" and distant past at the expense of addressing contemporary issues is inextricably linked to the ground-level realities of planning, constructing, and supporting memory sites that necessitate capital investments from "governmental, corporate, and philanthropic donors."[65] And while their narratives are generally confined to the safe past, these civil rights memorial landscapes, according to critics, are often removed from traditional spaces of power (downtown districts or near city hall) and located in de-facto segregated and economically marginalized areas in Black communities, a stark reality we discovered tracing the MFT during our visits to the state, which we explore in chapter five.[66]

It is in this complex and often problematic public memory milieu that Mississippi began promoting—and continues to promote—its civil rights history to tourists. Although economic motives can never be divorced from any form of tourism, civil rights tourism in Mississippi seeks to achieve a more nuanced set of goals not typically associated with the broader leisure market. In the next section we discuss them in greater detail.

Goals of Civil Rights Tourism

The primary goals of civil rights tourism are three-fold: economic development, image management, and social justice.[67] These goals are interrelated and interdependent, and are similar to other regional tourism efforts as well as Mississippi's more established blues tourism industry. The influx of new tourist dollars, along with opportunities to employ local residents at museums and other civil rights-related businesses, are tangible economic goals associated with Mississippi's newest form of cultural tourism. This is especially apparent at the joint complex housing the MMH-MCRM in Jackson, which has attracted hundreds of thousands of visitors since opening at the end of 2017. In some parts of Mississippi, this economic aim is facilitated by cross-marketing civil rights and blues tourism together. Although the extent to which these two forms of tourism can work together is still unclear, the town of Greenwood has connected Emmett Till and blues icon Robert Johnson through a series of advertisements published in *Living Blues* and other outlets (a problematic juxtaposition we explore more fully in chapter 3). In addition, in March 2018 the Grammy Museum Mississippi, located in Cleveland, hosted an event celebrating the life of Martin Luther King Jr. that included performances by soul blues artists Bobby Rush and Betty Wright. Civil rights-blues music cross-promotional efforts portend future intra-tourism collaboration that is congruent with their shared theme of social protest.[68]

Although the state may benefit financially from civil rights tourism, it is unclear if this will lead to a concomitant positive economic gain for Mississippi's African American communities. Instead, ironically, it may be the case that the state's white citizens will be the primary beneficiaries of a memory industry that condemns white supremacy and domestic terrorism and heralds a movement that advocated for racial-democratic reforms. While tourism is like other for-profit businesses that seek revenue, anthropologist Ronald Loewe cautions against overemphasizing the economic imperative, arguing that this ignores "the many tangible, if small scale, efforts at memorializing and honoring civil rights activists in Mississippi over the last forty years" as well as the "very sincere attempts to educate a new generation of students on civil rights history and, ultimately, improve race relations."[69]

Not only does tourism-based economic development have its own unique set of tensions and ironies, the second goal of civil rights tourism in Mississippi, image management, is particularly vexing for state politicians and tourism officials. Historically, the state has downplayed its civil rights history in an effort to draw attention away from Jim Crow and segregation, violence and lynching, and other atrocities. Interestingly, several regional and state tourism organizations as well as individual businesses now allude to or accentuate *truth* as an important value in telling the state's civil rights history. In *Telling Our Stories*, a book published concurrently with the opening of the MMH-MCRM, historian John E. Fleming—who helped design the Civil Rights Museum's exhibit—argued that its main function is truth-telling:

> Our primary goal in developing this exhibition was to tell the truth. The exhibition does not shy away from the unspeakable horrors of the

Jim Crow era and the atrocities that were committed in the name of preserving white privilege. The exhibition tells the stories of individuals with indomitable spirit who not only survived these horrendous acts of violence, but also emerged triumphant in their search for freedom and the American Dream."[70]

Balancing truth telling with image management becomes both an opportunity and a challenge for state tourism officials, especially as the economic goal casts a shadow over the development and marketing of the state's civil rights memorial landscape.

Perhaps nowhere is this more apparent than in the tiny Delta town of Glendora, home of the Emmett Till Historic Intrepid Center (ETHIC) museum. The museum—the first of its kind to commemorate Till—offers an unvarnished, at times even confrontational approach to detailing Till's gruesome lynching. The town's controversial use of state and federal grant money to fund a commemorative infrastructure around Emmett Till illustrates the complex relationship between tourism, economic development, and truth-telling, a relationship that Tell examines at length in his book.[71]

Within the truth-telling frame, civil rights tourism allows the state to remember leaders and activists of the Mississippi Movement as well as serve an important pedagogical function. Describing the MFT as both a "visitor attraction and an educational tool," the Mississippi Development Authority argues it "recognizes the bravery and courage of the men and women who were a part of the movement in the 1950s, '60s and beyond."[72] The same state organization also uses civil rights tourism as a platform to disseminate an ideology of racial progress and cultural optimism: "Today, Mississippi has more elected African-American officials than any other state in the country, as the civil rights movement continues as a strong element of political, social and daily life."[73]

The promotion of this image of a racially progressive state portends the third goal of civil rights tourism: social justice and the twin concerns of racial reconciliation and social activism. Unburdening truth from denial, telling stories and initiating difficult, but long-overdue conversations, the cooperation between African Americans and whites in shaping how the movement and Mississippi will be remembered are crucial elements that comprise the reconciliation process. In this way, Mississippi's civil rights tourism industry shares common goals with blues tourism in the state, which also seeks to improve the state's image and achieve some measure of reconciliation between Black and white residents.[74]

Racial reconciliation is rooted in Mississippi engaging in "genuine and comprehensive dialogue about its racial past."[75] It involves excavating the truth (especially regarding atrocities inflicted on the state's Black community), communicating that truth in a public way, and taking steps to restoring justice for the victims of white supremacy. Douglas A. Foster cautions us not "to assume ignorantly that racial reconciliation is a search to restore a mythical harmony that once existed," for in doing so we "distort and cover up the truth."[76] Of course, that harmony never existed, as the country's long history of slavery, Jim Crow, and racism makes clear. Instead, racial reconciliation seeks cooperation through dialogue. Even the act of truth-telling, considered by many to be an essential component of any reconciliation process, is fraught with complications. As Ronald W. Walters reminds us, "memory is politicized, raising the question of what constitutes the 'truth' of the past and how to reconcile the contentious perspectives of different versions."[77] Legal scholars Charles J. Ogletree Jr. and Austin Sarat frame racial reconciliation through the lens of respect, noting, "building respect involves producing the conditions for an embrace and appreciation of difference, for a desire that it exist in the world not just grudging acceptance."[78] One strategy for achieving this goal that is currently in practice in Mississippi is the act of the apology, perhaps best exemplified by the Emmett Till Interpretive Center (ETIC) in Sumner. Visitors to the center participate in an *apologia* ritual where they read a resolution crafted by the Emmett Till Memorial Commission (ETMC) that apologizes to the Till family for the violence done to Emmett Till. The extent to which civil rights tourism can foster improved relations between the state's Black and white citizens remains an open question. However, ignoring and denying the current material inequities of race, class, and gender is certainly an impediment to this goal.

In addition to racial reconciliation, social activism calls for tourists to transform into visitor-activists who channel the lessons learned on their sojourns in Mississippi's memorial landscape to fighting for justice in *their own* communities. We argue that this goal is unique to civil rights tourism insofar as it is not common in other forms of leisure tourism, or even blues tourism, in Mississippi, which also strives for racial reconciliation. On some level it is not surprising that a tourism infrastructure based on historical narratives of activism and struggle would seek to inspire similar activism in the present-day, but one of the criticisms of civil rights public memory sites, as we have discussed in this chapter, is its relegation of movement activities to the distant past. But a primary tenet of public memory is that the past is always in the present, and one of the more remarkable elements of Mississippi's civil rights sites—especially its vernacular and official museums, less so its historical markers—is their insistence on asking visitors to continue fighting against injustice. In the next section, we consider who these visitors are.

Civil Rights Tourists: Who Are They?

Even in the midst of a global pandemic, over 24 million visitors chose Mississippi as their destination in fiscal year 2021 (up from 20 million in fiscal year 2020 and similar to the 24.6 million who visited during fiscal year 2019), spending $6.25 billion as they traveled throughout the state.[79] Those numbers continue to grow. By fiscal year 2022, they surpassed 25 million visitors spending $7 billion.[80] It is no surprise that the Mississippi Development Authority's director describes tourism as "one of our top economic drivers."[81] Although it is impossible to accurately determine what percentage of this total came for civil rights-related tourism, interviews with tourism officials and our own experiences as civil rights tourists (and one of us a former long-time resident of Mississippi) provide some insight into the composition of this segment of the overall market.

In developing a profile of the civil rights tourist, it is helpful to consider the state's other popular cultural tourism engine, the blues. One of the authors spent several years studying blues tourism and its effects on the state, culminating in the book *I'm Feeling the Blues Right Now: Blues Tourism and the Mississippi Delta*. There King argues that blues tourists tend to be white fans of the music, which tracks the demographic shift in the genre's audience since the 1960s.[82] This audience is not entirely domestic, as international travelers also come to Mississippi in search of authentic experiences through the blues.[83] Rickey Thigpen, the president and CEO of Visit Jackson (the official tourism office in the state capital) and a member of the US Travel Association's national board of directors, said that the demographic driving blues tourism is "pretty parallel" to civil rights tourists. "Typically, we have an 80/20," Thigpen observed. "Twenty percent African American tourists are interested in civil rights when they come to Jackson. Eighty percent Caucasian."[84] This appears to be true in other states as well. In an interview with the chairperson of the American Civil War Museum's Board of Directors (located in Richmond, Virginia), Davis learned "that the vast majority of those interested in visiting museums, and Civil War museums in particular, are white."[85] Danielle Morgan, Executive Director of the Mississippi Tourism Association, agrees with the demographic overlap with blues tourism, while also noting that "there's a lot of international interest" in the state's civil rights history (by contrast, Thigpen mentioned that at least in Jackson, most international travelers are primarily interested in blues, not civil rights).[86] Moreover, Thigpen finds that Jackson's popularity with the family reunion market and "hub and spoke" tourism, where visitors make Jackson a base for multiple day trips to other parts of the state, is enhanced by the state's trail marker systems and the MCRM. Those public memory sites are "added value" when not the primary driver of visitors' travel plans.[87]

At the risk of oversimplifying what is, admittedly, a shifting and variable demographic, we can nonetheless categorize civil rights tourists into two major groups. The first (and largest) group is comprised of white visitors. Insofar as those visitors overlap with the prevailing demographic for blues tourists, they are more likely to be educated, middle (or upper) class baby boomers, and driven by an interest in history or social justice. Pamela Junior, the director of the MMH-MCRM, notes that the Civil Rights Museum was especially popular with white visitors when it first opened. "We get a lot of whites from everywhere," she told us, including some who travel from overseas.[88] The second, smaller group are African Americans, many who visit Mississippi to see family. According to a study by Mandala Research, this African American segment of the leisure tourism market is less likely than other tourists to spend money on heritage tourism, including visiting sites related to civil rights, thus providing quantitative evidence for Thigpen's observations.[89]

We observed this "80/20" demographic split during our multiple trips to the state. Although we were often the only tourists in sight when visiting markers on the MFT, in every instance where another visitor was there, they were white. The same was true of our tour of the Medgar and Myrlie Evers Home National Monument in Jackson, where we joined another white couple; "white" also seemed to be the dominant racial category for visitors we saw during our multiple trips to the MMH-MCRM.

Reading Texts, Fieldwork, and Oral History

Terror and Truth is rooted in rhetorical criticism, place-based fieldwork, and oral history. During the six-year period between 2016 and 2022, we not only analyzed various tourism rhetorics from print advertisements to tourism websites, but also travelled in Mississippi to broaden and enrich our understanding of how Mississippi is promoting its civil rights heritage. While in Mississippi, we conducted archival research, fieldwork and participant observations, as well as oral history interviews. We participated in over a dozen interviews recorded face-to-face in Mississippi, and later, via Zoom and telephone during the COVID-19 pandemic. We interviewed museum directors, tourism officials, local civil rights entrepreneurs, a historian, and former members of the Mississippi Movement. This mixed-method approach is consistent with projects that engage memory sites including museums, interpretive centers, murals, statues/monuments, ceremonial events, performative rituals, and other rhetorical elements of public memory.[90]

Our primary fieldwork included two joint trips to Mississippi. For a seven-day period in July 2016, we spent much of our time driving through the Delta locating, photographing, and analyzing ten MFT markers installed in multiple locations, from neighborhoods to church grounds to thoroughfares in Money, Ruleville, Belzoni, Marks, Clarksdale, Cleveland, Mound Bayou, and other communities that comprise this well-known region of the Magnolia State. It was during this trip that we encountered the white cyclist in Money and marveled at Helen Sims's brilliant performance at the Mississippi Heritage Consortium, an experience we discuss in detail in chapter 2. Curious about our interest in the "'Black Power' Speech" MFT marker located in Broad Street Park in Greenwood, state senator David Jordan—who as a young man attended Bryant and Milam's trial in September 1955—noticed our out-of-state license plates and stopped to engage us in conversation. We toured the Amzie Moore House Museum and Interpretive Center in Cleveland and made the first of many visits to the Fannie Lou Hamer Memorial Garden in Ruleville. We embarked on a brief journey to Parchman prison in a vain search for the elusive "Parchman Penitentiary" MFT marker. Although the sign was part of the first set of markers in the trail series created in 2011, tourism officials we spoke with were unsure if the Parchman marker was ever installed at a site accessible to the public. Once listed as "under repair" on the state's Visit Mississippi website, it is no longer mentioned there at all. Finally, we heeded the advice of a sign on Highway 49W urging visitors to stop only in case of emergency in this "State Penitentiary Area."

On the same trip, we also created our own Emmett Till tour of sorts. Starting in Tutwiler, which bills itself as the place "where the blues was born," we found a terminally, economically depressed downtown area mired in ruins and the remains of the Tutwiler Funeral Home where Till's body was prepared for the journey to Chicago. A historical marker identifying the site had suffered damage caused by a massive iron beam that had fallen from the crumbling structure. We visited Sumner and toured the ETIC and the restored courthouse where the Till trial was held nearly sixty years ago. During our visit, we heard a story about a white man who tried to remove the state historical marker (identifying the murder trial site) by placing a chain around the marker and hitching it to his truck. (Fortunately, the antagonist was dissuaded from committing this act of vandalism.) Susan Nieman writes about the same story in her excellent *Learning from the Germans: Race and the Memory of Evil* after visiting Sumner in 2017.[91] We also learned about an enraged white man who allegedly chased a fleeing Black man across a field in a military tank. That white man was apparently John W. Whitten III, a local retired defense attorney (and son of John Whitten Jr., who successfully defended Till's murderers): "In 2009, the NAACP accused him of a hate crime for organizing a vigilante mob to pursue an untried, unarmed African American man whom he believed was guilty of burglary. He chased the man in a World War II–era armored tank."[92]

We also played spontaneous blues tourists—a more popular and a more fully state funded form of Mississippi heritage tourism that has been cross-marketed with civil rights tourism in limited ways. We stopped at Dockery Farms, located between Cleveland and Ruleville, where Charley Patton and other blues musicians worked and performed during the early twentieth century. We visited Robert Johnson's "legitimate" gravesite on Money Road en route to see the "Bryant's Grocery" MFT marker and the remnants of the building. We took photos of the colorful juke joint Po' Monkey's, recently closed after its proprietor, Willie Seaberry, had died six days earlier. One of the authors stayed at Clarksdale's two most famous blues lodging haunts: the Riverside Hotel, one of the town's oldest Black-owned businesses, which served as a refuge for African American musicians during Jim Crow, and the much newer and more controversial Shack Up Inn, located on a plantation. The night's lodging was in a rented sharecropper shack decorated with Black Mamie dolls.

Each day during this trip we separately recorded our experiences by hand in notebooks and transcribed them on a laptop in the evening. This double narration helped establish a more accurate and detailed account of our experiences. As noted earlier, this trip was revelatory—it deepened our understanding of the dynamics of civil rights tourism. It also provided continued evidence of the value of seeking alternative epistemologies to the dominant "textual paradigm [that] privileges distance, detachment, and disclosure," a position communication scholar and ethnographer Dwight Conquergood argued years ago.[93] Although our study is not grounded in performance theory, as Conquergood's advocacy was, we did witness performances—some spontaneous and some rehearsed—and followed his call to "go beyond the text" into the immediate, fluid, and indeterminate present and embody the ever-increasing interest among rhetorical scholars to embrace fieldwork and other forms of experiential-driven methodologies.[94]

Nearly three years later, in May 2019, we traveled to the state capitol of Jackson for ten days to continue our fieldwork. The MMH-MCRM had opened a year and half earlier to universal acclaim, as detailed in chapter 6. While we spent most of our time immersed in exploring the MCRM, we visited the nearby Smith Robertson Museum and Cultural Center, housed in the Smith Robertson School that operated as Jackson's first public school for African Americans from 1894 through 1971 and interviewed its director. This museum features a wide-ranging exhibit on Evers and a re-creation of lunch counter protests and violence during the 1960s. Another exhibit, "From Africa to Mississippi," reaches back further in time to trace the rich history and culture of the African continent, the horrors of the transatlantic slave trade (complete with a replica slave ship visitors can step into), and post–Civil War America. One visitor from Nebraska praised the museum, calling it a "hidden gem." "Seeing the bloody clothing of Evers's neighbor hanging on a fence really brings home the lack of justice available for African Americans," they write. "Walking through a cramped and darkened slave ship was eerie and impactful."[95] We couldn't agree more. We also toured the Medgar and Myrlie Evers Home National Monument at 2332 Margaret Walker Alexander Drive, where we listened in awe as Minnie Watson, Medgar Evers's friend and the site's longtime interpretive guide, narrated the final moments of the late civil rights leader's life. Taking advantage of Jackson's status as a geographic hub of movement activity, we were able to visit an additional thirteen MFT markers on this trip, many that were located in the city itself. We toured the Emmett Till Historic Intrepid Center (ETHIC) in Glendora and interviewed the town's mayor and museum director, Johnny B. Thomas, in a field as he took a break from planting crops there. Excursions to Canton, Oxford, McComb, and Hattiesburg rounded out the itinerary. In the years between these two trips in 2016 and 2019, one of the authors would return to the Delta at least twice a year to conduct additional research.

It was during our 2019 trip that we sat down to conduct our first oral history interview. Rickey Thigpen, the CEO of Visit Jackson, welcomed us to his office in downtown Jackson and spoke at great length about growing up there, his education, and work experience. He answered a range of questions about the state's efforts to promote its civil rights history. Thigpen's insightful comment that "tourism is emotions" embodies the experience of the interviewing process itself. The trajectory of most of the interviews led into deeper waters as we explored systemic racism, generational inequity and injustice, and the possibilities of reconciliation and forgiveness. Most of these conversations hit an "emotional core," revealing what blues tourism arguably tries to hide and what civil rights tourism must embrace: the historical realities of America—slavery, lynching, segregation, mass incarceration and other horrors—and their impact on the present. Other interviews in Jackson, Canton, Glendora, and Oxford followed. When the COVID-19 pandemic forced us to cancel a planned two-week trip in the summer of 2020, we recorded the remaining interviews via Zoom or by telephone. Following the best practices of oral history, we engaged with everyone we spoke with as a unique *narrator* who was invited to share their story and with whom we would cocreate a narrative together (rather than an "interviewee" from whom we would attempt to extract useful information). Those conversations were loosely structured around a set of open-ended questions covering topics such as each narrator's life history, their experiences with civil rights tourism in Mississippi, and their perceptions about that industry's strengths, weaknesses, and goals. Each interview was cocreated through the process of informed consent and transcribed by hand and carefully audited for accuracy. Our decision to incorporate oral history as a fundamental component of this book was driven by a desire to "stand beside, advocate with, and learn from vernacular communities," as well as official representatives working in the state's civil rights tourism industry.[96]

This book could never have been written from the relative comfort of our offices in Texas and Pennsylvania, hundreds of miles from Mississippi. One of the authors can recall a conversation years ago with a respected scholar in the field who described an "occupational hazard" among rhetorical critics who never leave their computer keyboards to engage directly with the rhetors, audiences, and contexts they analyze. Such disconnectedness is especially problematic in public memory work, where the public's engagement with physical sites becomes an integral aspect of the text itself. Given its subject and scope, *Terror and Truth* necessitated we embrace on-the-ground fieldwork, that "nexus where rhetoric is produced, where it is enacted, where it circulates, and, consequently, where it is audienced."[97] Although our rhetorical fieldwork approach did not involve the level of immersion one finds in a more strictly ethnographic study, the deeply affecting experience of being in the field, experiencing sites firsthand, and conversing with Mississippians necessitated an acute awareness of our own identity and its impact on both our perceptions and those of everyone we interacted with along the way.

Throughout the project, we continuously and carefully reflected on our own positionalities as white tourists. John Van Maanen was writing specifically about ethnography when he argued that the method "carries quite serious intellectual and moral responsibilities, for the images of others inscribed in writing are most assuredly not neutral."[98] This is equally true of other forms of fieldwork, where "the power of one group to represent another is always involved."[99] Accepting that responsibility and reflecting on it at every stage of the process—from our fieldwork in Mississippi to writing and revising the book itself—was a charge we took seriously. In many ways, we are the target demographic for the Mississippi Development Authority's tourism division, Visit Mississippi: both white, college educated, middle to upper-middle class, socially conscious, lifelong blues fans, with a keen interest in heritage sites and African American history especially. Although neither of us is a Mississippi native, King lived in the Delta for nearly twenty years, where he taught at Delta State University in Cleveland before relocating to Illinois in 2013 and, later in 2018, to Austin, Texas, where he teaches at St. Edward's University. He still visits Cleveland each year, giving him a unique insider-outsider perspective as both a one-time resident and a tourist. Gatchet, a California native and one-time Austin resident who is currently a professor at West Chester University of Pennsylvania, first visited Mississippi in 2013, full of romanticized images of the state shaped by years of exposure to Visit Mississippi tourism ads in the pages of *Living Blues* magazine (both King and Gatchet are long-time contributors to the magazine, which is housed in the Center for the Study of Southern Culture at the University of Mississippi). He, like many tourists, has been struck by the region's beauty, cultural history, and crippling poverty. Despite our academic backgrounds in public memory and our research on the Mississippi Movement, visiting the state's civil rights sites was an extraordinary experiential learning opportunity as it deepened our understanding of the movement on both intellectual and affective levels. As Thigpen rightly put it, at its core, tourism is an inherently emotional journey.[100] Our collective experiences, our subjectivities, and our positions of privilege necessarily shape our impressions of civil rights memory sites in Mississippi, impacting our interpretations and analysis throughout this book. Wherever possible, we tried to live up to Jamie Landau's call for rhetorical critics "to share their feelings in print" while also being consciously aware of the subject positions we occupy that led our feelings to materialize the way they did.[101] In interviewing others, experiencing civil rights memory sites as tourists, and critiquing them as rhetorical critics, we were mindful of Jacqueline Jones Royster's warning of the "considerable consequence" works such as ours can have on those "whose own voices and perspectives remain still largely under considered and uncredited."[102]

Chapter Preview

Volumes have been filled tracing the history and contemporary implications of the civil rights movement and the Mississippi Movement specifically. Equally significant is the collective work on public memory, some of which has focused on civil rights memory, including sites in the Magnolia State. *Terror and Truth* distinguishes itself from this body of scholarship as the first book-length study of the state's civil rights tourism enterprise. Mississippi is one of the last southern states in the union—certainly decades behind Alabama, Georgia, and Tennessee—to actively market its civil rights history to tourists. In chapter 1, we offer a synoptic history of the Mississippi Movement (1945–1970) and the memory-building practices that emerged some thirty years after the decline of the movement. In doing so, we present both a comprehensive history of the state's tourism industry and the emergence of civil rights tourism in the early 2000s. Although civil rights tourism currently constitutes a small percentage of the state's overall tourism industry, this chapter charts the rapid growth of civil rights memory sites, suggesting it has become an important source of revenue for Mississippi.

The remainder of the book offers a close examination of a constellation of memory sites that comprise the state's civil rights tourism industry. We focus our attention on civil rights memorialization efforts occurring in the capital city of Jackson as well as the Delta region, located in the northwest part of the state. While most of the state's reported civil rights activities occurred in both locations, we acknowledge that movement activities and the memory-building practices that followed occur throughout other regions as identified by the *Mississippi Official Tour Guide*: the Hills (e.g., Oxford), the Pines (e.g., Philadelphia) and the Coast (e.g., Biloxi, Hattiesburg).[103] In chapter 2, we begin with a study of the grassroots efforts to create sites of civil rights memory in Mississippi. Long before the state was involved with its promotion in any meaningful, sustained way, local people such as Helen Sims were establishing makeshift museums and staging public performances, often on shoestring budgets and with volunteer support from the local community. Here we examine Sims's Mississippi Heritage Consortium in Belzoni, the Fannie Lou Hamer Museum and Fannie Lou Hamer Memorial Garden in Ruleville, and the Canton Freedom House Civil Rights Museum as examples of vernacular civil rights tourism. Perhaps more than any other public memory sites associated with civil rights in the state, these grassroots efforts exemplify the goal of social justice in its most palpable form.

No segment of Mississippi's memorial landscape has been analyzed more closely than that associated with Emmett Till, and in chapter 3, we explore two sites, the Emmett Till Interpretive Center in Sumner and the Emmett Till Historic Intrepid Center in Glendora, as well as promotional ads featuring Emmett Till produced by the Greenwood Convention and Visitors Bureau. This chapter builds on Tell's work on Till memorialization in Mississippi by offering a close analysis of the exhibits in both locations, thus highlighting the conflicting demands that are made of Emmett Till's body, story, and legacy. Chapter 4 turns its attention to the historic house museums established at the family homes of Amzie Moore in Cleveland and Medgar and Myrlie Evers in Jackson. Mississippi has long been an attractive destination for historic house tourism, and this chapter explores their rhetorical dimensions as sites of civil rights memory, as opposed to the focus on Civil War or antebellum history that is so often associated with historic homes, especially in Mississippi.

Chapters 5 and 6 examine the two major investments in civil rights tourism at the state level, the Mississippi Freedom Trail and the Mississippi Civil Rights Museum. The MFT (the focus of chapter 5) marks the first coordinated effort to create a statewide tourism attraction centered around civil rights, while the Civil Rights Museum (chapter 6) represents a decades-long effort culminating in the first state-sponsored civil rights museum. Although distinct in form and concept, both the marker trail and the museum offer case studies in the strengths and weaknesses of civil rights tourism. Finally, the concluding chapter offers an assessment of Mississippi's civil rights tourism industry goals and its potential to not only generate revenue for an impoverished state, but also achieve meaningful justice in the process.

CHAPTER ONE

FROM MOVEMENT TO MEMORY

A Rhetorical History of Civil Rights Tourism in Mississippi

> I'm worried because so many cultured people have really begun to hate Negroes. My sister, for example, always enjoyed Negro people. Now she can't stand them. It's because the Negros have changed. They want more. They don't want to stay in their place.
> —MISSISSIPPI DELTA "COMMUNITY LEADER," July 1962

> Mississippi cannot change America by itself, but America cannot change without Mississippi.
> —VICTORIA J. GRAY, National Conference for New Politics Convention, September 2, 1967

In a largely rural state with a population just under three million, civil rights tourists who visit Mississippi must typically make the journey by car, navigating highways and backroads, searching for what was, enveloped in a heritage tourism industry steeped in memory. Even tourists who fly into the state's capital city of approximately 150,000 will find, as Deborah D. Douglas did in her 2021 *U.S. Civil Rights Trail* guide, that "Jackson is synonymous with car culture and not entirely walkable given the distance of venues and the scorching heat in summer and early fall."[1] Our experience was no different. Whether discovering Aaron Henry's MFT marker in Clarksdale's African American downtown district, reading the gruesome timeline of Emmett Till's lynching at the ETHIC in Glendora and the aftermath at the ETIC in Sumner, or exploring the visually stunning, but emotionally exhausting, MCRM, these tourists will be alternately appalled and angry, educated and inspired. As a *Washington Post* reporter noted in one of his many visits to Mississippi, tourists are visiting a state haunted by its past: "This state seems always haunted by one regret or another, near or far, temporal or spiritual."[2]

Despite decades of silence and denial, Mississippi is now featured prominently among fourteen other states in the US Civil Rights Trail, a sprawling network of memory sites that stretch across the country. The state-funded MMH-MCRM, MFT marker series, and sections of the state's official tourism website devoted to civil rights and African American history all point to a growing tourism industry based around Mississippi's role in the US civil rights movement. Despite these noteworthy and progressive additions to the state's tourism offerings, however, civil rights tourism is still only a small segment of Mississippi's overall tourism industry and, ironically, it continues to compete with other prominent markers of the state's past, including Confederate statues and memorials.

This chapter is the first systematic effort to narrate the history of Mississippi's civil rights tourism industry. While we frame this history more or less chronologically, we acknowledge that historical events do not always transpire in a logical sequence. Events often collide and overlap in real time, and memory building is always a selective affair mediated by the dialectical tension of remembering and forgetting. While many other southern states—including Alabama, with its own appalling record on civil rights—have aggressively marketed their civil rights history for decades, Mississippi has been a laggard in doing so. As we will see, although early grassroots efforts by Helen Sims and others were met with indifference, concern, and even anger, the establishment of the state-sponsored MFT in 2011 helped legitimize a movement, a history, a cause, and a people that many Mississippians would rather forget. The MCRM and its associated media coverage, much of it glowing, has elevated the state's commitment to its civil rights history. One can expect the state to accelerate efforts to promote its story of the civil rights movement—the Mississippi Movement—as part of an overall shift to relying on tourism as a source of revenue. To better understand the places, events, and individuals who comprise the state's civil rights memory landscape, we open with a synoptic history of the Mississippi Movement from the premovement phase (1945–1955) to the movement's decline (early 1970s).

A Synoptic History of the Mississippi Movement, 1945–1970

Laying the Foundation: Premovement Activity and the "Birth" of the Movement

As part of a broad, statewide promotional strategy, Mississippi has grounded its allure to tourists in origin stories and appeals to authenticity that enhance its image as the cradle of musical genres and historical movements. For example, the state bills itself as the "birthplace of America's music," especially with regard to the blues, despite the impossibility of pinpointing a singular geographic starting point for such diverse cultural forms.[3] Given Mississippi's success using birthplace myths as a promotional vehicle for attracting blues tourists, it is no surprise that it employs a similar tactic to build its civil rights tourism industry. This is especially apparent in Money, where the "Bryant's Grocery" MFT marker asserts that "Till's death . . . is widely credited with sparking the American Civil Rights Movement." This claim circulates in countless texts, including as recently as the 2021 comprehensive tour guide to the US Civil Rights Trail, where it is mentioned no less than four times.[4] Claims of authenticity are deeply ironic, argues Dorit Wagner, for "tourism itself is actually extremely inauthentic, as it is merely about experiencing the reenactment of the lives of others."[5]

Dave Tell astutely tracks the historical roots of this birthplace narrative back to the 1960s and shows how it has more recently been used as a rhetorical strategy to fund commemoration and historical preservation projects in other parts of the state, especially in Tallahatchie County, where Till's murderers were tried.[6] Contrast the, at times, problematic mythic use of Till's memory with John Dittmer's *Local People*, a landmark historical study of the local heroes behind the Mississippi Movement. Although Dittmer acknowledges that "in the long run the Till lynching had an impact unforeseen by observers at the trial," he stops short of declaring it, or any one person, place, or event, as solely responsible for the movement's founding.[7] Instead, he criticizes the "arbitrary" assignment of beginning and end dates for the movement and identifies a *range* of factors and historical precedents that contributed to its early stages, many of which are dated decades before Till's train ride from Chicago to the Mississippi Delta.[8]

Chief among them were the experiences of African American military personnel who served their country during World War II. In her analysis of Black resistance in the Delta, historian Nan Elizabeth Woodruff argues that the wartime experience fundamentally changed how African Americans, particularly in the South, viewed their own plight back home:

> World War II, which followed massive changes created by the Great Depression and New Deal, expanded the political consciousness of African Americans. . . . Southern black people—men and women— fought all over the globe in a war to make the world safe for democracy. Having battled side by side with white American troops, as well

as "coloured" soldiers . . ., they returned to the Delta with a renewed determination to fight Jim Crow and to secure equality and freedom. The war had also raised the expectations of those who had remained behind to work in the fields and factories.[9]

As James C. Cobb notes in his history of the Mississippi Delta, the war served as the foundation for "escalating racial tensions in the Delta as blacks became more independent and assertive and whites viewed with alarm both the leftward drift of the national Democratic party and the inclination of Delta blacks to look to Washington for security and support."[10]

At the same time, while the war reinforced the belief of many white southerners serving abroad regarding the "virtues" of white supremacy, others in the ranks started to "question their own world of segregation and disfranchisement."[11] Despite the emerging racial skepticism of some whites, upon returning home to Mississippi, Black veterans (similar to after World War I) continued to experience the full onslaught of white supremacy and Jim Crow, which in turn inspired "intensifying black activism in Mississippi" after 1946.[12] Historian Michael Vinson Williams argues that southern whites viewed Black veterans as a direct threat to the racial social order because these returning veterans were "trained soldiers with military experience in combat zones where *white men* had been identified as enemies of democracy and freedom and where nations had banded together in a global war to prevent their success."[13] Ultimately, as Glenda Elizabeth Gilmore notes in *Defying Dixie: The Radical Roots of Civil Rights 1919–1950*, the war in Europe was a "war against racism" as the Allied forces successfully ended Hitler's Final Solution to exterminate Europeans Jews because of their racial identity.[14]

In the years leading up to the US Supreme Court's 1954 decision in *Brown v. Board of Education of Topeka* that abolished racial segregation in public schools, the Mississippi Movement "began slowly and developed unevenly across the state" and was comprised primarily of what historian Dernoral Davis calls "scattered episodes of protest" focused on voter rights and desegregating public education.[15] Brothers Medgar and Charles Evers, who would go on to become prominent movement leaders based in Jackson, led one such effort in their hometown of Decatur, where they and other African American war veterans were confronted by an armed mob of white locals who prevented them from casting ballots in the 1946 Democratic primary.[16] On the education front, Black activists brought legal challenges to address injustices associated with the separate-but-equal doctrine, what one historian argues "constituted one of the most glaring inequities in Mississippi."[17] One such challenge was filed in 1948 by science teacher Gladys Noel Bates of Smith Robertson Junior High School (now home to the Smith Robertson Museum and Cultural Center), which sought to match the notoriously low salaries of Black teachers to that of their white counterparts. Bates and her husband were fired for their efforts, and a judge dismissed the case the following year.[18] Historian Françoise N. Hamlin notes that although the lawsuit was unsuccessful, it "brought attention to the extent of the educational inequalities in the state, ringing warning bells throughout Dixie."[19]

During this premovement period, the Regional Council of Negro Leadership (RCNL), founded by Mound Bayou surgeon Dr. T. R. M. Howard in 1951, played a prominent role in voter education and registration efforts, especially through the work of one of its leaders, Amzie Moore.[20] Howard's biographers characterized the civil rights leader as advocating "a message of self-help, mutual aid, thrift, and equal political rights."[21] The MFT marker in Mound Bayou dedicated to Howard notes how he "led voter registration drives, supported boycotts, and lobbied Washington for services and hospitals." Moreover, this work was augmented by the Mississippi Progressive Voters' League, which promoted "civic education and participation through motivation and literacy" and strengthened the NAACP's presence in the state.[22] Although it is impossible to pinpoint its precise starting point, not long after Medgar Evers assumed his post as the NAACP's first field secretary in Mississippi in 1954—and in the wake of *Brown v. Board of Education*, Till's lynching, and the formation of the first Citizens' Council office in Indianola—the Mississippi Movement had begun.[23]

Amzie Moore and Regional Movement in the Delta

Historian Charles M. Payne notes, "If asked to choose one person as the forerunner of the work they did in Mississippi in the 1960s and particularly of their work in the Delta, veteran SNCC workers would overwhelmingly choose Amzie Moore."[24] Unfortunately, Moore's significance to the civil rights movement, both in Mississippi and nationally, is woefully underappreciated. The development of a tourism infrastructure, built on the work of civil rights historians, has helped elevate his profile as a significant movement leader—particularly in present-day Cleveland, where multiple public memory sites dedicated to Moore form the core of the town's civil rights tourism offerings. Born in 1911, he grew up as part of a farming family, worked the fields and other labor-intensive jobs, and struggled through poverty and hunger, an economic situation made worse by the Great Depression.[25] These experiences laid a foundation for his future activism. During "the Depression days in the

Delta," Moore remembered, "we had so many banks closings and jobs were so few. And the Red Cross was issuing a small piece of meat with some brown flour. That was the extent of what we had."[26] In 1942 Moore was drafted, and his wartime experience proved to be a personal turning point during his formative years. As he noted in one interview,

> I just really didn't have any knowledge of the world about me and what was going on. I think what God really did with me, in this particular thing, was to put me on a ship and send me around the world. And let me live in different environments and be in contact with different people and to really and truly find out what was behind it because I certainly didn't know.[27]

Like Medgar Evers and many of his other Mississippi contemporaries, Moore experienced firsthand the hypocrisy of fighting a war for freedom only to return to Mississippi's feudal sharecropping economy and segregated society.

When Moore returned to civilian life in 1946, he tapped into a strain of Black nationalism that called for economic independence from white control. Over the next three decades, he would work with a number of leaders in the Mississippi Movement, including Fannie Lou Hamer, Medgar Evers, Aaron Henry, T. R. M. Howard, Robert Moses, and others. Moore, who was a postal employee, established a combination gas station, café, and beauty store in Cleveland and quickly became a regional civil rights leader through his work with the RCNL. Its purpose, according to Moore, was to "teach Negroes first-class citizenship, the preservation of property, the paying of taxes, the holding of public office, the changing of the economic standpoint."[28] "Amzie was the lead person [in Mississippi] for anything about civil rights," remembers civil rights veteran Charles McLaurin, who worked closely with Moore in the years leading up to 1964's Freedom Summer project.[29] Moore was particularly concerned about the Delta's oppressive plantation culture, lack of employment for its African American citizens, and food insecurity. In 1955 he was elected president of Cleveland's chapter of the NAACP (which he grew to be the second largest in Mississippi), and it was through Moore that activist Robert (Bob) Moses became involved in the Mississippi Movement.[30] According to his biographer, Laura Visser-Maessen, Moses is "widely acknowledged as one of the civil rights movement's most compelling and beloved" figures because of his skills as a grassroots organizer as well as his belief that he, like Moore, needed to stand with local activists in Mississippi even if that meant compromising his own safety.[31] As a result, Moses became known "as one of the most prominent individuals between 1961 and 1965 within the group-centered leadership of the Student Nonviolent Coordinating Committee."[32] SNCC's presence in the state can be traced to Moore as well.[33]

Moore's activism intensified throughout the 1960s, despite efforts from the local Citizens' Council to bankrupt him. Started in Indianola, Mississippi in 1954, the Citizens' Council—a "country club" version of the Klan[34]—claimed in its founding document, "Birth of an Idea," that it was "dedicated to the preservation of our way of life by maintaining segregation by legal means."[35] Moore was pivotal in bringing SNCC into the state and was an early inspiration for a SNCC voter registration drive in 1961.[36] He helped lay the groundwork for the Mississippi Freedom Democratic Party's founding in 1964 and started a local chapter of Head Start in 1966.[37] Moore also played a central role in helping impoverished African Americans gain access to low-income housing.[38] Moore retired from the post office in 1968, and he would continue his civil rights work until he died in Cleveland in 1982 at the age of sixty-nine.[39] An MFT marker (one of two state historical markers that flank his family home in Cleveland, now a historic house museum) cements his legacy as "a principal architect of early civil rights activism" in Mississippi.

Movement in the Capital and Beyond: Medgar and Myrlie Evers

"If Amzie Moore was a living symbol of resistance to people in the Delta," Payne writes, "Medgar Evers had the same meaning to Blacks across the state."[40] Of all the civil rights leaders active in the Mississippi Movement, perhaps none has been lionized for their leadership more than Medgar Evers. Both Mississippi natives, Medgar Evers and Myrlie Beasley were born in central Mississippi—Medgar in the small town of Decatur in 1925, and Myrlie in Vicksburg in 1933. One of seven children, Medgar was deeply influenced by his parents James and Jessie Evers, who refused "to cower in the presence of segregation and white supremacy."[41] Myrlie, whose parents divorced when she was young, was raised by her aunt and grandmother in Vicksburg.[42] In direct contrast to Medgar's upbringing, Myrlie's caregivers explicitly discouraged her from challenging the racial caste system in Vicksburg and the state.[43] Although primarily recognized for her civil rights work after leaving the state following her husband's murder, Myrlie Evers provided critical support during Medgar's tenure with the NAACP, and her experiences growing up in a segregated society primed her for a life of activism later on.

Medgar enlisted in the US Army during World War II, where he fought in the European theater and served as part of the Red Ball Express, a convoy of supply trucks that carried desperately needed supplies to Allied forces during the war.[44] When he returned home to Mississippi with an honorable discharge in 1946, Medgar—like Moore—arrived "with renewed convictions that African Americans claim citizenship in its entirety."[45] Medgar and Myrlie would eventually meet at Alcorn Agricultural and Mechanical College (now Alcorn State University), the first public historically Black land grant university in the country, in 1950. Medgar, who was a junior and a star football player at Alcorn at the time, already had a reputation on campus for being a "rabble-rouser" who was "always talking about registering and voting," Myrlie recalled.[46] After marrying in 1951, the couple relocated to Mound Bayou, a small, all-Black city in the Mississippi Delta, where they both found employment at T. R. M. Howard's Magnolia Mutual Life Insurance Company.

Dittmer describes Medgar Evers's position at Magnolia Mutual as an "apprenticeship for his life's work."[47] Traveling throughout the Delta as a door-to-door salesman, he further witnessed the devastation wrought by segregation in Mississippi and was soon "using his job as a cover for political work."[48] Medgar attempted to desegregate the University of Mississippi before accepting a position as the NAACP's first field secretary for the state of Mississippi in late 1954, where he "toiled in relative isolation and barely contained rage, gathering files on lynchings, beatings, and endless discrimination cases common to the Jim Crow era."[49] One of those was the lynching of Emmett Till in 1955, an investigation he completed with Moore. Medgar's tireless work cataloging acts of brutality inflicted on the state's Black population—itself an act of resistance to white supremacy—would later become a prominent theme across many of the state's civil rights tourism sites, especially the historical markers and museums that detail how African Americans' struggles for freedom through organizing and agitation were met by white terror and violence. Writing in 1967 of her husband's assassination, Myrlie said that Medgar "was carefully chosen. No other victim would have served at that moment in time. Medgar was killed specifically because of what he represented, of what he had become, of the hope that his presence gave to Mississippi Negroes and the fear it aroused in Mississippi whites."[50]

During Medgar's time as NAACP field secretary, Myrlie worked closely with him, managing his office and even serving as his speechwriter on occasion.[51] Over time, Medgar began to play a more direct role in movement organizing, especially after Clarksdale pharmacist Aaron Henry ushered in a "new militancy" when he took over as the NAACP president for the state of Mississippi in 1960.[52] This included a leadership role in the successful 1960 boycott of the central shopping district on Jackson's Capitol Street, an action that historian Stephanie R. Rolph describes as "the first organized civil rights protest" in the city.⁵³ Evers also played a critical role in increasing youth involvement in the movement.⁵⁴

Medgar Evers's important work came to a sudden and traumatic halt in June 1963. As he was exiting his car and walking up the driveway after returning home from a late-night organizing meeting in Jackson, Klan and Citizens' Council member Byron De La Beckwith fatally shot him in the back with a .30-06 high-powered rifle. Medgar died shortly after. Speaking of the months leading up to her husband's assassination, Myrlie said,

> We came to realize . . . that our time was short, it was simply in the air. You . . . knew that something was going to happen, and the logical person for it to happen to was Medgar. It certainly brought us closer during that time. As a matter of fact, we didn't talk. We didn't have to. We communicated without words. It was a touch; it was a look; it was holding each other; it was music playing. And I used to try to reassure him and tell him, nothing's going to happen to you, the FBI is here, everybody knows you, you are in the press. They wouldn't dare do anything to you. Medgar's approach was a much more realistic one, and he would say, "honey, you've got to be strong, I want you to take care of my children, it probably won't be too long."⁵⁵

Beckwith was tried—twice—in 1964; both trials resulted in hung juries. In the aftermath, Myrlie and the Evers's three children relocated to Claremont, California. As she reflected in her 1967 autobiography, *For Us, the Living*, "Slowly, with many detours—with relapses into a numbing emptiness—my life has begun to begin again."⁵⁶ Once established on the West Coast, she earned her college degree, transitioned into a corporate position as a community affairs director, and ran for Congress.⁵⁷ While serving as commissioner of the Los Angeles Board of Public Works (the first Black woman to do so), a third trial in 1994—thirty-one years after the assassination—finally brought justice to the Evers family when Beckwith was convicted and sentenced to life in prison. The following year Myrlie was elected as chair of the NAACP's Board of Directors.⁵⁸

Fighting for Freedom on Multiple Fronts: Movement Efforts, 1960–1968

As the Mississippi Movement transitioned into its second decade, Davis notes that "by 1960 the number of organizations participating in the Civil Rights Movement had doubled from a decade earlier."⁵⁹ This two-fold increase was certainly felt in Mississippi, with the Congress of Racial Equality (CORE) and SNCC establishing a presence there starting in 1961. Cobb documents the ethos of CORE and SNCC's younger membership, who were "unwilling to accept the conservatism of the NAACP approach and anxious to reach out to blacks at the grassroots level."[60] The Council of Federated Organizations (COFO), a Mississippi-based coalition of groups including the NAACP, CORE, and SNCC, was at its "peak" during the first half of the decade (the COFO office in Jackson is an important civil rights public memory site in the capital city, with a dedicated MFT marker posted nearby).[61] COFO characterized itself as embodying "the effort of all civil rights workers in Mississippi to coordinate their efforts in one direction for maximum efficiency."[62]

Coordinated action around the state signaled the Mississippi Movement's growing momentum. On March 27, 1961, nine students from Tougaloo College, an HBCU in the Jackson area and an important site of civil rights organizing, engaged in a sit-in to desegregate the Jackson Public Library. Demonstrations and violence erupted after their arrests and trial, and Dittmer argues it "initiated a burst of activity by black youth in Mississippi."[63] Today, visitors can learn more about the sit-in through a large display in the MCRM's permanent exhibit and an MFT marker posted outside the old library building, which notes that the students' actions "inspired African American protests . . . against segregated public parks, swimming pools, stores, and movie theaters." Later that summer, C. C. Bryant, who served as president of McComb's NAACP chapter for several decades, worked with SNCC field secretary Bob Moses to organize a voter registration drive in Pike County, Mississippi. A historical marker posted outside Bryant's former home in McComb recounts his story, describing him as a "major force" in the Mississippi Movement.

Movement successes continued to be met with the full force of white supremacy. Cobb observes that in "the early 1960s the white planter's word was still the law" in Mississippi, "and even his most audacious pronouncements stood as unchallenged statements of fact."[64] A prime example of this were the Freedom Rides of 1961. Launched by CORE and later bolstered with the involvement of SNCC members, this nonviolent direct-action campaign saw small groups of white and Black activists ride buses and trains into the South to test the Supreme Court's decisions declaring segregation in interstate transportation facilities unconstitutional. The riders "encountered enormous levels of white violence," including mobs who burned buses and beat the Freedom Riders.[65] A Ku Klux Klan poem, "T. W. A. K. Confederate Mother's Day—1961," celebrated the grotesque violence with images of "clubs

... swinging" as the Riders "caught hell again."⁶⁶ Hezekiah Watkins, a civil rights activist and staff member at the MCRM, became the youngest Freedom Rider when he was arrested outside the Jackson Greyhound bus station at the age of thirteen. Contradicting the advice of others to steer clear of the riders when they arrived in Jackson in the summer of 1961, Watkins and his friends rode their bicycles to the station's entrance on the chance they could see, and perhaps even touch, one of the riders. "As a joke, my friend pushed me inside, and ran," Watkins remembers.⁶⁷ He was arrested and immediately transported to Parchman Farm, the notorious Mississippi State Penitentiary in Sunflower County, where he was placed in a death row cell with other convicted prisoners. In a state of confusion and fear, the inmates led Watkins to believe he may be executed. "It was a hell of an ordeal that I went through," Watkins recalls. "I was only there for five days, and those five days were like five months to me. Not being able to sleep. Being physically harassed, sexually harassed." Later, at the urging of SNCC and SCLC activist James Bevel, Watkins would continue his work with the Mississippi Movement, experiences he now shares with visitors at the MCRM.⁶⁸

Speaking of her experience with a group of riders traveling from New Orleans to Jackson, another Freedom Rider, Helen Singleton said, "You begin to sort of feel like a soldier getting ready to go into enemy territory."⁶⁹ Like Watkins, Singleton and dozens of others were arrested after entering the portion of the Jackson station reserved for whites only. Later, as she and other riders were transferred by bus to Parchman Farm, Singleton recalled, "I thought, as a region of the country, this could be a great tourist place, if they would just get their social act together."⁷⁰ She had no way of knowing it at the time, but decades later, the prison would become an official tourist stop on both the Mississippi Blues Trail and the MFT.⁷¹

The work of Watkins, Singleton, and other Freedom Riders in Jackson (including a young Stokely Carmichael) was so significant they "thrust the state head-first into the heart of the movement," including inspiring Clarie Collins Harvey, who ran a funeral home in Jackson, to found Womanpower Unlimited, an organization dedicated to supporting the Freedom Riders and empowering Mississippi women for a life of social activism and leadership.⁷² The following year, in 1962, James Meredith's success desegregating the University of Mississippi (and the riot that followed) became "a flashpoint for the civil rights movement, dramatizing racial injustice to the entire world."⁷³ More organized campaigns followed, as membership in the Ku Klux Klan rose in the wake of Beckwith's first two trials for Medgar Evers's assassination.⁷⁴ Faced with continued disenfranchisement at the polls and what Dittmer calls "a lull in movement activity" with national media "attention shifting to Capitol Hill and the debate over the civil rights bill," the COFO organized a mock election for Black voters in the fall of 1963.[75] Known as the "Freedom Vote," the campaign opened with a convention in Jackson that nominated a slate of candidates, and in November, over eighty-three thousand ballots were cast.[76] The successful effort paved the way for Freedom Summer the following year. As part of this broader project and with support from the COFO, a network of approximately fifty freedom schools (the brainchild of SNCC activist Charles Cobb) were set up "in church sanctuaries and basements, in local community homes, in storefronts, and in 'Freedom Houses' built by civil rights activists." These sites offered African American children "a humanities-based curriculum that taught political efficacy, social critique, and the organizing strategies employed in the civil rights movement."[77]

Youth involvement in the Mississippi Movement was arguably at its peak in the Freedom Summer of 1964. Released in the spring of that year, the "Prospectus for the Mississippi Freedom Summer" identified Freedom Summer as the "massive participation of Americans dedicated to the elimination of racial oppression."[78] It saw local Black volunteers collaborate with white college students from out of state (in an alliance that was uneasy at times) to canvass neighborhoods and register voters.[79] It was also one of the most violent summers on record in the state.[80] Retaliation from white supremacists, organized in the form of the Citizens' Councils, a reinvigorated Ku Klux Klan, and the state Mississippi Sovereignty Commission, was swift and often deadly, as in the case of CORE volunteers James Chaney, Andrew Goodman, and Michael Schwerner, who were executed by KKK members near Philadelphia, Mississippi, in June 1964. Dittmer calls it "the most depressingly familiar story of the Mississippi movement."[81] Despite this horrific violence, the Meridian COFO office pledged to continue the fight, as reported in the *Jackson Daily News*: "Our ultimate hope is that James Chaney, Andrew Goodman, and Michael Schwerner and the supreme sacrifice that they paid will light an eternal fire of diligence in the heart of America."[82] And while the Freedom Summer project "enjoyed some successes," the number of Black voters volunteers registered fell short of expectations.[83]

One of those successes was bringing Black community leaders "from their fields and shops to the gates of power at the Atlantic City Democratic Convention" in 1964.[84] It was there that the Mississippi Freedom Democratic Party and its vice chair Fannie Lou Hamer—perhaps the most celebrated woman in Mississippi's civil rights tourism industry—"threw a monkey wrench into the president's plans for an orchestrated convention" when they argued their claim to Mississippi's slate of delegate seats.[85] Hamer's passionate testimony to the Credentials Committee, where she famously asked, "Is this America, the land of the free and the home of the brave, where we have to sleep with our telephones off of the hooks because our lives be threatened daily?" was later broadcast on prime time television after an angry Lyndon Johnson interrupted it with a press conference.[86] Johnson's unsuccessful attempt at brokering a compromise with the Mississippi Freedom Democratic Party's delegation (most of whom rejected an offer of two voting seats at the convention) bespoke an uneasy relationship between his administration and Mississippi Movement leaders just one month after the passage of the Civil Rights Act of 1964. Two years later, James Meredith's "March Against Fear" was temporarily thwarted by Aubrey James Norvell, a white man, who shot Meredith from the side of the road on the second day of his solitary march from Memphis to Jackson.[87] With Meredith recuperating in a Memphis hospital, civil rights leaders and activists from around the nation descended upon Mississippi to complete the march, culminating in a massive rally at the state capitol anchored by speeches from Martin Luther King Jr. and Stokely Carmichael. In his book-length treatment of this pivotal event in the nation's civil rights history, historian Aram Goudsouzian argued that "the march expressed both the depth of black grievances and the height of black possibilities."[88] The March Against Fear and Carmichael's fiery declaration of "Black Power" at the Broad Street Park in Greenwood (where an MFT marker now stands to commemorate the event) popularized—in an unprecedented way—the rise of a new militant movement that had its roots in Black nationalism and organizations such as an Ohio-based student group, Revolutionary Action Movement, and the Afro-American Association, based in the San Francisco Bay Area, as well as Robert Williams and Malcolm X.[89] We discuss the Black Power movement in Mississippi in more detail in chapters 5 and 6.

By 1968, the Mississippi Freedom Democratic Party was fractured, signaling the symbolic "end of the grass-roots" Mississippi Movement.[90] Although imperfect, Hamlin notes the movement was "a calculated success" as evidenced by the progress achieved on multiple fronts.[91] The Mississippi Sovereignty Commission, an official "state agency that used spy tactics, intimidation, false imprisonment, jury tampering and other illegal methods to thwart the activities of civil rights workers" in Mississippi from the 1950s through the 1970s, closed in 1973.[92] And Black participation in the political process increased at every level—both as voters and candidates for local, state, and national office—buoyed by the passage of the Voting Rights Act in 1965. After years of resistance following *Brown v. Board of Education*, integration of the state's public school system progressed in the 1970s (although fraught with problems, including the establishment of private academies that maintained de-facto segregation and drained public system resources).[93]

Assessing the impact of the Mississippi Movement, Dittmer argues that even though it achieved "extraordinary changes in a state that had been locked up in the caste system for nearly a century," that progress "reminds us of the distance still to be traveled."[94] Payne similarly notes our collective "tendency to reduce the movement to a 'civil rights' movement, taking that narrow label more seriously than did the people who participated in the movement. To many of them, the overriding question is still, How do you open up the society?"[95] From that perspective, the movement continues—albeit in a much different form than its existence in the 1950s and 1960s—while our memories of earlier stages of the movement live on in public memory sites throughout the state. SNCC, CORE, COFO, and other organizations central to the movement no longer exist, but their memory does. Examining how that memory is articulated through the state's civil rights tourism infrastructure is the backbone of this book. In the next section, we chronicle Mississippi's early efforts, some thirty years after the decline of the movement, to market the state for tourism purposes with special attention directed at the emergence of what would become a civil rights tourism industry, the latest addition to the state's ever-expanding heritage tourism portfolio.

Civil Rights Tourism and Mississippi: An Evolving Industry

As is true in other southern states, the tourism landscape in Mississippi has changed dramatically over the past several decades. And although civil rights tourism is a relatively new, twenty-first-century expansion of the state's tourism industry, Mississippi's earliest, official efforts to promote the state as a tourist destination can be traced back to at least the late 1930s, when Governor Hugh L. White helped launch the Balance Agriculture with Industry (BAWI) program in the wake of the Great Depression. White hoped to diversify Mississippi's agrarian-centric economy with state-subsidized investments in manufacturing and industry, and the Mississippi Advertising Commission, which would later transform into the Agricultural and Industrial Board, was formed to aggressively promote a state perceived by many to be "a backward region without much promise."[96] According to communication scholar Burt Buchanan, "marketing the state's possibilities for manufacturing sites and travel and tourism was a new and bold concept."[97] Although the commission's primary charge was to attract investments in manufacturing, framing

Mississippi Advertising Commission Ad, 1937. Courtesy of the Archives and Records Services Division, Mississippi Department of Archives and History.

Mississippi as "a haven for the out-of-state tourist" and "a playground for year-round recreation" was central to its overall marketing strategy, and it soon began producing a number of advertisements, publications, and tourist guides to help achieve this goal.[98] In one example, a 1937 print ad lauds Mississippi's "friendly spirit" and notes that "Mississippi is known as a land where gracious hospitality has always reigned."[99] Another newspaper ad,

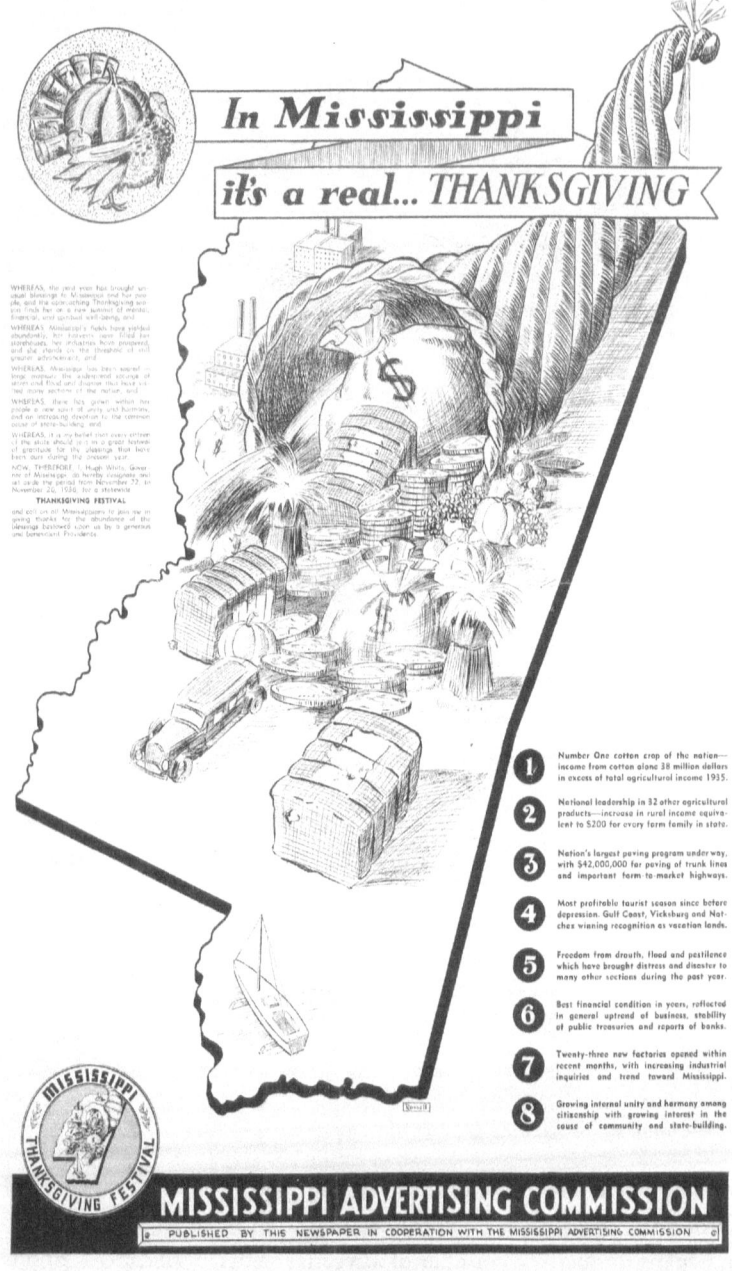

Mississippi Advertising Commission Ad, 1936. Courtesy of the Archives and Records Services Division, Mississippi Department of Archives and History.

published in 1936, claims that the state had recently enjoyed its "most profitable tourist season since before depression," lists several regions that are "winning recognition as vacation lands," and boasts of "growing internal unity and harmony among citizenship with growing interest in the cause of community and state-building."[100]

The official tourism literature produced by state authorities, which focused primarily on opportunities for recreation and economic investment, often highlighted locations and structures that reflected a narrow vision of the state's past. These included plantations, mansions, battlegrounds, and other similar sites that continue to be popular destinations for many southern heritage tourists. In those rare instances where African Americans appeared in these promotional materials, the representations often drew on racist stereotypes and other offensive depictions of the state's Black population.[101] For example, the 1941 *Mississippi Tourist Guide* lauds political institutions of power ("The Old Capitol"), mansions and antebellum homes, outdoor and recreational activities, a new and "modern" highway system, the Civil War (described as the "War Between the States"), and the state's ethos of hospitality. The only Black faces appear toward the end of the guide. Set in a cotton field, a photo shows what is presumably a Black sharecropping family (a man, woman, and infant) using a water pump. Underneath the photo is the caption, "Delta Pickaninnies," a common racial slur at that time.[102]

The state's whiteness campaign remained consistent for decades. For example, historian Ted Ownby notes that African Americans are completely absent from an official guidebook published in the mid-1970s by the Mississippi Agricultural and Industrial Board.[103] The magazine-style guide is dense with color photographs that show white Mississippians fishing, hunting, relaxing outdoors, riding on river boats, and enjoying other recreational opportunities. The only people of color who appear in photographs are members of the Choctaw tribal nation, and these exoticized depictions reflect a constricted vision of the state's indigenous peoples that portrays them as primitive, trapped in the distant past and willingly performing their culture for white tourists' consumption.[104] Equally troubling, the guide conspicuously whitewashes the state's history by asserting that enslaved Africans and other ethnic groups "heard of the rich lands in Mississippi and came here before the turn of the century."[105]

Despite the Mississippi BAWI program's success in luring tourists to the Magnolia State, by the 1990s, even independent guidebook and travel writers continued to find it necessary to actively challenge the state's negative reputation, a consequence of the civil rights battles of the 1950s and

1960s. For example, the authors of *The Insiders' Guide to Mississippi*, first published in 1994, made this plain, asserting that Mississippi's virtues had been obfuscated by the state's past "injustices": "Unfortunately, what some people outside of the state remember most clearly are stories of injustices written years ago. Accomplishments are not nearly as newsworthy, so the rest of the story has not always been told."[106] The guide's occasionally defensive tone resurfaces at the end of the opening narrative. "A great deal has been documented and speculated and imagined about this sometimes misunderstood and often underestimated state," its authors assert. *The Insiders' Guide* extolls Mississippi's virtues, from its music and literary history to its natural beauty and culinary delights, culminating in a "brand of genuine Southern hospitality that has reached legendary status."[107] In keeping with the guide's implied denial of the state's history of racial and economic injustice, civil rights leaders' voices are silenced in the guide's narrative. As we will see, however, despite the guide's efforts to selectively remember the past, other institutional voices, including the MDAH, would begin to use its legitimate power to document and memorialize the Mississippi Movement and other nondominant groups.

The role of the MDAH in laying the foundation for a civil rights tourism industry cannot be overstated. Given its role in preserving and promoting the state's civil rights heritage, it is ironic—but not surprising—that the MDAH's inception at the turn of the twentieth century was motivated by larger political interests to promulgate the state's Lost Cause narrative.[108] According to current MDAH director Katie Blount, it was the visionary and "fearless" work of former MDAH Museum Division director Patti Carr Black who, starting in the 1970s, advocated for the MDAH to widen the scope of its collection efforts, gathering stories and other material artifacts from traditionally marginalized groups including the Mississippi Movement:[109]

> The department has changed gradually over the years. But it's a completely different place by now. And there were a number of kind of inflection points in that, but one of them was Patti's interest beginning in the 1970s in broadening the department's vision for collecting and telling stories. She was very interested in the civil rights story, she was very interested in the Native American story, she was very interested in folk art, culture, music, and she really expanded the department's vision of its role as a historical agency. . . . I really credit Patti with, again, having an expansive sense of the department's role that took in communities that had not earlier been represented by our work.[110]

In 1985, Black helped curate the first permanent civil rights exhibit in the United States, "The Struggle for Equal Rights," in a small room in the Old State Capitol building.[111] Blount visited the exhibit soon after she moved to Mississippi. "It was a powerful exhibit," she remembers, and one that "told honest stories."[112] In his assessment of the exhibit, historian Neil R. McMillen argued that while "The Struggle for Equal Rights" might appear initially incoherent to visitors, it offered a much-needed critique of the state's long-standing efforts to portray its history as noble: "Indeed, no reasonably attentive visitor could experience this installation without learning that the struggle protrayed [sic] was one for basic human rights and that the full power of the state of Mississippi in this conflict was arrayed on the wrong side."[113] Not surprisingly, in 1987, the American Association for State and Local History bestowed the exhibit with the Award of Merit.[114] Meanwhile, the MDAH continued its pioneering work by installing civil rights–related historical markers as part of its official state marker series, notable for the green metal signs that recognize a broad range of historic sites around the state. The first green marker spotlighting civil rights, "Freedom Summer Murders," was unveiled in 1989, some two decades before the MFT was created in 2011. It is worth noting that the green marker signs are proposed and financed locally by those who desire these official markers of remembrance.

Although civil rights were by no means the focus of the state tourism office's broad promotional strategy during this period, behind the scenes, a foundation for a civil rights tourism infrastructure was being laid as the result of various grassroots efforts around the state. Some of these efforts were led by scholars. For example, in 1977, the University of Mississippi launched the nation's first regional studies center, the Center for the Study of Southern Culture.[115] Folklorist and blues scholar William R. Ferris was the center's first director. Not only did Ferris play a major role in "legitimizing the blues as a serious cultural artifact,"[116] but he also was an important catalyst in justifying the importance of documenting the state's civil rights history.[117] A decade later, in 1987, the University of Mississippi organized a series of public programs to celebrate the twenty-fifth anniversary of James Meredith's admittance to the institution.[118] Five years later, the Civil Rights Commemoration Initiative, a multiracial student group, collaborated to "commission an artwork to honor those who struggled for and achieved equal access to educational opportunities in Mississippi."[119] The group's effort led to the construction of a civil rights commemorative site in 2002 on campus.[120] Four years later, a bronze statue of James Meredith was added to the site. Meanwhile, in 1988, the Civil Rights Research and Documentation Project at the University of

Mississippi sponsored a commemoration of Medgar Evers. The project produced a publication for the public that details information about Evers's history, activism, and legacy and notes that it is "one component of a much larger and sustained effort to focus on aspects of the experiences of black people and race relations in the Deep South."[121]

Although these programs were confined to the campus of one university in the state and are not tourism attractions per se, they are indicative of a growing interest—both among scholars and the general public—in preserving and sharing Mississippi's African American history. Another significant development was the establishment of the William Winter Institute for Racial Reconciliation (known as the Alluvial Collective starting in early 2022) on the University of Mississippi campus in 1999. Led by former Mississippi governor William Winter, the center is arguably the state's first, and most expansive, initiative to attempt to heal the state's bitter racial wounds through a series of reconciliation projects. As we will see in chapter 6, Winter played an important role in moving the MCRM from idea to reality.

Meanwhile, the publication of a state-sponsored guidebook in the 1990s, *African-American Heritage Guide*, was a significant turning point in recognizing the value of promoting the state's African American heritage, even if the motivations were largely economic. Deploying the oft-used "hospitality" slogan, the guide acknowledged—albeit opaquely—that its African American population had long suffered under the system of Jim Crow. In text set against a photograph of the Medgar Evers statue in Jackson, it reads: "Welcome to a world of startling contrasts, a kaleidoscope of images, dark and light, struggle and triumph, pain and progress, a past filled with hostility and a future brimming with hope."[122] The guide lists cities, attractions, churches, events, houses, cemeteries, historical markers, even plantations, throughout the state—although it did not list civil rights museums, interpretative centers, markers, or other concrete tourism sites because outside of a few MDAH green roadside markers, a civil rights infrastructure did not yet exist. Interestingly, the guide asks Black tourists to reframe their implied negative impressions of Mississippi: "Today, we invite you to see and put into perspective the events of the past by visiting our sites and attractions. More importantly, we invite you to share in Mississippi's future."[123]

Given the Mississippi Movement was largely based in Jackson and the state's Delta region, it is not surprising that civil rights tourism infrastructure started to emerge in these key places, along with other important sites throughout the state, including Oxford, Tupelo, Philadelphia, McComb, Hattiesburg, and Biloxi. Years later, Rickey Thigpen would characterize Jackson's marketing plan using a wheel metaphor: Jackson is the tourism "hub" while the surrounding regions are the "spoke":

> Although we promote Jackson and that's our job, when people come in the door and they come and they talk on the phone we promote the entire state. Because if they are going to be here for four days and they are interested in the blues, we want them to get a hotel room in Jackson. And we call it "hub and spoke." So, we want them to go to Cleveland and Indianola and then come back and spend the night in Jackson. Eat dinner and get up the next morning and go to Vicksburg and spend a day there and discover the state. Because we're so centrally located.[124]

By the 1990s, efforts were underway to memorialize and legitimize the work of civil rights leaders and activists who literally died for the cause. In particular, the city of Jackson has been instrumental in remembering Medgar Evers. In 1992, a five-hundred-pound bronze statue of Evers was unveiled in front of a city library named after him. *Jet* magazine reported on the ceremonial event, quoting Tougaloo president Adib Shakir, who praised the city and the state: "I am so pleased that this city and this state had the courage, strength and conviction to erect a statue in honor of Medgar Wiley Evers."[125] In 1995, WFT Architects submitted a proposal to renovate the Evers house, which was maintained as a rental property in the decades after his 1963 assassination. The plan stated that "with his home and the site of his assassination virtually unaltered today, there is an extraordinary opportunity to showcase them and the story they tell."[126]

While Jackson has largely been responsible for memorializing Evers, the town of Philadelphia—located in the southeastern part of the state—has turned murder into memory as the site where Chaney, Goodman, and Schwerner were killed in June 1964. After decades of collective forgetting, Philadelphia held the first of two public memorial events. After the release of the 1988 film *Mississippi Burning* and subsequent media coverage, Philadelphia's first ever public commemorations drew more than one thousand visitors from across the country.[127] The film's success also led to the eventual prosecution of one of the murderers, Edgar Ray Killen, in 2005.[128] Fifteen years later, the Philadelphia Coalition, a multiracial organization comprised of business and political groups, along with civil rights organizations, was tasked with organizing another landmark commemorative event at the city's Neshoba County Coliseum and the Mt. Zion United Methodist Church.[129]

Today, tourists who visit the city's downtown welcome center, a converted train depot, will find a brochure that outlines a driving tour that traces the trio's tortured final hours.[130]

By the turn of the century, other efforts—largely grassroots in nature— were underway to remember the movement. As noted earlier, in 2000, Helen Sims opened what she claims is the first civil rights museum in the state. According to Sims, both white and Black Mississippians were opposed to her idea of creating a civil rights museum.[131] Other local museums—the Smith Robertson Museum and Cultural Center in Jackson, the Jacqueline House Museum in Vicksburg, the Ida B. Wells-Barnett Museum in Holly Springs, and the African American Military History Museum in Hattiesburg—also address topics related to civil rights and African American history but are not part of a cohesive, statewide civil rights tourism strategy.

Also in 2000, the US House of Representatives passed a bill to honor civil rights activist Aaron Henry, a Clarksdale native born on a plantation in Coahoma County in 1922 (although the bill was never passed in the Senate, it would have renamed the Clarksdale Federal Building and Post Office the "Aaron E. Henry Federal Building and United States Courthouse").[132] A World War II veteran, Henry graduated from Xavier University's pharmacy school in 1950 and returned to Clarksdale to pursue his pharmacy career.[133] He became the first president of Clarksdale's chapter of the NAACP as well as a member of other civil rights organizations in Mississippi, including the RCNL and the Mississippi Freedom Democratic Party.[134] Like many of his contemporaries, including Amzie Moore and T. R. M. Howard, Henry faced violent white backlash, including verbal harassment, arrest and imprisonment, economic sanctions, and death threats. White authorities got creative and even arrested Henry on a morals charge (for allegedly sexually propositioning a white hitchhiker) in 1962.[135] In Clarksdale, Henry's name also appears on a medical center and a chapter of Head Start. Today, Henry has his own MFT marker on Fourth Street in Clarksdale's Black section of the city's downtown area. The marker is located in an empty grass lot where his pharmacy once stood (for years, a sign posted there has proclaimed it the future home of the North Mississippi Civil Rights Museum). Most recently, a second memorial has appeared near his MFT marker: a silhouette of Henry with his hands spread out and accompanied by the declaration, "Aaron Henry Stood Tall Here." And, located on US Highway 61 between Cleveland and Clarksdale stands the Dr. Aaron E. Henry Memorial Highway marker, part of a larger Mississippi Department of Transportation Memorial Highway marker system which is designated by its brown color signage.

Despite these hopeful signs that Mississippi was finally beginning to recognize its civil rights heritage, by the early 2000s, the memories of the Mississippi Movement could hardly be found in a state teeming with statues, memorials, homes, and other material memory sites, many dedicated to revering the Confederacy and the Civil War. Published in 2004, *A Traveler's Guide to the Civil Rights Movement* laments the lack of civil rights memorialization in the state, describing the collective output as "modest" and "hard to find":

> There is one small, central museum in Jackson, one small community display in Port Gibson, and, sadly, many scattered headstones. Except in Jackson and Philadelphia, road signs to civil rights history are nonexistent. In towns with some of the most heroic events—McComb, Greenwood, Hattiesburg—a Confederate soldier on a pedestal still rules the public space. A stranger wandering Mississippi would have almost no idea that a revolution envied by the world took place there.[136]

The development of the state's blues tourism industry in the early to mid-2000s mirrors the process by which civil rights tourism has grown in Mississippi. Whereas blues tourism was limited initially to the uncoordinated efforts of grassroots blues enthusiasts throughout the state between 1977 and 2004, Stephen A. King notes that it eventually became "recognized as an important type of economic development and is financially supported by state government, politicians, and other legitimate institutional bodies."[137] In addition to popular museums such as the Delta Blues Museum in Clarksdale and the B.B. King Museum and Delta Interpretive Center in Indianola, one of the most visible examples of this burgeoning industry is the Blues Trail. Inaugurated in 2006 by the Mississippi Blues Commission, the trail has grown to encompass more than two hundred historical marker signs located throughout Mississippi and in other states, including Alabama, Illinois, California, as well as in Europe. Because so many of the Blues Trail's markers are dedicated to African Americans or the places they lived, labored, and performed, the trail reflects a clear and growing interest in Mississippi's African American history (and, of course, in marketing that history for economic gain). "Once ignored and scorned," King writes, "an important part of the state's African American culture and heritage is now being recognized and celebrated."[138] Because these efforts attracted growing numbers of tourists, official efforts to promote the state's civil rights history were expanding as well.

After a decade of planning, the designation of the Mississippi Delta as a National Heritage Area (MDNHA) in 2009 was an important new development in building a sustainable civil rights tourism infrastructure. With the mission of fostering "preservation, perpetuation and celebration of the Delta's heritage through a climate of collaboration and sustainable economic development," the MDNHA focuses on five heritage themes, including civil rights.[139] Delta State University's Delta Center for Culture and Learning is the management entity of the MDNHA, and is administered by a fifteen-member Board of Directors. Luther Brown, its first director (2000–2014), spearheaded the idea of a Mississippi Delta National Heritage Area. In 2014, Brown noted the collective effort involved in moving the idea of a national heritage area to reality: "Many people and numerous entities have worked hard to make this Heritage Area possible, and some have worked for over a decade to see this happen."[140] Not long after current director Rolando Herts took the helm of the Delta Center for Culture and Learning in 2014 following Brown's retirement, he recognized that some tourism efforts in the state, particularly in the area of blues tourism, supported a prevailing "narrative created around a nostalgia for a past that not everybody was able to experience and that did not allow everyone to live their best lives." Consequently, the Delta Center and the MDNHA started developing community programming, often based in oral history, to "bring in some other narratives."[141] One example is the Delta Jewels Oral History Partnership, an award-winning project that interpreted and celebrated the experiences of African American church mothers who lived through the Jim Crow era and civil rights movement in the Mississippi Delta. As of this writing, the Delta Center and the MDNHA is actively participating in a campaign to create an Emmett Till and Mamie Till-Mobley National Park with historical sites in Mississippi Delta as well as Illinois. The MDNHA also is the first National Heritage Area to be designated to the National Park Service's African American Civil Rights Network.

Similar to the state's success in marketing its blues culture and history, civil rights tourism has shifted from the local to the state level—with politicians and state tourism officials now financially supporting and celebrating the state's role in the civil rights movement. The first and most significant development in Mississippi's official efforts to promote civil rights tourism came in the form of yet another historical marker trail, a subject discussed in more depth in chapter 5. In 2011, the MFT joined the state's Blues Trail and the Country Music Trail with its first marker near the Bryant's Grocery building in Money. The MFT now includes more than thirty markers and has become an important, if imperfect, medium for narrating the people, places, and events that define the state's civil rights history. State, regional, and local tourism organizations highlight the MFT in promotional materials, and the Mississippi Development Authority's *Fiscal Year 2021 Annual Report* notes, collectively, "Mississippi's Trails Programs are highlights of the state tourism industry."[142]

The MFT is administered by the Mississippi Development Authority with funding provided by various agencies, including the Mississippi Department of Transportation and the MDAH. Interest in the trail paved the way for the construction of the MMH-MCRM. The December 2017 opening represents the most expansive and high-profile effort to scale up the state's promotion of its civil rights history. As we will see in chapter 6, the idea of a state civil rights museum was especially controversial in Mississippi, which had long engaged in cultural amnesia and rhetorical exaggerations of racial reconciliation between its white and Black residents. The controversy surrounding the construction of the MMH-MCRM was one of the many reasons why the project suffered from multiple delays over a fifteen-year period.

Ironically, while the state is expanding its civil rights memory work, other significant civil rights sites continue to deteriorate or have been outright destroyed. *Clarion-Ledger* journalist Jerry Mitchell has documented many of these destroyed sites, including Aaron Henry's home in Clarksdale.[143] The *Clarion-Ledger* quoted Leslie B. McLemore, a civil rights veteran, who condemned the destruction of the civil rights site: "It is now just a slab on Page Avenue in Clarksdale. Tearing down these landmarks really dishonors the people who paved the way."[144] The Bryant's Grocery building's slow deterioration is perhaps the most well-known example of the complexities associated with civil rights historical preservation. While material remains of civil rights sites throughout the state continue to disintegrate, the creation of the MFT and the opening of the MMH-MCRM are, without a doubt, significant memory milestones in the state's burgeoning civil rights tourism industry. In the next chapter, we discuss an important, but often underreported, element of Mississippi's civil rights tourism infrastructure: grassroots or vernacular tourism. While civil rights tourists will undoubtedly visit the MMH-MCRM in Jackson or stop at various MFT markers positioned throughout the state, these same tourists also have the opportunity to experience other, more localized efforts to remember the movement.

CHAPTER TWO

BREAKING GROUND

Vernacular Efforts in Mississippi Civil Rights Tourism

> The museum was . . . a grassroots, and still is, effort. A lot of people recognize the struggle to want to do. I want to do whether anyone else want to or not. There was a calling on my life to tell these stories so that my children's children and others will know them.
>
> —HELEN SIMS, founder of the Mississippi Heritage Consortium

In 2021, the MDNHA partnered with the MDAH to conduct a study of underdeveloped and endangered civil rights sites connected to the Mississippi Movement. The Civil Rights Sites Resource Study focused on eighteen counties in the state's Delta region, identifying over two hundred sites as candidates for historic preservation and heritage tourism development. Led by Memphis-based architectural historian Judith Johnson, the survey uncovered a vast array of buildings and locations, including public schools, community centers, and churches. As MDNHA executive director Rolando Herts told us, "there's so much here that people don't know about. You know, you pass by sites every day and don't realize that they're there. . . . There is absolutely an opportunity to have well over two hundred of these Freedom Trail markers in the Delta alone, let alone the state."[1] Among those sites is the former location of a COFO office and Freedom School in Sunflower, Mississippi, a building Johnson called "an excellent example on a national level of what was happening in Mississippi in terms of educating the voters and educating the population."[2] Despite the availability of state and federal grants to rehabilitate sites such as these, the sheer number identified in this study (which represents less than a quarter of all the state's counties) makes it likely that many will remain unmarked, if not forgotten. In the same way that local grassroots efforts are needed to preserve these civil rights sites, similar local efforts have been essential to telling the story of the Mississippi Movement, particularly in the absence of organized state support for civil rights tourism.

Sites such as these, notable for their inaccessibility, rural locations, and relative obscurity, exemplify a vernacular, grassroots civil rights tourism ever present in Mississippi's memory landscape. While much of the public's attention has been directed at the more recent and high-profile official representations of civil rights tourism, including the MFT and the MMH-MCRM, an equally important material element to the state's overall civil rights offerings are grassroots initiatives that emanate from "the people." Vernacular expressions take the form of museums (Emmett Till Historic Intrepid Center in Glendora), run-down buildings (SNCC headquarters in Greenwood), parks (Amzie Moore Park in Cleveland), artwork (the silhouette of Aaron Henry next to his MFT marker in Clarksdale), and streets and neighborhoods (Farish Street in Jackson, a mostly abandoned and deteriorating historic center of Black commerce). These grassroots representations are inconsistently promoted in tourism guides, brochures, pamphlets, postcards, and online. And while many vernacular expressions predate the MFT and the MMH-MCRM, others have emerged in the wake of the state's commitment to promoting its civil rights history.

Rather than attempting to conduct a rhetorical analysis of the myriad vernacular forms that dot the entire state, we focus our attention on four representative examples of grassroots civil rights tourism noted by their diversity and the varying degrees to which they embody vernacular expression: a house, an oral performance, a museum, and a memorial garden. First, we explore the memory building efforts of Glen Cotton, who renovated the Canton Freedom House, transforming it from the former Madison County headquarters of the Congress of Racial Equality in the 1960s to the Canton Freedom House Civil Rights Museum in 2013. With an exhibit curated by Cotton and the local community, the museum asserts itself as an authentic testament to the Mississippi Movement and its contemporary legacy. Next, we travel to the state's Delta region and visit Helen Sims's Mississippi Heritage Consortium, which houses the Rev. George Lee Museum of African American History and Heritage, the Pinetop Perkins Blues Museum and Cultural Arts and Heritage Center, and the Fannie Lou Hamer Civil Rights Museum (hereafter, "Sims Museum"). Located in a field just northwest of Belzoni, it offers unsuspecting visitors an unorthodox museum experience focused on the oral performance of history. Finally, we travel to Ruleville, home of the Fannie Lou Hamer Museum and the Fannie Lou Hamer Memorial Garden. While the museum was built primarily through grassroots work in Ruleville, the garden's development was only possible through complementary vernacular and national efforts that span several decades. Collectively, both sites present a glowing and inspiring remembrance of Hamer centered in the same themes Hamer represented and championed during her life: bravery, courage, and community.

Vernacular Culture, Vernacular Tourism

While the MCRM and the MFT are the most publicized and recognized elements of the state's civil rights tourism industry, there are numerous local and community-based efforts to remember the Mississippi Movement. Billing itself as the first museum in the state dedicated to civil rights, the Sims Museum is one of the earliest examples of a vernacular civil rights museum in Mississippi. Maja Mikula describes museums like this—also sometimes referred to as a "DIY museum" and "lay museum"—as a public-private space that is communal, democratic, rooted in local politics, and often infused with performance and storytelling.[3] Patricia G. Davis argues that museum staff performances "empower visitors to become active participants" and "use their own personal and shared memories to fill in the gaps in dominant history."[4] Located in an old farmhouse off US Highway 49W and led by professional storyteller Helen Sims, the museum captures the essence of the vernacular approach. Sims's electrifying oral performance showcases the elements of performative protest, a rhetorical form which, in many cases, demarcates vernacular expressions from their official counterparts.

While official culture reflects the interests of the powerful who desire to remember the past in a way that primarily serves dominant ideological interests, vernacular culture "come[s] from ordinary people who often oppose the representations of official culture."[5] At its most fundamental level, vernacular tourism is cultural expressions from ordinary citizens, "the folk." Vernacular tourism is characterized by hyperbolic statements ("first," "smallest," "largest"), local "heroes" exhibited in quasipublic spaces, the reappropriation of land for museums and other memory places, rural museums, historical markers that remember past events and people, as well as folk art. Places of vernacular expression are also characterized by general inaccessibility—one must forgo public transportation and drive (and walk) to these "folk" sites.[6]

Vernacular tourism is also oppositional, with ordinary citizens assuming an activist role in remembering a past that others would often rather forget. Indeed, vernacular tourism embodies a sense of personal agency and ownership over one's immediate surroundings and political context. Interestingly, this protest element can also be enacted at the group level where protesters disrupt other types of tourist activity. For example, citizens who deface, destroy, and attempt to remove Confederate memorials or statues are also challenging efforts to perpetuate white supremacy and Civil War tourism. Angered by official culture's oppressive and dehumanizing portrayal of the past, vernacular expressions resemble what John M. Sloop and Kent A. Ono call "out-law discourse." "We see out-law discourses as loosely shared logics of justice," they write, arguing that out-law discourses promote "ideas of right and wrong that are different than, although not necessarily opposed to, a culture's dominant logics of judgment and procedures for litigation."[7] In their review of the rhetorical characteristics of out-law discourse, Sarah Hagedorn VanSlette and Josh Boyd find that it "exposes and challenges sedimented ways of thinking" and, ultimately, serves as an opportunity for change. Not surprisingly, out-law discourses are interpreted by official culture as "illogical, immoral, or illegal."[8] As noted earlier, the decision to open the Sims Museum in 2000 was met with local opposition by both whites and African Americans who considered such a move controversial; one local politician even warned Sims not to be an "agitator," she told us.[9] In addition to their oppositional and agent-centered approach, museums, interpretive centers, and other expressions of vernacular tourism emerge from the "bottom up" (like social movements), are more obscure than official representations (e.g., lacking traditional advertising and media coverage), and do not rely on state funding. They operate with irregular hours or by appointment only, are often managed by one person with minimal staffing, are frequently located in marginalized and economically distressed areas, are perceived as more "downhome," "funky," and "authentic," and are often only tangentially connected to the larger tourism infrastructure.

While there are distinct differences between official and vernacular tourism, there are at least four instances where there is overlap and integration between the two touristic expressions. First, civil rights memory places sometimes contain both official and vernacular memory objects. The Fannie Lou Hamer Memorial Garden, located in an African American neighborhood in Ruleville, contains the gravesite of both Hamer and her husband, a statue of Hamer, and an assortment of other memory objects alongside an MFT marker honoring Hamer's significant contributions to the civil rights movement. In this space, the vernacular (metal plaques recognizing local residents, flowers left on the gravesite) and official (state MFT marker) are in seamless harmony rather than discordant opposition. Second, vernacular objects and places sometimes emerge over time to become official representations of culture. The MFT markers commemorate sites of vernacular protest ("'Black Power' Speech" in Greenwood; "Capitol Rally" in Jackson) and civil rights organizing and planning ("William Chapel" in Ruleville), along with civil rights leaders, the "folk," who were viewed by Mississippi's power structure as agitators, communists, and enemies of the state (Medgar Evers, Aaron Henry, Unita Blackwell, Amzie Moore). In another example, the *idea* of a state-funded museum dedicated to the Mississippi Movement certainly originated at the grassroots level before finally becoming fully realized as part of the state's official culture. Third, official culture sometimes contains vernacular discourse and knowledge as in the case of the MCRM, which engages the state's horrific record of lynching and other acts of racial genocide—a history that the state of Mississippi is only now beginning to formally acknowledge. Yet, this history was certainly well known in communities of color. Finally, while some memory spaces and objects are not promoted as part of the state's official civil rights narrative, local and regional tourism organizations do incorporate and legitimatize these vernacular cultural expressions. In the end, it is more accurate to reconceptualize official and vernacular public memory sites as existing on a continuum. The sections that follow are organized according to where each site might fall on such a continuum, beginning with those that received no funding or official support beyond that provided by their local community and concluding with a site that was made possible, in part, thanks to a national fundraising campaign. First, we stop in Canton, home of one of Mississippi's last standing Freedom Houses, where the building itself holds the key to its touristic appeal.

Last House Standing: The Canton Freedom House Civil Rights Museum (Canton)

As an official stop on the US Civil Rights Trail, the Canton Freedom House Civil Rights Museum (hereafter, "Canton Freedom House") is located in an economically distressed neighborhood in Canton, the seat of Madison County and twenty-six miles north of Jackson. The Canton Freedom House enjoys a slightly higher profile than some of the other vernacular sites in Mississippi's civil rights tourism industry. Opened to the public in 2013 by Canton resident Glen Cotton, who inherited the home from his grandparents, George and Rembert Washington, the Canton Freedom House served as the state headquarters for CORE, which established its first voter registration project in Mississippi there under the direction of George Raymond in the summer of 1963.[10] The house was built by the Washingtons in 1958 on a lot across the street from their gas station and grocery market. In 1963, they rented the house (and some time later a second small building next door) to CORE to serve as its base of operations in Mississippi after Raymond was unsuccessful securing other properties in town. The Washingtons suffered retaliation from local whites for doing so. "The city ... basically tried to put them out of business," Cotton told us.[11] Vendors refused to provide goods, gasoline, and equipment for their store, leading the local Black community to create its own supply chains, often under the cover of darkness, to keep the business running.[12] This retaliation would turn violent in the months leading up to the Freedom Summer campaign of 1964, when George Washington was harassed, arrested, and assaulted by local police and dynamite bombs were placed on and around their store.[13] Flonzie Brown-Wright, an activist who managed Canton's NAACP office, noted that the Washingtons "took a big risk in renting" CORE the house. "They endured a lot of atrocities but were determined."[14]

Despite dire threats to their lives and property, the Washingtons continued to rent the buildings to CORE, who used them as a communication center, a site of organizing and planning, as storage for donated clothing and books, and, of course, as housing for CORE volunteers. Cotton took care to emphasize that the house had a working telephone installed inside (a feature not common at the time). "The phone was just a lifeline," he said, a means of communication for CORE volunteers "when they got in trouble and when they felt intimidated."[15] Indeed, Cotton described the Freedom House as a safe house; the original windows were spray painted black and covered with chicken wire to repel bombs and other projectiles and to prevent law enforcement from peering inside.[16] This need for security was not unwarranted, as the Freedom House was the target of multiple drive-by shootings and bombings in May, June, and August 1964.[17]

Cotton grew up just down the street from the Freedom House. Following his grandfather's death in 2000, he kept the building as a boarding house until 2008, at which point it languished in a state of disrepair. In 2012, a letter from the city required a difficult decision: either repair the house and make it structurally sound or tear it down. Tom Manoff, a CORE volunteer who worked in the Freedom House in the 1960s, encouraged him to preserve it.[18] This, in addition to the fact that tourists would often drive by the property to look and take photographs (despite its lack of promotion as a memory site), inspired Cotton—a building contractor with forty years' experience in the construction industry—to save it from ruin on his own. Cotton's goal was to "keep it as original as I could."[19]

Canton Freedom House Civil Rights Museum. Photo by Roger Davis Gatchet.

Over an intensive two-month period in 2012, Cotton replaced the flooring, rewired the entire house, and rebuilt the interior walls. He removed two rear bathrooms from the original floor plan in order to create more exhibit space and make room for a small community computer lab. He also installed central air and heating, replaced the roof, sealed up all the windows (to prevent light from damaging photographs and other exhibited documents), and painted the interior. With the renovation complete, Cotton turned his attention to creating the exhibit. With no formal training in curation or museology, Cotton educated himself on the house's history and relied on community input and donations for the displays. Locals offered photographs and newspaper clippings from their personal collections, and he sourced other materials, especially picture frames, from local pawn shops and thrift stores. The remodel cost approximately $20,000, which he largely paid for himself after attempts to secure historic preservation funds through the MDAH proved unsuccessful. Although Mississippi State Senator Barbara Blackmon and her husband, Mississippi House Representative Edward Blackmon Jr., have regularly advocated for Cotton's museum since at least 2016, to date he has received no state support to fund it.[20]

This "labor of love," as Cotton told us during a 2020 interview, opened to the general public as the Canton Freedom House Civil Rights Museum in 2013.[21] "The house is worth every bit of effort that I've put into it for its preservation," he told us, noting that the museum is "contributing to the preservation of our history."[22] In contrast to the intermittent operating hours at so many vernacular memory sites, Cotton has managed to keep his museum open on a regular weekly schedule with a staff composed entirely of unpaid volunteers. Visitors who come on weekdays will find the museum open from 9:00 a.m. to 4:00 p.m., with appointments available on Saturdays. Citing Canton's endemic poverty as a major barrier to access, Cotton decided to operate the museum on a donations-only basis to increase the likelihood that local residents would visit more regularly. He sees one or two visitors per week, mostly white tourists from out of town (including some international tourists), and receives only enough donations to cover half of his operating costs. Although the museum has lost money every year since its opening, Cotton perseveres, seeing his work as similar to his grandparents' commitment to support CORE's use of the house. The museum is a local "jewel," he asserts. "I'm still happy about it because I still feel like I'm contributing to the community."[23]

A small room just off the front entrance doubles as the museum's welcome desk and main office, interspersed with displays dedicated to George Raymond and other local civil rights leaders. It is there that one of the authors met museum volunteer Wesley Rushing, who explained the house's history and its significance to the Madison County movement. Cotton was also there to conduct the main tour, drawing attention to displays dedicated to his grandparents, Jim Crow laws and slavery, *Brown v. Board of Education*, and other seminal campaigns of the Mississippi Movement which, as with the MCRM, are the museum's primary focus. Most of the displays in the handful of rooms throughout the house stand on their own, with no obvious chronological narrative connecting them.

Indicative of the process through which it was created, the Canton Freedom House possesses a certain haphazard quality. In stark contrast to its appearance when it served as a Freedom House under CORE, the interior walls are painted red throughout. Displays reflect the DIY spirit that made the museum possible, with framed photos hung askew and newspaper clippings tacked directly to interior walls. Some of the displays bring together photographs and documents that cohere around a specific theme (e.g., March Against Fear, Freedom Summer), including several that offer pictorial evidence of the Madison County movement's success in the form of African Americans more recently elected to local office, serving as judges, or in law enforcement. Other displays are best described as a bricolage, a hodge-podge of unrelated artifacts and materials. In one example, an old washboard and rusted set of hand-crank egg beaters are displayed alongside photographs of local individuals, images of southern Confederate currency, and a poster displaying national civil rights figures—all along a wall labeled "*Brown v. Board of Education*" and "Voting Rights." Another wall dedicated to pastors of the movement inexplicably includes iconic images of heavyweight boxer Muhammad Ali and Tommie Smith and John Carlos with their fists raised at the 1968 Summer Olympics. Some rooms have materials stacked in corners or scattered on tabletops, waiting for a space on one of the walls.

The amateur nature of the exhibit gives it a quaint, homey quality that would seem out of place in a professionally curated museum but certainly feels appropriate within the confines of a house museum that was built with grassroots support. Affectively, the Canton Freedom House *feels* right; it is, in the most literal sense, the neighborhood's museum. Its primary appeal, particularly for visitors who have already experienced the MMH-MCRM in nearby Jackson, is not necessarily the exhibit but the house itself. As one of the last Freedom Houses still standing in Mississippi (and, to our knowledge, the only one that has been turned into an active museum), the building embodies a type of authenticity that is categorically distinct from other museum sites on Mississippi's memorial landscape. History happened *here*. Even with the changes to its original floor plan, visitors can still walk through the same rooms where CORE volunteers organized, socialized, slept, and lived. One online reviewer highlighted this, calling it a "very realistic" place.[24] Upon starting the tour of the house, Rushing was careful to point out that the chicken wire on the outside of the windows is original; that was the actual wire that kept actual Molotov cocktails from crashing through the windows during Freedom Summer. Cotton mentioned that until recently, the concrete sidewalks outside the house still bore the cracks caused by those explosions.[25] Clearly, the Canton Freedom House is a visceral testament to the truth-telling function of civil rights tourism. Whereas the MCRM mostly relies on its exhibit displays to do that, the Canton Freedom House's very existence accomplishes this act. Although its economic impact on the local community is negligible, the Freedom House's importance should not be measured in strictly economic terms. It has been used for civil rights commemorative events since its opening, and its continued presence at the same site and in the same residential neighborhood where CORE established its regional headquarters some sixty years ago speaks to a persistent resilience that is common in vernacular memorialization. A similar resilience is at work fifty-seven miles away on the outskirts of the Delta town of Belzoni, where a very different vernacular museum is named after two civil rights leaders: Fannie Lou Hamer and Reverend George Lee. We now turn our attention to that site.

Lessons from Lula, the Old Storyteller: The Mississippi Heritage Consortium (Belzoni)

Leaving the Canton Freedom House, visitors who head west on Highway 16 eventually hit Highway 49W, leading them into the Delta and to an old farmhouse in the middle of a field on the outskirts of Belzoni. It actually houses three distinct museums whose official names belie the makeshift, almost haphazard nature of the site: the Rev. George Lee Museum of African American History and Heritage, the Pinetop Perkins Blues Museum and Cultural Arts and Heritage Center, and the Fannie Lou Hamer Civil Rights Museum. In truth, each museum is a series of modest displays housed in different rooms inside the same building, whose rustic surroundings, limited exhibit space, appointment-only hours, and focus on performance over traditional curated displays makes this an exemplar *par excellence* of a vernacular museum. Geographically speaking, the decision to open the museums in Belzoni—a town of around two thousand that touts itself as the "Catfish Capital of the World"—makes sense insofar as it is the birthplace of Pinetop Perkins (a respected blues pianist) and the home of Reverend George Lee. Based in Belzoni, Lee operated a printing shop and grocery, preached the gospel, and was intimately involved in the struggle for civil rights as a coorganizer (with Gus Courts) of the Belzoni chapter of the NAACP and vice president of the RCNL before he was assassinated.[26] Dedicated on May 10, 2013, "The Reverend George Lee" MFT marker, located in Belzoni, recounts Lee's assassination at the hands of two unknown white assailants.[27]

In December 2000, Helen Sims founded her museum despite opposition from locals who feared a civil rights museum would dredge up an uncomfortable past.[28] Calling the museum "grassroots," Sims views it as a powerful educational tool to narrate the state's civil rights history—a story Mississippi's official culture was still reluctant to tell when she founded it nearly two decades before the MMH-MCRM opened.[29] In a 2012 interview, Sims reaffirmed why the state's civil rights history must be told: "I think that, if history is not accurately portrayed—if history is not available to the people of the present—then they will live a life in the future miseducated, misinformed."[30]

A far cry from the newer multi-million-dollar MMH-MCRM in Jackson, Sims's humble enterprise is open by appointment only. The museum sits amidst fields just outside the city limits on Highway 49W and is relatively

Museums of the Mississippi Heritage Consortium. Photo by Roger Davis Gatchet.

easy to spot from the road. According to the museum's website, a "feasibility study revealed the best location for the Cultural Heritage Project was on Highway 49, a major traffic flow, where more than an estimated 9,000 travelers travel each day, making this the ideal location for the Cultural Heritage Project."[31] However, despite the fact that Highway 49W is a major thoroughfare, the museum's location is not where a typical tourist—or anyone for that matter—would be likely to walk by. There are no sidewalks, no paved parking lot, and, as with so many of the state's vernacular memory sites, no tourism infrastructure.

We made arrangements speaking with Sims by phone to visit the museum on July 18, 2016. After parking in a grassy field serving as a parking lot, visitors pass a red, metallic heart-shaped sculpture as they walk along pavers that form a makeshift path leading up to the front entrance. Various signs affixed to the beige siding of the building identify the three museums housed there, including one that asserts its authenticity as the first civil rights museum in the state. The signs, with their DIY aesthetic and scattered typos, lend a folksy charm to the site. Two sharecropper shacks can be seen in the field that extends behind the museum. As part of Sims's as-yet-unrealized efforts to create a "Heritage Village," at some point the shacks were relocated to the museum site to enhance its cultural setting (and, apparently, to provide future homes for each museum in the consortium).[32] The shacks accentuate the rural poverty that is ever-present in the Delta. The modest website for the museum consortium suggests a larger, ambitious vision, with descriptions

Fannie Lou Hamer Civil Rights Museum Sign. Photo by Roger Davis Gatchet.

of a Reenactment Society that works "exclusively" with the museums, as well as a proposed civil rights memorial to lynching victims in the state.[33] "And we're just proud of the things . . . and the insight he [God] has given us here to break ground on," Sims has said, implying the museum is a space through which she can do God's work.[34]

The museum's small size led us to anticipate a rather quick and uneventful visit. Put simply, we expected to be underwhelmed. Nothing written on the museum's website or mentioned during a brief phone conversation with Sims when scheduling our tour, however, would prepare us for an experience we alternately described in our fieldnotes as "powerful," "unorthodox," and "surreal." Upon walking through the front door, Sims greeted us in character, we would later learn, as Lula, the "Old Storyteller." Dressed in a long cotton dress and a white curly wig, Sims asked us to join several African American teenage students who were seated in front of a small platform stage on the far side of the entrance. We did not pay an entrance fee but were encouraged to leave a donation upon our exit.

Waiting for further direction from Sims as we sat with the group gave us an opportunity to take in the space. Like many other vernacular memory sites that fall outside the state's purview, the quality of the displays reflects the museum's limited funding. Unframed, ruffled posters bearing photographs and biographies of civil rights movement figures (Emmett Till, Rosa Parks, Lamar Smith, and others) dominated one side of the room, along with displays recounting historical information about slavery, sharecropping, Jim Crow laws, and the March Against Fear. Two large posters described Sims's plans to install a lynching memorial on the grounds of the museum, while period artifacts (a washboard and cotton bale, oil lanterns, cast-iron cookware) filled the remaining space around the stage, which was designed to resemble the covered, weathered front porch of a sharecropper shack.

Eventually, Sims—Lula, the Old Storyteller—sat down in a wooden rocking chair on stage, with a small fabric doll, adorned with a similar white wig as that of Sims, adjacent to her in a miniature rocking chair of its own. Speaking in multiple voices that ranged from a gentle grandmotherly rasp to a southern Baptist preacher delivering a fiery Sunday sermon, the Old Storyteller launched into a nearly two-hour, *tour de force* performance that traced African American history from the origins of the slave trade through the present day. A modern-day griot of sorts, her mythic narrative—told without breaks or intermission—recounted the US Civil War and emancipation, sharecropping and the prison system, and important periods and figures in the Mississippi Movement, including Freedom Summer, Fannie Lou Hamer, and the Rev. George Lee, whom she described as the "father of the civil rights movement." While Sims's narrative was mostly concerned with the past, she did discuss the present, including police shootings of unarmed Black men in Ferguson and Baton Rouge. She also intertwined the past and near-present by discussing how Mississippi finally voted in 2013 to officially ratify the Thirteenth Amendment, the abolition of slavery. For Sims, the civil rights movement is not a thing of the past, but part of an ongoing struggle for human rights.

Despite the frequent looks of boredom from the students in attendance (some of whom slept during our visit; one got the impression this was not their first experience at the museum), we were captivated by the Old Storyteller's performance. In character, Sims's narration was delivered with such authority that it allowed one to believe, if only temporarily, that she had firsthand experience with an impossibly expansive arc of historical events going back decades, even centuries. Much of her performance that day described the indomitable spirit and faith that inspired African Americans in the freedom struggle after the Civil War. Consciously channeling the "spirit" of Hamer, Sims offered living witness to horrors both past and present, describing Mississippi as a "hub of darkness and hatred" and the lynching capital of the world.[35]

In narrating that history, Sims regularly wove biblical tales and verses throughout her performance, connecting stories from the book of Genesis to the civil rights movement and asserting that Satan is the root cause of all racism. This was the most fascinating and surprising element of her performance, and something that distinguishes her museum from other civil rights public memory sites in Mississippi. By shifting blame to Satan as the primary cause of racism and racial tension (past and present) between African Americans and whites in the United States, Sims forwards an explanation that reflects Hamer and Lee's Christian worldview (both were deeply religious) but whose meaning can be interpreted in a number of ways. From one perspective, the history of white supremacy in the United States is so horrendous that only a cosmological explanation—Satan himself—can fully account for it. During our multiple visits to the state, we found no other sites that framed the Mississippi Movement in this particular way. An ironic consequence of this perspective, of course, is that it implicitly, and problematically, absolves the state of Mississippi of its responsibility for perpetuating racist systems of violence and oppression. An alternate reading might consider the religious references as metaphorical rather than literal, a kind of coded performance-within-a-performance similar to what James C. Scott calls infrapolitics, "a politics of disguise and anonymity that takes place in public view but is designed to have a double meaning or to shield the identity of the actors."[36] From this perspective, Satan stands in for Mississippi in a coded critique that avoids directly criticizing whites or the state and is thus more palatable for white audiences who visit the museum.

This kind of immersive and affective experience, wholly unique on Mississippi's memorial landscape, offers a breathtaking survey of civil rights and Mississippi Movement history; the lasting impression is qualitatively distinct from anything tourists will get from a more traditional museum or memorial. One Google reviewer described Sims's performance as "inspirational" and her museum "a must visit place" for anyone seeking to better "understand the civil rights movement in Mississippi."[37] In some ways, Sims's site is an antimuseum. We were politely shooed out of the building shortly after her performance with no opportunity to closely peruse the artifacts on display. Ironically, the actual space, which bills itself as a three-museum consortium and cultural center, is presented as an afterthought, a cover of sorts that offers a legitimizing, authenticating place for the real show and focal point that is the Old Storyteller. Sims described hers as the "Po' Monkey's of Museums" (a reference to the Po' Monkey's blues juke joint near Merigold) and emphasized (on more than one occasion) that up to that point her museum had never received a single dollar of state or federal funding, noting at the end of the performance that she is "proud" of that fact. Her comments suggest that she sees the museum as a direct response to institutionalized efforts by the state (and even the nation) to memorialize Fannie Lou Hamer, Rev. George Lee, and the Mississippi Movement. Here, it seems, tourists get to hear the *real* story about African American history and culture from a wise woman (or character) who has learned that history as it was handed down to her through oral traditions. Her performance as the Old Storyteller, which she has enacted at schools, churches, and public ceremonies over the years, can be considered a form of social activism, one element of civil rights tourism's goal of social justice. Rather than confine history to the past or in static museum displays located at one site, she connects those stories to the present in a living, breathing, and dynamic fashion in multiple sites. The inclusion of present-day anecdotes of injustice underscores her commitment to social activism. This focus on motion and indeterminate meaning is unique to vernacular memorialization. As we will see, the Mississippi Heritage Consortium is not the only civil rights tourism site to remember Fannie Lou Hamer. In Hamer's Mississippi Delta hometown of Ruleville, located forty-five miles north of Belzoni on Highway 49W, are two different, but equally compelling, sites of memory that honor the legacy and heroism of the late civil rights leader: the Fannie Lou Hamer Museum and the Fannie Lou Hamer Memorial Garden.

Standing Tall in the Delta: Fannie Lou Hamer Museum and Fannie Lou Hamer Memorial Garden (Ruleville)

> She really was the prophet feeding the people the truth. And she really was the fearless person going forth not on her own power but with the power of God. I don't think she saw her role in the movement as that of a historically great leader, but simply as an extension of her religion, from Luke, of tending to the sick and bringing liberty to the captives.
>
> —L. C. DORSEY, Mississippi Movement activist[38]

The Fannie Lou Hamer Museum (hereafter, "Hamer Museum") and the Fannie Lou Hamer Memorial Garden (hereafter, "Memorial Garden") are located in this largely impoverished African American community with a population of around 2,600 residents. Although Hamer was born in Montgomery County, situated just east of US Interstate 55 and the state's Delta region, her sharecropping family moved to a Delta plantation in Sunflower County near Ruleville in 1919 when Hamer was two.[39] Until she became involved in the Mississippi Movement in 1962, Hamer worked as a sharecropper on plantations in the Delta with her family and, later, with her husband, Perry "Pap" Hamer, whom she married in 1944.[40] In August 1962, Hamer attended a civil rights meeting, sponsored by SNCC and the Southern Christian Leadership Conference (SCLC), at Ruleville's William Chapel Missionary Baptist

Church.[41] The meeting was a transformative experience for Hamer, and for the next fifteen years, she became intimately involved in the movement—as an organizer, a leader, and an inspiration to many, including former SNCC member June Johnson, who praised Hamer for expanding "the political consciousness about true democracy in this country."[42]

A powerful orator and singer, Hamer's early efforts—as a SNCC field secretary—involved leading voter registration drives to expand the African American vote in Mississippi. In 1964, she cofounded the Mississippi Freedom Democratic Party (MFDP), a racially inclusive grassroots "independent political organization."[43] The MFDP was "conceived to give Negro citizens of Mississippi an experience in political democracy and to establish a channel through which all citizens, Negro and white, can actively support the principles and programs of the National Democratic Party."[44] Through her civil rights work, Hamer became a powerful symbol of resistance whom Charles McLaurin, a SNCC activist and Hamer's campaign manager, called "our champion for civil rights and human rights."[45] She also paid dearly for her unwillingness to accept the racial edicts of Jim Crow. She was fired and evicted from Marlow Plantation, where she lived and worked prior to attempting to register to vote in 1962.[46] She was verbally harassed and threatened, physically and sexually assaulted, and the target of failed assassination attempts. In one particularly horrific event, Hamer and other movement activists were arrested in Winona, Mississippi, in 1963 while returning from a voter registration drive in Charleston, South Carolina.[47] Hamer and others were jailed and tortured. Although Hamer survived her gruesome assault by both law enforcement and Black prisoners (who were goaded into beating her by the officers), she never fully recovered from her injuries, the victim of "racial and sexual brutality that scarred her literally and figuratively."[48] As Maegan Parker Brooks describes that night in her rhetorical biography of Hamer, "Hamer's debilitating physical pain was not all that kept her from the rest her battered body so badly needed. The ongoing screams echoing through the jailhouse as the remaining group members received their beatings made sleep impossible."[49]

Hamer's gut-wrenching speech at the 1964 Democratic National Convention brought the former sharecropper to national attention. In her analysis of Hamer's vernacular style, Brooks argues that her power as a speaker was "built upon her ethos as a representative of the country's most oppressed people by suggesting that those furthest from the center hold valuable insight regarding the national malaise."[50] In the following years, Hamer traveled across the United States and abroad to speak at civil rights meetings, including her first overseas trip to Guinea in 1964.[51] Between 1964 and 1971, she ran—unsuccessfully—for political office, including a bid for Mississippi State Senate in 1971. She participated in the 1964 Freedom Summer campaign and marched with Martin Luther King Jr. during the 1966 March Against Fear after James Meredith was shot. In 1969, Hamer purchased Freedom Farm, a forty-acre cooperative designed to give Sunflower County's poor Black citizens "access to their own land and the fruits of their own labor," a social experiment designed to "free them economically and psychologically from the 'plantation mentality' that crippled many black Mississippians and kept them dependent on white paternalism."[52] Hamer continued to be politically active throughout the early 1970s. Yet, by the mid-1970s with her health failing, her civil rights activities slowed. She underwent breast cancer treatment in 1976 and died March 14, 1977, from heart failure brought on by complications from diabetes and cancer.[53]

Today, Fannie Lou Hamer is the "face" of Ruleville. Ruleville greets locals and visitors alike with "Home of Fannie Lou Hamer" welcome signs. The town even renamed its post office, a daycare center, and a residential street after the civil rights icon.[54] In 2019, the Fannie Lou Hamer Cancer Foundation announced the groundbreaking of a "state-of-the-art" headquarters to be built in the town that will include both a medical center and another museum honoring Hamer.[55] Brooks is correct when she asserts that "it would be impossible to drive through Ruleville and not realize that this was where Hamer lived and worked, that she played a pivotal role in redefining race relations in this small Delta town, and that she is sorely missed."[56] In contrast, the memory of Democratic US senator James O. Eastland, the segregationist Mississippi senator (1941, 1943–1978) who ruled over Sunflower County and strongly opposed the civil rights movement, is largely absent from Ruleville's and Mississippi's growing memory landscape. In the *Senator and the Sharecropper*, historian Chris Myers Asch observed that even Eastland's family members "seemed eager to distance themselves from him, or at least his reputation."[57]

The Fannie Lou Hamer Museum is located at the corner of L. F. Packer Drive and Byron Street. Located just down the street from the late civil rights leader's Memorial Garden, the museum shares space with Head Start and Early Start. The Hamer Museum–Head Start contiguous pairing is appropriate considering this federal initiative, inspired by President Johnson's "War on Poverty" and a byproduct of the Economic Act of 1964, was created to break the cycle of poverty through early education intervention—a goal shared by civil rights leaders and organizations, including SNCC.[58]

Former Ruleville alderwoman Hattie Robinson Jordan is acknowledged as the primary force behind creating the Hamer Museum. Born in Morgan City,

Mississippi, Jordan moved to the small hamlet of Doddsville (near Ruleville) at the age of two.[59] Jordan and her family sharecropped on the Eastland Plantation, an experience that led her to understand education as a vehicle for economic uplift: "I lived on a plantation, chopped cotton, and I picked cotton. But I saw education as being a mechanism that would move me from that condition to a better lifestyle."[60] She earned her BA at Mississippi Valley State.[61] After college, her first goal was to emancipate her family from the plantation: "I couldn't be comfortable, happy, teaching school and having a dollar in my pocket and knowing that my sister and daddy were still on that plantation and not being comfortable."[62] Jordan was successful, and she and her family moved into a house on Fannie Lou Hamer Drive in Ruleville.[63] Jordan went on to have a career as an educator, including being the first Black faculty member at Rosedale High School in 1967. Not surprisingly, she was subjected to social isolation and racial taunts.[64] She served on Hamer's Freedom Farm Board.[65] She characterized Hamer as an "activist for human rights and all political rights"; Hamer, according to Jordan, "touched every aspect of our lives," from expanding voting rights to providing food and other material resources to help the citizens of Ruleville.[66] Jordan died in 2019.

The museum has no dedicated website or regular hours of operation, and the source of its funding is unknown.[67] In fact, the museum barely has an online presence at all, and its address cannot be confirmed using Google Maps (those who search for it using Google's mapping service are instead directed to Sims's museum in Belzoni). The Ruleville museum, which opened in 2012 on Hamer's ninety-fifth birthday, has yet to be featured in any major civil rights tourism guide, including the 2021 *U.S. Civil Rights Trail*.[68] Tourists are unlikely to know of its existence except by happenstance, and once discovered, they will approach the building only to find that to tour it, they must contact one of two individuals (Georgia Sibley or Bobbie Bound) whose phone numbers are displayed near the front door.

After repeated efforts and delays stemming from the museum's temporary closure in 2020 due to the COVID-19 pandemic, one of the authors was able to gain access to the museum during the summer of 2021 by calling Georgia Sibley, who is a member of the Fannie Lou Hamer Memorial Garden and Museum Foundation, on a Friday and inquiring about visiting the museum (the author visited the museum again in March 2022). Sibley said she was available to open the museum the following Monday at 2 p.m. She asked the author to call her on Monday morning to confirm the meeting time. The author called on Monday, and Sibley indicated that she anticipated arriving at 2 p.m. but might be delayed because of a potential work conflict. Unlike official museums with a fulltime staff and regular operating hours, vernacular museums like the Hamer Museum are open by appointment only. They rely on volunteers who, like Sibley, are employed elsewhere and must find time to field inquiries by visitors, drive to and open the museum, and remain until visitors have completed their tour.

The author arrived at 2 p.m. and, after gaining access to the building via a Head Start–Early Start employee who did not appear to be associated with the Hamer Museum, waited in a hallway that serves as the only access point to the museum exhibit. The building's cinderblock walls and fluorescent lights typify the building's mid-twentieth-century Brutalist architecture. To the left of the museum's front door is a sign announcing, "Welcome to the Fannie Lou Hamer Museum Center: 'Her Light Still Shines.'" To the right, a notice reminds visitors of several museum rules, including, "Keep a safe distance between you and each work of art" and "Running, pushing, and roughhousing are not allowed in the Museum." Photography is also not permitted.

Sibley arrived offering a warm greeting and some introductory remarks before the author started his self-guided tour. The museum's admission fee is five dollars (interestingly, the author had to initiate payment). The museum's exhibit spans five self-contained rooms with corresponding titles: (1) Plantation, (2) William Chapel, (3) Civil Rights, (4) Library, and (5) Contributions. In one of the few places where one can find information about the Hamer Museum online, a succinct description of the exhibit notes that it positions "Hamer's activism in the larger context of the fight for civil rights in the Delta as well as the state of Mississippi."[69] Indeed, the museum is a study in individual recognition and celebration, humility and community. As we will see, the use of a variety of artifacts—photographs, posters, drawings, artwork, political cartoons, newspaper clippings, agricultural implements, and more—highlights Hamer's struggles and extraordinary accomplishments within the context of the larger collectivity of the Mississippi Movement.

Unsurprisingly, a museum dedicated to the late civil rights activist would, of course, prominently feature its biographical subject. Hamer's presence is experienced both visually and emotionally throughout the museum in the form of multiple Hamer timelines and brief biographical narratives, famous quotations (the oft-cited "I'm Sick and Tired of Being Sick and Tired"; "Nobody's Free Until Everybody Is Free"), artwork ("Fannie Lou Hamer's First Home in Ruleville, MS"), political posters, photographs, Hamer's own discourse in the form of handwritten letters and testimonies, and other archival materials. Hamer's civil rights initiatives and grassroots organizing projects are also featured; for example, the "Contributions" room includes a variety of materials, ranging from the "Freedom Farm Corporation" to "Garment Factory," from "Pig Bank" to "Head Start." Rather than offer an exhaustive biographical account, the exhibit instead highlights key moments from Hamer's life. Here, her courageous truth-telling leadership is evidenced by the price she paid for her activism through stories of her experience working (and being fired from) the Marlow Plantation, the physical abuse and sexual violence she endured inside that Winona jailhouse, and her searing testimony in front of the Credentials Committee at the 1964 DNC. All are relived through various rhetorical fragments scattered throughout the museum. It is no accident that Hattie Robinson Jordan and others who assembled the museum's artifacts positioned a large poster, "Fannie Lou Hamer[:] Always Telling It Like It Was!" in a prominent place at the beginning of the exhibit. Visitors who enter the museum cannot miss it.

At the same time, Hamer's powerful biographical presence is shared through the voices and stories of others, especially her friend and fellow civil rights activist Charles McLaurin, who himself is honored in the form of multiple certificates of appreciation and recognition. Hamer's humility is evident from the outset. The lyrics to her signature song, "This Little Light of Mine," are posted near the museum's front door, the words printed on a white background and set in a black frame. This gospel song not only conveys Hamer's fervent belief in the power of agape love to conquer division and hate,[70] but it also suggests, via the diminutive "little," that Hamer considered herself a part of a larger struggle against racial tyranny. As McLaurin told us in a 2021 interview, the museum emphasizes "that the work of Fannie Lou Hamer is alive" and is part of a larger "effort to keep the little light shining."[71] Indeed, the museum shares "the light" by celebrating the contributions of other civil rights leaders and activists including Amzie Moore, Mae Bertha Carter, T. R. M. Howard, Charles McLaurin, Unita Blackwell, Medgar Evers, Rev. George Lee, and James Meredith, among others. The room's title, "Contributions," also reinforces the sense of collective action. Interestingly, the museum spotlights members of the Mississippi Movement to the near exclusion of national figures such as Martin Luther King Jr.

Similar to the DIY aesthetic of the Canton Freedom House and other vernacular museums, the Hamer Museum does not contain professionally crafted displays or sophisticated technology, nor does it offer visitors interactive or immerse experiences. There are no touchscreens or audio installations here. Although the museum does include a television and one DVD/VHS player, they were not turned on during the author's visits. Instead, stationary photos, posters, artwork, and other memory items affixed to cinderblock walls dominate the exhibit. Some objects are placed directly on the floor, and harsh fluorescent lighting casts an unyielding glare throughout the museum. In this context, the lighting offers a stark, unromanticized memory of Hamer and the Mississippi Movement. Unlike the fifteen-million-dollar B.B. King Museum and Delta Interpretive Center located in nearby Indianola that remembers the "King of the Blues" through a linear narrative of elevating transcendence,[72] Hamer's nonlinear biographical treatment in the Hamer Museum has no discernable beginning or end; instead, her story is interspersed with narratives of other movement activists, an effect that reinscribes both her modesty and a sense of collective action. Finally, while five of the rooms are labeled according to a specific theme, items appear to be "misplaced" in some of the rooms, a curatorial practice noticeable in the Canton Freedom House as well. For example, the William Chapel room, dedicated to remembering the William Chapel Missionary Baptist Church in Ruleville, includes a blurry photo of a child picking cotton with adults positioned in the background. This photo's importance is not to be discounted, for it documents the vile use of child labor. However, the photo's relevance to the William Chapel church is uncertain.

While the museum celebrates Hamer's activism and accomplishments as well as acknowledges the contributions of other civil rights leaders and activists, it also makes clear that the Mississippi Movement did not operate in a vacuum—white supremacy and racial terrorism are ever-present in the exhibit. The "Plantation" room, which contains a variety of household items (chamber pot) and farm implements (plow), reminds visitors of the difficult working and living conditions on the plantation. This room also tells the story of Hamer's material struggles before she joined the movement in 1962. In addition to the photo of child labor, the "William Chapel" room includes a copy of a 1964 issue of *Look* magazine with a striking quotation displayed in large print: "If any of my niggers try to register, I'll shoot them down like rabbits." At the same time, while visitors are reminded of Mississippi's hostile environment, these representations of the state's closed society never overwhelm the museum's collective sense of history. The number of artifacts dedicated to remembering Hamer and the Mississippi Movement outnumber representations of racial oppression. In a sense, then, the museum communicates how Hamer and the Mississippi Movement achieved victory against a state which engaged in legal and extralegal means to maintain its racial and political hegemony.

While the museum's collection focuses most of its attention on Hamer and the movement prior to her death in 1977, other artifacts are more recent, with many serving to honor the late civil rights leader. In the hallway leading to the five rooms, visitors will find newspaper clippings from the 2000s, including a report about the unveiling of the Hamer statue that is the centerpiece of the Fannie Lou Hamer Memorial Garden. A nearby display calls attention to a 2017 resolution honoring Hamer on what would have been her one hundredth birthday. Finally, friends and admirers pay respect to Hamer's legacy through art and literature, including a poem by Hermand Bennette Jr. called, simply, "Fannie Lou."

Although the Hamer Museum's location in a municipal building lacks the kind of architectural authenticity of the Canton Freedom House, it is an important vernacular element of the broader civil rights tourism industry in Mississippi and emblematic of the kinds of local resources that culturally (but perhaps not economically) sustain it. Visitors looking for a more traditional museum experience won't find it in Helen Sims's performance at her Fannie Lou Hamer Civil Rights Museum in Belzoni (which, ironically, covered few biographical details about Hamer), but they certainly will in Ruleville. Leaving the Hamer Museum, visitors need only walk or drive two blocks east on Byron Street, past William Chapel Missionary Baptist Church, before transitioning into a largely African American neighborhood and arriving at the final site explored in this chapter: a memorial garden dedicated to Fannie Lou Hamer that was decades in the making.

Before her death in 1977, Hamer told McLaurin, "Mac, I lived on a plantation all of my life. Please don't let them bury me on a plantation."[73] Not realizing at the time that she was just weeks away from dying, McLaurin "committed to it. Because I figured . . . she would outlive me."[74] McLaurin faced numerous challenges planning Hamer's funeral at a time when most African Americans were buried on plantations. "All the burial spots are on a plantation," McLaurin said in a 2016 interview, remembering that period. "They're all on a plantation."[75] He eventually determined that Hamer's Freedom Farm Cooperative was an ideal location for her final resting place. Unfortunately, this forty-acre plot—all that remained of Hamer's cooperative—was designated as private property, and Ruleville's zoning laws prevented human burials there. With the assistance of civil rights attorney Cleve McDowell, McLaurin reached an agreement with the Freedom Farm Board and the City of Ruleville to transfer ownership of the property back to the city and in the process reclassify it as public property, allowing Hamer's burial to proceed.[76]

At the time, that property was little more than an open field, McLaurin told us, a far cry from the prominent public memory site it would become decades later.[77] "There was no memorial, there wasn't nothing out there but her gravesite," he remembered, "and . . . I hoped that some day, somebody here, in this town, would pick this up, and run with it."[78] In fact, the construction of a monument at the burial site within three years was an explicit condition of the agreement McLaurin and his attorney negotiated with the City of Ruleville.[79] A Ruleville resident who worked for the local Head Start program raised funds to install a proper headstone for Hamer's grave,[80] but a little over two years after her burial, Hamer's gravesite was vandalized by thieves who stole the tombstone and a commemorative plaque that was placed there.[81]

Development of the gravesite into a public memory site took a number of turns during that initial three-year period and in the decades that followed it. As Brooks discusses in a fascinating chronicle of those efforts, Ruleville's elected leaders first approved a proposal submitted by McLaurin that called for a grand "Greco-Roman-inspired white marble structure honoring his fallen hero."[82] "When an important national figure passes, they are buried in Arlington," McLaurin told us. "And so I wanted to create Fannie Lou Hamer's Arlington."[83] With input from Hamer's husband and boosted by a fundraising effort led by Linda Jones Malonson, McLaurin's vision was eventually rejected and replaced with an alternate design created by students at Howard University's School of Architecture and Planning. The project stalled after Malonson's fundraising efforts were unsuccessful, however, and for the next decade those who attempted to visit the site found it largely "untended," even as efforts to preserve Hamer's memory and build upon her legacy continued elsewhere.[84]

Those stalled efforts gained new momentum in 1999, over twenty years after Hamer was buried, when Patricia Thompson and the nonprofit organization she founded, Repaying Our Ancestors Respectfully (ROAR), started organizing local residents and politicians to make improvements to the Fannie Lou Hamer Memorial Garden. ROAR also initiated the first Fannie Lou Hamer celebration there in 2000.[85] Between 1999 and 2008, Hamer's burial site was further developed as Hattie Jordan led a private fundraising drive and secured a $100,000 Mississippi Development Authority grant to expand the site into the Memorial Garden.[86] Ruleville celebrated a rededication of the Memorial Garden in July 2008, and in 2009, a sixteen-member Fannie Lou Hamer Statue Committee was established to raise funds for a memorial statue. The composition of this diverse committee led by McLaurin and Patricia Reid-Merritt, a professor of Africana studies and social work, is indicative of the quasivernacular nature of the Memorial Garden. The project was always deeply rooted in the Ruleville community and the labor of local leaders and activists; however, they were part of a broader coalition that was national in scope and whose successful two-year fundraising effort saw donations from individuals and corporate sponsors across the country.[87] Evidence of this effort can be found on two large plaques affixed to stone pillars that flank the statue; the plaques prominently feature dozens of contributors, many of whom, such as the New Jersey–based National Black United Fund are well outside Ruleville and the state's borders.

The Hamer Statue Committee played the lead role in designing the memorial. "I wanted her standing tall in the Delta and in Ruleville," McLaurin remembers:

> A lot of people, especially around Ruleville in the Delta, didn't really see her as having been that significant. You know, they didn't understand where she had gone and what she had done that was helping to make their and my life more livable now. So I didn't want her life to be little. . . . But my original idea was that she should not be forgotten.[88]

Although the design process was contentious at times, it was successful, and the statue was finally unveiled in a public ceremony on October 5, 2012.[89] Although Hattie Robinson Jordan lamented the fact that most of the funds for the statue came from contributors outside of Ruleville, she described the Memorial Garden as her "biggest accomplishment" during her tenure as alderwoman.[90] Online reviews from several visitors confirm the site's impact. "Truly a must-see place," one reviewer wrote. "You can feel the power of Fannie Lou Hamer's life and legacy when you're here."[91]

The Memorial Garden is roughly one-half acre in size. A black iron fence standing approximately four feet tall encloses the area that one enters from the street through a tall, gated metal archway. Although the Hamer Museum and Memorial Garden are distinct sites with distinct histories, their connection is emphasized by a large white sign affixed to the garden's main entrance gate that has contact information for the Hamer Museum. The Memorial Garden includes a number of memory objects dedicated to the late civil rights leader: the Fannie Lou Hamer MFT marker, the bronze statue, a fountain, a metal sign ("Let Your Light Shine"), an engraved stone marker highlighting some of Hamer's accomplishments, and a large red-roofed pavilion. Several plaques list the names of local civil rights veterans, members of the Fannie Lou Hamer Memorial Garden Committee, and donors. While the Memorial Garden celebrates and honors Hamer's crucial role in the movement, it is also hallowed ground, a serene, protective site where Hamer simultaneously stands tall and is at peace. Silk flowers were placed on each side of Hamer and her husband's gravesites during our visits. The well-manicured grounds complement a message of gratitude from the citizens of Ruleville that can

Entrance to Fannie Lou Hamer Memorial Garden. Photo by Stephen A. King.

be found on one side of the stone marker: "Thanks for your vision, courage, and leadership—citizens of Ruleville."

Upon entering the site, visitors first encounter Hamer's MFT marker (unveiled in 2011). With its twelve lines of text on the front panel and its more detailed rear panel (complete with five paragraphs of text and assorted photos), the MFT marker provides visitors with a biographical sketch of Hamer's transformation from plantation worker to civil rights leader. Located to the right of the MFT marker is a "Fannie Lou Hamer Voting and Civil Rights Pioneer" stone marker that highlights her distinguished civil and human rights record, from joining SNCC in 1962 to founding the Freedom Farm Cooperative to being named to the Board of Trustees of the Martin Luther King Center for Nonviolent Social Change in 1974.

In assessing the combination of official and vernacular memorializing at the Memorial Garden, three rhetorical themes dominate the site. First, Hamer is remembered as a woman of unparalleled courage and tenacity, a rhetorical agent who rejected passivity and was not afraid to speak truth to power. The centerpiece of the Memorial Garden is the bronze statue of Hamer that stands at eight feet and sits atop a four-foot-tall stone pedestal.[92] The statue shows Hamer striking a strong, defiant, and empowered pose. She speaks into a megaphone, her voice symbolically amplified through a small speaker resting at her feet. The statue augments her rhetorical agency by depicting Hamer engaged in oratory, a physical act that dissolves the illusory speech/action binary. This statue, which was created by sculptor Brian Hanlon, appears to be modeled after a photo taken of Hamer speaking to an

Statue in Fannie Lou Hamer Memorial Garden. Photo by Roger Davis Gatchet.

audience of mostly MFDP sympathizers during a trip to Washington, DC in September 1965.[93] Standing tall with her left hand raised toward the sky, the defiant Hamer is posed in an act of civil dissent unbound by labor (a slave-sharecropper stooped picking cotton) or nonverbal subservience (e.g., stepping off a sidewalk when encountering whites). "When a person walks in that gate," McLaurin noted, "their head automatically goes up as they approach the statue. Looking up at her."[94] As is the case in the Hamer Museum, this image of Hamer as the immovable orator is balanced by Hamer the singer whose signature song, "Little Light of Mine," is inscribed at the front base of the statue: "This little light of mine, I'm gonna let it shine." References to the song can be found elsewhere in the Garden, including a black iron art piece (*Let Your Light Shine*) and her MFT marker. A deeply religious person, Hamer believed that truth and love ("the light") always has the potential to transform the hearts of even her most cruel, bigoted, and racist detractors.

Complementing the first theme, Hamer is also remembered here as a civil rights martyr—she literally sacrificed herself for the movement. For example, the statue's assertive speaking stance displays a significant degree of kinesic openness. With her torso exposed, Hamer is not protecting herself from potential body blows from her many adversaries. Instead, her open posture reveals her vulnerability, courage, and truth-telling qualities. The theme of self-sacrifice is reinforced by the story of her Winona prison experience that appears in two places in the Memorial Garden. Hamer's self-sacrifice is also evident in etched photos affixed to the statue's base. One shows a photo (circa 1960s) of Black women holding signs (e.g., "WE DEMAND AN END TO BIAS NOW!") marching toward the camera. Hamer's quotation appears under the photo: "I'm never sure when I leave home whether I'll make it back or not . . . but if I fall, I'll fall five feet and four inches foward [sic] from freedom and I'm not backing off it!" Another photo shows a weary Hamer holding a "Freedom Now" sign. Underneath is another Hamer quotation, her most famous: "I'm sick and tired of being sick and tired." This rhetorical fragment is also inscribed in Hamer's gravestone as well as on the rear side of her MFT marker.

Not surprisingly, the final rhetorical theme is one of community—a community comprised of the living and deceased, the movement and ordinary citizens. A social movement is a rhetorical community that possesses both material and physical connection. Indeed, the modern civil rights movement has been affectionately called the "beloved community." Hamer cherished this beloved community and referenced the concept of interconnectedness in one of the quotations that appears at the base of the statue: "Whether you have a Ph.D. or no D, we are in this bag together. Whether you're from Morehouse or Nohouse, we're still in this bag together." While the Memorial Garden venerates Fannie Lou Hamer's legacy and influence, she is literally surrounded by the memory of other civil rights leaders and those sympathetic to the movement. In the covered pavilion, four small plaques are mounted around the inside of the structure that display the names of "Ruleville Civil Rights Veterans" (e.g., Mary Tucker, Fred Brown) who were influenced or inspired by Hamer (only the names are given; no other information is on display, and these individuals are not contextualized in any way). As noted earlier, additional plaques list the members of the Fannie Lou Hamer Memorial Garden Committee as well as individuals (e.g., Alice Walker), organizations (e.g., Mississippi Freedom 50th Foundation) and corporate donors (e.g., Double Quick) who provided the financial support for the construction of the Hamer statue. The fact that the Memorial Garden is built on land that was once part of Hamer's Freedom Farm only reinforces the movement's goal to achieve freedom, justice, and equality.

The Memorial Garden also signifies community by its placement in a residential neighborhood, with modest houses across the street. On the day we visited, young children were jumping on a trampoline in the front yard of the house that sits directly across from the garden's main entrance. A group of people arrived by car to the adjacent park and engaged in recreational activities. Unlike some public memory sites, the Memorial Garden is part of, not separate from, the larger community. Unlike most museums, there is no admission fee to enjoy the Memorial Garden. Beyond having easy access to this memory site, it also features a community gathering place and pavilion for special events. Considering the rhetorical impact of the site, and the statue specifically, Maegan Parker Brooks (who was a member of the Hamer Statue Committee and directly involved with commemorative events at the Hamer Museum and Memorial Garden) wondered if the fundraising effort "had unwittingly created a larger-than-life hero out of an activist with whom we had hoped young people in Hamer's community would relate" and in the process developed a monument that was "potentially *disempowering* to Delta-area students."[95] This concern notwithstanding, here, in her final resting place, we find Hamer's memory transformed into an empowering force in a neighborhood and town that is clearly still struggling to overcome decades of white supremacy and material deprivation. In this living, vernacular space, the defiant Hamer statue is not just speaking out against some *past* injustice, but rather is a symbol of the need to continually engage the *present* injustice through oratory, a constitutionally protected form of nonviolent action.

To date, the Fannie Lou Hamer Memorial Garden is the most significant memory site for the late civil rights leader in the state. In recent years, sites preserving Hamer's memory have expanded beyond Ruleville. For example, in nearby Indianola, another Fannie Lou Hamer historical marker was unveiled on the grounds of the city's courthouse in October 2020.[96] Her story also appears in multiple galleries that comprise the MCRM in Jackson. When we spoke with McLaurin in late 2021, he expressed hope for the continued expansion of the Memorial Garden in Ruleville: "We always saw that to be a work in progress, that it's not finished, you know."[97]

Vernacular memory sites like the Canton Freedom House, the Sims Museum, and the Fannie Lou Hamer Museum and Memorial Garden play a critical role in Mississippi's memory landscape. Taken together, they exemplify vernacular cultural expressions of the "folk": the emphasis on remembering local heroes, the irregular hours, the DIY approach to museum curation, the accessibility issues, the economically marginalized surroundings, the personal agency, and the rhetoric of resistance imbued in both the stories told and the grit and determination necessary to construct these memory sites in the first place. In the case of the Memorial Garden especially, they also show

how local sites are often developed with financial and logistical support from well beyond the local community. Like other vernacular or quasivernacular sites that largely predate the state's official investment in civil rights tourism, they laid the groundwork for this growing industry and continue to provide deeply meaningful touristic experiences that help augment and sustain it. Indeed, sustainability remains a central issue for sites such as these, where funding is often largely dependent on local donations and volunteer labor. At the Mississippi Heritage Consortium museums, which are reliant on Sims's performances, one wonders what will happen when she is no longer able to perform as the Old Storyteller. In the absence of support from the state or local government, the Canton Freedom House hinges on Glen Cotton's willingness to maintain and subsidize it out of his own pocket and on local volunteers who are committed to its success. At the Hamer Museum, tourists must actively plan their visits in advance, coordinating with local community members who do not have the luxury of working full-time at a museum that does not appear to operate with a consistent revenue stream.

A lack of reliable funding portends an uncertain future for vernacular sites and the enriching opportunities they offer civil rights tourists in Mississippi; however, some vernacular memory workers frame this financial uncertainty in beneficial terms. Sims, for example, once worried that an excess of external resources from beyond the local community could water down visitors' experiences. "Sometimes, we can have too much resources," she says. "Sometimes, we can take the struggle out of the struggle and lose the authenticity of the reason why we're here. And, when we do that, it's no longer genuine.... When I tell the story, I can tell it with conviction and compassion because I lived the injustices."[98] Sims's tenacity notwithstanding, local museums in Mississippi may stand a greater chance of receiving state and federal government funding as the state's civil rights tourism industry continues to grow. With the assistance of the Mississippi Humanities Council, president Biden's 2021 American Rescue Plan issued a $15,000 grant to the Canton Freedom House as part of a larger effort to support local cultural organizations struggling during the COVID-19 pandemic.[99] The following year, Mississippi congressional representative Bennie Thompson helped facilitate a $50,000 grant from the Southern Poverty Law Center for Sims's Fannie Lou Hamer Civil Rights Museum in Belzoni (only five museums nationwide were selected for these awards). It was a first for the museum, which up to that point had never received grant funding.[100]

Sims, Cotton, McLaurin, the volunteers, and other local people dedicated to creating and maintaining vernacular sites assume the role of memory activists. Not only are they preserving memories and spaces that might otherwise be forgotten or destroyed, but they also connect historical memory to the present. The Old Storyteller does this explicitly in her performances at the museum and around the state. Likewise, Cotton implies a desire for racial reconciliation by connecting the historical movement to contemporary issues when he told us that his museum "opened up a door for dialogue, especially with our younger people."[101] In Ruleville's Hamer Museum, the vernacular memory work signifies that the struggle must continue as intimated in Hamer's own words, "Nobody's Free Until Everybody's Free." And the Memorial Garden situated near that museum, with the defiant Hamer statue as its centerpiece, engages the present through symbolic oratory. This site, more than any other examined in this chapter, highlights the quasivernacular nature of many civil rights heritage sites across Mississippi's memorial landscape, where cooperative partnerships between local people and national supporters is necessary to realize public commemoration. In the case of the Freedom House and Sims's humble museum consortium, it remains to be seen how the recent infusion of much-needed grant funding will impact their financial stability, vision, and operation in the years ahead. All four sites emerged to tell the truth, often hidden historical truths, and, in doing so, provide a rhetorical counterbalance to official retellings of the past and the present that can traffic in erasure, misdirection and ambiguity, and mythic hyperbole. In the next chapter, we turn our attention to the memory of Emmett Till and how local communities and the state of Mississippi have wrestled with developing tourism and memorialization practices surrounding this sinister chapter in the state's history.

CHAPTER THREE

REMEMBERING THE LYNCHING OF EMMETT TILL
From Experiential to "Dark" Tourism

> If Mississippi rivers were drained, just how
> many bodies would have been discovered?
> —EXHIBIT AT THE EMMETT TILL HISTORIC INTREPID CENTER, Glendora, Mississippi

> The signs dedicated to the memory of Emmett Till have been stolen,
> thrown in the river, replaced, shot, defaced with acid, and spray
> painted with the letters "KKK." ... It is hard to understand how it can
> be so difficult to honor the memory of a murdered child—even today.
> —EMMETT TILL INTERPRETIVE CENTER, Sumner, Mississippi

Of the hundreds of memory sites associated with the civil rights movement in Mississippi, none has attracted more public attention than those connected to a fourteen-year-old African American teen who was kidnapped, beaten, and murdered in the Delta in August 1955. In a state that has made a concerted effort at local and state levels to develop a tourism infrastructure related to the people, places, and events of the Mississippi Movement, the memory of Emmett Till, whose brutal lynching was a galvanizing force of the modern civil rights movement, has become a lightning rod that vividly illustrates our affective and contentious relationship with the past.[1]

After two white men kidnapped Till at gunpoint from his uncle's home in Money, Mississippi, the final hours of Till's short life were marked by sadistic violence that brought into stark relief the extent to which some whites would go in order to maintain systems of power and privilege in the South. As attorney John W. Whitten III, a Sumner resident and son of one of the defense attorneys at the Till trial, said in 2019, "Fella [Emmett Till] who came down here and got in trouble—overstepped his bounds to a degree some folks thought. And they cured him of his problems."[2] Over fifty years later, many of the memorials erected in his memory have borne the brunt of another kind of violence. In July 2005, Mississippi's first official act of memorializing Till was to rename a segment of US Highway 49E the Emmett Till Memorial Highway.[3] Within the first year, vandals had defaced the sign, spraying the letters "KKK" across it.[4] Sadly, this was just the beginning.

In 2008, the ETMC erected historical markers in front of eight locations that are central to remembering Till's story. One of those signs, "River Site"—so-named for its placement on the banks of the Tallahatchie River where Till's body was likely pulled from the water—was vandalized on at least three separate occasions. Less than a year after its installation, the original marker was gone and likely disposed of in the river.[5] A new sign installed in its place suffered a similar fate: vandals sprayed the sign with bullets.[6] It was removed in 2016.[7] The third replacement sign stood unmarred for thirty-five days before it was found riddled with bullet holes.[8] In a 2019 National Public Radio interview, Jessie Jaynes-Diming—a long time member of the ETMC and local civil rights tour guide—likened the shooting of this sign to assaulting other sacred religious and political symbols: "It would be the same thing if I had a Bible up there, or if I had the flag up there and you shot it up."[9] In July 2019, a photograph surfaced of three smiling, gun-wielding University of Mississippi students posing in front of the bullet-riddled marker. The students were later suspended from their fraternity, and the photo was turned over to the Civil Rights Division of the Justice Department.[10]

For the fourth iteration of the sign, the ETMC replaced it with a 500-pound bullet-proof marker that included surveillance cameras and other security devices.[11] In early November 2019, less than a month after the new marker was unveiled to the public, members of a white supremacist group calling themselves the League of the South filmed what has been described as a propaganda video in front of the marker. Before a security alarm caused the group to flee the scene, one of its members could be heard saying, "We are here at the Emmett Till monument that represents the civil rights movement for blacks. What we want to know is where are all of the white people—?"[12]

In another disturbing example of the continued violence visited upon Till's memory, the MFT marker that stands near the remains of the Bryant's Grocery building was vandalized during two separate incidents in 2017 that left the sign severely damaged. The marker's detailed rear panel, with its lengthier historical narrative and captioned archival photographs, was the primary target. Vandals peeled away the vinyl face of the marker and used "a blunt tool" to scratch its surface.[13] Four years later, in September 2021, the same MFT marker was reported missing. Allan Hammons of Hammons and Associates, a Greenwood-based advertising agency responsible for the design of the MFT marker series,[14] believed the cause was likely an accident because the marker "was not defaced in any way."[15] He surmised a large truck may have accidently knocked down the sign.[16] According to the *Clarion-Ledger*, LeFlore County Road Department employees removed the marker and placed it in storage until Hammons could evaluate the damage.[17] Given the history of violence associated with Till memorialization efforts, it is not surprising that the Emmett Till Interpretive Center was suspicious of the cause. As Patrick Weems told the *New York Times*, "Regardless of whether this was an accident or not, there is a clear pattern of violence against these signs, and we think it's time for the federal government to step up and take responsibility for this national American story."[18]

The rhetorical power of the site in Money continues in full force, even with the sign's absence. This reflects what public memory scholar J. David Maxson characterized as "residual memory" or "the remaining rhetorical potency that clings to a commemorative site after the focal object or structure of memorialization is removed."[19] While Maxson's case study focused on the removal of a prominent Confederate monument in New Orleans, the Liberty Place Monument, and the ritualistic performance of an activist group, Take 'Em Down NOLA, that celebrated the monument's removal, the missing MFT marker and the controversy that followed demonstrates the power of memory to remain after its material fragments have been removed.

These acts of material and symbolic violence on Mississippi's memorial landscape—shooting, defacing, silencing, even *erasing*—have important implications in a state that is making significant investments in scaling up its civil rights tourism infrastructure. It should be noted that civil rights crimes at memory sites are not isolated to those associated with Emmett Till. In 2016, Austin Reed Edenfield, a former University of Mississippi undergraduate, pled guilty to assisting another student place a noose and a Confederate flag (an outdated version of the state flag of Georgia) around the neck of the James Meredith statue that sits prominently in front of the university's main library.[20] According to a *Washington Post* reporter, "Edenfield admitted that he knew the rope and flag would be threatening and intimidating to black students."[21] Collectively, acts such as these galvanized the public's imagination and challenge the state's efforts to deploy civil rights tourism to serve the interdependent goals of economic development, image management, and social justice.

As we will see, Mississippi presents markedly different images of Emmett Till through its promotional materials, museums, and other touristic artifacts.

Admittedly, the task of positioning the face, body, and image of a fourteen-year-old lynching victim as part of the state's tourism industry is fraught with questions and concerns related to exploitation and profit as well as opportunities for reconciliation and racial healing. It is not an exaggeration to suggest that tourism organizations associated with remembering Emmett Till and promoting Till memory sites are faced with an extraordinary challenge.

Additionally, three important promoters of the Emmett Till story—Greenwood's Convention and Visitors Bureau (CVB), the Emmett Till Interpretive Center (ETIC), and the Emmett Till Historic Intrepid Center (ETHIC)—focus on a specific aspect of Till's lynching to serve specific touristic goals. Through the use of experiential tourism narratives, Greenwood's CVB transports potential tourists to Money Road and what it calls the "Emmett Till saga." At the same time, these narratives arguably hide Till's brutalized face, depersonalizing the fourteen-year-old victim as part of an event and landscape. With its focus on the encounter between Till and his accuser, Carolyn Bryant, and the resulting aftermath, Greenwood's CVB highlights the mythic claim that Mississippi is the "birthplace" of the civil rights movement. In contrast, the ETIC in Sumner and, especially, the ETHIC in Glendora, provide openings for social justice by revealing Till's face and confronting visitors with the gruesome realities of lynching. Both differ, however, in degrees of emphasis and their pursuit of distinct goals. The ETIC exhibit's narrow focus on the trial, the acquittal, and the silence that followed highlights the need for racial reconciliation through restorative justice. Meanwhile, the ETHIC's decision to spotlight the vivid, raw, and excruciating timeline of events in Till's barbaric lynching illuminates a culture of systemic white racism. These contrasting touristic enterprises highlight the conflicting demands that are made of Emmett Till's body, story, and legacy when tourism and public memory intersect in the state of Mississippi.

Emmett Till in History, Public Memory, and Tourism

Over the past several decades, historians, documentarians, and artists have expended considerable effort exploring every possible facet of Emmett Till's story. There is no shortage of book-length historical studies on Till,[22] and two documentary films—PBS's *The Murder of Emmett Till* and Keith Beauchamp's *The Untold Story of Emmett Louis Till*—brought Till's story to the screen in the early 2000s.[23] Books such as Devery S. Anderson's exhaustive *Emmett Till: The Murder That Shocked the World and Propelled the Civil*

Rights Movement (2015), Timothy B. Tyson's *The Blood of Emmett Till* (2017), and Elliott J. Gorn's *The Story of Emmett Till: Let the People See* (2018) offer definitive historical accounts that narrate Till's life and legacy from his early childhood up to the present, while Bob Newman's *Shadows of Emmett Till* (2022) takes the form of an extended photographic essay that examines the murder's impact on the Delta today. In January 2022, ABC's limited television series *Women of the Movement* premiered. Based on Anderson's book, the six-episode primetime series focuses on Till's mother, Mamie Till-Mobley, and the story of her son's lynching.[24] Two months later, in March 2022, John Jay College in New York premiered a controversial opera—written by white librettist Clare Coss—based on Emmett Till's murder.[25] Also in early 2022, the passage of bipartisan legislation by the US Congress continued to evoke Till's memory. In January, Congress awarded a posthumous Congressional Gold Medal to both Emmett Till and his mother.[26] And in March, President Biden signed the Emmett Till Antilynching Act, a historic piece of legislation that declared lynching a federal hate crime.[27] By year's end, Chinonye Chukwu's film *Till* opened in theaters to critical acclaim. Dave Tell rightly notes that "the story of Till's death has remained a staple of the American imagination."[28] Without question, his memory continues to both haunt and fascinate us in equal measure.

Rhetorical critics have complemented the rich body of historical literature on Till with several studies, including those that appeared in a 2005 special issue of the journal *Rhetoric and Public Affairs*. One area that has yet to be fully explored in this literature, however, is Till's appropriation as an object of tourism. In what is one of the few rhetorical studies to address tourism directly, Dave Tell's groundbreaking 2019 book, *Remembering Emmett Till*, explores how geography, memory, forgetting, and tourism intersect in various Delta communities. In addition to his critical-rhetorical work on Till and public memory, Tell himself has been involved in Till memorialization efforts through the Emmett Till Memory Project. Funded by the University of Kansas and the Institute for Museum and Library Services, the Emmett Till Memory Project is a joint collaboration between the ETMC, ETIC Public Engagement and Museum Education Director Benjamin Saulsberry, and communication scholars including Tell, Davis Houck, and Pablo Correa.[29] The project, according to Tell, "uses a website and a smartphone app to commemorate fifty sites in and around the MS Delta."[30] On its website, the Emmett Till Memory Project is described as a "complete guide to the legacy of Till's murder.... At each site, the app provides expert-vetted narratives, access to relevant archival documents, and a collection of historic and contemporary photographs."[31] Having used it during our fieldwork in the state, the authors can attest to the high quality of the app and its careful and nuanced site descriptions. Tell notes that the technology "capture[s] the two things that tend to be forgotten by traditional memorials: the contingency of history and the influence of politics in the stabilization of the past."[32] The Emmett Till Memory Project features three tours, "The Essential Emmett Till," "Tallahatchie Civil Rights Driving Tour," and the "Chicago Tour."[33] The first two focus on Till's lynching and the Sumner trial, while the "Chicago Tour" captures Till's wider biography. "The basic idea," Tell says, considering the violence inflicted on Emmett Till memorials, "is that you can't shoot an app."[34]

Emmett Till: The Whistle, Trial, and Aftermath

Born in Chicago in July 1941, Emmett Till was the only son of Mamie Carthan and Louis Till. Emmett's mother was born near the small Mississippi Delta town of Webb, located between Glendora and Sumner. As part of the Great Migration, Mamie emigrated to Argo when she was two years old.[35] Her marriage to Louis was brief and unhappy, and familial neglect and abuse seemed to define the Till household.[36]

Raised by his mother and grandmother, Emmett was, by all accounts, a happy, precocious, and boisterous child who suffered a bout of polio at the age of six; the aftermath left him with muscle damage and a stutter.[37] Although the Carthan family fled Mississippi because of oppressive working conditions and racial violence, Mamie later returned to Mississippi for brief visits with her extended family, including trips with Emmett when he was young.[38] In *Death of Innocence: The Story of the Hate Crime That Changed America*, Mamie recalls that while visiting relatives in Chicago in August 1955, Emmett's uncle, a sharecropper and preacher named Moses "Mose" Wright, described the rural delights of the Mississippi Delta. Emmett was intrigued. When he learned that his cousins, Wheeler Parker and Curtis Jones, were planning to visit Wright on his Mississippi Delta farm, Emmett tried to convince his disapproving mother to permit him to travel south. She finally relented, allowing Emmett a two-week sojourn at Wright's tenant house in East Money.[39] Before his departure, she tried to prepare her son for the harsh realities of race relations in Mississippi. "Chicago and Mississippi were two very different places," she instructed him, "and white people down South could be very mean to blacks, even to black kids."[40] Before departing on the *City of New Orleans* train for Mississippi on Saturday, August 20, Till decided to wear one of the few possessions his father left him—a ring with the inscription "L.T."

During his visit, Till, his cousins, and other family members stayed with Wright on the twenty-five acres of land that he had been leasing from the Grover Cleveland Frederick Plantation since the 1920s.[41] During the evening of August 24, Till, his cousins, underage driver Maurice Wright, and children from the neighborhood drove three miles to downtown Money after dropping off Moses and Elizabeth Wright at the East Money Church of God in Christ.[42] Unfortunately for Till and his companions, Bryant's Grocery was one of the town's few businesses.

Observing a checkers game outside of Bryant's Grocery, the group stopped to investigate. Owned by Roy Bryant and his spouse, Carolyn Bryant, Bryant's Grocery and Meat Market catered to the local African American population.[43] When the group arrived, Carolyn Bryant was working alone behind the register. Wheeler Parker first entered Bryant's Grocery to purchase some snacks. Parker quickly made his purchase and, as he was leaving, Till entered the store and was alone with Bryant for a brief period of time.[44] (Anderson argues there is credible evidence to suggest that another unidentified adolescent urged Till to go inside the store to see the former high school beauty queen.[45]) It is unclear what occurred next. Perhaps Till violated southern racial etiquette by placing change in Bryant's hand rather than on the counter, as at least two eyewitnesses later recalled.[46] Other sources speculate that Till inadvertently violated other racial codes, including not using the "proper" form of address ("Yes, ma'am").[47] According to one witness, as Till was exiting the store, he waved at Bryant and said "good-bye."[48] It is unclear what prompted Bryant's next act: she immediately left the store to retrieve a gun from her sister-in-law's car.[49] Multiple witnesses testified that, at that moment, Till whistled at Bryant, an act described by Parker and others as a "wolf whistle."[50] Some of Till's companions were perplexed by Till's whistle, including Simeon Wright, who reported decades later that "many of the books and stories said that we dared him to do it. But that's not the truth. He did it on his own, and we had no idea why."[51] Various theories have emerged over the years to explain the behavior, including his mother's contention that whistling helped her son pronounce words when he was stuttering.[52] Whatever the explanation, Till and his companions left quickly, returning to his uncle's house. During the trial, Bryant changed her story, claiming that Till physically assaulted her.[53] In an interview with Timothy B. Tyson decades later, she finally admitted that the physical altercation was a fabrication. She also said that "nothing that boy did could ever justify what happened to him."[54]

Nearly three days later, a young angler found Till's body in the Tallahatchie River. In *A Death in the Delta*, historian Stephen J. Whitfield graphically captured Till's grisly end:

> The lower half of the badly beaten corpse protruded above the surface of the Tallahatchie River. Though a fan weighing about a hundred pounds had been attached to the neck with barbed wire, only the right side of the head was intact, suggesting terrible torture.... The protruding tongue was eight times normal size, and one eye dangled. Above the right ear was a hole the size of a bullet, and on one finger was a ring inscribed with the initials L. T.[55]

Shortly afterward, Roy Bryant and J. W. Milam were arrested and later indicted for Till's murder.

What occurred over the course of those three days? The answer depends on which account one believes. During the early morning of Sunday, August 28, Bryant and Milam had arrived at Wright's doorstep, demanding to "see the boy from Chicago" who had insulted Bryant's wife with his "smart talking."[56] Bryant and Milam kidnapped Till in front of multiple witnesses.[57] Similar to what transpired in the Bryant's store days earlier, it is unclear what happened next. One discredited version that was supported by Bryant and Milam's defense team argued that they simply questioned Till and released him in close proximity to Bryant's Grocery. This "one county" narrative confines the Till story to LeFlore County, the home of Greenwood, the Delta town which has invested resources to promote Till as part of the city's history and tourism offerings.[58] The prosecution's alternate "three county" story confirms Bryant and Milam's role in the lynching: the abduction of Till (LeFlore County), Till's lynching in a barn on the Milam Plantation (managed by Milam's brother Leslie) near the small town of Drew (Sunflower Country) some thirty miles west of the abduction site, and the return of Till's body to Tallahatchie County, where Bryant and Milam used barbed wire to attach a heavy cotton gin fan around Till's neck before dumping him in the Tallahatchie River.[59] Another account places Till's execution in Tallahatchie County. According to this narrative, Roy Bryant shot Till in the head; later, Till's body was dropped from the Black Bayou Bridge into the waters below.[60]

Attracting the kind of national and international media attention most Mississippians did not want, the Till trial, not surprisingly, was a farce. As Tyson notes, "the one fixed opinion that everybody from Tallahatchie County seemed to share was that the jury would find the accused not guilty."[61] The prosecution presented its three-county version of events, and Mose Wright served as a key eyewitness to the abduction of Till. Defense attorney John W. Whitten Jr. attempted to discredit the state's witnesses and claimed that the body found in the river could not be positively identified as Till's despite the "L. T." ring that was found on the body. The defense also argued that Till's murder was a hoax hatched by Wright, Till, and the NAACP. Without providing evidence, the defense suggested that Till was still alive, hiding out in Chicago or Detroit.[62]

After hearing compelling evidence of Till's kidnapping and execution, the jury deliberated for approximately sixty-seven minutes before rendering a not guilty verdict.[63] Jackson's *Clarion-Ledger/Jackson Daily News* and Memphis's *Commercial Appeal* and other southern newspapers found the prosecution's case lacking.[64] The Mississippi press, in particular, "called belatedly for a collective forgetting."[65] Meanwhile, the national and international outcry was monumental. Vowing to continue its investigation to unearth witnesses to the crime, the *Chicago Defender* proclaimed that "this miscarriage of justice must not be left unavenged."[66] The *Commonweal* magazine denounced the acquittal, arguing that the death of Till was a "cruel example of a moral disease" that plagued the entire nation.[67] The headline of one *Daily Worker* editorial expressed the sentiments of many who were appalled by the verdict: "The Shame of Our Nation."[68] Published in the *Norfolk Virginia Pilot*, one letter to the editor—authored by "Another Negro"—argued that Till's lynching was decidedly antidemocratic: "The Till boy's death and a thousand other acts are communism at its worst. I know what to expect from Russia; this country is supposed to be a democracy, but our actions are too often to the contrary."[69]

Public outcry was also measured in the massive number of people who turned out to view Till's brutalized corpse; Till's mother's decision to allow the public viewing exposed the unspeakable cruelty of white supremacy. Beginning on a Friday in Chicago, the public viewing continued until the following Tuesday, drawing "tens of thousands" of spectators to Till's open casket.[70] Visitors recoiled in disbelief and anger, and *Jet*'s published photos of Till's corpse shocked the world.[71] Julie Buckner Armstrong argued that Emmett Till's lynching "seemed incongruous to a country that fought two global wars for democracy and proclaimed itself as the world's protector of peace and justice."[72] With the Till verdict arriving three weeks later, large protests erupted in Chicago, Detroit, Baltimore, and other cities, including Paris, France.[73] Rosa Parks and other civil rights activists claimed that Till's lynching served as a catalyst for their own activism. Without question, Emmett Till was an important touchstone for the modern civil rights movement, a prime example of Karlos K. Hill's assertion that narratives of Black lynching victims marshal great rhetorical power in the public sphere.[74] Indeed, the outrage, anger, and activism that followed can be attributed, in part, to the violence that marked Till's face and body, the fact that he was a child, and the shifting cultural meaning of lynching itself.[75] The nineteenth-century understanding of lynching as a "variant of criminal justice" had been supplanted with a new one by the middle of the twentieth century. Lynching was now a "national crime."[76]

The Promotion of Emmett Till

Until recently, Mississippi's official culture has largely avoided promoting memory sites associated with Till as tourist destinations. To wit, there is little hyperbole in ETIC executive director Patrick Weems's observation that after Milam and Bryant confessed to Till's murder in a 1956 article published in *Look* magazine, "our community tried to put it behind them. And so, for fifty years, the community did not mention the word[s] 'Emmett Till.'"[77] Prior to the 2000s, visitors hoping to explore Till's story through Mississippi's memorial landscape would have found little to no official recognition that Till even visited the state, let alone that he was lynched there. The most visible example of this intentional silence is the Bryant's Grocery building in Money. In a 2000 article about his trip there, journalist Paul Hendrickson noted, "There is no plaque from a state historical commission. The building is just here, a shrine in ruin, forgotten, recalcitrant, collapsing in on itself, set against memory and the wind"; likewise, when Houck visited the site a few years later, he traveled down "an unmarked narrow road in an unmarked place" and relied on a human guide to locate it.[78] As noted earlier, it was not until 2011—more than a half century after Till was murdered—that a historical marker was finally placed near the decaying building identifying it as the site where Till encountered Carolyn Bryant.

A memorial landscape that was once defined by a community's eagerness to forget has transformed dramatically in recent years. Tell's exploration of the relationship between Till, public memory, and place shows how the Mississippi Delta has transformed into a "burgeoning Emmett Till memory industry" that "is now literally dotted with Till memorials."[79] Indeed, after decades of relative silence, Till's memory has emerged in signifiers that stretch across the state, from historical markers and the restored service station that stands adjacent to the Bryant's Grocery building, to exhibits in cultural centers and the MCRM, to a variety of locally produced brochures and promotional advertisements. In the section that follows, we examine some of the more provocative texts to emerge from this memory industry in recent years. We focus on how Till has been appropriated and presented to heritage tourists in three Mississippi locales: Greenwood, Sumner, and Glendora.

Experiential Narratives and Money Road

Although Emmett Till was not lynched in Greenwood, the city actively draws on Till's story as part of its broader tourism strategy. The Greenwood CVB's decision to promote this story is reasonable given the city's proximity to the Bryant's Grocery building as well as the fact that it possesses a tourism infrastructure that Money and Glendora simply lack.[80] As we will see, the Greenwood CVB—through both print advertisements and its website—has deployed various rhetorical strategies to renarrate the events surrounding Till's lynching. These strategic efforts reflect what former Greenwood CVB director Danielle Morgan calls "experiential tourism"—situating tourists directly in the scene to experience a journey on Money Road.[81] For example, in advertisements that appeared in the national publication *Living Blues* magazine in 2015 and 2016, Greenwood's CVB encourages tourists to explore Money Road, where they will find "memorable sunsets and much more," including a church featured in the film *The Help*, Robert Johnson's burial site, and the "Bryant's store in Money where the Emmett Till saga began."[82] If the goal of this tourism discourse is to intrigue and entice potential visitors to visit this part of the Delta to experience the alluring and mysterious Money Road and its haunting memory, it succeeds. The advertisement does what it is designed to do. Unwittingly, however, this narrative (and other iterations of it) transforms Till's traumatic death into a less threatening tale of historical places and events in a land known for its "beauty" and "culture-changing history."[83] In this ad's brief narrative, Till was not lynched; instead, he is incorporated into a longer mythical "saga" that is left unexplored, and the Bryant's Grocery building is transformed from a site of trauma to just one of several interesting and "authentic" historical locations for tourists to consume. As historian Michel-Rolph Trouillot reminds us, silences in historical narratives such as this one "are neither neutral or natural. They are created.... One engages in the practice of silencing."[84]

In contrast to this adventurous description of the Till "saga," a different ad sensationalizes Emmett Till by pairing him with another doomed Black body—blues artist Robert Johnson. The pairing of Till and Johnson is one of the few, but growing, examples of how blues tourism has intersected with

Mississippi's civil rights tourism industry. Johnson's gravesite is most likely located between Money and Greenwood on Money Road. On August 13, 1938, Robert Johnson was performing on the western outskirts of Greenwood at the Three Forks juke joint, where he ingested corn liquor spiked with mothballs.[85] The use of mothballs was a "common way of poisoning people in the rural South."[86] The perpetrator, R. D. "Ralph" Davis, spiked the bottle of liquor after discovering Johnson was having an affair with his wife, Beatrice Davis.[87] In 2015, the Greenwood CVB released an advertisement that oddly juxtaposes both Till and Johnson through narrative and visual elements. Although Johnson died seventeen years before Till's murder, the ad reads, "Find America's soul laid bare on Money Road.... Two lanes. Ten miles. A sound that rocked the world. And a night that changed the nation."[88] The ad fuses the two historical figures through time, proximity, and visual placement. Johnson's legacy is associated with "blues in the night" (evening), while Till is linked to a "nation waking up" (morning), collapsing time in the process.[89] Johnson and Till are also united through Money Road, which connects Bryant's Grocery and the cemetery where Johnson is buried. Furthermore, faded, cracked archival photographs of Johnson and Till appear next to each other in the advertisement, symbolizing death—one rhetorical quality that both have in common.

This ad positions the city of Greenwood as an agent of radical, progressive change—Johnson's music "rocked the world," while Till's lynching "changed the nation."[90] Of course, the city of Greenwood assumes geographic authority for two historical events whose relationship is purely coincidental. Both Johnson and Till were temporary visitors—tourists if you like—and not residents of Greenwood.[91] Rather than a beacon for racial justice, Greenwood has historically been one of the Delta's most racially oppressive cities. During the social upheavals of the 1950s and 1960s, the "intensity of the hatred and cruelty exhibited by Greenwood whites was shocking even by the standards of Mississippi."[92]

More problematic is the advertisement's misappropriation of Till's motives. The ad implies that Till was somehow a participant in his demise, as if he willingly sacrificed himself to "ignite" a movement for racial justice. In *A Grammar of Motives*, Kenneth Burke articulates key elements that comprise his rhetorical theory of human motive: "What is involved, when we say what people are doing and why they are doing it?"[93] To address this question, Burke developed the pentad, which includes the following five elements: the act (what transpired), the scene (the act's location), the agent (the person who performed the act), agency (the means by which the act was carried out), and the purpose (the agent's goal for committing the act).[94] In Burkean terms, the ad subtly implies that Till was a willing agent who controlled both act and agency in this particular scene. Of course, Till was at best a passive agent, ultimately a powerless victim of the scene and the violence of Bryant, Milam, and their conspirators. Rather than being cast as a victim, Till is described in positive terms—his act and agency "sparked" the birth of the modern civil rights movement, changing the nation as a result.

Words such as "spark," "catalyst," and "propelled" have been deployed to describe the Till lynching and the rise of the civil rights movement.[95] For a state that claims to be the birthplace of the blues, country music, and even "America's music," it is not surprising that Greenwood (and the state) appropriates Till's lynching as evidence of another mythic origin story. Greenwood stakes its claim with references to the movement's origins in various promotional materials, including describing itself on its website as the "epicenter for the Civil Rights Movement."[96] In another tourism brochure produced by the Greenwood CVB and the Mississippi Delta National Heritage Area, *Remembering the Struggle for Civil Rights: The Greenwood Sites*, the familiar photograph of Till's smiling face appears below the proclamation, "Change Began Here." Using similar language as the ads appearing in *Living Blues*, the brochure states that Till's "brutal murder . . . awakened the nation and mobilized the American Civil Rights Movement."[97] The brochure further implies a link between Till's lynching in 1955 and a seemingly inevitable movement toward change, noting, "In the middle of the 20th century, Greenwood and Leflore County witnessed a slow but certain shift in the winds of justice, a gathering spirit of hope and promise and determination that what had been taken for so long would be taken no more."[98] As Anderson argues, the relationship between Till and the civil rights movement must be qualified:

> He has been called a martyr and the catalyst that started the civil rights movement. . . . Emmett Till was never a willing martyr and was certainly indifferent to the issues that consumed countless folks before or after him. . . . To say that the murder of Emmett Till started the civil rights movement is to ignore the work of politicians, ministers, grassroots activists, and organizations as early as the 1930s and is an oversimplification. . . . Yet the death of Emmett Till and the injustice that followed galvanized a people like few events have.[99]

By September 2020, Greenwood's CVB had stopped running the Johnson-Till ad in *Living Blues* but was featuring three separate entries on its website:

"Legend of Robert Johnson," "Mississippi Blues Trail," and "Money Road." Featuring the image of a setting (or rising) sun illuminating a desolate rural road, the "Money Road" narrative still associates Johnson's "chords of devilish blues" with the "murderous anger" that Milam and Bryant unleashed after Till's encounter with Carolyn Bryant. Unlike the 2015 advertisement, however, this new "Money Road" narrative obfuscates Johnson and Till—both are unnamed, invisible, and repackaged as part of a sinister and mythic scene:

> It's Leflore County Road 518, a 20-mile stretch of two-lane asphalt that runs from Greenwood to Mississippi Highway 8, and just one of a million little local roads all across America, just a way to get from here to there and back again. However, the history that took place on this storied road is seared into the nation's consciousness and the chords of devilish blues and the depths of murderous anger infuse it like a curse, winding along with it as it hugs the banks of the Tallahatchie River. Passing farms with names like Sweet Home and Wildwood, taking the curve past a storied churchyard, and forever vibrating with that fateful night when all hell broke loose at a simple country store, this pavement carries America's memories on its back.[100]

Tourists unfamiliar with Till's story may not make a connection between Till's lynching and "murderous anger" or the "simple country store." For those who can decode the referent, Till's identity as a lynching victim has been transformed into a scene, a place: Money Road and Bryant's Grocery. In this ad, Emmett Till is no longer a person. He has become a thing to be promoted for tourists. Not surprisingly, Greenwood's CVB never uses the word "lynching" in its ads and other promotional materials. In this advertisement, the abduction, torture, and execution of Till is reduced to a "murderous anger" and a "fateful night." Till's lynching and Johnson's mythologized supernatural dealings have seemingly placed a curse on Money Road that neither local citizens nor the world will ever forget.

In another example, the Greenwood CVB website offers tourists the choice of a number of itineraries with names such as "Delta Blues," "Culinary," and "History[,] Culture," with the latter introducing visitors to the Till story and Money Road. According to the website's description, "crumbling walls . . . are all that remain" of Bryant's Grocery—"one of the darkest chapters in American history." The word "lynching" does not appear in this retelling either. In fact, it is Till's act—not the acts of Bryant and Milam—that is highlighted in this cause-effect narrative: "When Emmett Till *stepped across* the threshold of that store on an August afternoon, he set in motion an explosion of terror and retribution that would rock the nation. The Civil Rights Movement, a landmark 20th-century social upheaval, traces its birth to that sagging store."[101] Interestingly, the Mississippi Tourism Association deployed the same language on its "Pivotal Civil Rights Sites: A 3-Day Itinerary" website.[102] Till's actions justified a violent and swift response in the eyes of racists who felt compelled to restore the white social order. As Christine Harold and Kevin Michael DeLuca argue, both Bryant and Milam claimed that their actions were justified in the defense of white supremacy and the sanctity of white womanhood: "Significantly, this specific instance of violence was, for its perpetrators, 'caused' by Till's failure to keep his *body* in line. That is, he supposedly committed . . . the worst crime a young black man could: being sexually suggestive toward a white woman."[103] Thirty years later, Roy Bryant invoked the same "race role" violation argument when he told two Mississippi reporters, "I feel this way: If Emmett Till hadn't got out of line, *it* probably wouldn't have happened to him."[104] Although the CVB ad narrative does not in any way justify Till's lynching, it arguably uses the same implied cause-effect relationship between act and action—Till crossed a "threshold" and "terror and retribution rocked the nation." Significantly, while the "nation" is "rocked," Till's mutilated Black body remains conspicuously absent, invisible.

Perhaps the most unsettling appropriation of Till's image can be found in Greenwood's *Unique Delta Experiences* brochure. The brochure includes a photo of a smiling Emmett Till on his bicycle along with a brief description of how his murder "rocked the world." This prelynching photo—with its encoded meaning of joy, contentment, and childhood bliss—is a queasy rhetorical rewinding of time and forgetting.[105] This prelynching photo is the most direct example of how contemporary civil rights tourism in Mississippi has transformed Till from a brutalized corpse back into the smiling, happy young adolescent he was before leaving Chicago. This image is much easier to sell to tourists, particularly to white tourists.

As one of the official voices promoting Emmett Till, Greenwood's CVB has alternately transformed Till's lynching into a seemingly natural part of the city's scenic elements, as a geographic claim for the state's civil rights origin story, and as tacit evidence that it was Till's transgressive actions that led to his murder. Danielle Morgan acknowledges that "promoting something that is so serious and meaningful" is "definitely a challenge" and that she worked closely with the agency that produced the ads to ensure they struck the right tone.[106] Greenwood's use of Till in its ads and promotional materials points to the allure of experiential tourism and the inescapable challenges inherent

Emmett Till Interpretive Center. Photo by Roger Davis Gatchet.

in promoting sites of trauma. As we will see in the town of Sumner, however, the ETIC seeks restorative justice as its mission in narrating the Till story.

Seeking Justice in Sumner

Like Greenwood, the small town of Sumner, Mississippi, has a connection to Till, making it one of the more significant geographic sites for civil rights tourism in the state. In addition to being the location of the infamous trial that allowed Till's murderers to go free, Sumner is also home to the Emmett Till Interpretive Center, a museum and cultural outreach space that formally opened to the public in 2015.[107] This unique community center, located directly across the street from the historic courthouse that anchors Sumner's modest downtown square, features a permanent exhibit that chronicles the Till murder trial and its aftermath, a small screening room and library, and meeting space. The ETIC's museum is open to the public during regular weekday hours (booking an online appointment is encouraged), and its executive director, Patrick Weems, has spearheaded partnerships with local high school student interns who assist with guided tours of the museum and courthouse.

The ETIC was established by the ETMC of Tallahatchie County, a group formed by former president of the Tallahatchie County Board of Supervisors, Jerome G. Little, in 2006.[108] In his rhetorical history of the ETMC, Tell praised Little—who grew up sharecropping on the Mitchener Plantation in Sumner—for his dedication to confronting issues of racial injustice.[109] Jessie Jaynes-Diming, one of the founding members of the ETMC, called Little the "originator of race reconciliation" in Mississippi.[110] For Little and others, addressing social injustice meant eradicating silence, particularly Sumner's longstanding practice of forgetting Till's lynching. "In order to properly remember and honor Emmett Till," the ETMC "needed to first break the silence and take responsibility for their role in the injustice."[111] Although the ETMC's membership was initially all Black, the commission would transform itself into a multiracial organization, including inviting Susan Glisson to participate before the commission had its first official meeting.[112]

Glisson was a pivotal figure in the ETMC's historical development and direction, but her influence on promoting and organizing state-wide racial reconciliation efforts is perhaps her greatest contribution to racial healing and justice. Indeed, her social justice résumé is impressive—she founded the William Winter Institute for Racial Reconciliation in 1999 and became its first executive director, played a role in the formation of the Philadelphia Coalition in 2004, and worked with groups and communities to develop public apologies to confront and address historical injustice, one of which is featured in our analysis in this chapter as well as the book's conclusion.[113] Part scholar (with a doctorate from the College of William and Mary), community organizer, and "memory activist,"[114] Glisson is the cofounder of Sustainable Equity, a "healing and equity consulting firm" that promotes itself as having "helped make Mississippi a leader in healing old wounds, especially in places most haunted by racial violence."[115] She also helped recruit another white woman and respected advocate for civil rights, Mississippian Betty Pearson, to join the commission.[116]

In stark contrast to Greenwood's appropriation of Till's image for touristic purposes, the ETIC employs the memory of Till for pursuing a less commercialistic—and more elusive—goal: statewide racial reconciliation. The center's website describes its mission as rooted in social justice, one of the three primary goals of civil rights tourism: "The Emmett Till Interpretive Center exists to tell the story of the Emmett Till tragedy and to point a way towards racial healing."[117] In a 2015 interview, Weems noted, "Reconciliation begins by telling the truth, and that's a big piece of the mission of the Interpretive Center—how do we tell the truth, and how do we tell it honestly?"[118] The answer to that question lies in the center's approach to framing the Till narrative for its visitors through its exhibit and a short film, and culminating with a tour of the courthouse, whose interior was restored to more closely resemble its original appearance in the 1950s. The center's work in the local community is channeled through a metaphor of restorative justice, an inclusive conflict resolution strategy that involves "not only an interpersonal relationship between victim and offender but also the communities of which they are a part."[119]

As Weems explained during our visit, the center explicitly strives for restorative justice because justice was not achieved during Milam and Bryant's trial in 1955. This message was echoed by Bill Foster, Little's cousin and an ETIC volunteer who assisted with our tour, who often spoke of the center's work in chords of harmony, forgiveness, and transcendence. Reflective of restorative justice's focus as the centerpiece of its mission, all visits to the center begin with a reading of a resolution crafted by the ETMC, "The Apology," that was presented to members of the Till family in a public ceremony on the steps of the Sumner courthouse in 2007. It is an extraordinary document, especially considering the conflicting views that divided the commission along racial lines early on. As Tell writes, Black members of the group were primarily concerned with "racial justice," whereas its white members were more interested in the "economic benefits" of restoring Sumner's courthouse.[120] The statement's opening paragraph tacitly admits that Mississippi is a state that continues to be rife with racial conflict; Mississippi's history, it argues, plays a central role in that conflict and holds the keys to its potential transcendence. "We the citizens of Tallahatchie County," it opens,

> believe that racial reconciliation begins with telling the truth. We call on the state of Mississippi, all of its citizens in every county, to begin an honest investigation into our history. While it will be painful, it is necessary to nurture reconciliation and to ensure justice for all. By recognizing the potential for division and violence in our own towns, we pledge to each other, black and white, to move forward together in healing the wounds of the past and in ensuring equal justice for all of our citizens.[121]

The statement goes on to summarize the details of Emmett Till's kidnapping in the summer of 1955, his brutal murder, Milam and Bryant's trial, and the FBI's reopening of the case in the 2000s.

The conclusion of "The Apology" is noteworthy for the way it speaks to the case's impact on later generations of Mississippians, the systemic problems that enabled Till's lynchers, and, more subtly, the connection between Till's lynching and contemporary examples of racial violence and injustice—all issues that are rarely addressed in civil rights tourism in Mississippi. "We ... acknowledge the horrific nature of this crime," it reads. "Its legacy has haunted our community. We need to understand the system that encouraged these events and others like them to occur so that we can ensure that it never happens again. Working together, we have the power now to fulfill the promise of liberty and justice for all."[122] Yet, "The Apology" is not without its critics who dismiss such efforts as superficial and inconsequential, as we detail in the concluding chapter. And as Weems noted in a 2019 interview with us, the focus on reconciliation transforms the expectations of some who originally expected to "see" and "experience" the act itself and the gruesome aftermath.[123] Dallen J. Timothy describes this as a type of dark tourism where tourists seek to "satiate an interest in risk, morbidity and death."[124] Lynching sites and stories are associated with dark tourism, which attracts visitors to places of incarceration (e.g., concentration camps, slave forts), natural disaster zones (e.g., volcanic eruptions, earthquakes), and crime scenes.[125]

The ETIC's museum exhibit—a reproduction of a traveling exhibit developed at the Delta Center for Culture and Learning at Delta State University[126]—focuses on a narrow, yet central, chapter in the Emmett Till story: the 1955 trial. Composed of ten tall, framed, wall-mounted poster displays that detail different moments and key players in the trial's narrative, the decidedly low-tech exhibit casts visitors in the role of historians in a curated archive. In contrast to what is typically found in most museums' historical exhibits, none of the displays is accompanied by interpretive cards or notations. Instead, they are comprised entirely of reproductions of primary-source documents. Contemporary newspaper clippings populate each frame and are supplemented with a mosaic of court documents and excerpts of typed and handwritten letters, all of which are superimposed over black-and-white photographs. Without the text-based or audio guides many visitors are accustomed to relying on when interpreting a museum's exhibits, the center instead relies on the historical documents themselves as the primary means for cultivating a sense of narrative coherence and fidelity.[127] This was especially true during our visit, when we examined the exhibit without an interpretive guide.

And what of those documents and the story they tell? The ETIC's emphasis on truth telling and its relationship to racial reconciliation through restorative justice suggests that the exhibit, at least from the center's perspective, offers a definitive account of the trial rather than one that is open to individual interpretation. Its narrative, in other words, is channeled through the authoritative voice of History itself, a voice that is initially framed by "The Apology" that visitors are invited to read. The displays themselves are all identical in design.

A brief title at the top of each poster describes that respective display's focus in large font (examples include "Scene of Trial," "The Jurors," and "Mamie Bradley"), followed by the words "Emmett Till Trial." Although contemporary journalistic accounts of the trial dominate the displays, the additional documents that accompany them reflect a range of viewpoints, from those who were sympathetic to Till's family and supported the state's case against Milam and Bryant to others who resolutely insisted on the killers' innocence.

The exhibit's first frame presents a single, enlarged black-and-white image of a smiling Emmett Till, taken in a south Chicago suburb approximately five years before he was lynched. With suspenders over each shoulder and one hand resting playfully atop a bicycle's handlebars, the image captures a sense of childlike innocence that quickly fades from the exhibit's remaining displays. Interestingly, the exhibit does not include the horrific *Jet* photograph of Till's crushed face.[128] Instead, the ETIC exhibit contextualizes Till's photo with other documentary evidence that speaks to the violence he later suffered. For example, the author of one unsigned letter displayed in "Preparation" notes "the cruelty shown to this Negro boy" and questions whether "the people of Mississippi still have barbarians in their state"; in another display, "Sumner, MS," deep irony permeates a photograph of a sign on the edge of town that advertises Sumner as "A good place to raise a boy."

The final poster in the exhibit, titled simply "Resolution," includes a newspaper headline that reveals how the jury deliberated for a little over one hour before acquitting the accused men. An excerpt from a William Faulkner essay that references Milam and Bryant's murder confession the following year sits uneasily alongside news accounts of the verdict. Here, the story ends with a juxtaposition that makes it clear that, in fact, there was no satisfactory resolution to this terrible crime. Although an approximately nine-minute film screened for visitors fills in some additional details (including Till and his mother's biography, the lynching's impact on the civil rights movement, and Till's funeral), much like the exhibit, it makes no attempt to provide narrative closure to the case itself. In light of that, the ETIC becomes the mechanism for restoring justice that the system failed to achieve in 1955 and again, decades later, when the DOJ twice reopened the case. And that work continues in new and novel ways. At the time of this writing, the ETIC had collaborated with the Emmett Till and Mamie Till-Mobley Institute and members of the Till family to create a new traveling exhibit, "Emmett Till and Mamie Till-Mobley: Let the World See," that will eventually be housed at the ETIC in Sumner after completing a national tour that runs through the end of 2023.

Perhaps more than the exhibit, the center's location is interesting rhetorically insofar as it is placed in one of the most important geographic sites associated with the public memory of Till. Whereas the historical markers associated with sites related to Emmett Till tend to present their locations as places where specific events happened, the ETIC uses history as a vehicle for addressing contemporary concerns that go beyond individual historical events.

Moreover, the ETIC's physical relationship to the courthouse lends the center a kind of spatial agency that amplifies its rhetorical power. A towering stone monument erected in 1913 by the United Daughters of the Confederacy—an organization that has promoted Lost Cause narratives and installed Confederate memorials and monuments throughout the South—still stands in a place of prominence next to the courthouse. Thus, the courthouse and ETIC not only face but confront one another. When we toured the restored courthouse with Weems, our main guides were a group of local African American high school interns participating in the Sumner Youth Institute. They discussed the building's restoration, pointed out where key figures in the trial stood, and showed us the small room and table where twelve white men rendered their verdict. These students' very presence in that space and their intimate participation in the center's efforts bring Till's memory to life in a way that differs markedly from the dry, authoritative voice of the state historical marker that identifies the courthouse as the site of Till's murder trial. And while it may be too soon to assess the center's effectiveness at restoring justice and moving a divided community closer to racial reconciliation, through their voices, a symbol of injustice and white supremacy is transformed into a place of racial healing. Meanwhile, another rural community just eleven miles south of Sumner has created an entirely different space for telling Till's story.

Confronting the Past at the Emmett Till Historic Intrepid Center

Tell is correct when he asserts that the small village of Glendora (estimated population 132[129]) possesses the "greatest density of Till memorials anywhere in the world" that includes dozens of marker signs, a dedicated park, a bus tour (the alliterative Till Trail of Terror Tour), and the first Emmett Till museum in the world, the Emmett Till Historic Intrepid Center.[130] Founded by Glendora's mayor Johnny B. Thomas, the museum opened its doors in 2006 and later, after a period of extensive renovations, "re-opened" in 2011.[131] Tell characterizes the first incarnation of the museum, which was "quietly funded" using portions of a USDA Community Connect grant whose purpose was not to construct a museum but rather to bring broadband internet

Emmett Till Historic Intrepid Center. Photo by Roger Davis Gatchet.

service to Glendora, as essentially vernacular in nature: amateurish, bereft of a single original artifact, and mired by low-tech displays, historical inaccuracies, and bogus photographs.[132] Needless to say, professional curators were not contracted to build the exhibits. Instead, students at Mississippi Valley State University in nearby Itta Bena and Prairie View A&M University in Texas spent approximately two weeks researching Till's background and trial before constructing the museum's primary display, a historical timeline that included Till's lynching.[133] After several failed attempts to obtain a historical preservation grant, Thomas's close relationship with Bennie G. Thompson, Mississippi's longstanding congressional representative, finally helped secure the necessary financial support (a $400,000 earmark) to significantly renovate the museum.[134] As Tell noted in his description of the current exhibit, "the improvement to the museum is uncontested and extensive."[135]

Before arriving at the museum, visitors entering Glendora drive past a number of purple Emmett Till historical markers ("King's Place," "Milam's House," "Glendora Gin") that were installed by the ETMC in 2008. The museum is housed on the ground level of a cotton gin where Till's murderers may have retrieved the fan used to weigh down Till's body, according to the ETHIC's version of how he was lynched (the MDAH has disputed this claim). In addition to its reputation as a site for Till memorialization, Glendora—like many small Delta towns—is mired in unimaginable poverty, high unemployment, little to no business infrastructure, and a dearth of resources necessary for the community's survival. Using the word "misery" to illuminate Glendora's predicament, Tell observed that "the impoverishment of Glendora is astounding, even by Delta standards."[136] As a case in point, we conducted our May 2019 interview with Mayor Thomas in a field where he and another man were tending to their crops. Thomas explained that growing vegetables is essential to the community's survival because Glendora is a food desert, with the nearest supermarket a considerable distance away.[137]

Located near the patch of farmland where we interviewed Thomas is another of the mayor's memory projects, the Emmett Till Memorial Park and Interpretive Nature Trail.[138] Built on the edge of the Black Bayou, the walking trail's dilapidated condition when we visited mirrors the rural surroundings and the town's desperate poverty. Some of the green signs were stained with dirt and skewed, and the wooden benches were in disrepair. Similar to Greenwood's efforts to cement its birthright status, one of the signs argues that Glendora is the rightful birthplace of the civil rights movement. Dated April 30, 2010, the untitled marker quotes Thomas, who vigorously (and hyperbolically) proclaims: "It's a pleasure to be given the opportunity to serve this Historic Community that SPARKED THE CIVIL RIGHTS MOVEMENT as Mayor for the past 24 years." Thomas also claimed that the ETHIC museum "sparked the beginning of the RACIAL HEALING OF OUR NATION and WORLD."

In an interview with us and in other published accounts including his own autobiography, Thomas has freely admitted that the impetus for founding the museum was not solely motivated by his desire to memorialize Till. The collapse of Thomas's sweet potato farming venture in the 2000s[139] forced the mayor to reconsider his options: "We thought about our history and we decided that we would go with our history. The Emmett Till case and the African Americans here that had to do with it."[140] While this may be the case, Thomas's motivations are also tied to the economic survival of Glendora (which Tell explores in his book) and to the mayor's own role in the Till story. As Thomas wrote in his autobiography,

> Everyone knew that my father [Henry Lee Loggins] was one of the "right hand" workmen of J. W. Milam, who later confessed to the murder of Emmett Till, and it was rumored that Milam forced him to participate in the Emmett Till kidnapping and possibly the murder, and help dump Till's body in the Black Bayou to destroy evidence of the crime. . . . Shortly after Emmett Till was murdered, my father was arrested by Sheriff Strider and secretly hidden in jail in nearby Charleston, Mississippi to prevent him from testifying and was later banished out of town to an unknown location.[141]

Some aspects of Thomas's narrative, particularly the Black Bayou being the dump site for Till's body, are contested by the MDAH. Weems notes that the lack of documentation confirming the historical veracity of this competing narrative has led some to wonder if "boosterism was a major factor in starting that museum."[142]

The ETHIC acronym is appropriate given the museum's mission, which focuses on civil and human rights, and its vision to "promote justice, equality, civility, and fair treatment for all persons."[143] After watching an eighteen-minute film on the town of Glendora and the Till lynching (including an interview with Loggins, who denied any involvement in the murder), visitors move into an exhibit curators would later characterize as the "circle of truth." The exhibit can be divided into two primary sections. The first provides a broader historical context that includes interpretive panels on a wide range of subjects, including slavery and segregation, the village of Glendora, Tallahatchie County, the area's Native American history, the Illinois Central Railroad, religious institutions, a Black veterans' war memorial, and famed blues musician Sonny Boy Williamson II (Aleck "Rice" Miller), who was born in Glendora. The entire exhibit also features several timeline displays. The first display, "Significant Events in the Struggle for Civil Rights and War against Human Wrongs," chronicles events from 1865 (end of Civil War) to 1947 (CORE and the first Freedom Rides).

The second part of the exhibit begins with another timeline display (1950 to 1959, with commentary on Emmett Till) and is devoted to a detailed, painful account of Till's lynching—parts of which are comprised of details of questionable historical veracity.[144] Although the museum's temporal narrative moves quickly during the first half of the exhibit (from slavery to 1950), time begins to slow down during the second half, allowing visitors to contemplate, even investigate, the events that led to Till's death. Here visitors first encounter a physical replica of the Bryant's Grocery and Meat Market storefront. Positioned on the structure's right is a dark orange sign that reminds them of "The Reality of Racism," fifteen of which are featured throughout the exhibit space. Each of these signs, particularly in the second part of the museum, serves as a guidepost marking critical moments in the Till lynching. After encountering the Bryant store, visitors pass through several individual exhibits: (1) "Abduction: Home of Moses Wright," (2) "The Truck of Torture," (3) "The Barn," (4) "Glendora Cotton Gin," (5) "The Trial," (6) "The Funeral that Sparked the Movement," (7) "The Place of Rest," and (8) "Lasting Impressions." Till's killers are named, Mississippi, Jim Crow, and white supremacy are assailed, and Till is described as "the young victim of multiple physical and mental violations of human rights by incensed racists." Following popular crime investigation television series as inspiration, one interpretive display called "ETHIC Crime Scene Investigation" asks visitors to review the evidence and "be the judge." Part of the evidence displayed considers the "real cause" of Till's death. What follows is a prosecutor's list of violations: (1) Assault and Battery/Torture, (2) Cut/Stabbed, (3) Assault with a Deadly Weapon, (4) Lynching and (5) Drowning/Asphyxiation.

After Till's death is thoroughly investigated, visitors arrive at Till's Chicago funeral. In the center of the room lies an open casket. A mannequin representing Till is dressed in a suit, its face battered and mutilated (the *Jet* photograph of Till's actual face hangs on a nearby wall, providing documentation that validates the abuse he suffered). Thomas identified this feature of the ETHIC as one of the things that distinguishes his museum from the ETIC in Sumner. "They don't show the kid's body as we display it here," he said. "In Sumner you won't find the casket or the body display, which I think is a crucial part of everything."[145] To the left of the casket sits another display, "Burr Oak Cemetery" in Chicago, with an Emmett Till headstone. To the right is a sign that reads: "Roberts Temple Church of God in Christ." The Till casket is the emotional centerpiece of the exhibit, as Thomas noted in his 2019 interview with us: "We get an array of emotions from that. People normally be crying and those kinds of things. Kind of rough. Makes me do the same . . . it hits hard."[146]

In one of the final displays, entitled "ETHIC Hall of Expressions," visitors are asked to remember Emmett Till as a "living sacrifice" for civil and human rights and are encouraged to continue to serve as change agents for social justice, with the express purpose of serving the goals of racial unification and reconciliation:

> The purpose of this "experience" is for you to remember the legacy of Emmett Till and others, not in their deaths, but as living sacrifices for us. . . . As we reflect on THEN and NOW, it is evident that we have come a long way, yet there are more strides that we the people need to take. . . . Let's not focus totally on the problems, but on the promises and triumphs. . . . Allow the echoes to serve as educational healing agents for peace, unity and reconciliation. . . . Now, look into Emmett's piercing eyes and tell him that you are worthy of his sacrifice and commitment to being a Healing Agent, a Warrior for Human Rights.

Like the ETIC, the ETHIC offers a critical response to Till's lynching in the larger context of civil rights memory work in the state. Emblematic of its explicitly confrontational approach, the exhibit includes a drawing of the state of Mississippi with a noose draped over the state. Similar to the ETIC exhibit, the museum's curators do not allow Till to be airbrushed out of history or superseded by the Delta landscape, as is the case with many of the promotional efforts deployed by the Greenwood CVB. Interestingly, while the ETHIC mission statement references "justice" and "equality," the museum's rhetorical emphasis is on recreating and documenting the horrors that transformed Till's body into an unrecognizable corpse, with social justice as a secondary consideration.

It is significant that of the three geographic sites examined in this chapter, it is the ETHIC in Glendora that most directly confronts the traumatic final days in Till's short life. Located in what is arguably one of the most rural and impoverished communities in the state (especially when compared to Sumner and Greenwood), it is also the least likely to be a primary destination for tourists. Tell has thoughtfully traced how poverty is inextricably yoked to representations of Till's memory in Glendora.[147] There is a troubling irony in this confluence of extreme poverty and federal funding that makes the museum possible. Some communities throughout Mississippi depend on tourism as a means for generating much-needed revenue. Although Glendora clearly has much to gain from civil rights tourists who might visit the village as they follow Till's story throughout the Delta, if Tell's assessment is accurate, then the ETHIC depends on a continual cycle of poverty for its very existence. Although it does not thrive on poverty, without it, the museum would lose the funding that keeps its doors open. Under these conditions, the ETHIC and its critical, race-conscious message—a message that is all but absent from the many Till narratives that dominate Mississippi's tourism industry—is not likely to emerge from the perpetual obscurity that prevents it from reaching a broader audience. The museum's marginalized geographic location, critical approach to telling Till's story, and dependence on the poverty of the very community it hopes to support all point to the difficulties that rural southern communities face when telling difficult stories about their past.

Although the ETHIC and ETIC have similarities in telling the Till story, the two entities have rarely—if ever—collaborated on Till-related projects. Similar to the fragmented and sometimes contentious relationship between local communities invested in selling the blues which characterized blues tourism's early years, some elements of local civil rights tourism are marked by competitiveness, fragmentation, and resentment.[148] For example, in his autobiography, Thomas characterizes his relationship with the ETMC as largely negative. He is critical of the decision to create a 50–50 percent Black and white membership: "I had an uneasy feeling about the whites coming in and trying to dictate the rules."[149] Chastising the commission's African American membership for being too docile, Thomas described himself as the "most outspoken African American on the Commission, which turned off both blacks and whites. They thought my suggestions were too radical and controversial."[150] Thomas also believes that while Glendora is still mired in poverty, racism, and neglect, Sumner is profiting from Till's lynching, as he told *Mississippi Today* in 2018: "To this day you find the community where the trial was held is now reaping benefit from that murder—financially and through tourism. Communities such as Glendora who suffered in every sense of the act continue to be repressed and looked over."[151]

In separate interviews, both Thomas and Weems expressed disappointment about a lack of collaboration in Till's memorialization. Thomas's animus is centered on the Sumner-based ETMC, but it is clear from our interview with the mayor that the perceived lack of collaboration extends to the ETIC:

> I'm a part of the Emmett Till Memorial Commission up in Sumner that house[s] the courthouse and the Interpretive Center. There's no, there's no togetherness on it. They won't seem to come together and let everybody survive. Everything is brought to Sumner. . . . We've tried to do everything together, and I served on the commission so that we could try to do things together. But . . . we don't do much together in Tallahatchie County whatsoever.[152]

According to Weems, efforts to work collaboratively on projects, including a tourism brochure, have been unsuccessful. From Weems's perspective, collaboration is a fruitful approach given the motivation of tourists who visit the area:

> What I've tried to express to him, and it might not be true, but what my thought process has always been, if you're going to travel from California to come to the Emmett Till Interpretive Center, you're most likely going to go five miles down the road and go to Glendora. And vice versa. If you're going to come all the way to visit Glendora, you're most likely going to come to the courthouse. And so, the idea is, you don't want just one casino, you want ten casinos. That way it draws people from all over the world and they go to each one. But I don't think he sees it that way. I think he sees it as, either he wins or we win, kind of scenario.[153]

While Weems and Thomas's disagreements are reflective of tensions bound in regional tourism efforts elsewhere, both believe Emmett Till's memory should serve the larger goal of the present: social justice. Similarly, Jessie Jaynes-Diming has pressed for remembering and honoring Till's memory as a mechanism for racial justice. In a 2021 roundtable discussion moderated by Dave Tell, she recalled the climate of collective forgetting reflected in local community resistance by both local whites and African Americans during the formative years of the ETMC: "The Emmett Till Commission, when it was first being formed, we had African Americans and whites talking about, 'Why are you all bringing this up? You know, I didn't have anything to do with it. You know, why don't y'all let sleeping dogs lie?' But those days are over with."[154]

Jaynes-Diming grew up in Chicago and was aware of Till's story years before she moved to Mississippi. In addition to her work with the ETMC, she is the owner of a local tourism organization called Mississippi Delta Experience Touring.[155] In a 2019 *National Parks* article, journalist Kate Siber highlighted Jaynes-Diming's work as a tour guide as the two explored various Till memory sites, including the courthouse in Sumner and the Tallahatchie River site where Till's body was discovered.[156] Jaynes-Diming continues to educate young people about Till's lynching and promote the values of social activism. During the fall of 2021, eighteen students from Wabash College embarked on a civil rights tour of Mississippi. On the third day of their visit, Jaynes-Diming took them to the Milam Plantation, where Till was most likely lynched, and encouraged the students to enter a life of activism: "I hope this experience will spark a fire in the belly of all of you," she said. "A lot of times, when young people witness the injustices of the world, it ignites them to stand, to be strong and to fight back to make a difference. That is my hope for all of you."[157]

Without question, the appropriation of Emmett Till as an object of tourism in the state of Mississippi has been fraught with tension and conflict. From its early reluctance—if not outright refusal—to acknowledge Till's memory to recent efforts that actively promote his story for sojourners visiting the state, the discordant mélange of Till-related texts and discourses that increasingly populate Mississippi's memorial landscape are symptomatic of the challenges that many communities face when the past is repurposed for the present. Moreover, the various and at times conflicting ways in which Till's story is framed draws attention to how we choose to remember traumatic events from our past, especially when those histories speak to contemporary issues that present-day communities continue to grapple with. How are we to remember Emmett Till? Through the euphemistic lens of a cheerful Chicago teen who "rocked the world" and sparked the civil rights movement, or as a Black victim who was kidnapped at gunpoint, tortured, shot in the head, and dumped into the Tallahatchie River by white men who wanted him permanently silenced? Or do we remember Till's mutilated body and face that were on display in that open casket over sixty years ago? In the next chapter, we examine the rhetorical dynamics of two historic house museums, the Amzie Moore House Museum and Interpretive Center in Cleveland and the Medgar and Myrlie Evers Home National Monument in Jackson. As we will learn, Amzie Moore survived multiple threats against his life, while Medgar Evers suffered a similar fate as Emmett Till—the victim of white racism and violence.

CHAPTER FOUR

PRIVATE SPACES, PUBLIC MEMORIES

Mississippi's Civil Rights Historic House Museums

> There was no escape for any of us from the
> strain of living at the edge of disaster.
>
> —MYRLIE EVERS

A modest house sits at 614 South Chrisman Avenue in Cleveland, Mississippi, right in the heart of the state's Delta region. Like the other homes that dot the neighborhood's streets, this inconspicuous structure of brick and wood, with its lone bush and small, unfenced lawn, would go unnoticed by most if it were not flanked by two historical markers. In fact, this house, which was designated a state landmark in 2007,[1] once served as a civil rights "command center," a space that "was always churning with ideas, conversation, and planning."[2] Its former owner, Amzie Moore Sr. was a seminal figure in the grassroots struggle for civil rights in Mississippi during the 1950s and 1960s. Active with the NAACP, SNCC, and the Regional Council of Negro Leadership (RCNL), Moore fought for social justice on a number of fronts.

As one of many safe houses located throughout Mississippi, including the Canton Freedom House highlighted in chapter 2, Moore's house provided a place of security and fellowship for exhausted civil rights workers in their struggle for social justice. Despite concerns that it would be attacked by members of the Ku Klux Klan and other white supremacists, the house was also a "central headquarters" and "orientation center" for activists.[3] Over three decades following his death in 1982, Moore's home was transformed into the Amzie Moore House Museum and Interpretive Center (hereafter, "Moore House"). According to the mission statement displayed in the museum, the Moore House "attempts to share the life of an unassuming man who had a passion and a drive to encourage social justice."

Amzie Moore House Museum and Interpretive Center. Photo by Roger Davis Gatchet.

An equally modest house museum can be found at 2332 Margaret Walker Alexander Drive in Jackson, a two-and-a-half-hour journey southeast of Cleveland. Like the Moore House, an MFT marker was installed on the property. One of dozens of similar ranch-style houses in the historic Elraine Subdivision developed in the 1950s by two African Americans, Winston J. Thompson and Leroy Burnett, the house's humble exterior belies its tragic history. Shortly after midnight on June 12, 1963, NAACP field secretary Medgar Evers returned home after attending an evening rally at the New Jerusalem Baptist Church. Under the cover of darkness 150 feet away, Citizens' Council and KKK member Byron De La Beckwith shot Evers in the back as he walked up the driveway to meet his waiting family.[4] The shot proved fatal, with Evers the latest victim of a system determined to maintain white supremacy at any cost. It took over thirty years and three separate trials before Beckwith was finally convicted of murder in 1994.

After her husband's assassination, Myrlie Evers kept the house after relocating her family to California. She maintained it as a rental property for the next three decades, and in 1993, she donated the home to Tougaloo College; it completed restorations in 1996 with funding from the state legislature.[5] Unlike the lesser-known Moore House, the Evers House and its surrounding neighborhood have been granted a dizzying array of official designations. The home became a Mississippi state landmark in 1993 and was later added to the National Park Service's National Register of Historic Places in 2000.[6] The Elraine Subdivision was recognized as the Medgar Evers Historic District in 2013,[7] the house was designated a National Historic Landmark in late 2016,[8] and in 2018 federal legislation paved the way for its addition to the African American Civil Rights Network.[9] The following year, it became a

Medgar and Myrlie Evers Home National Monument. Photo by Roger Davis Gatchet.

national monument, with ownership officially passing from Tougaloo College to the National Park Service in 2020.[10] Now known as the Medgar and Myrlie Evers Home National Monument (hereafter, "Evers House"), the site "commemorates the legacies of two civil rights activists who, from their modest, 3-bedroom ranch home, devoted their lives to ending racial injustice and improving the quality of life for African Americans."[11]

Despite the similarities between the outward appearance and historical significance of both sites, the Moore House and Evers House museums draw on distinct rhetorical strategies that evoke contrasting experiences and emotions for visitors. Save for a couch and a few other items, the Moore House is almost entirely devoid of home furnishings and decorative displays. The interior of the Evers House is curated in a manner consistent with many other historic house museums around the country, where most of the rooms are staged with furniture and artifacts to resemble its lived-in state as the Evers family home. Whereas visitor experiences in the Moore House are rooted in metonymy, a rhetorical trope that simplifies the sweeping historical narrative told in the house's exhibit, at the Evers House architectural elements and curatorial presentation explicitly frame it as an authentic site dominated by the memory of Medgar Evers and his civil rights work. While both houses create points of identification between tourists, the activists who lived there, and the goals of the Mississippi Movement, the Moore House does so by deemphasizing Amzie Moore as a biographical subject (even as it reveals the details of his life) and instead using him as a symbolic vessel through which it tells the larger story of the Mississippi Movement. The Evers House, by contrast, has a more singular focus on Medgar Evers, especially his assassination, and relegates Myrlie Evers—an important civil rights leader in her own right—to the role of mother and grieving widow. In doing so, the Moore House becomes a safe house, and the Evers House a house of death.

Historic Houses as Sites of Public Memory

Unlike many museums or exhibitions in places whose geographic connection to the subject matter is minimal or even nonexistent, historic houses have a direct, tangible relationship to the people who lived there or the era they represent. As private-living turned-public spaces, historic houses derive their power as sites of memory from their potential to evoke a profound sense of intimacy, domesticity, and authenticity. According to some historians, the first public historic house museum in the United States was established in 1850 at the Hasbrouck House in Newburgh, New York, which served as headquarters for General George Washington during the latter part of the American Revolutionary War.[12] Historic house museums have proliferated across the United States since the Hasbrouck House's public dedication nearly two centuries ago. According to one estimate, some five hundred were in operation by the outset of World War II and another six thousand created between that war's end and the year 2000.[13] Historian Linda Young argues that historic houses constitute their own unique museum genre and represent approximately 10–15 percent of established museums.[14] The "museumization" of these homes, as she calls it, transforms the "conventional domestic scope of the house" into "the vehicle of larger narratives about the character of the nation or the locality."[15]

Of course, Mississippi is no stranger to historic houses, which have been drawing tourists to the state for nearly a century. Historian Susan T. Falck traces enthusiasm for historic house tourism in Mississippi back to at least the 1930s, when an organized pilgrimage brought "carloads of tourists" from across the nation to Natchez to visit the many antebellum homes there.[16] This nascent form of tourism was boosted by full-page newspaper ads produced by the Mississippi Advertising Commission as part of the state's BAWI program, an initiative described in chapter 1. In one example from 1937, a large map of historical sites around the state showcased eight historic house locations.[17] Interest in exploring the state's antebellum mansions continued through the decades. An official 1970s-era Mississippi travel guide cataloged dozens of historic houses open to visitors, including thirty-five in Natchez alone.[18] Historic house museums continue to be featured prominently in the state's official tour guides and on the list of historic sites at VisitMississippi.org, the tourism website operated by the Mississippi Development Authority. Many of the historic house museums throughout Mississippi represent the state's antebellum past, while the number of house museums connected to the Mississippi Movement are fewer in number. Although the Evers House is undoubtedly the most visible on the national level, other "movement" homes have the potential to be renovated, including the Indianola Freedom House, the C. C. Bryant House in McComb, and the Unita Blackwell House in Mayersville.[19]

Young's typology of historic house museums separates the genre into distinct categories according to what the museum foregrounds; these include heroic figures who lived there, the building's architectural design, and the social history it signifies.[20] The Moore House and Evers House exemplify one of Young's categories, the hero house, which "constructs purposeful narratives of greatness" that amplify the work of their activist-residents—especially in the case of Moore, one of the lesser-known leaders of the movement.[21] Young also notes that this very feature of hero houses "gives them special strength as agents of a nationalist agenda," including perpetuating Great Man historical narratives.[22] This potential pitfall is tempered somewhat in both the Moore House and Evers House by their focus on social history—one of Young's other categories—and the grassroots work of Mississippians in the fight for civil rights. This twin focus on memorializing the heroism and emphasizing the activism of Amzie Moore and Medgar Evers (and to a much lesser extent, Myrlie Evers) makes the Moore House and Evers House museums especially unique, if at times underappreciated, features of Mississippi's growing civil rights tourism industry. Although the Canton Freedom House Civil Rights Museum is also a historic house museum, we explored it in chapter 2, rather than here, because it is a prime example of vernacular tourism. Unlike the Canton Freedom House, whose only major source of government funding to date was a one-time relief grant due to the COVID-19 pandemic, the Moore House and Evers House were professionally curated and funded through grants and other government appropriations. In the next section, we turn our attention to the Moore House and the stories it tells.

A Safe House: The Amzie Moore House Museum and Interpretive Center

Today, Cleveland is an increasingly popular Delta destination for blues tourists due to its close proximity to Dockery Farms (a plantation that was home to blues musician Charley Patton) and the Grammy Museum Mississippi located less than a mile from the town's downtown area. Cleveland's civil rights tourism infrastructure, however, largely hangs on Amzie Moore and the sites and commemorative activities that have coalesced around his memory, including a city park named after him that was dedicated in 2001. In Jim Carrier's *A Traveler's Guide to the Civil Rights Movement*, he describes Moore's home as a "safe house for fleeing, scared, and exhausted activists."[23] Noting at the time of the book's publication in 2004 that the house was privately owned, he argued, "it deserves to be a monument to one man's courage and impact."[24] A decade later, Carrier's hope was realized.

In 2011, the Bolivar County Board of Supervisors was awarded $210,000 through the Mississippi Department of Archives and History's (MDAH) Mississippi Civil Rights Historical Sites grant program to restore the structure and establish it as a museum.[25] Although the grant application focused primarily on the house's architectural condition and restoration, it also emphasized its potential to draw tourists to Cleveland. "Cleveland, MS is a tourist destination attracting many in their search for Blues history," the application reads. "Tying blues music and the struggle for civil rights is a natural progression in our tourism development."[26] By the time work started on restoring the Moore House, it was in significant decline and marked by years of neglect, vandalism, and termite infestation. Restoration was completed in January 2015 and the first informal tours started approximately a year later. At the 2016 ribbon-cutting ceremony and with Moore's son, Amzie Moore II, in attendance, Will Hooker, Bolivar County administrator, remarked: "Therefore today is not only a commemoration of actions of the past from one foot solider, Amzie Moore, but also perhaps more importantly to learn from his actions and carry his legacy forward."[27]

While the promotion of the Moore House has been inconsistent since the ribbon cutting ceremony in 2016—due largely to the fact that the MDAH grant did not extend to its operation after the restoration work was complete—it stands as the most significant civil rights site in Cleveland. Local tourism brochures list the Moore MFT marker and house as part of the town's civil rights and blues history,[28] and the 2021 issue of the *Cleveland and Bolivar County Welcome Guide* devotes space to Moore and his home.[29] Likewise, a recent edition of the state's official tourist guide includes references to the Moore House and MFT marker (while simultaneously lauding the town's downtown shopping district—a conspicuous reminder of the economic goals that also drive civil rights tourism).[30]

The dual state historical markers posted outside the house immediately frame the site as historically significant. In contrast to the Evers House and other historic house museums in Mississippi, furniture and artifacts are largely absent from the Moore House.[31] Instead, the focus is on polished interpretive displays and, more importantly, the house itself. As Young argues, in historic houses, "the whole ensemble itself communicates meaning to the visitor," and this is especially true in the Moore House, as we will discuss later in this chapter.[32]

Visitor experiences at the Moore House are framed through the lens of metonymy. Metonymy refers to a form of reduction, as when one "convey[s] some incorporeal or intangible state in terms of the corporeal or tangible."[33] For Barry Brummett, metonymy is essential for "rendering judgments about an impossibly complex world."[34] Likewise, Victoria J. Gallagher and Margaret R. LaWare describe how metonymy "relies upon the use of a single characteristic to identify a more complex whole, or the use of a single attribute to create identification with a larger whole."[35] By reducing complex, difficult to understand elements of a community's history to a more manageable signifier, metonyms shape the public's understanding of a historical period or series of events in powerful ways. Claire Sisco King argues that metonymies "should also be understood as having political and ideological implications."[36] She draws attention to the "ideological work of metonymy as a form of displacement, visualizing the process of subjectification in which individuals come to know (or, more precisely, imagine) themselves in relation to something or someone else."[37]

The Moore House exhibit is primarily housed in five rooms. All visitors begin their tour in room 1 (the living room); room 2 served as a dining room, while rooms 3, 4, and 5 were bedrooms. Visitors must make an appointment to visit the museum, whose displays follow an approximate chronological timeline as they track Moore's work and its connection to the broader movement. During our visit in 2016, we were accompanied by Will Hooker and Delta State University archivist Emily Jones, who offered some background information on the museum's history. Our tour of the house was primarily self-guided. In the following analysis, we focus on three themes that emerge from its exhibit: local resistance, violence and economic terrorism, and the Mississippi Movement's influence on the national civil rights movement.

Local Resistance

While the museum acknowledges the national civil rights movement in displays such as "Moving the Movement," the focus of the Moore House is decidedly local in nature—geography, activists and citizens, the Mississippi

Movement, Moore as a biographical subject, even the house itself. The titles of some displays, including "Amzie Finds His Calling: Local Leadership" and "Civil Rights Leader: Amzie and the Evolution of Grassroots Strategies," emphasize the indigenous nature of the Mississippi Movement. In an untitled display that provides an overview of the Moore House as museum, the word "local" is used twice—as a description of Moore's activist identity as well as the goal of the space: "encouraging exploration and understanding of the civil rights movement on a local and national level." With regard to Moore's biography, the museum narrates his early life, military service, return to the Mississippi Delta in January 1946, and early involvement in the movement.

Situated in the Black community, the materiality of the Moore House reinforces its importance as a central hub for local activism. This, in turn, supports its metonymic function in the context of the broader civil rights movement. Civil rights leaders and activists met in a variety of private-public spaces throughout the South, including churches and homes. The Moore House, in particular, was viewed by civil rights leaders and members of the movement as a refuge and sanctuary from white intimidation and harassment, violence and murder, as well as a "safe haven," according to one display, for planning and organizing. "I was more than relieved when the screen door opened and I stepped inside the house of Amzie Moore," remembers Danny Lyon, a SNCC photographer quoted in the display "Civil Rights Leader: Amzie and the Evolution of Grassroots Strategies." Visitors also learn that, in 1963, Moore turned his house into "the center of food and clothing distribution in Cleveland." One display includes a large black-and-white photo of activists (both African American and white) sitting on a couch. As visitors enter the Moore House, they, too, are invited to sit on a couch positioned underneath the display. The Moore House contains little in the way of additional furniture except for one green chair, a television set, and a black, cloth-covered display table that was empty during our visit. Unlike museums housed in buildings that have no historical or material relationship to the past, the Moore House has existed since he built it in 1941, and its life cycle—from birth to near death to recent resurrection—is literally rooted in the soil of the Delta and the Chrisman Street neighborhood.

In addition to Moore's biography and the house itself, the museum focuses on the Mississippi Movement and its various groups (e.g., RCNL, Delta Ministry, COFO) and affiliations with larger, national organizations, including the NAACP, CORE, and SNCC. The Moore House also references social movement campaigns, including Freedom Summer and Freedom Vote, a Mississippi voter registration drive that occurred the previous year. One display,

"Foot Soldiers," alludes to Saul Alinsky's famed "rules for radicals" approach to community organizing.[38] The display recommends that "for the best and lasting results," the Mississippi Movement should train "local leadership" rather than "importing" outsiders who will not have the same type of long-term commitment as the local citizenry. This display also provides a list of local leadership in the Delta, a rhetorical strategy that not only emphasizes the local over the national, but places Moore's activities within the larger frame of an organized collective agitating for change. At the same time, the museum highlights localized activism through the use of testimony, including passages from John Dittmer's definitive book on the Mississippi Movement, *Local People: The Struggle for Civil Rights in Mississippi*. Dittmer praised the Mississippi Movement for its strength and tenacity and is quoted describing the "character" of the Mississippi Movement as shaped by "local people themselves" and an "indigenous leadership." Documenting the workload associated with this ground-level civil rights work, the museum features a display, "Paper Trails: Evidence of the Front Lines." This display shows a large photo of a white woman feeding paper into a typewriter. In one of the few physical artifacts presented in the Moore House, two tall stacks of paper rest on the floor beneath the display. An antique Royal typewriter sits on one stack; an interpretive card rests atop the other. The description on the card explains, "These two stacks of paper represent the volume of work required by one volunteer to reach out to one citizen over four years to encourage them to register to vote in one election." In short, perseverance, hard work, determination, and success at the local level are prominent values embodied in the museum's metonymic chronicle of the state's role in the broader civil rights movement. In the next section, we focus on the museum's representation of the primary threats to the Mississippi Movement's success.

Violence and Economic Terrorism

For many visitors to the Moore House, their experience begins before they enter through the front door, with the two state historical markers posted on the grounds outside. One, a green MDAH marker, was unveiled in 2008 and is in close proximity to the front of the house. Four years later, another historical marker—an MFT marker—was installed at the rear of the house. Although the MFT marker devotes little space to the structure itself, a single sentence offers an intriguing glimpse into the important role it played as a safe haven for activists arriving in Cleveland. "He offered his home to visiting activists and for numerous civil rights efforts," the sign reads, "despite continual threats of violence and economic pressures, especially regarding mortgages on his home and service station." As historian Charles M. Payne has noted, "Moore often carried a gun. His home was well armed, and at night the area around his house may have been the best-lit spot in Cleveland."[39] Charles McLaurin, the civil rights veteran who lived and mentored with Moore for a year in the 1960s, confirmed as much when he told us that Moore had "guns set up strategically" in the house, which "was certainly a place that was well-observed by the opposition."[40] Another scholar went so far as to describe the house as "a veritable armed fortress."[41] This theme—preparing for violence and the constant threat and enactment of economic terrorism—is a central feature of the narratives in the museum's exhibit, and the Moore House offers a metonymic means through which visitors can understand these threats beyond Cleveland's city limits.

Without question, images of horrific violence—Emmett Till's lynching, assassinations, police dogs unleashed on activists—are seared into our collective memory of the national civil rights movement. Rather than chronicle these human rights abuses, the Moore House instead uses Moore and his home as a metonymy that stands in for those atrocities. One of the more striking signifiers of the threat of violence is encoded in the architecture of the house itself. Room 3 (a bedroom) stands out among the others due to a window located much closer to the ceiling than what is typically found in a residence. A display titled "Shattered Silence" explains: "High windows and tightly closed curtains were subtle but physical reminders of the constant threat to the lives of those involved in any civil rights activities. Stories of high-paced road chases, bullets flying into cars and homes at all hours of a [sic] day and night and taunting phone calls were just some of the commonly heard conversations among SNCC workers in Mississippi."

During our visit, we learned that this space served as a bedroom for visiting activists, and it was part of an extension to the house that Moore built himself.[42] Although the exhibit offers no evidence to suggest that Moore's home was specifically targeted (a fact that McLaurin reiterated in our interview), we learned that an African American resident of the neighborhood once scared off a potential white assailant who had planned to shoot through the bedroom window. When combined with the Moore House's broader narrative, this incredible story uses the home as a metonymy that personalizes, in a very clear and concrete way, the violent realities of civil rights workers in the 1950s and 1960s. While reading about the violence and seeing photographic evidence of it, visitors can personally witness its material reality in the high window's wood and glass.

Other displays in the museum have a similar effect, while also extending the terrain of white violence to the economic well-being of African Americans. Amzie Moore is portrayed as a local entrepreneur whose business enterprises in Cleveland played an important role in the RCNL's campaigns to challenge Jim Crow laws in the South. As we learned in chapter 1, Moore's entrepreneurial activities included owning the Pan-Am service station, which doubled as a safe space for African Americans to use the restroom, purchase gas, and enjoy a hot meal. As "The Pan-Am Change & Service" display details, however, "the gas station would prove to be a bitter battle for Amzie, almost costing him everything for which he had worked." The display contains reproductions of typewritten letters that depict Moore "in a constant battle with insurance companies and petroleum providers as he defended his ability to run his businesses."

In room 3, visitors learn that Moore's situation was, indeed, dire. An unlabeled display contains a magazine story centered in a simple glass frame that further illuminates the confluence of violence and economic terrorism that threatened Moore and other civil rights activists. The title of the two-page spread notes that "Moore may lose $20,000 home and life." The story leaves no uncertainty as to the perpetrators' race, reporting that Moore "was warned by whites that he stood to lose his $20,000 ranch home, a $29,000 combination gasoline station-cafe-beauty shop, some $15,000 worth of equipment and maybe even his life." Although the exact nature of the violent threat to Moore's life is not explained, the source of his financial woes is clearer. As the story explains, it was the Citizens' Council that "plotted his downfall" and convinced "local banks, stores and wholesale supply houses" to cut his credit and require payment on his outstanding debts. A black-and-white image of Moore's service station in the magazine display further reinforces the story's narrative, noting, "Whites . . . threatened to 'blow up' [the] station." Despite this constant threat of violence and economic terrorism, Moore continued the fight, and his efforts would have an impact beyond the state. This leads to our discussion of the third theme in the Moore House: the prominent role activists in Mississippi played on the national stage.

The Mississippi Movement's Influence on the National Civil Rights Movement

While localism is a predominant theme, the Moore House also connects the Mississippi Movement to the national civil rights movement. The title of one display, "Moving the Movement: Amzie Reaches Beyond the Delta," highlights Moore's skills as a negotiator as he soothed tensions between the NAACP and SNCC over a planned school walkout in 1961 in McComb. In addition, national figures, including Martin Luther King Jr., Roy Wilkins, Stokely Carmichael, Andrew Young, and Jesse Jackson Jr. are listed and sometimes quoted (visitors are also treated to audio recordings from King, Carmichael, and James Forman). Many of these national figures, including King, Young, and John Lewis stayed at the Moore House during the 1950s and 1960s.[43] Moore's activism was also connected to the larger political structure, specifically the Johnson administration's "War on Poverty," an important goal that Washington and the movement shared. One display dedicated to Robert F. Kennedy's visit to the Delta in 1967 focuses on the senator's experience witnessing the abject poverty there. During his visit, Moore served as Kennedy's host. The following excerpt from this display ("War on Poverty: Senator Robert Kennedy Visits the Delta") emphasizes the relationship between the local and national: "It is suggested that Kennedy stopped in Annie White's home on Chrisman Avenue before continuing on to Mound Bayou and Winstonville. Kennedy, appalled at the level of poverty in the Delta, urged Miss Marion Wright to tell Dr. Martin Luther King Jr. to bring the poor to Washington, resulting in the Poor People's Campaign in 1968."

The museum also uses metonymy to place Moore's activism and the Mississippi Movement within the larger historical struggle for civil rights. "Across the Threshold: Carrying Amzie's Legacy Forward" traces the struggle for civil rights back to slavery, chronicles the failure of Reconstruction, and situates the rise of the modern civil rights movement in the 1950s. Similarly, the display "This Is Jim Crow," which takes up an entire wall in room 2 (the dining room), begins its narration in 1865 with the end of the Civil War and the immediate efforts to stall Black freedom as it was "unlawful for any freedman, Negro, or mulatto to ride in any first-class passenger cars used by white people." This Jim Crow timeline centers on three themes: "voting rights," "education," and "transportation" and concludes in 1971; placed underneath this timeline is another sequence of events which highlights Moore's accomplishments as a civil rights leader, from co-founding the RCNL in 1951 to his involvement with Head Start and the Child Development Group of Mississippi in the late-1960s.

As visitors walk counterclockwise through the house, it becomes evident that although the exhibit does not offer a clear, straight-line chronology of Moore's life, the movement's "won cause" narrative is evident in individual displays such as "This Is Jim Crow," as well as the sequence of events (the Mississippi Movement in the 1950s and 1960s) that are introduced in room 1 (the living room) and conclude in room 5 (a bedroom) with "Across the

Threshold," a display that accentuates the movement's documented successes, including the significant increase in registered Black voters from 1956 to 1968 and the rise of Black political power in the 1980s and 1990s (featuring key figures such as congressmen Mike Espy and Bennie Thompson). The museum also highlights how, by 1992, Mississippi had elected more Black politicians than any other state. Interestingly, this is the same evidence that local and state tourism officials employ, including at the MCRM, to intimate that Mississippi has eliminated the worst excesses of Jim Crow and progressed to a more enlightened state of race relations.[44] The Moore House shows how Moore and others participated in a movement that affected real social and political change.

While the Moore House provides ample evidence of the movement's successes, its chronological narrative ends abruptly in 1993, and, not surprisingly, the museum makes no reference to the present other than encouraging visitors to carry on the struggle for civil rights in "Across the Threshold": "As generations before them had equipped them to take these steps, they realized that it would be the generations who followed them who would inherit their works and carry on the responsibility of enlightenment, engagement and hope." As Dwyer and other critics have noted, most civil rights memorializing circumvents the present because acknowledging it might jeopardize sources of support and funding from the larger political structure.[45]

Moore's role as a civil rights leader serves a metonymic function by standing in for the interrelationship between the grassroots and the national movement. Although one of the purposes of this house museum is to educate the public about Moore and his civil rights activities, any reasonable retelling of history would need to contextualize Moore within the larger civil rights movement. The deployment of visual and verbal references to national civil rights leaders, timelines that signify the transcendence from oppression to enlightenment vis-à-vis the larger US cultural value of progress, and Amzie Moore's role as a facilitator to heal intragroup conflict all recognize the relationship between the local and national. The physical presence of national civil rights leaders in the Moore House (leaders who presumably interacted with local activists) further reinforces metonymy's role in the museum's narrative, as individuals representing different spheres of activism stand in for the broader relationship between the local and the national. A very different kind of rhetoric frames the state's most recognized civil rights–related historic house museum. We now turn our attention to that site, the Evers House, to explore its place on Mississippi's civil rights memorial landscape.

A House of Death: The Medgar and Myrlie Evers Home National Monument

The assassination of Medgar Evers had a dramatic impact on the eventual development of civil rights tourism in Mississippi. As Carrier notes, Beckwith's violent act that night in 1963 "scarred" Jackson, leading the city to do "more than any other midsized city in the South to face its racist past and make it a lesson for citizens and visitors."[46] One of those acts of commemoration was the transformation of the Evers family home into a public memory site. Little time was wasted in restoring it after Myrlie Evers gifted the house to Tougaloo College in 1993. An appropriation from the Mississippi state legislature paved the way for its restoration, which was completed in 1996.[47] Tougaloo worked with the Jackson-based architectural firm WFT Architects, who described the house as "an extraordinary opportunity to showcase" Mississippi's civil rights history and their "primary goal" as "a careful renovation/restoration of both the house and the grounds to their 1963 appearance."[48] As is often true with historic structures, authenticity was a focal area of concern at the Evers House from the very beginning. In the structural report written by WFT Architects in 1995, the authors lament that "there is very little documentation of interior furnishings and arrangements."[49] Even with the help of Myrlie Evers (who is identified as the probable sole source of information regarding the interior's original state), the report acknowledges the challenges with locating period-specific furniture from the 1950s and 1960s when the Evers family lived there. Nonetheless, "the authenticity of the furnishings is important," the report asserts. "An attempt to the fill the house with unrelated pieces would serve only to diminish the significance of the project as a whole."[50]

As it turned out, state funding for the house's restoration did not extend to interior furnishings, and when the authors toured it in 2019, Minnie White Watson, a former Tougaloo College archivist, the museum's longtime curator and tour guide and friend of Medgar Evers, confirmed that the house remained empty and devoid of artifacts for nearly three years early on. That changed when it was selected as a location for scenes in the 1996 Rob Reiner film *Ghosts of Mississippi*. As Willie Morris notes in his book *The Ghosts of Medgar Evers*, the film's crew quickly went to work transforming the home's interior and exterior to its 1963 appearance, decorating and furnishing the rooms and even transplanting a large oak tree that the Evers planted in the front yard after moving in.[51] Once filming concluded, Castle Rock Entertainment donated a majority of the furnishings, window dressings, and artifacts to Tougaloo to enhance the house museum.[52] Those materials remained in the house during our 2019 tour, giving the Evers House the unusual distinction of being a historic site whose appearance and exhibit is a direct result of having once been a movie set.

Like the Moore House, the Evers House was open to tourists by appointment only throughout Tougaloo's stewardship. Prior to ownership transferring to the National Park Service, Tougaloo president Beverly Hogan noted that budgetary limitations prevented the museum from hiring a full-time staff.[53] Instead, one had to phone Watson directly for a guided visit. Watson served as the museum's primary curator and tour guide from its opening until it became a national monument (the authors were some of the last to tour the home with Watson before her retirement). Incredibly, even with such limited staffing, Hogan said that thousands visited the house every year,[54] and interest is likely to increase with its national monument designation and Jackson's stature as a civil rights tourism hub in the state. In what follows, we examine how authenticity shapes visitor experiences at the Evers House before turning our attention to its gendered representations of Medgar and Myrlie Evers.

Experiencing Authenticity in the Evers House

Like the Moore House in Cleveland, the Evers House is similarly inconspicuous, a "humble home in a neighborhood of modest homes."[55] Touring the house both inside and out, visitors will find their experience framed in terms of authenticity. When understood as a "rhetorical phenomenon," argues Stephen A. King, "absolute, genuine, 'true' authenticity does not exist."[56] In public-memory settings, authenticity is actively constructed through curatorial efforts. Although it may be "an invented and manufactured phenomenon," this form of authenticity—*constructive* authenticity—asserts influence even at civil rights memory sites where real people lived and real events transpired.[57] Both faces of the MFT marker in the front yard call attention to an oft-mentioned detail defining the site's authenticity—the assassination of Medgar Evers in 1963. The deadly violence Evers suffered at the hands of Beckwith is described in a single sentence on the front panel: "Just after midnight, on June 12, 1963, he was assassinated in the driveway as he returned from a meeting."

In his guidebook of prominent civil rights sites around the nation, Charles E. Cobb Jr. describes the Evers House as "moving" due to "the access it gives to its owner's personal life."[58] To be more precise, it is his assassination—a watershed moment in the Mississippi Movement—and the numerous acts of harassment and violence leading up to it that most affect the visitor experience at the Evers House. Entering it allows one to fully appreciate the force of Beckwith's violent act. During our tour with Watson in 2019, she recounted, in vivid detail, the violence the Evers family endured when they lived in the house.

After a chronological summary of Medgar Evers's time in college, his early relationship with Myrlie and T. R. M. Howard, his efforts to register Black voters, and his position as the NAACP's field secretary, Watson described how Evers chose the house site from several available options with his family's security in mind. He avoided selecting available corner lots because they were more vulnerable to attack, and he altered the original design plan so that all bedroom windows were raised higher up the wall to make it more difficult for potential attackers to see inside (a design feature it shares with the Moore House). Moreover, he decided that the carport would serve as the location for the house's main entrance, rather than placing a door in the more vulnerable front exterior wall facing the street.

As Evers expected, attacks on the house and his family came quickly. Within their first year there, Watson told us, someone shot through one of the front windows, which led the family to relocate a piano and couch to avoid bullets. According to Cobb, "abusive and threatening telephone calls constantly harassed the Evers family."[59] Myrlie Evers described how these threats impacted seemingly mundane aspects of the family's home life. "There were even places in the house where they [the children] couldn't sit," she wrote; "the furniture had to be arranged away from the windows; and where the television set was placed, we couldn't use the chairs to watch at night. We had to sit on the floor or present inviting targets through the front windows."[60] After additional gun attacks pierced the master bedroom window, Medgar and Myrlie Evers took the precaution of resting bed mattresses directly on the floor (some of the prop beds left from the film are arranged in this manner). Watson recalled another evening when Myrlie was forced to barricade the house's back door with a refrigerator to thwart someone attempting to break in.

Speaking with an authoritative voice aided, no doubt, by her own friendship with Evers and decades of experience touring thousands of visitors during her tenure as the Evers House curator, Watson went on to recount the details of Evers's assassination in painstaking detail. His biography and accomplishments, while still an important part of the overall visitor experience, are deemphasized in deference to a narrative focused primarily on his violent final moments. She paid special attention to the fatal bullet's pathway after exiting Evers's body, tracing its trajectory and showing where its marks on the house are still visible today. These include one of the more interesting features that contribute to the house's authenticity, a hole left by the bullet when it passed through an interior wall between the living room and kitchen. Although this hole was patched sometime after Evers was killed, it was "carefully reopened" during a 2013 renovation before the museum was rededicated on the fiftieth anniversary of his death.[61] This physical imprint of the violence that took Evers's life—once covered and then restored decades later—emphasizes the memory of that violence revisited in the name of architectural preservation and civil rights memorialization.

Although the bullet's entrance hole in the house is gone, the memory of its impact is preserved in black and white in a photograph on display that shows where it penetrated the window in 1963. Similar photos (all taken by the Jackson Police Department) are displayed throughout the house, offering visitors a careful reconstruction of the crime scene, a sort of memory echo, that validates Watson's narration. Watson brought us into the kitchen, showing where the bullet's mark can still be seen on two original damaged wall tiles and the door of a refrigerator (the appliance is in fact a prop from the filming of *Ghosts of Mississippi*). As we explored the carport at the conclusion of our visit, she identified spots on the concrete driveway still stained with Medgar's blood nearly sixty years later. It was a moment whose affective power was palpable and rarely matched during our experiences touring the state. Jackson's top tourism official, Rickey Thigpen, described a visit to the house with Myrlie Evers when she first identified the blood stains as his most "significant" moment as a civil rights tourist. "I walked that driveway dozens of times. Walked on top of those stains. And she said, 'This is Medgar's blood here. They can't get it.' And guess what? For awhile they tried to get it up. Talk about how tourism has evolved.... Now ... people sit there, students sit there and touch and write on pads, and tears coming out of their face while they're writing as they're touching the sidewalk."[62] Thigpen's account is echoed in visitors' online reviews, many who describe crying during their tours. The stain becomes an impossibly dense signifier, preserving the memory of an entire movement and the violence of white supremacy in a few square inches of concrete. Watson's identification of the stain at the climax of our tour seemed only to emphasize the finality of his assassination.

Assuming our experience was typical of most tours, Watson's narrative is *the* framing device for the visitors' tour, the lens through which they experience and interpret the lives (and death) of its former inhabitants. Without that narration and the knowledge of the extraordinary event that happened there, the museum itself would seem rather unremarkable. All but one of the rooms mimic the house's state when the Evers family lived there. Film prop furniture and staged artifacts capture a snapshot in time before their lives were violently disrupted: a casserole dish rests in a drying rack near the kitchen sink, framed school portraits of the Evers children are perched atop a piano in the living room, hosiery hangs from clips in the shower, and spare change is piled on a dressing table in the master bedroom, as if someone had just emptied their pockets.

Even though Watson calls attention early on to the fact that these items were never the actual property of the Evers family, we experienced them as such nonetheless. A framed certificate bearing the seal of Tougaloo College hanging in the dining room commemorating the museum's rededication in 2013 describes the house as a "sacred place," and it is this ability to evoke a combination of sacredness and quotidian domesticity that makes the Evers House such a unique public memory site in Mississippi. Given the freedom to wander through the house on our own, the overwhelming sense of intimacy and horror created by the rooms and bullet marks made it easy to forget that we were walking through a film set. The staged inauthenticity of the artifacts becomes moot when subsumed by the overwhelming affective power of the place itself. In fact, unlike the Moore House, only one room in the house explicitly hails the house as a museum. This bedroom, completely devoid of furniture, contains a small blue rug with the Tougaloo College seal (asserting the university's ownership of the property) and a large multipanel display titled "Medgar Wiley Evers" that spans three of the room's walls. A small portion of the display is partially dedicated to Myrlie Evers. Although the room is an anomaly in the house, and the display's small text discourages engagement from all but the most dedicated civil rights tourists (to wit, the other white guests with whom we toured the house spent no time reading it while we were present), it contributes to a stark difference between the portrayals of Medgar and Myrlie Evers.

Gendered Representation at the Evers House

The gendered representation of male visibility and female inconspicuousness in the Evers House mirrors how critics of civil rights memorialization have described a consistent pattern of male privileging at the expense of women who "played significant roles at all levels of the Civil Rights Movement, yet too often . . . remain invisible to the larger public."[63] Nearly all of the artifacts, displays, and elements of the narrated tour at the Evers House orbit around Medgar Evers. He is presented as a man of action, an unflinching change agent whose accomplishments were achieved despite the constant threat of danger. Myrlie, by contrast, is presented as a largely passive woman confined to a limited range of domestic roles. This is apparent before visitors step foot in the house, where Myrlie is mostly absent, her importance minimized. The US Senate bill that declared the home a national monument initially left Myrlie Evers's name out entirely, requiring Congress to pass an amendment acknowledging her presence there. A metal plaque affixed to the house's front exterior wall identifies it as "The Home of Medgar Wiley Evers."[64] Likewise, the MFT marker posted in the front yard describes it as the "Medgar Evers Home." Its front face text does mention Myrlie by name, describing "Medgar and Myrlie Evers" as parents who "moved into this home with their children." Quickly, however, their surname becomes shorthand for Medgar himself, where "Evers" references only Medgar, "an outspoken activist for voter registration and social justice." Myrlie, meanwhile, is subsumed under "the family" that "moved to California and deeded the home to Tougaloo College" after his death. He is the activist, she the mother. Similarly, the marker's rear face describes Myrlie as Medgar's "wife," while images and captioned photographs frame her as a mother, a pianist, and a grieving widow. Meanwhile, Medgar's accomplishments are listed in detail: "Speaking at mass meetings, documenting acts of brutality, working with the NAACP legal defense team, encouraging voter registration, and coordinating protests." Although the marker was installed in 2011, its narrative extends only to 1963 (excluding a brief reference to Beckwith's conviction in 1994); Myrlie's activism and work leading the NAACP after Medgar's assassination are conspicuously absent, leaving her as simply the mother, along with Medgar, who were "pleased to have room for the growing family" and the secretary "who helped her husband in his office."

The gendered representations of Medgar and Myrlie Evers are reinforced through displays inside the house as well. In the living room, visitors can peruse black-and-white photographs of Myrlie playing with her children and posing with other family members, and the cover of an issue of *Life* magazine that captures a poignant image from Medgar's funeral, where Myrlie, dressed in black, comforts her distraught son. The cover does not mention Myrlie by name; instead, she is defined in terms of her relationship to her husband, as "Medgar Evers' widow." Images of Medgar are absent from all but one room of the house, a fact that alternately reinforces his identity, in both life and death, as a *field* secretary at work or a martyr of the freedom struggle who is now gone. Even in his absence, the museum frames Medgar Evers as someone who is actively *doing*, whereas Myrlie is the more passive mother and widow keeping the family together. Visitors who take the time to read Tougaloo's rededication certificate on display in the living room will initially find no mention of Myrlie's name; rather, she is Medgar's "devoted wife," whereas Medgar is "a noble, courageous, and dignified leader," and the museum is "a monument" to his "legacy and inspiration." An allusion to Myrlie's activism is framed in terms of her husband's work, where she is part of "the family that breathes life back into *his memory* and unfailingly works to advance *his dreams*" (emphasis added). Only at the end of the certificate is she explicitly connected to civil rights activism, where she and Medgar are called "two iconic American heroes."

As noted earlier, the sole room that features interpretive displays is devoted almost entirely to cataloging Medgar Evers's life journey and his accomplishments as a movement leader. It is a large display, spanning three walls in the room. Myrlie Evers appears in eight photographs, most of which are incorporated into the seven multiparagraph columns that comprise the display's text. In the first photo, we find a seventeen-year-old Myrlie as a college freshman at Alcorn A&M College, an image that complements the display's description of her courtship with Medgar while they were students there. Her relationship to Medgar as bride, wife, and eventually mother of their children, is the primary focus of this early narrative, and it is reinforced through a photo of the happy couple cutting cake at their wedding, followed by a family portrait. As the display continues, the crippling poverty Medgar encountered working as an insurance agent throughout the Delta inspired him to extend the NAACP's reach in the state. While Medgar's attitude towards systemic oppression against the state's African Americans is presented in terms of action, Myrlie's position is more consistent with her photographic representation as a mother. For example, when the display recounts Medgar's attempts to desegregate the University of Mississippi in 1954, it notes that "Myrlie was fearful about the fact that Medgar had not considered the effect that this financial strain and separation would have on their family. Then she found out she was pregnant again and begged him to withdraw his application." When the display does depict Myrlie as an active agent in a photograph where she is taking notes next to Medgar in his NAACP field secretary office in Jackson, she is described simply as "his secretary," with no details of the nature of her work.

After detailing Medgar's assassination, the display's final panel shifts to addressing his legacy. Although the panel's images again depict Myrlie as both a grieving widow and strong mother keeping her family together in the wake of her husband's death, it also includes a 1997 newspaper article clipping that lauds her election as chairperson of the NAACP's Board of Directors in 1995, making her "perhaps the most powerful African American woman in the U.S."

Rather than learn about her accomplishments in that important post, however, visitors who read the article will instead find that she hesitated to run for the position. Speaking of her second husband, Walter Edward Williams, who was suffering from cancer, Myrlie is quoted, "My first priority was to be there for Walter, as he had always been there for me and my children." Here again, and now at the height of her work as the national leader of the largest civil rights organization in the country, Myrlie Evers is framed as a dutiful, loving wife. In contrast to the article clipping, the panel's text devotes three paragraphs to describing Myrlie's many accomplishments after relocating her family to California. Finally, visitors are given a fuller description of Myrlie's education, professional and political career, and work with the NAACP, where she "brought fiscal and organizational stability" and "strengthened its membership and prominence." The display quickly resignifies her successes in terms of Medgar, however, whose "legacy lives on in Myrlie's work." A lengthy list of gains in the freedom struggle follows, all of which are made possible, at least in part, by "the courage and commitment of Medgar Evers." By inextricably tying Myrlie's achievements and leadership to Medgar's, rather than letting them stand on their own or framing them as an extension of the broader civil rights movement, the Evers House unwittingly reinforces a gendered understanding of the movement that minimizes the contributions not only of Myrlie Evers, but of all women who were integral to its success.

Together, the historic residencies of Amzie Moore and Medgar and Myrlie Evers represent how white terrorism yielded no quarter—even the sacred privacy of home was not immune to violation. Eschewing the furnishings and artifacts that are typically found in historic house museums, the Moore House metonymizes Moore via his role in a larger collective. In doing so, the museum becomes a safe house—a place of refuge against white violence, a space to reaffirm group solidarity, and a base of operations for organizing. If the Moore House is a safe house, the opposite is true of the Evers House. Walking through its staged film-set pieces, witnessing the documentation of Beckwith's violent act, and listening to Minnie White Watson's authoritative tour, visitors experience it as authentic, a family home under the constant threat of white violence, and, as the bullet holes and blood-stained concrete driveway bring into stark relief, a house of death. The Evers House simultaneously minimizes Myrlie Evers's influence and accomplishments, mostly relegating her to the role of wife, mother, widow, and steward of Medgar's legacy.

As representatives of the hero house category of historic house museums, both the Moore House and the Evers House reify their namesakes, elevating their accomplishments and status in the Mississippi Movement and the national civil rights movement. In addition to his military service, Moore is presented as a hero because he survived despite great odds. Just as Moore becomes a metonymy for the movement, so the Moore House metonymizes the civil rights hero—all the activists, regardless of race, who risked (or lost) their lives for the freedom struggle. Medgar and Myrlie Evers and their children are heroes, too. While the Evers House associates Myrlie's heroism with Medgar's legacy, Medgar achieves this status as a martyr, with the house's authenticity as material evidence. Without question, both museums are unique and important additions to Mississippi's civil rights tourism sites. As historic house museums that venerate African American civil rights heroes, the Moore House and the Evers House confront a state memorial landscape saturated with antebellum mansions and Confederate monuments. Both museums assert a crucially important counternarrative to historic house museums that offer a partial, sanitized telling of Mississippi's history. Like other sites explored in this book, they also fall short of critiquing present-day racism in Mississippi, thus limiting their ability to address contemporary social justice issues through racial reconciliation and social activism even as they confront the present with the truth of the past. Equally compelling complexities are at play in the MFT marker series, which marks the state's first major official effort to promote Mississippi's civil rights heritage. We explore the rhetorical dynamics of those signs as public memory in greater detail in the next chapter.

CHAPTER FIVE

MARKING THE PAST

The Mississippi Freedom Trail and Signs of Racial Truth

> In the battle for historical memory, every
> word matters—and every marker does, too.
> —*SMITHSONIAN MAGAZINE,* 2017

In 2006, blues tourism in Mississippi began its transformation from localized, grassroots efforts to a state-sponsored campaign to sell the blues with the unveiling of the first Mississippi Blues Trail marker honoring Charley Patton. Five years later, Mississippi's early struggles to promote its civil rights history and legacy achieved a similar newfound legitimacy at the state level as part of another trail series: the MFT. The MFT is comprised entirely of official state markers that commemorate people, places, and events related to the struggle for civil rights in the state. On May 18, 2011, politicians, members of Emmett Till's family, and others gathered in Money to witness the unveiling of the first MFT marker, "Bryant's Grocery"—a marker that officially memorialized Till's lynching in August 1955. Till's cousin, Reverend Wheeler Parker Jr. unveiled the marker and noted in his public remarks to the crowd that "Emmett Till still speaks fifty-six years later."[1] Jerome G. Little, Tallahatchie County supervisor and the organizer of the Emmett Till Memorial Commission, argued that the unveiling of the first MFT marker is "going to help us move the state forward. It's going to give the state of Mississippi a new vision, a new look for the other part of the country and the world."[2]

Mississippi's efforts to promote its history and heritage (and, in the process, bring much-needed revenue into local economies) with the MFT was the first significant move to organize Mississippi's complex and contentious history of racial struggle for touristic consumption. As we discussed in chapter 1, an earlier effort by the Mississippi Department of Archives and History, commenced during the 1980s, resulted in a series of state civil rights–related markers but no coherent, centralized plans for marketing the state's civil rights history. The MFT, along with the MMH-MCRM in Jackson, demonstrates that civil rights tourism had become an important site—if not *the* site—of struggle over Mississippi's civil rights legacy.[3]

Since the unveiling of the first marker in 2011, the MFT has, with a few exceptions, been warmly received and praised for its economic value and candor. Jim Carrier listed the MFT project as part of a series of "consequential efforts" in 2011 including restarting plans to build a state civil rights museum.[4] In his assessment of the "culinary delights" of Mississippi's food culture, a *New York Times* reporter noted in 2016 that the Mississippi Tourism Association's heritage trail projects, the Mississippi Blues Trail and the MFT, "helped create a greater flow of tourists to the region."[5] Two years later, the headline of another *New York Times* article characterized the MFT as a "chronicle of outrage and courage" and an "indictment of the cruelty of racism and a commemoration of those who fought against it."[6] In 2022, the MFT's scope expanded to the digital realm in the form of several MFT-branded episodes in a US Civil Rights Trail podcast.[7]

The Mississippi Development Authority coordinated the efforts that led to the selection of multiple themes and locations that launched the initial markers in the MFT—during the same year the nation was celebrating the fiftieth anniversary of the Freedom Rides; at that time, twenty-five of those were chosen from some three hundred submissions from around the state with the help of "a task force of scholars, historians and veterans of the Civil Rights Movement."[8] As indicated on the markers themselves, the MFT is funded in part by grants from the US Department of Transportation Federal Highway Administration, the Mississippi Department of Transportation, and the MDAH. Additional funding sources include the Mississippi Legislature, Tougaloo College, and private donations.[9] In this way, the MFT is quite distinct from the state's first historical marker program, which began in 1949 and is overseen by the MDAH. Those markers are initiated by local applicants and privately sponsored. MFT markers, by contrast, are administered by the state's primary tourism development agency, a reminder of the economic goals that are inextricably tied to civil rights tourism.

Although, for marketing purposes, the MFT is presented as a discrete trail, much like the state's Blues and Country Music Trails, the notion of a "trail" is in fact a rhetorical construction that creates the illusion of geographic intentionality and navigability. While there is a clear logic to their individual placement insofar as each marker is located on or near the site it commemorates, the trail itself is not a distinct route that visitors can easily traverse in its entirety. Tourists must invest a considerable amount of time and energy driving around the state to visit all MFT markers, which are largely concentrated in the Delta region and Jackson.

This chapter explores the rhetoric of the MFT and draws primarily on our fieldwork. At the time that fieldwork concluded, we had visited twenty-three of the trail's twenty-eight markers (by 2022, the total number of MFT markers had grown to more than thirty).[10] Although images of both panels of all the existing trail markers are available on the Internet, we only examine markers we visited in-person for two primary reasons. First, the smaller text and photos that compose each marker's rear panel are challenging to decipher in online images posted to Visit Mississippi, the state's official tourism website; in some of the images, the photo captions are impossible to make out altogether.[11] Second, and more important, Web-based research makes it difficult to offer a nuanced critique of the deeper narratives that emerge from each marker site; this can only be achieved through onsite fieldwork. Michael S. Bowman's work on the performative elements of tourism and its emphasis on attending "to the embodied nature of tourists' movements and encounters" underscores how difficult it is to understand tourism discourses through a computer screen.[12] For example, photographs of the Bryant's Grocery MFT marker on the Visit Mississippi website do not show the marker's immediate surroundings (which include the remains of the Bryant's Grocery building), nor do they permit one to understand where the site is situated in the community, its accessibility, or other important rhetorical features that impact how tourists experience it.[13]

Mississippi's selective efforts to present the people, events, and locations that are part of its civil rights history via official trail markers can be understood in terms of a dialectical relationship not only between the past and the present, but between public acts of remembering and forgetting. This dialectic suggests an intriguing rhetorical turn away from Mississippi's collective forgetting, with the state no longer actively marketing itself to tourists in a way that "minimizes or ignores the historical realities" of slavery, sharecropping, and other state-sponsored systems of oppression.[14] Perhaps the MFT's more important contribution is officially documenting the myriad acts of violence that engulfed the state during the 1950s and 1960s. Civil rights leaders and activists knew all too well that protesting the state's Jim Crow laws risked injury, imprisonment, and death. The MFT also fills a conspicuous gap in the historical record by raising public awareness of underrecognized figures and events in the Mississippi Movement. At the same time, its narrative underemphasizes the central role that women played in that movement as well as privileges narratives about activism that embraced the very system that disenfranchises African Americans. Furthermore, the markers that comprise the MFT present the struggle for civil rights as something that is confined to the past. In doing so, official memory workers in Mississippi limit the MFT's ability to speak to contemporary racial struggles in the present. Finally, many markers are located in de-facto segregated Black spaces, although some markers can be found near traditional centers of white political power in the state's capital city.

Public Memory and Historical Markers

Despite the growing body of scholarship on rhetoric and public memory, scholars have focused relatively little attention on historical markers, even as they have become a quotidian feature dotting America's memorial landscape.[15] Derek H. Alderman calls them "one of the most widespread, yet under-analyzed commemorative landscape features in the United States."[16] For Alderman, the "commonplace nature of highway historical markers arguably contributes to their rhetorical power, making their inscriptions appear to lie beyond the political complexities and debates of life."[17] Unlike the richness and complexity associated with museums and cultural centers, historical markers are, by design, limited repositories of memory. Some historians and cultural geographers have even referred to historical markers as "history on a stick" or "history by the spoonful."[18]

Although highway historical markers are limited in their ability to selectively remember the past, this does not necessarily diminish their significance. As Bob Brinkman, coordinator of the Texas Historical Markers Program, argues, "state markers are the government's official endorsement not only of what happened, but what is worthy to be remembered."[19] Markers, according to cultural geographers Samuel M. Otterstrom and James A. Davis, can be deployed in the "exploitation of certain historical interpretations." They argue that "government entities, including federal and state governments, use historical markers to identify heritage and cultural sites of interest and value to their respective jurisdictions, and the process helps define the territorial extent of the entity placing the marker."[20]

Much can be understood about civil rights tourism and public memory through the study of this mode of memorialization, as the limited literature on the topic demonstrates. In their analysis of African American history and historical markers in Fredericksburg, Virginia, Stephen P. Hanna and E. Fariss

Hodder found that "slavery and emancipation remain incredibly scarce in the city's commemorative landscape."[21] Likewise, North Carolina's markers tend to overlook "the violence, racism, and struggle that characterized the larger African American experience in the United States," and they neglect to mention the horrors of lynching altogether.[22] Next, we offer an interpretation of both the markers' material form and a thematic analysis of twenty-three MFT markers.

Mississippi Freedom Trail Markers

Historical markers, located in neighborhoods, downtown city streets, state highways, and other public spaces, are found across the country and vary in content and form.[23] Some markers—commonly associated with highway or roadside markers—are thick, aluminum cast signs set atop a long metal post, with large (up to three-inch tall) letters that attempt to convey complex people, places, or events in a short message that approximates the length of a tweet.[24] Other markers take on greater complexity, including narrative length and readability as well as the incorporation of visual images. Ironically, while historical signs "mark" important persons, places, and events, importing markers to a landscape inevitably adds a new symbolic texture to the physical context. But as Otterstrom and Davis note, "signs can be necessary to locate and identify historical happenings and artifacts, even if they introduce a foreign element into the very landscape that they are commemorating."[25] With the passage of time, however, markers blend in, as if they were a natural part of their cultural and memory landscape.

MFT markers mirror their counterparts that comprise the state's Country Music Trail and Blues Trail. Although their height above the ground varies by location, each metal marker is approximately forty inches wide and thirty-seven inches tall. An oval featuring the words "Mississippi Freedom Trail" and the silhouettes of approximately twelve marching civil rights activists (many holding signs) crowns the top of each marker. The image of Black activists is set against an orange background. Each marker's front panel also showcases a title in large font followed by approximately ten to twelve lines of text that provide a brief historical account of the subject the marker commemorates. The narrator's voice is what one would expect from a historical marker: authoritative, neutral, and objective.

The marker titles themselves are relatively easy for pedestrians and, in some locations, motorists to briefly pause and read without having to

"Madison County Movement" Mississippi Freedom Trail Marker, Canton, Front Panel. Photo by Roger Davis Gatchet.

"Madison County Movement" Mississippi Freedom Trail Marker, Canton, Rear Panel. Photo by Roger Davis Gatchet.

approach the markers for closer inspection, ostensibly giving casual tourists and unsuspecting passersby the ability to claim they have seen a marker without ever stopping to actually read it in its entirety. Each marker's rear panel, by contrast, offers a richer, more detailed display that features several paragraphs of text exploring the marker's subject and placing it in historical context, quotations from noted historical figures (politicians, civil rights movement leaders, and so forth), and captioned photographs and images of relevant artifacts. Unlike the front panel, the left side of the marker's rear

"William Chapel" Mississippi Freedom Trail Marker, Ruleville. Photo by Roger Davis Gatchet.

panel contrasts both an objective retelling of the past with a more subjective, more emotional narrative tone, while the right rear side provides documented evidence from black-and-white or color photographs, letters, quotations, and newspaper articles. The greater amount of information and related content and the much smaller size of the text on display on each marker's rear panel requires one to make the conscious decision to approach and engage with it, thus rewarding visitors willing to endure the oppressive heat and humidity and other inconveniences associated with some marker locations (mud, insects, overgrown grass and weeds) with a more nuanced understanding of Mississippi's civil rights history. In some cases, such as the marker for Reverend George Lee in Belzoni, motorists may be able to *see* both sides of a marker without leaving their vehicles; however, it is impossible to easily read the rear panel without making a conscious effort to do so. In another example, the "William Chapel" marker's front panel faces the street while the opposite side is directly positioned in front of the church itself. Visitors must walk onto church property to access the rear panel. With few exceptions, the front panel of the markers faces a street or sidewalk, while the back panel is obscured. And while many MFT markers are not near highways, the series adopted the form commonly associated with a highway or roadside marker.

Each marker contains additional salient rhetorical elements. First, the color orange signifies agitation while the image of protesters holding up signs and marching represents only one type of agitation. In reality, civil rights activists deployed a variety of rhetorical means to protest, ranging from legalistic and discursive methods (e.g., petitions) to body rhetorics (e.g., sit-ins) to physical confrontations with establishment surrogates (e.g., police). Second, the circle or oval that appears at the top of the markers communicates unity and community—a rhetorical theme that serves as a reoccurring trope among many, if not all, of the MFT markers. While it is certainly true that the civil rights movement, like all movements, existed only within the context of some collective rhetorical action, the movement was, in fact, comprised of multiple groups (local, regional, and national) that were often at odds with each other over tactics, strategies, and goals. Next, we discuss the MFT's four dominant rhetorical themes.

Black Resistance, White Violence

The MFT depicts the Mississippi Movement as engaging in nonviolent direct action and other forms of agitation to dismantle "the Southern way of life": voter registration drives, oratory and song, mass rallies, boycotts, freedom rides, sit-ins and wade-ins, petitions and judicial redress, fundraising drives and letter writing campaigns. In fact, nowhere in the MFT's historical retelling of the movement are African Americans depicted as deploying violence to achieve their civil and human rights goals, particularly as it relates to dismantling the state's segregation policies as well as significantly expanding voting rights. This is in stark contrast to long-standing white racist fears of Black criminality, including murder, rape, and theft. Mississippi civil rights leaders—Fannie Lou Hamer, Medgar Evers, C. C. Bryant, Aaron Henry, Amzie Moore, and others—"campaigned," "sang," "addressed," "registered," "pressured," "march[ed]," and engaged in other assertive, nonviolent acts of dissent. Other African American protesters are depicted as college students who "quietly sat in at the Jackson Municipal Library, which served only white patrons" ("Jackson Municipal Library Sit-In") and "sat down at the white lunch counter" ("Woolworth's Sit-In"); James Meredith ("University of Mississippi") and Clyde Kennard ("Clyde Kennard") sought, independently, to "desegregate" a prominent public state university; CORE activists "staged a boycott, created Freedom Schools, and implemented mass voter registration drives" ("Madison County Movement"); and a Jewish rabbi formed the "Committee of Concern" with other "diverse ministers" to raise money "for Black churches burned by the Klan" ("Bombings in Jewish Community"). In the cases of the "Jackson Municipal Library Sit-In," "Woolworth's Sit-In," and other MFT markers that memorialize turning points in grassroots protests, civil rights activism inspired more street-level dissent.

As part of the truth-telling goals associated with civil rights tourism, a graphic description of white retaliatory violence contributes to the MFT's narrative theme. In contrast to the more sanitized narratives that define many state historical markers in place throughout Mississippi, MFT markers selected for our study do not shy away from acknowledging violence motivated by hatred and racism. The front panel of the "Tougaloo College" marker accentuates this reoccurring cause (Black resistance) and effect (white violence) relationship, quoted here in its entirety:

> The courage of Tougaloo College students, faculty, and staff fueled the Jackson Civil Rights Movement. *Inspired by the bravery and resolve of Medgar Evers, students and faculty attempted to integrate Jackson's main public library, restaurants, and churches. In demonstrations and sit-ins, they suffered insults, beatings, and jailings.* A private institution, Tougaloo was not governed by racist state policies but did risk the revocation of its charter as it became Mississippi's safe haven for activists fighting for dignity, equality, and justice. (Emphasis added)

Indeed, almost all the markers we visited address violence in some form or another, with most framing it as individual acts of violence against particular civil rights activists and some focusing on the perennial threat of violence that terrorized African Americans in Mississippi. The "Amzie Moore" marker in Cleveland addresses both. Visitors learn that Moore "offered his home to visiting activists and for numerous civil rights efforts, despite continual threats of violence and economic pressures," and that the New Hope Baptist Church (located next to the Moore House and MFT marker), an important site for community organizing, "was burned to the ground after an NAACP meeting there." Similarly, the "William Chapel" marker in front of the William Chapel Missionary Baptist Church in Ruleville suggests that African American churches throughout the South were under the constant threat of attack when used as meeting places for civil rights activists; the William Chapel itself, which is still an active church today, "was in fact firebombed after a civil rights rally in June 1964." A quote on the rear panel recognizing Fannie Lou Hamer, one of the most prominent leaders to rally organizers at William Chapel, emphasizes the mortal danger that activists faced: "Sometimes it seem like to tell the truth today is to run the risk of being killed."

If any heritage tourists are inclined to read Hamer's words with skepticism, there are several markers along the trail that reveal the astonishing lengths to which some aggressors would go to maintain white power and privilege in the South. White opposition to the Mississippi Movement is identified as the police and the highway patrol, the Mississippi Army National Guard, prison guards, a "mob," as well as specific individuals. The "Jackson State Tragedy" MFT marker details how members of the Jackson police and the Mississippi Highway Patrol gunned down two Jackson State students and injured other students in 1970 as police attempted to suppress protest by firing into one of the university's dormitories and the nearby area.[26] Another marker, "Woolworth's Sit-In," describes how an "angry mob" attacked "nonviolent protesters" in 1963 who sat at a whites-only lunch counter, reproducing similar "sit-ins" dating back to 1960.

It is important to consider how agency is attributed in narratives of violence such as these, especially when the use of passive voice obscures or conceals the identity of those who use violence as a tool of oppression. Although the voice narrating these graphic depictions of violence often shifts between active and passive, it usually, but not always, identifies those responsible for inflicting violence on African Americans. For example, the marker dedicated to Fannie Lou Hamer in Ruleville briefly addresses the abuse she suffered after being arrested for violating Jim Crow laws, noting, "Police had two other black prisoners brutally beat Hamer in jail." As noted in chapter 2, Reverend George Lee, a co-founder of the local NAACP branch in Belzoni, is described as a "martyr" in his marker. "Lee was driving on a street in Belzoni," it reads, "when a car pulled up alongside his and assailants shot him in the face. He lost control of the car and crashed, and died on the way to the hospital." Additional text provides grim details of Lee's assassination, this time in passive voice: "An examination of Lee's body by two black physicians revealed that two to three rifle shots were fired—one at point-blank range into the cab—ripping off the lower left side of his face." While the killers are not identified by name, the marker does mention two men—Sheriff Ike Shelton and Mississippi governor Hugh White—who were complicit in the state's refusal to fully investigate the crime. In the case of the assassination of Medgar Evers addressed in the "Medgar Evers Home" marker, the same passive voice is used, obscuring—on the front panel—the name of Byron de la Beckwith, the Klansman and Citizens' Council member who murdered Evers. "Just after midnight, on June 12, 1963, he was assassinated in the driveway as he returned from a meeting." The rear side of the marker (left side, bottom) contains a single reference to Beckwith. These descriptions underscore just how much was at stake for civil rights leaders and activists in Mississippi at the time.

Even though violence is represented in MFT marker discourse, perhaps no marker foregrounds it as clearly as the "Bryant's Grocery" sign in Money. As noted in chapter 3, this marker narrates one of the most publicized (and horrific) moments in the early civil rights movement—the lynching of Emmett Till—in explicit detail:

> On August 28 at around 2:30 in the morning, store owner Roy Bryant, Carolyn's husband, and his half-brother, J. W. Milam, kidnapped Till from his great-uncle's home three miles east of Money. According to the FBI, they brought him back to this store before driving him to the Shurden Plantation in Sunflower County where he was beaten and shot with a .45 caliber pistol. His murderers secured a 75-pound gin fan to his neck with barbed wire and dropped his body into the Tallahatchie River. The next day, Milam and Bryant were arrested on charges of kidnapping. Three days after his abduction, Till's body was pulled from the Tallahatchie River.

Even when the marker shifts from active to passive voice to describe Till's murder—"where he was beaten and shot"—it leaves no question that Bryant and Milam were responsible for the heinous crime or that the trial that led to their acquittal was a gross miscarriage of justice. By contrast, the viciousness of the murder is somewhat de-emphasized by a reproduction of a page from an issue of *Jet* magazine that published the iconic photos of Till's mutilated body at his open-casket funeral in Chicago. The *Jet* photograph is much smaller than seven other images depicted on the marker and is also partially obscured by an image of the *Jet* cover; the photographs also appear on the rear of the marker where they are not visible to passing motorists. Ironically, the marker notes that *Jet*'s publication of these photographs in 1955 was "widely credited with rallying black support and white sympathy across the U.S." and was a catalyst for the modern civil rights movement. Their diminutive size creates tension with the verbal description's emphasis on the sheer brutality of the killing.

In light of the relative dearth of state historical markers that offer candid interpretations of the experiences of African Americans, the MFT begins to fill a noticeable gap in the state's memorial landscape by highlighting the violence that civil rights activists faced in their march towards justice—from well-publicized figures like Hamer and Evers to lesser-known leaders such as Reverend Lee. There is tragedy, anger, and sadness in the biographical stories of Emmett Till, Medgar Evers, Fannie Lou Hamer, Aaron Henry, C. C. Bryant, and Clyde Kennard. The markers also highlight activists' determination and resolve, courage and bravery, and a well-spring of optimism for a brighter, more racially inclusive and democratic Mississippi.

With the exception of repeated references to the police, the markers devote less (and in some cases, no) space to addressing the wider context of systemic racialized violence in Mississippi and the extent to which it was embedded in social and political institutions. For example, only two markers of the twenty-three we visited mention the Mississippi State Sovereignty Commission. Moreover, only two markers ("Bombings in Jewish Community" and "C. C. Bryant") explicitly mention the Ku Klux Klan,[27] and one marker ("University of Mississippi") identifies the state's ultrasegregationist governor, Ross Barnett.[28] Even more surprising, the words "lynch" or "lynching" do not appear on any of the markers we viewed. With few exceptions, they rarely appear on historical markers in Mississippi. In a recent development, the Equal Justice Initiative has commemorated several lynching sites, including installing four markers in Mississippi to date, two of which focus specifically on lynching: "Lynching in America" and "The Lynching of Elwood Higginbottom," both located in Oxford.

The "Tougaloo College" marker, with its reference to "racist state policies," perhaps comes the closest to redirecting blame from rouge individuals to state power. None of the markers comes close to depicting Mississippi, in the words of District of Columbia representative Eleanor Holmes Norton, as a "wide open terrorist country in the United States of America."[29] By limiting the scope of the violence discussed in the MFT to a particular individual or event that is the focus of each respective marker, these specific violent acts lack the metonymic power they might otherwise have if they were portrayed as representative of the state's willingness to use violence to perpetuate white power throughout Mississippi (something that the MCRM does much more effectively, as we will address in chapter 6). Moreover, the trail's exclusive focus on the past—as is common with historical markers across the state—further limits its ability to speak to racialized violence in the state today.

Agitating and Organizing

Given that the MFT's primary focus is on the state's civil rights history, it is no surprise that a central theme across the twenty-three markers is the role that African American Mississippians played in the movement. The emphasis on the collective work of local people at the grassroots is accomplished through solidification strategies—tactics that foster a sense of communal identification among movement members. This agitation strategy took many forms, from the "Fannie Lou Hamer" marker's description of Hamer singing "This Little Light of Mine" to dejected bus passengers when they were denied the right to register to vote in the summer of 1962, to the marker dedicated to T. R. M. Howard in Mound Bayou, which notes his efforts to create the RCNL in Cleveland, Mississippi.[30]

In *The Rhetoric of Agitation and Control*, John W. Bowers, Donovan J. Ochs, Richard J. Jensen, and David P. Schulz make a distinction between two primary strategies enacted by movements for social change. When they engage in vertical deviance, groups "accept the value system of the establishment but dispute the distribution of benefits or power within that value system." By contrast, lateral deviance is a more radical strategy comprised of movement efforts that "dispute the value system itself and seek to change it or replace it with a competing value system."[31] In public memory, the mainstream civil rights movement is framed predominantly as a nonviolent movement whose leaders—most notably, King—were committed to *vertical*, rather than lateral, deviance, and the MFT makes no effort to challenge that dominant narrative.[32] Even the "'Black Power' Speech" marker in Greenwood, which notes that Stokely Carmichael's speech "revealed a growing difference between the nationalist philosophy of SNCC and the more moderate stances of the NAACP and SCLC," downplays the Black Power movement's influence in the larger civil rights movement. The same can be said for the "Capitol Rally" marker in Jackson. Its front panel makes one reference to Black power toward the end of the brief twelve-line narrative; the rear panel also makes a single reference to Black power in the form of a rebuttal from SNCC activist Floyd McKissick, who claimed in a speech at the rally that "there's nothing wrong with black power. It's just an adjective inserted before a noun . . . you can call it orange power, green power, or whatever you want. But we want power." The McKissick quotation is an intriguing choice: he both deescalates the fear and misrepresentation of the phrase "Black power," while undercutting the need for African Americans to strive for power. In any case, neither MFT marker explains the radical philosophy of Black power or the subsequent Black Power movement that espoused the illegitimacy of the very system other (earlier) civil rights leaders accepted. And none of the markers we visited mentions Malcolm X or the Black Panther Party.

Although the "'Black Power' Speech" and "Capitol Rally" markers make passing references to the more radical, more militant philosophy, the two markers do highlight the "birth" of the "Black Power" slogan and the resulting new schism in the larger civil rights movement. As one observer noted, the ecstatic reception of Carmichael's calls for "Black Power" "captured the deep questioning among a growing number of blacks regarding the efficacy of nonviolence" and a turn toward "armed self-defense."[33] In turn, the emergence of the Black Power movement created a widening split in the civil rights movement with members from the NAACP and Urban League condemning the new movement as advocating violence and racial exclusivity, while CORE and SNCC embraced the new philosophy.[34] Yet, as the markers tell the story, Black power's presence in Mississippi is confined to the popularization of a new slogan. But this is, of course, a selective retelling of the past. For example, consider one manifestation of Black power, the armed self-defense group Deacons for Defense and Justice. Founded in Jonesboro, Louisiana, in 1964 under the name "Jonesboro Legal and Defense Association," the Deacons for Defense and Justice established several chapters in Mississippi, starting with one in Natchez in 1965.[35] Although civil rights groups from the NAACP to SNCC had long had "informal associations of armed blacks willing to provide self-defense," the Deacons for Defense and Justice were unique in the history of the Mississippi Movement: a self-styled paramilitary group comprised of ordinary citizens who "viewed themselves as filling the vacuum left in the African American community by federal, state, and local law enforcement personnel who were either sympathetic or neutral to white supremacist violence."[36] John Dittmer notes that some members of the Mississippi Movement found the abstruseness of the Black power slogan to be useful, "enlisting it in behalf of boycotts, voter registration drives, and economic self-help endeavors such as the cooperatives."[37] Moreover, a Black separatist movement, the Republic of New Afrika (RNA), opened up a headquarters near the Jackson State University campus in 1968. The group "hoped to establish a separate and self-sufficient nation for black people—and one safe from the violence routinely inflicted on them by whites, including police officers right here in Jackson."[38] In August 1971, a joint operation between the FBI and Jackson police involved breaching the heavily guarded RNA headquarters, resulting in numerous arrests and the death of one police officer.[39] One of the group's members, Chokwe Lumumba, later served as Jackson's mayor from 2013 until his death in 2014.[40]

Yet, at the same time, according to Dittmer, both SNCC and CORE had started to withdraw their presence from Mississippi by the latter part of 1966 for internal reasons, including conflicts over how to define Black power.[41] And the Black Power movement's antiwhite sentiment "did not attract a large following among local people."[42] Not surprisingly, none of the markers characterizes sympathetic whites in pejorative terms; white involvement in the movement is either absent or portrayed as a symbol of racial integration and social justice (e.g., see the "Greyhound Bus Station," "Bombings in Jewish Community," and "WLBT-TV" markers). In another example, the "COFO

Central Offices" marker is located near the front door of the COFO office in Jackson; on the front door is an image of a Black hand and white hand forming a handshake superimposed over the state of Mississippi. Despite the historical muddiness, it is clear some elements of the Black Power movement and its new radical philosophy existed in Mississippi after 1966.

In contrast to the Black Power movement's condemnation of the "system," MFT markers present Mississippi's civil rights pioneers almost exclusively as people who were passionately committed to the American Dream and the country's founding values and whose activism sought to make that dream universally accessible to Black Americans. This is accomplished in two primary ways: through references to local leaders' entrepreneurial spirit and success in business, and through their participation (or persistent attempts to participate) in politics, education, and other state institutions. For example, Reverend George Lee is described as a "successful entrepreneur" in his marker. Amzie Moore's marker similarly highlights his multiple business operations. In some cases, these endeavors also created spaces for community organizing. The marker for Aaron Henry notes that he operated a pharmacy in Clarksdale that "became a hub for political and civil rights planning for three decades." Photographs on the rear of the marker of his storefront and of Henry at work in the pharmacy reinforce his contributions to both the movement and the local economy in Clarksdale. This theme is most apparent in T. R. M. Howard's marker. Its front panel (the side most visible to motorists) describes him first as a "businessman and physician," while the rear panel further notes that he "promoted an agenda of black entrepreneurship, maintaining that political power required financial power." As "a physician, banker, insurer, and farmer, Howard launched several businesses in the Mississippi Delta of the 1940s and was chief surgeon at the Knights and Daughters of Tabor hospital in Mound Bayou before setting up his own clinic. He also built a small zoo and a park as well as the first swimming pool for blacks in Mississippi." The biography detailed in the marker for C. C. Bryant, who presided over the NAACP McComb chapter for more than three decades, suggests another type of entrepreneurial leader who operated in a liminal space apart from the mainstream white power structure. Bryant worked for the railroad and, thus, "was not dependent on local whites for his living, as many local blacks were." He also "operated a barber shop in his front yard, where he offered a library of African American newspapers, magazines, and broadsides to the community."

Although the authoritative voice narrating these brief anecdotes presents them as neutral biographical accounts, their rhetorical impact has deeper implications. Indeed, they are exemplars of the discursive genre known as tokenist biography, or what Dana L. Cloud defines as "biographical narratives that authorize a person from a marginalized or oppressed group to speak as a culture hero *on the condition* that the person's life story be framed in liberal-capitalist terms."[43] By establishing this connection between African Americans' active and successful participation in a capitalist economy and their effective advocacy for civil rights in Mississippi, MFT markers participate in a rhetoric of tokenism that reinforces that these economic systems were (and are) fundamentally devoid of harmful ideologies that support white hegemony. White power is located in bad actors who reside *outside* the system, not within it. In fact, as noted earlier, although agents of Mississippi's power structure (e.g., Governor Barnett, police) and its white domestic terrorist organizations (Ku Klux Klan) are occasionally named, the markers do not, as a whole, indict Mississippi as a terrorist state. Through this problematic ideological lens, civil rights are won largely through strategies of vertical agitation that facilitate African Americans' access to these systems. If Lee, Moore, Henry, and Howard can be successful—even when living under the threat of, or ultimately succumbing to, white violence—then the American Dream must be sound.

This rhetorical vision presented in the MFT markers finds additional support in the narratives describing Mississippi civil rights activists' engagement with politics and community organizing. At the national level, Hamer's efforts leading up to her testimony before the Credentials Committee at the 1964 Democratic National Convention are prominently featured in her marker. The narrative highlights her perseverance in the face of opposition from the party establishment when "In Freedom Summer 1964, civil rights activists challenged the all-white Mississippi delegation to the Democratic National Convention on the grounds that blacks had been systematically excluded from voting." Hamer's work did not end in 1964, as the marker makes clear. She would go on to serve as a delegate for the Democratic Party the following election cycle, establish a "Freedom Farm with a goal of providing food and some economic independence to local people," work in support of Head Start programs, and run for a State Senate seat in Mississippi in 1971.

While the MFT explores the work of Mississippians in the national movement for civil rights, its trail markers do challenge the "Great Man" version of history by devoting more space to addressing agitation and politics at the state and local level; however, it also reifies this ideological rendering of history by foregrounding the actions of men more so than women. For example, Aaron Henry's marker in Clarksdale chronicles his service as a long-running president of the NAACP's Mississippi branch, as a founding member of the Mississippi Freedom Democratic Party (where he worked closely with Hamer), and as an elected representative in the Mississippi House of Representatives. James Meredith's historic effort to gain admission to the University of Mississippi in 1962—which is the focus of the marker located on the university's campus—is another noteworthy example. In another, Amzie Moore's MFT marker documents his tireless efforts organizing voter registration drives in the state, founding a Head Start program in Cleveland, and coordinating with student recruits and SNCC on various civil rights projects. As noted in the previous chapter, while Myrlie Evers was a member of the Mississippi Movement and would later go on to chair the NAACP Board of Directors, the "Medgar Evers Home" marker does not include her name as part of the marker's title, and her positionality is one of domestic partner and mother. Alas, there are only two women featured in the entire marker series: Fannie Lou Hamer and Unita Blackwell.

The MFT's thoughtful counternarratives of Black Mississippians' achievements—both in business, in community organizing, and in gaining access to powerful institutions from politics to higher education—make important strides towards recognizing African American history in a public medium that has routinely silenced the voices of marginalized groups. The markers frame this history, however, in a way that subtly valorizes the very systems that oppressed African Americans. In this iteration of history, African Americans appear as if they are marching in nearly perfect unison and inevitably towards racial equality, a message that is reinforced not only by the marchers' silhouettes that appear at the top of every marker on the MFT, but by the form of the markers themselves. The absence of any careful critique of oppressive systems and their role in maintaining the hegemony of white power suggests that King's dream has been realized thanks to the incredible sacrifices made by the local heroes of the movement. While some aspects of this dream have been achieved, the premise of this book is that the fight for civil rights is obviously an ongoing struggle, not only in Mississippi, but throughout the nation. As we will show, by disconnecting the past and the present, the MFT mutes this continuing struggle for racial equality in the United States.

Time: The Past Is Not the Present

With one minor exception, MFT markers confine their narratives to the past. As noted earlier, markers that spotlight people typically include biographical information, including birthdate and date of death, profession, early involvement in the civil rights movement, membership and association with specific civil rights organizations, heroic examples of leadership, personal struggles, and victories. In most cases, mortality and death signal the end of the narratives, which range from Lee's assassination (1955) to Henry's death (1997). Not surprisingly, markers that highlight events, such as "'Black Power' Speech" (1966) and "Marks Mule Train and Poor People's Campaign" (1968) as well as places, such as "Bryant's Grocery" (1955), "University of Mississippi" (1962), "Capitol Rally" (1966), and "Jackson State Tragedy" (1970), have considerably condensed time frames. The "William Chapel" marker is the only one in our sample that references the present, and that single sentence is both fleeting and noncontroversial: "Today it [the church] stands as a symbol of the freedom struggles of the Mississippi Delta."

The "'Black Power' Speech" marker dramatically signifies the devastating consequences when the past is denied its relationship to the present. The marker is positioned prominently at one corner of Broad Street Historical Park in Greenwood, a town of approximately fifteen thousand and the seat of Leflore County. Dedicated in early 2013, it is the tenth MFT marker and commemorates Stokely Carmichael's famed 1966 speech that was delivered on the site where the marker is now located. Not to be confused with a similarly titled address that Carmichael gave a few months later at the University of California campus in Berkeley, it was this speech, as noted earlier, where the term "Black Power" was first popularized, and where Carmichael proclaimed, "We have got to get us some Black power." It was a pivotal moment. Describing the atmosphere surrounding Carmichael's rousing speech, historian Peniel E. Joseph notes, "As the crowd chanted 'Black Power' in unison, the rhythmic call and response between speaker and audience electrified some, frightened others, and marked a turning point for the African American freedom movement."[44]

While the placement of the Black Power marker is appropriate given the site of the 1966 protest, the marker's location also represents a cruel and unforgiving irony—the promise of Black power as an ideal unfulfilled. Broad Street Historical Park is located in a desperately impoverished African American neighborhood. Roofs sag on some of the houses lining the streets, and trash litters the grounds around the marker and in the park. What we found on our visit to Greenwood was not Black power, but clear evidence of white power. As we exited Greenwood to visit the "Bryant's Grocery" marker in neighboring Money, we drove down Grand Avenue and gaped at sprawling, opulent homes set off from the boulevard. Many of these enormous properties were flanked by rows of trees that created strategic barriers between the homes and one of the main boulevards through town. For even the most passive tourist, it is immediately clear that Greenwood remains divided by race and class, with devastating poverty in the Black community and material signs of prosperity in the white community. This juxtaposition of poverty and affluence is common throughout the Delta.

The critique we offer in this section begs an obvious counterresponse: the MFT is a *historical* marker series that should, by its very nature, focus exclusively on the past—history—and not be in the business of commenting on the present. On its face, this criticism makes sense. Rolando Herts, who leads the Delta Center and the MDNHA and has worked with the task force that developed the MFT, argues that this may be an inherent limitation of a historical marker sign's material form: "By its appearance and the way that it is set up, constructed like that, it speaks of something that's in the past," he told us. "It's not moving, it's not doing anything. It's just there. How does a person really engage appropriately with a marker beyond just reading it and taking pictures? It's just a limited mode of information or knowledge transfer."[45] Well aware of this limitation, the MDNHA has created programming that Herts describes as "experiential learning." "We have found that to be a more impactful, transformative educational tool," he observes. "It's just a question of what we choose to make the experiential learning about. And who we choose to have there sharing stories. That's where we get into issues of power and privilege and selective narrative, and controlling those narratives.... It's a very powerful tool. It's transformative for people who participate in it."[46]

Beyond a marker's form, however, one might consider the difference between discontinuity and continuity. For example, Pennsylvania state historical markers devoted to the Revolutionary War typically focus on a discrete event that occurred in the past and is confined to the past. However, a marker series devoted to remembering a movement for social change, such as the Mississippi Movement, *should* acknowledge that such strivings are predicated on the continual struggle and advancement for social justice. Seeking justice, inclusion, and equity *are never past*, to paraphrase Mississippi writer William Faulkner. Instead, for many visitors this category of marker likely embodies the very essence of public memory—the intellectual and emotional connection to the past and its relationship to the present. Beyond a tourist's own personal reflections on the imperfections of the present, the compelling evidence of present-day racial injustice—as reflected most prominently in the protests that engulfed the nation after police officer Derek Chauvin murdered George Floyd in 2020—makes it more difficult for observers to still believe the United States has reached a transcendent and mythical "postracial" utopia.

Yet, by avoiding the temporal relationship between the past and the present, the MFT unwittingly tells a privileged and comfortable story: Although the struggle was unquestionably violent, even in the face of impossible odds, the Mississippi Movement "won," and the struggle is over. This understanding of history delegitimizes contemporary civil rights efforts and reinforces larger promotional strategies that highlight how Mississippi is a unified state that has transcended its racist past. It helps the state achieve one of its goals with civil rights tourism, but at a cost. This disconnection between the past and present may also impact how Black communities (especially in locations where markers are placed) understand civil rights in Mississippi. For Mississippi's current generation, are these markers simply history lessons from a past era?

Black Places: Sacred and Secular Spaces

Most of the MFT markers are located in the Delta and Jackson. This is not surprising considering these areas were hotbeds of civil rights activism. The remaining markers are scattered throughout the state from southern Mississippi ("C. C. Bryant" in McComb; "Biloxi Beach Wade-In" in Biloxi) to the northeast ("Carpenters for Christmas" in Blue Mountain). Markers are located in neighborhoods and parks, in rural and urban downtown areas, in mixed residential and commercial spaces, on university campuses and church grounds, in a memorial garden, and at other locations.

While marker placement is certainly not restricted to one part of the state or a single geographic type (e.g., only in residential neighborhoods), a majority of markers selected for this study are located in either de-facto segregated and marginalized African American neighborhoods or on major thoroughfares in predominantly African American towns such as Mound Bayou and Marks. This pattern is consistent with the observations from Dwyer and others who noted that African American heritage landscapes are often confined to marginalized, poverty-stricken Black areas. The placement of the markers in these neighborhoods makes sense given where activists lived and where events transpired; however, these spatial dynamics concretize the same segregation patterns that the civil rights movement was supposed to eliminate, to say nothing of the hesitation or fear some white tourists may experience when traveling into predominately Black communities. Those fears at times emerge in visitor reviews posted online. For example, one visitor reviewing the Canton Freedom House noted that "the area is poor, but you will be safe."[47] It is worth noting that during our visits to each marker site, the authors were, with one exception, the only tourists there.

Within these Black places, the MFT markers—in both physical placement and in discursive form—embody a constellation of multiple overlapping places and spaces: sacred and secular, private and public. Civil rights activists required these places and spaces to create a rhetorical community, develop strategies to promote movement goals, and effectuate change on the streets and in the halls of justice. For example, within the relative safety of the church, African Americans could engage in dissent—heated discussions, planning sessions, speeches, sermons, and freedom songs. Located on the highway running through Marks, the "Marks Mule Train and Poor People's Campaign" marker describes a Mule Train "march" to call attention to poverty in the United States. Martin Luther King Jr. visited Marks in 1966 and, appalled by the obscene poverty and plight of the African American community there, returned to the Delta town in March 1968 with plans to seek support for a second Poor People's Campaign (the first one was staged in 1963). For this second campaign, King "decided to launch the campaign's march on Washington, DC, from Marks, using mule-drawn wagons to dramatize its theme." The following description from the marker demonstrates the important role the church played in providing a space for organized dissent:

> When Dr. King was assassinated in April 1968, his lieutenants decided to go on with his plan for the campaign. Ralph David Abernathy, Andrew Young, James Bevel, and Willie Bolden came to Marks and began to organize, meeting with community activists at the Eudora A.M.E. Zion church, and planning three rallies prior to the Mule Train march. Marchers began to converge on the town, staying with local families, in churches, and in tents.

In another example, the "William Chapel" marker is located on the grounds of the church in Ruleville. Because the marker is located in front of the church (several feet away from the street), visitors who desire to read the rear panel must leave the street and walk onto private property. Indeed, as we can testify, stepping on the green, well-manicured lawn to read the marker's rear panel felt like an act of invasion. The front panel of the marker emphasizes the relationship between the church and movement activities: when members of SNCC and SCLC visited Ruleville in 1962 to agitate for a voter registration drive, a "mass meeting" was held in the church where Fannie Lou Hamer became inspired to join SNCC. Under the direction of another civil rights hero, Reverend J. D. Story, the church scheduled mass meetings every Friday. Story's decision is keeping with the church's historical pattern of activism.

Visitors to this marker learn that the church, since its founding in 1922, had served as a "meeting place for civil rights activists before the organization of the modern civil rights movement." While Black churches served as a sanctuary for civil rights activism, angry whites made it a habit of burning and blowing them up in protest. Unfortunately, the William Chapel Church was no exception. It was firebombed in 1964 after a civil rights rally.

While the William Chapel Missionary Baptist Church is the only church—outside of the "Bombings in Jewish Community" marker located on the grounds of the Beth Israel Congregation synagogue in Jackson and the "Hopewell Missionary Baptist Church" marker in Itta Bena—to have received an MFT marker, other markers are located on church property or in close proximity to a church. For example, the marker for Reverend George Lee is located on the grounds of the Green Grove Baptist Church in Belzoni. In Clarksdale, the "Aaron Henry" marker is located near several churches within a two-block radius, and in Cleveland, the Amzie Moore House (and his two historical markers) are positioned in close proximity to two churches, including the one Moore attended, St. Peter's Rock Missionary Baptist Church. The church-movement relationship should not be surprising given the fact that many members of the movement were deeply religious, and some in the leadership (e.g., Martin Luther King Jr.) were ministers themselves.

While churches served as sanctuaries for the movement, private residences served as safe houses for activists. As noted in the previous chapter, the Amzie Moore House Museum and Interpretive Center in Cleveland illuminates the role of secular space in organizing dissent. While the Moore house exemplifies the important role of private/secular space, in the eyes of some activists the secular-sacred dialectic might not be a dialectic at all. It could be argued activists perceived the church and private residence as part of a larger indivisible whole.

Although it is true that many of the markers inhabit Black segregated spaces, it is also the case that some markers—particularly in downtown Jackson—are placed near historical and present-day centers of (white) political power. Located near the state Capitol, the "Capitol Rally" marker exemplifies this break with normative past memory practices. As one of only two markers to give voice to the Black Power movement, the "Capitol Rally" marker remembers the "largest civil rights demonstration in Mississippi history," as the crowd swelled to fifteen thousand to mark the conclusion of the three-week march precipitated by James Meredith's "March Against Fear" campaign.[48] Jackson's downtown also features other MFT markers that remember pivotal events, including the "Greyhound Bus Station" (the arrival of Freedom Riders to Jackson in 1961) and the "Jackson Municipal Library Sit-In." In all three cases, these markers showcase Black bodies challenging and breaching white power and exclusion. In the case of the "Greyhound Bus Station" marker, the group of African American and white Freedom Riders from the north used their physical presence to challenge Jim Crow laws on multiple occasions prior to arriving in Jackson.

As one of many cultural trails in Mississippi, the MFT narrates the people, places, and events that comprise the Mississippi Movement of the 1950s and 1960s. To be sure, the MFT and the growing civil rights tourism industry in Mississippi are long-awaited correctives to official historical and touristic accounts that minimize or outright deny Mississippi's long and tragic record of racial oppression. Indeed, MFT markers chronicle assassinations, beatings and sexual assault, church burnings, and lynchings (although, as noted earlier, this word never appears in the narratives but does appear as part of the Equal Justice Initiative's marker project). Exposing historical truths in a stable public setting is a crucial first step in any reconciliation effort.

Moreover, the MFT documents the lives of local activists in Mississippi who too often have been neglected in the rush to narrate the civil rights movement through the lens of its national leaders. Through their descriptions of collective organizing and the development of networks, MFT markers make it clear that the movement's success in challenging white supremacy was achieved through a constellation of individuals working within a larger rhetorical collective. In addition, unlike museums, which often require an admission fee, historical markers are relatively permanent repositories of memory that are free to the public and always "open." They serve as opportunities for identity construction and community building. As part of the public sphere, no one is denied access to historical markers. Yet, for all of its rhetorical import, our critique aligns with similar concerns directed at civil rights tourism in general—male privilege, a focus on the "safe" past, and the placement of a majority of markers in historically segregated African American spaces. In the next chapter, we explore the state's most significant and, arguably, its most successful effort to remember the Mississippi Movement—the MCRM.

CHAPTER SIX

"THIS LITTLE LIGHT OF MINE"

Truth Telling at the Mississippi Civil Rights Museum

> There's no healing if we lie.
> —PAMELA JUNIOR, director of the MMH-MCRM

On December 9, 2017, the MCRM first opened its doors in a ceremony that was decades in the making. For a museum that had been in development since at least the 1980s, what should have been a watershed moment organized to coincide with the state's bicentennial celebration instead became a day roiled in controversy when then-president Donald J. Trump attended the opening day ceremonies. Despite the optimism expressed by MCRM Foundation chairperson and former Mississippi Supreme Court Justice Reuben Anderson, who said of the opening ceremonies, "It's going to be just a magnificent event, and I don't think anything can dampen it," Trump's decision to tour the museum and speak there afterwards seemed to do just that.[1] Several prominent figures boycotted the event, including congressional representatives John Lewis and Bennie Thompson, former Mississippi governor Ray Maybus, Mississippi State Senator Sollie Norwood, and Jackson mayor Chokwe Antar Lumumba, while a group of approximately two hundred others staged a protest near the museum.[2] Pamela Junior, the museum's director, also elected not to escort Trump through the exhibit.[3] Press coverage focused as much on the reactions to Trump's presence as it did the museum exhibit; "a slap in the face," as one resident described it.[4]

The critique of Trump's visit on opening day points to the MCRM's significance not only as a repository for artifacts and historical information about the Mississippi Movement, but also as a public memory site that marshals immense rhetorical power. As the first state-funded museum in the country dedicated solely to civil rights, the MCRM has quickly become the keystone of Mississippi's civil rights tourism industry and the state's second

Museum of Mississippi History (left) and Mississippi Civil Rights Museum (right). Photo by Roger Davis Gatchet.

major initiative after inaugurating the MFT in 2011. The MCRM's accessible downtown location in the capital city of Jackson as part of a two-hundred-thousand-square-foot dual-museum complex shared with the MMH has contributed to its early success.[5] Unlike vernacular museums which might only draw a few hundred visitors a year, official museums like the MMH-MCRM attract tens of thousands. Together, both museums drew over 350,000 visitors in the first two years after opening,[6] and the MCRM saw nearly 3,000 visitors on Dr. Martin Luther King Jr. Day in 2020.[7] Moreover, it has been the subject of glowing reviews from journalists and academics alike. One journalist praised it for its lack of "closure" and refusal to "sugarcoat history," noting that the museum is successful because it "leaves us upset, its story unresolved."[8] Jackson's own *Clarion-Ledger*, a newspaper that once condoned lynching and promoted segregation, called it "poignant and moving."[9] And Mississippi Movement historian John Dittmer even described it as "the most impressive" civil rights museum in the entire South.[10] "It just does everything," he said, noting in particular its representation of women central to the movement.[11]

In many ways, as we will see, the MCRM serves to expand, illuminate, and emotionally magnify many of the themes inscribed in the MFT, particularly the Black resistance–white violence dialectic as well as the emphasis on vertical rather than lateral deviance. Although the MFT markers, by their very design, represent an unchanging and static discursive and pictorial narrative, the MCRM accentuates these themes in vivid fashion through audio and video clips, interactive displays, and other technological advances in museology, elements that visitors increasingly expect from museums. On the other hand, the MCRM effectively connects the past to the present and future, a temporal dynamic not found in the MFT, whose rendering of history (and memory) is confined to the "safe" past. In addition, while many MFT markers can be found in Black de-facto segregated neighborhoods, the MCRM's downtown location is in close proximity to the Capitol building near the center of white political power in Jackson. Despite these differences, the MCRM serves as an effective extension of the memory-building practices of the MFT. In many ways, the MFT is the précis to the story of the Mississippi Movement. The MCRM is the book.

This chapter offers the first comprehensive rhetorical assessment of the MCRM, and it is based on extensive field work we conducted there in 2019.[12] Through a historical account of its genesis and a thematic analysis of its exhibit, we interrogate the museum's role in Mississippi's efforts to pursue larger economic and ideological goals through tourism. More specifically, we argue that although the MCRM is the state's most aggressive example of the truth telling and antiracist functions associated with civil rights tourism, it does so by privileging a more narrow narrative of social movement tactics that deemphasizes the influence of the Black Power movement in the state. By subtly minimizing the more revolutionary and radical elements of the Mississippi Movement, the MCRM minimizes the possibility of alienating some (white) visitors, a rhetorical strategy that facilitates the state's goals of economic development, image management, and social justice through civil rights tourism.

Rhetoric, Museums, and Public Memory

As museums grow more complex and technologically sophisticated, they have developed into one of the most powerful places of memory building on the memorial landscape. Likewise, museums have been an especially popular object of criticism in the communication discipline, as evidenced by the numerous essays that have examined this common public memory site from a rhetorical perspective.[13] Once viewed as unquestioned repositories of "truth," museums are now understood as rhetorical sites where the past is selectively re-presented to audiences.[14] Rhetorical scholars have studied museums and identity, authenticity, transcendence, vernacular communities, and audiences, among other areas of interest.[15] Collectively, a recurring thread running through this work is their focus on how museums reinforce or challenge hegemonic norms and values through artifacts, narratives, and, in some cases, physical space itself. For example, Nicholas S. Paliewicz argues that the National September 11 Memorial Museum "affirms the legitimacy of the museum as an institution capable of organizing disparate remembrances to facilitate public memory, but it also risks appropriating subjective grievances for political purposes."[16]

Understanding museums as rich and complex rhetorical representations of the past reflects what rhetorical scholar M. Elizabeth Weiser calls the "narrative turn" in museum exhibits noted by a shift from "object analysis to human relations."[17] As Weiser elaborates, curatorial and administrative power guide the use of "storytelling and other interactive enterprises" that "have become such major components of museums—with large panels, touchscreens, films, audio guides, docents, and performers competing for the audience's attention."[18] Museums do not simply replay the past; they tell stories. And the stories they tell are not just about the past. It is no coincidence, then, that the title of the 2017 book that accompanied the opening of the MMH-MCRM is *Telling Our Stories*.[19]

Museums are more public memory than past history. In her review of museum scholarship, public memory, and rhetoric, Susan Mancio argues that "museums attribute meaning to the past by presenting memory accounts imbued with contemporary concerns."[20] She also notes that "museum rhetoric remains a powerful source in shaping public memory, constructing cultural authority, and enabling public forgetting."[21] In his "rhetorical pilgrimage" of the US Holocaust Memorial Museum (USHMM), Marouf Hasian Jr. explores how the museum's memory architects craft and reinterpret memories of the Holocaust through the lens of American intervention. "Given the magnitude of the Holocaust and the multi-vocal nature of all evocative artifacts," Hasian writes, "it should come as no surprise that the USHMM has become a contested site of memory."[22] In particular, the USHMM has served as a flashpoint for debates on "some past and present failures of American foreign policy initiatives."[23]

Rhetorical scholarship on civil rights museums has received limited attention. Bernard J. Armada's analysis of the NCRM in Memphis, Tennessee; Deborah F. Atwater and Sandra L. Herndon's cross-comparison analysis of the National Civil Rights Museum and MuseuMAfricA in Johannesburg, South Africa; and Marouf Hasian Jr. and Nicholas S. Paliewicz's exploration of the National Memorial for Peace and Justice (often referred to as the "Lynching Memorial") in Alabama are exemplars of what could be a fruitful area of museum scholarship.[24] Indeed, the addition of several high-profile museums and memorials dedicated to civil rights around the country in recent years, including the National Museum of African American History and Culture in Washington, DC, in 2016 and the MMH-MCRM a year later, may portend an increased interest among rhetorical scholars to understand how museums remember the civil rights movement. In the next section we recount the events leading to the opening of the MCRM, which now stands as the focal point of Mississippi's civil rights tourism industry. As we will see, the museum's decades-long gestation period was fraught with conflict and uncertainty and serves as a metaphor for the gradual emergence of civil rights tourism in Mississippi.

A History of the Mississippi Civil Rights Museum, 1985–2017

The genesis of the MCRM can be traced back to early efforts in the 1980s to commemorate the state's civil rights movement. As noted in chapter 1, in 1985, the MDAH sponsored the first permanent civil rights exhibit in the United States, "The Struggle for Equal Rights," featuring burned wooden crosses and other period artifacts.[25] During the rest of the decade, the MDAH played a key role in serving as one of the only official spaces in Mississippi where the history of the movement was retold.

In the early 1990s, the MDAH proposed replacing the exhibit with a new museum; however, nearly a decade passed before state politicians initiated political action to transform the idea of a civil rights museum into material reality. Between 2000 and 2006, a number of bills were introduced in the Mississippi legislature to establish and fund it. All failed. As Glenn Eskew notes, "Controversy swirled around the proposals, as conservative white politicians resisted a museum to the black freedom struggle, while African Americans feared the state's telling would temper the truth."[26] In 2006, then-Mississippi governor Hailey Barbour created the Commission to Establish a National Civil Rights Museum in Mississippi to push the project forward. Barbour's role in the creation of the MCRM is fraught with irony, as his memories and views on race have been criticized, particularly after he publicly downplayed Yazoo City's (Barbour's hometown) Citizens' Council chapter and its role in sparking fear and violence in Mississippi during the 1950s and 1960s.[27]

In contrast to the MCRM's focus on Mississippi, Barbour initially believed the state should be the location of a new *national* civil rights museum.[28] Led by cochairs and former judges Reuben Anderson and Charles Pickering, the commission recommended funding the museum through a $50 million bond and private funds.[29] The commission also believed that the campus of Tougaloo College, the historic African American college that served as an important site for dissent and protest in the Mississippi Movement, would be an appropriate location to build the new museum.[30] The Jackson chapter of the Veterans of the Mississippi Civil Rights Movement agreed with the commission's recommendation.[31] Some, including state senator David Jordan, argued that the new museum should be built in the Delta city of Greenwood. Alluding to the movement birthplace myth, he claimed the city was the first location where police dogs were used to disrupt voter registration efforts: "Why shouldn't the museum be put there?" he said. "This is where the movement actually took off, had its origin."[32] Other Mississippi communities, including Hattiesburg and the Delta region, were also proposed as potential sites.[33]

Meanwhile, a concerted effort was underway, led by Barbour, to build the museum in downtown Jackson, the largest population center in the state. Debates about the museum's location raged on for years. Claiming that Jackson had the "infrastructure to support the economics of operating a state museum that seeks national stature," a *Clarion-Ledger* editorial argued that Jackson State University, another site of civil rights unrest and the location where two students were killed in 1970 in clashes with police, "would merit at least as much consideration as Tougaloo."[34] In the same year, a *Clarion-Ledger* staff writer, Ronnie Agnew, acknowledged that while Tougaloo College certainly has credibility as a civil rights site, the "quaint campus is not in a location that will drive museum traffic." Instead, he argued that Jackson was the logical choice: "No other population centers exist in Mississippi with enough critical mass to make this a success. The rancor over where this museum should go should end now. Its home should be Jackson.... Prudent thinking should prevail here and not territorialism."[35]

As part of his 2007 budget, Barbour proposed a half million dollars for the MDAH to plan the museum and advocated the need for private capital to help fund it.[36] In his 2006 address to the commission, he argued, "if we just let the state government pay for this, it will be much less successful than if the private sector, foundations and individuals are participating. I really do think it will have more success if it is participatory."[37] Although Barbour believed in pursuing a public-private funding strategy, he also asserted in his 2007 State of the State Address that "we stand ready to do what it takes to make sure the National Civil Rights Museum in Mississippi . . . does justice to this subject."[38] Fundraising efforts eventually netted $470,000 dollars but were eaten up by consulting fees, leaving only $108,000.[39] The collapse of global financial markets the following year and the subsequent recession effectively ended efforts to raise funds for the proposed museum.[40]

By 2010, some were questioning whether state leaders were still genuinely interested in opening a civil rights museum, including State Senator Jordan, who remarked, "It comes to a point that I don't think Mississippi wants her history clearly told."[41] After several years of inactivity, that changed when the Mississippi legislature approved $20 million in bond funding in 2011.[42] From 2011 to 2016, the legislature increased that total to $90 million.[43] It was decided that the new museum would be connected to an already proposed state history museum, and the two museums finally broke ground in downtown Jackson on October 24, 2013.[44] At this point, however, the museums were not fully funded and still lacked an estimated $30 million to complete.[45] By this time, the Mississippi legislature had passed a law that required a shared responsibility between the state and private funding to complete the exhibits.[46] Three years later, the Mississippi legislature passed a bill that included an additional $16.6 million for their completion, and the MMH-MCRM finally opened to the public in December 2017.[47] The MMH-MCRM, along with the MFT, serve as key symbols of how—like the state's blues tourism industry—prior grassroots efforts are being replaced by a more top-down, state-run approach to remembering the Mississippi Movement.

Because of his role in the creation of the museum, it is not surprising that Barbour cowrote the forward to the 2017 book, *Telling Our Stories: Museum of Mississippi History and Mississippi Civil Rights Museum*, published to coincide with the opening of the museums. Viewing the twin museums as a "tourism portal," Barbour and Anderson believed the museums would be successful in "drawing visitors into Mississippi and then sending them out across the state to the places where history happened."[48] Indeed, the MCRM's exhibit seems designed with this goal in mind; approximately twenty "Explore Mississippi" displays highlight local (and primarily vernacular) memory sites—museums, parks, memorials, and the like—throughout the state, encouraging the hub and spoke-style tourism that Visit Jackson CEO and President Rickey Thigpen associates with the state capital. Politicians and pundits alike predicted the MMH-MCRM would serve as an economic boon for the state as well as an opportunity to repair its negative public image. Four years before the museums opened, the Mississippi Development Authority and the MDAH anticipated that the construction of the museums alone would create a total of 775 direct and indirect jobs and another 320 jobs after their doors opened.[49] It was also predicted the museums would generate over $17 million in tourism.[50] These predictions, on balance, would prove to be accurate.

Curating the Freedom Struggle: The Mississippi Civil Rights Museum Exhibit

Overview of the Museum and Exhibit

Situated in downtown Jackson, the MMH-MCRM are located next to the MDAH building and in close proximity to a constellation of civil rights sites. Visitors pass through an electronic surveillance system before entering the main lobby that connects both museums and includes a gift shop and small café. Administrative offices and a temporary special exhibit space are located upstairs on the second floor. Although the scope of the MMH is significantly larger, and its layout and design are markedly different than its sister museum, portions of its exhibit are relevant to the Mississippi Movement, including galleries focusing on slavery and the Civil War, Reconstruction, and the civil rights movement. In this way the MCRM is not othered or isolated from Mississippi's larger historical context, but rather integrated into this official historical narrative.

Despite Barbour's desire for a museum whose focus would be national in scope, the exhibit concentrates primarily on the Mississippi Movement. Director Junior notes that

> the first thing they're [visitors are] looking for . . . is where is Martin Luther King? Where is Rosa Parks? And then they get in here and they understand that the movement was so much larger than those people. And once they realize that we hone in on Mississippi heroes and she-roes, then the perspective changes. They're like, "Wow! I had no idea that the movement was this large." It wasn't like Martin was coming into these cities and saving folks. Folks was already doing the work.[51]

This Mississippi story—a story about *local* people—is told through the MCRM's eight themed galleries, arranged chronologically (and with a primary focus on the years 1945–1976) in a floor plan that encourages visitors to move through them more or less sequentially. Gallery 1, "Mississippi Freedom Struggle," traces the struggle for civil and human rights from the introduction of slavery in 1619 to the American Civil War. Gallery 2, "Mississippi in Black and White," features a post–Civil War narrative that spans 1865 to 1941 and includes information about Reconstruction and its collapse, Jim Crow, lynching, and other acts of white violence, as well as African American leaders. Gallery 3, "This Little Light of Mine," is the symbolic heart of the museum. Located at the center of the exhibit, this circular room allows visitors access to all the other galleries except the first and last. Continuing the exhibit's linear timeline, gallery 4, "A Closed Society," focuses on civil rights activities from 1941 to 1960, as well as the lynching of Emmett Till in August 1955. In gallery 5, "A Tremor in the Iceberg," visitors encounter an early-1960s narrative highlighting the rise of the SNCC as well as the 1963 assassination of Medgar Evers. There they have the chance to speak with Freedom Rider Hezekiah Watkins, a veteran activist and museum staff member who is often found in this room. Moving into the final galleries of the museum, gallery 6, "I Question America," focuses almost exclusively on 1964's Freedom Summer and the murder of three civil rights activists (James Chaney, Andrew Goodman, and Michael Schwerner) near Philadelphia, Mississippi. Gallery 7, "Black Empowerment," showcases legislative victories, including the 1965 Voting Rights Act and to a lesser extent the rise of the Black Power movement and more aggressive forms of agitation. The exhibit concludes with gallery 8, "Where Do We Go from Here?" Devoid of a historical timeline, this final room provides opportunities for personal reflection and engagement through social activism, as the concluding chapter will discuss in more detail. There, visitors are encouraged to "read the words of Mississippians from all walks of life as they discuss the progress our state has made since the Civil Rights era and the challenges that remain."[52]

Uncovering the (Violent) Truth of the Freedom Struggle in Mississippi

As we discussed in chapter 5, violence—and especially violent acts born out of racism and perpetrated by whites against Black bodies—is a primary theme connecting the disparate historical markers on the MFT. A similar theme dominates most of the galleries in the MCRM, amplifying the overarching truth-telling function of the museum. Thigpen remarked, "as a tourism guy I'm immensely proud, not just that we have the museum, but it's done in a way that is truthful.... I was afraid that it was going to be a little watered down, so it would be a nice museum. And it's an *excellent* museum, because it tells truth."[53] Dittmer, who served on a committee of scholars who consulted on the museum's exhibit, agrees. "A number of critics felt, including movement people, that in the end the state is going to step in and say, 'You can't do this,' he told us. "And this is important: Not once did anybody from the state come in and say, 'You cannot do this.'"[54] To Thigpen and Dittmer's point, even passive visitors who exert minimal effort engaging the museum's numerous displays will find it impossible to avoid narratives uncovering the appalling history of white violence in Mississippi. Indeed, the opening display in the first gallery frames the main exhibit in terms of a freedom struggle. A quote from former Mississippi state representative and activist Aaron Henry superimposed over a massive image of African Americans demonstrating on the street defines this struggle in unmistakably violent terms: "There is no panacea to the end of freedom road.... You have to be prepared to take the chances and prepared to take the punishment." Displays throughout gallery 1 describe what this punishment entailed in the early years of the freedom struggle leading up to the American Civil War. Activists (including children) "risked their lives," according to one display. Other displays employ chronological timelines, physical artifacts, and first-hand testimonials to document the summary execution of enslaved Africans who organized rebellions, corporal punishment inflicted on runaway slaves ("lashes on the bare back, burned hands, maiming, and death"), and the horrors of defining humans as chattel.

As visitors progress through the remaining galleries, these narratives broaden in scope and intensify in tone. In a recurring display that appears in nearly twenty locations throughout the museum, a rough parallelogram elevated several feet from the museum floor simulates a broken window with yellow, orange, and red shards of plexiglass splintering from a bullet hole. Each one spotlights a violent episode, from Willie McGee's execution in 1951 after an all-white jury found him guilty of raping a white woman to the murder of NAACP member Herbert Lee, who was shot by E. H. Hurst (a white man serving in the Mississippi state legislature) in 1961. They chronicle a litany of firebombings, beatings, assassinations, and mob violence perpetrated by racist whites on Black activists, citizens, even children. Moreover, the displays are specific when describing the agents of this violence. In one display in gallery 2 focused on convict labor, "white legislators passed laws meant to secure white supremacy"; another, "Riot at Clinton," describes how "whites organized a special train to Clinton with armed white men" to intimidate and murder Blacks at a political rally there. In gallery 5, a similar display describes "hordes of snarling white folks . . . with bricks, baseball bats, pipes, sticks, and chains" who sought a violent end to local efforts to desegregate the beaches in Biloxi, Mississippi. The accumulation of these true and horrific stories in nearly every gallery of the museum reinforces a stark admission from SNCC activist Chuck McDew that appears in a display in gallery 5: "Nothing would happen in Mississippi, and in the South, unless somebody was willing to die." These displays are not the only avenue for truth telling, however. The exhibit also elicits narratives from visitors who spontaneously interact with fellow strangers. During one visit an African

American woman struck up a conversation with one of us. As we gazed at the same display, she recounted her own memories living in Jim Crow Mississippi and the dehumanizing experiences she endured as a child who was subjected to racism and hatred.

While these displays and experiences are a constant reminder that civil rights movement successes were tempered by systemic barriers to equality, assassinations, and white supremacy, few aspects of the MCRM can compare to the poignancy of gallery 2, "Mississippi in Black and White," which offers an unflinching narrative of lynching in Mississippi that chronicles decades of extrajudicial terror. Lynching, a term that is rarely evoked in official civil rights tourism discourses sponsored by the state, nonetheless dominates gallery 2. Suspended from the branches of a tree-like sculpture that extends throughout the dark, cramped gallery are five tall, black monoliths that list the names, race, and occupation of every documented lynching victim in the state from 1882 to 1949. The monoliths are a striking visual metaphor symbolizing five hanging Black bodies that metonymize the hundreds more who suffered these extrajudicial executions. Each victim's purported crimes—"writing insulting note" in one case, "annoying [a] white woman" in another—are meticulously cataloged in each display. Jim Crow–era product advertisements revealing a litany of offensive stereotypes form the "leaves" of each branch, making the tree a powerful symbol representing a wide range of human rights abuses in the state and beyond.

In a conversation with us on the exhibit floor, Junior described this gallery as the museum's "darkest tunnel," an assessment that is further emphasized by artifacts flanking the monoliths (including a full-size KKK robe and hood) and audio recordings of southern whites issuing verbal threats that are easily heard by visitors as they move through the space. "Hey, you best watch where you're going, now!" one man says, a dog growling menacingly in the background; "Y'all looking for trouble?" warns another, audibly pumping a shotgun. The gallery is deeply affecting; visitors (including us) wept at times. The displays provide further information and historical context, noting that "lynchings were committed openly" ("Abandoned by the Law") and quoting former Mississippi governor James K. Vardaman (1904–1908), who said in no uncertain terms, "If it is necessary, every Negro in the state will be lynched; it will be done to maintain white supremacy." In the truth-telling rhetoric of the MCRM, violence is the barrier to progress that simultaneously motivates the movement, pushing it ever forward in the museum's broader narrative—a dichotomy we discuss more fully in the next section.

Resisting White Supremacy

The MCRM's linear timeline across all eight galleries presents a rhetoric of African Americans' resistance to the abject cruelties of slavery leading up to the emerging movement of Black political power in Mississippi during the late 1970s and early 1980s. At the same time, resistance and progress toward freedom, equality, and justice are met, at seemingly every turn, with white retaliation both legal and extralegal, as well as ideological and physical violence. Although the MCRM devotes the most attention to the Mississippi Movement of the 1950s and 1960s, the museum situates its intimate portrayal of people, places, and events within a broader historical context. In gallery 1, this context begins in 1619 in Jamestown, Virginia, and the first arrival of slave ships from West Africa. Using drawings and captioned photos, the first panel documents the brutality of the transatlantic slave trade and parallel acts of resistance, from the 1739 Stono River Rebellion in South Carolina to Harriet Tubman's involvement in the Underground Railroad a century later. Gallery 1 establishes this theme of dialectical struggle common to nearly all the galleries except 3 and 8, where white oppression is met with Black (African) resistance, and Black progress is thwarted by white supremacy. In the long four-hundred-year arc of history, however, these forces are not perfectly balanced, as this progress towards freedom gradually overtakes white intransigence, and, as galleries 7 and 8 suggest, Black social and political progress is neither permanent nor ensured. While Mississippi can rightfully claim it has the highest number of Black elected officials in the nation, the open-ended aesthetic of the museum's final gallery obliquely suggests that the struggle continues.

As gallery 1 concludes with the Civil War, the defeat of the Confederacy, and the abolishment of slavery, gallery 2, "Mississippi in Black and White," documents a postwar America in turbulent transition between 1865 and 1941. The first section of gallery 2 radiates with the optimism of Black liberation (Freedmen's Bureau, Reconstruction, the rise of early Black political power) and the seething of southern white rage and resentment. As noted earlier, gallery 2's documentation of the wide range of draconian efforts to return the region to a quasifeudal slave state is perhaps the most affect-saturated space in the museum. And while gallery 2 charts Black progress in the areas of education and politics, white efforts are best summarized in a display showcasing an 1889 newspaper article that read, "Don't monkey with white supremacy; it is loaded with determinism, gun-powder, and dynamite."

Before entering gallery 2 a sign warns visitors of what is to come: "To present a true and accurate story, the stories told here include acts of violence, oppression, and injustice. Quotations and documents are presented in their original context, and some include offensive images and language." Similar to gallery 1, gallery 2 provides a "National Timeline" display chronicling the progress-resistance dialectic with the passage of the Thirteenth, Fourteenth, and Fifteenth Amendments alongside the passage of Black Codes, the rise of the first wave of the Ku Klux Klan (1865), and race riots in several southern cities. As visitors reach the end of the Reconstruction era and the subsequent passage of Jim Crow laws, the gallery displays become increasingly sinister. The advent of the convict leasing system in 1866, the construction of Parchman Penitentiary, lynching displays, KKK robes, burned crosses, "No Colored" signs, racist advertisements, and a display about the 1915 film *The Birth of a Nation* are just a handful of examples of white extremism on full display.

Yet, Black resistance confronts white hatred in the gallery's claustrophobic space. For example, visitors standing in front of two displays of Klan robes will also see a panel dedicated to Ida B. Wells, the pioneering journalist and antilynching crusader. Multiple displays documenting Mississippi's infamous reputation as the lynching capital of the nation are juxtaposed with an antilynching campaign display; signs of racist social etiquette ("Black men must lower their eyes in the presence of white women") are situated in close proximity to a panel featuring six prominent African American civil rights leaders; the story of Richard Wright and his influential novel, *Black Boy*, is positioned next to the display "Riot at Clinton," where twenty to thirty African Americans were killed in 1875. One visitor describing their experience in gallery 2 emphasized the room's gravitas, noting that "the sheer number of lynchings in Mississippi was devastating to learn about."[55] Emotionally exhausted from the gruesome revelations of state-sanctioned violence against its Black population, visitors have no choice but to enter gallery 3, "Little Light of Mine." In this march toward progress against white supremacy, here visitors find a much-needed respite from the intense exhibit.

Emerging from the darkness—both literally and metaphorically, as the low lighting of gallery 2 gives way to the much brighter gallery 3—visitors enter a space that functions symbolically as a "safe house." As noted in earlier chapters, during the 1950s and 1960s, churches, private residences, and commercial businesses became safe spaces where civil rights activists could seek solace from the lethal external environment and organize future rallies, marches, and other forms of agitation. In gallery 3, visitors may sit on cushioned seats to rest, listen to freedom songs such as "We Shall Overcome," and gaze upon the names and faces of civil rights leaders. During our multiple visits to the MCRM, we found visitors resting, conversing, sitting silently in deep reflection, singing, and even crying in this gallery. The museum's powerful effect on visitors is not hyperbole. By the time visitors reach gallery 3, they are psychologically exhausted. We found ourselves emotionally distressed at times, particularly when standing in front of displays of Ku Klux Klan robes in gallery 2. The exhibit is "very detailed and intense," noted an online review from 2020; "you got to be prepared to feel various emotions and come out like really needing to get yourself together."[56] The MCRM is certainly aware of the exhibit's affect, as emotions are part of the museum's promotional rhetoric. One advertisement featuring Fannie Lou Hamer, which appears in the 2022 *Mississippi Official Tour Guide*, encourages museum visitors not to "learn history," but to "feel it."[57] Thankfully, gallery 3 provides a temporary break from the unrelenting violence and death. Resting from their experience, visitors will see a twisting, glowing light sculpture that rises from the middle of the room to the ceiling, suggesting upward ascension from our earthly bonds to a transcendent heavenly realm. The MRCM's website implies how the living and the dead are united in purpose in this space: "As more visitors gather and interact with the sculpture—adding their own 'light'—it shines brighter and the music grows stronger."[58] Yet, like movement activists, visitors who experience release and, perhaps, physical and spiritual rejuvenation know that these experiences are fleeting, as sounds of violence from the surrounding galleries occasionally invade the room's peaceful atmosphere. At some point visitors must leave this safe haven and reengage with a world of uncertainty, violence, and death. For both the MCRM visitor and the civil rights activist, there is no easy escape.

The narrative of resistance continues after gallery 3, where visitors can select which historical epoch to explore by entering galleries 4, 5, 6, or 7. Paralleling their experience in gallery 2, those who wander through these later galleries must return to the center gallery 3 before moving into the next phase of the exhibit. Gallery 7 provides the only passage to the final room, where visitors are greeted with inspirational quotations and photo displays and are prompted to respond to questions such as, "What would you take a stand for?" and "How can we improve our relationships with others?" In direct contrast to the more limited narratives of the MFT markers, gallery 8 makes it clear that progress toward racial equality and empowerment is real, but white resistance is also very much a part of present-day Mississippi. In the next section, we analyze the museum's presentation of *how* civil rights activists engaged in dissent.

Reframing the Struggle

The story at the heart of the MCRM's exhibit is one of movement and agitation, of activism and the impact the Mississippi Movement had on changing the state and nation. Not all forms of activism are privileged equally in the exhibit, however. As we touched on in chapter 5, scholars make a distinction between two primary strategies enacted by movements for social change. Vertical deviance seeks social justice reform while, at the same time, it preserves the current political and social system structure. Lateral deviance, in contrast, is radical in its intent and imagination—a rejection of the established value system for a vision of a new world order through change or total replacement.[59] The MCRM's narrative clearly promotes the former by deemphasizing the more militant and nationalistic dimensions of the Mississippi Movement and, in some cases, reshaping them to appear more consistent with the vertical strategies of the mainstream movement throughout the country. This theme emerges gradually in some of the preliminary galleries before culminating in gallery 7. For example, in gallery 2, the display "Black Elected Officials" recounts the earliest efforts by newly freed Blacks to participate in democratic government. The display cites that by 1868, nearly 97 percent of adult Black males in Mississippi were registered to vote. This high figure is remarkable in its own right, and the display also notes that less than 81 percent of white males in the state were registered at the same time. In comparing these two figures, however, the display reinforces how passionately this emerging Black community was committed to (male) suffrage despite the risks—not in changing the political system itself. Only "intimidation and violence" were able to keep "many black people away from the polls." The display further indicates that despite this violence, more than one hundred Black Mississippians were elected to various state and federal offices in the 1860s and 1870s.

    In the MCRM's narration from 1945 to 1976, activists and freedom fighters are represented as vertical agitators who are deeply invested in gaining access to the system denying them the basic human freedoms whites enjoyed. In gallery 5 especially, visitors encounter displays that chronicle the most prominent vertical tactics used in Mississippi and across the nation, including sit-ins, marches, and boycotts. One such display, "Sitting In in Mississippi," emphasizes the use of strategic sit-ins in various cities and towns in the state in an effort to desegregate businesses that refused service to Black customers. Although the display acknowledges that sit-ins were a "confrontational tactic" when compared to other vertical strategies, it also reinforces that their emphasis on "nonviolent confrontation" made them successful. A similar display in the gallery tells the story of the nine Tougaloo students who staged a read-in in 1961 to desegregate the public library system in Jackson. The display notes that their peaceful act of civil disobedience mobilized others to use vertical strategies to support their efforts, including a prayer meeting, march, and boycott.

As African Americans continued to apply strategies of vertical deviance to desegregate public services and businesses, a similar approach sought equal access to public education and political participation. Gallery 4 draws attention to this struggle in the wake of the landmark *Brown v. Board of Education* decision in 1954. In one display, "Battle over Segregation Begins," a statement from the NAACP notes that the Black community would focus on "the removal of all racial segregation in public education and reiterate our determination to achieve that goal without compromise of principle." In gallery 6, visitors learn more about movement efforts to mobilize Black voters. Voter registration drives are a focal point in this gallery, further reinforcing the narrative of vertical over lateral deviance. One representative display, "Getting Out the Vote," recounts the work of the COFO in recruiting white students from Ivy League universities to canvas neighborhoods, prepare speeches, and assist with other field duties during the 1963 Freedom Vote campaign. Through text and images, the display advances a narrative of vertical deviance by positively framing well-established tactics like fundraising, the creation of polling sites, and public rallies.

The MCRM not only recounts the actual strategies that activists used to achieve social change through vertical deviance, but it also emphasizes the effectiveness and success of these strategies. One way the museum does this is through a recurring series of displays titled "Point of Light" that spotlight key figures who contributed directly or indirectly to the Mississippi Movement's success. In gallery 2, for example, one of these displays focuses on Blanche Kelso Bruce, a former enslaved man and the first African American to serve a full term in the US Senate. Elsewhere, other displays enumerate the economic success stemming from vertical deviance in the rise of Black-owned businesses, the production of Black newspapers, and the formation of Black agricultural communities such as Mound Bayou. In one Freedom Vote display in gallery 6, "The Vote Tally," activist Hollis Watkins describes the campaign's success: "It showed people how easy it would be for them if the system was just, and treated them fairly. And . . . it showed the power that black people had if they had the right to vote, and if they used the vote in a unified manner." A historical timeline display in this gallery notes major legislative victories for the movement that these collective efforts spawned, including the passage of the 24th amendment to the US Constitution that abolished the poll tax in 1964 and the Civil Rights Act signed into law that same year.

Of course, because the mainstream civil rights movement was primarily vertical and nonviolent in nature, the MCRM's emphasis on vertical deviance throughout the exhibit's galleries is not surprising. Activists in Mississippi and nationwide largely sought to repair, not overturn, faulty and racist systems, and the museum tells that story brilliantly and in a manner that is more comprehensive (and more engaging) than any other public memory site in Mississippi. Without question, the efficacy and subversiveness of the numerous and creative methods employed throughout the Mississippi Movement—strategies that often put Black bodies in mortal danger—should not be underestimated. What we draw attention to here is how the exhibit's rhetorical framing of movement strategies downplays the impact of lateral deviance and its role in the movement's success. This is most evident in gallery 7, "Black Empowerment," whose title subtly co-opts one of the more radical aspects of the civil rights movement—Black power—and reframes it as Black *empowerment*, a tonal shift that transforms a lateral form of agitation into one more consistent with the museum's overall narrative and support of the state's racial reconciliation and image management goals through civil rights tourism.

The shift from Black power to Black empowerment is emphasized in the first display introducing visitors to gallery 7. Rather than mention the Black Power movement by name, it instead alludes to intermovement disagreements as an unremarkable element of the larger freedom struggle, noting, "As is common in a democracy, they did not always speak with one voice." Despite these disagreements, the display notes that by the end of the 1960s, "black leaders [were] running Head Start programs and taking seats in the Mississippi state legislature." Marching—a central vertical strategy of the Mississippi Movement—is heavily featured in multiple displays in an entire section of gallery 7 devoted to the topic, "Why We March."

Similar to the MFT's memory-building narratives, the more radical elements of the Black Power movement in Mississippi (and elsewhere) are downplayed or simply not present in the exhibit. Gallery 7 rarely references the Black Panther Party or Malcolm X; indeed, the most prominent mentions of both are smaller, more easily overlooked entries among many in two "National Timeline" displays; one observes X's assassination in 1965 and notes the Black Panther Party's formation the following year, while the other references party members on trial for the murder of an FBI informant. The timelines' design offers little space for context or nuance; instead, X is described in uncontroversial language as a leader who "spoke out for black identity" and "campaigned against racism," while the Black Panthers are presented as a group that simply grew in popularity in 1966. Although the

Black Panther Party never established a major presence in Mississippi during the movement, this gallery makes no mention of NAACP activist Rudy Shields's efforts to bring various Black power groups to Mississippi for a state convention in 1970, including extending a special invitation to Black Panther Party cofounder Huey P. Newton to be the keynote speaker.[60] The gallery is also silent with regard to Shields's work establishing the Black United Front in Jackson, an organization that "advocated the creation of a paramilitary organization for the protection of the Black community" in the wake of the police violence at Jackson State University in 1970.[61]

Elsewhere in gallery 7, other displays subtly recast Black power or lateral deviance in Mississippi and their radical potential to upend established systems of power. For example, one display focuses on efforts by Black nationalists to form an independent country in the late 1960s, the Republic of New Afrika (RNA). Revolutionary in its scope and aim, the movement, which was headquartered in Jackson, adopted a provisional government and sought "complete independence and statehood of the Black nation," including reparations.[62]

Former RNA president Imari Abubakari Obadele is quoted at the top of the display, "In Mississippi we are following a simple and legal path to independence. We are organizing . . . an election in which the people may vote to be a free and independent nation." This emphasis on voting for *independence* is a stark contrast to mainstream movement efforts to integrate with white society that are cataloged throughout the museum. However, the quotation is juxtaposed with other RNA initiatives that closely parallel that mainstream movement, including economic cooperatives, education, healthcare, and "respect" for the law, all of which obscure the display's single brief reference to "militant self-defense" (which receives no elaboration). Much of the display focuses on the violence that broke out when law enforcement officers raided the RNA's Jackson headquarters, leaving the revolutionary ethos of the RNA largely unaddressed. That ethos is further overshadowed by adjacent displays that emphasize the success of vertical movement tactics, including marches and educational campaigns.

Moreover, two displays devoted to defining the meaning of Black power offer little insight into the more radical, system-challenging dimensions of the Black Power movement. Instead, they draw heavily on a selective framing of SNCC leader Stokely Carmichael's rhetoric. And while excerpts from Carmichael do describe Black power as a "revolutionary idea" in one of the displays, the revolution described is clearly one that does not seek to overturn any system. "Politically, black power means what it has always meant to

SNCC," Carmichael is quoted, "the coming-together of black people to elect representatives." Historical details with the potential to alienate some white visitors—and potentially undermine the state's civil rights tourism goals—are not addressed, such as Carmichael's association with the Black Panther Party and the All-African People's Revolutionary Party or the expulsion of SNCC's white membership in 1966. Instead, in the MCRM's telling, Black power is reframed almost exclusively as vertical deviance, a narrative that supports the larger economic development, image management, and racial reconciliation goals of the state.

Without question, and as we have mentioned throughout this book, the MCRM is the most significant addition to the state's civil rights tourism industry. Its very existence after a seemingly interminable period of development that was decades in the making is a testament to the commitment of the citizens, scholars, donors, MDAH staff, and state politicians who supported it along the way. The museum's truth-telling narrative is reinforced through detailed, specific, and overwhelming documentation. The sheer number of individual artifacts and displays that saturate the exhibit (requiring us to take more than three thousand photographs to fully document) create a sensation that approaches claustrophobia at times and rhetorically disarms silence and denial. By uncovering the truth, championing Black resistance to white supremacy, and deemphasizing the more militant aspects of the freedom struggle to service a consistent narrative of vertical deviance in the Mississippi Movement, the museum is positioned to help the state achieve its broader goals through civil rights tourism. Importantly, the MCRM's potential as the predominant force in the state's civil rights tourism industry does not come at the expense of sugarcoating the violence that was ever-present in the 400-year timeline the exhibit covers. Slavery, race riots, Jim Crow, the Ku Klux Klan, the convict leasing system, lynching, church burnings and bombings, assassinations of civil rights activists and leaders—all are meticulously cataloged throughout the museum, making it the most aggressive state-funded truth-telling narrative in Mississippi to date.

Yet despite the unrelenting violence visitors encounter in each gallery, the museum promotes a rhetoric of gradual and consistent progress that concludes with the dismantling of some of the more egregious elements of white supremacy and a celebration of the state having the highest number of African American elected politicians in the nation. Of course, the fact that Mississippi even has a state-sponsored museum dedicated to civil rights is material evidence of this progress. Grounded in the mythos of the American Dream, the MCRM's message is also streamlined by privileging vertical deviance as a means to both preserve the current political and economic system and move the nation closer to the political values embedded in the Declaration of Independence and the US Constitution. The role of Black nationalism, Black power, and other forms of agitation that are less amenable to Mississippi's desire to present itself as a racially healed state making progress toward racial reconciliation are minimized in the exhibit.

While the MCRM clearly articulates a message of hope and progress, the museum does signal in its final gallery the relevance of social justice as a civil rights tourism goal: progress is not permanent and the struggle for civil and human rights is not over. In the concluding chapter, we explore and assess the civil rights tourism goal of social justice and the related concerns of racial reconciliation and social activism. We also provide an overall assessment of the other two tourism goals this form of heritage tourism shares with its blues counterpart: economic development and image management.

CONCLUSION

> What would you take a stand for?
> Peace, love, and equality for all.
> —VISITOR RESPONSE ON DISPLAY AT THE MCRM

In the early 2010s, Mississippi's official culture initiated promotion of the state's civil rights history and heritage. While its neighbors to the east, Alabama and Georgia, had long been promoting their civil rights history and addressing their equally shameful record on civil and human rights, the state of Mississippi largely refused to do so. Excuses were offered, and silence reigned. During these early years, some white and Black Mississippians believed civil rights tourism would reignite racial hostility.[1] Others argued that civil rights tourism would unnecessarily retraumatize the state, perpetuating negative stereotypes and hindering efforts to rehabilitate its public image from a "deathplace" to a "birthplace."[2] Mississippi, the "birthplace" of the blues" and "of America's music," as some tourism officials would have us believe. The promotion of the state's civil rights history is also complicated by the fact that families of individuals responsible, directly or indirectly, for the state's antidemocratic, racial apartheid policies and unprosecuted crimes were and are still living in the state. Arguably, a volatile and toxic mix of defiance, denial, shame, and fear served as a strong deterrent to Mississippi marketing and promoting its civil rights legacy any sooner than it did.

Early resistance and fears proved to be an apparition. The nearly universal praise for the MMH-MCRM as well as the MFT was greeted with relief and the knowledge that silence was transforming into memory. In 2018, political scientist and historian Alvin Tillery pronounced the opening of the MMH-MCRM "an incredible cultural moment."[3] To the outside observer, it was the silence that was shameful. Indeed, truth telling was necessary for advancing, in the words of Myrlie Evers and William F. Winter, "a more just, vibrant, and healthy Mississippi for our future."[4] A consistent theme rings out in the high praise for the MMH-MCRM: the museum does not sugarcoat the past. The enormous force of white supremacy and its brutalization of Black bodies are uncovered for all to witness, and the museum has quickly become an indispensable part of any civil rights tourist's itinerary in the state.[5] "Now, at a time when our country is more divided than ever, and when school districts are still illegally ignoring federal desegregation orders, the state has given all Americans an opportunity to come to Mississippi and reflect on our dark and not-so distant past," proclaimed Liz Willen of *The Hechinger Report*. "The Mississippi Civil Rights Museum is a reason to go—and to learn. Change can't happen without knowledge."[6] Journalists, critics, and other observers all but begged readers to visit the museum.

Improving the state's public image is one of three major goals associated with civil rights tourism. And anecdotal evidence suggests that truth telling is actually good for Mississippi's public image. It is also good for business. Like blues tourism and other elements of the state's expansive heritage tourism landscape, civil rights tourism's ability to encourage out-of-state and international tourists can be traced, in part, by annual visitor attendance to museums like the MMH-MCRM. As the centerpiece of the state's civil rights tourism industry, the MMH-MCRM is an exemplar for the industry's most recent successes. For example, approximately seven months after the twin museums opened in Jackson, the *Clarion-Ledger* reported attendance of 185,000, exceeding the first-year goal of 180,000. In-state travel originated from all of Mississippi's 82 counties, and international travelers came from France, China, Brazil, South Africa, and beyond.[7] Based on those attendance numbers, both museums were awarded the Mississippi Travel Attraction of the Year Award in 2018.[8] In December of that year (just one year after the museums' opening), Visit Jackson estimated the economic impact in the capital city to be in excess of $20 million.[9] By July 2019, attendance at both museums topped 320,000 since opening its doors in December 2017,[10] and the museums would boast attendance milestones on January 20, 2020—the Martin Luther King Jr. federal holiday—when Jackson's WHTV reported that "almost 3,000 visitors walked through the doors" during an eight-hour period.[11]

Starting in 2020, the impact of the worst pandemic in a century demonstrated the fragility of tourism and the hospitality industry. When Mississippi was hit hard by COVID-19 infections and deaths during the first half of 2020, many state-run museums were closed for several months, including the MMH-MCRM.[12] The museums reopened on July 7, 2020.[13] Later that summer, we inquired about visiting the Fannie Lou Hamer Museum in Ruleville and were told the museum was closed indefinitely due to the pandemic, with no timeline for reopening. The situation in the state was so dire that the Mississippi legislature passed House Bill 1791 in 2020, which, in part, created the Mississippi Tourism Recovery Fund and the Mississippi Nonprofit Art Museums Recovery Fund to help support the distressed tourism industry.[14] The pandemic's impact on travel and tourism was felt in a decline in several metrics, including the estimated number of direct jobs (FY19: 91,400 vs. FY20: 80,000), visitor expenditures (FY19: $6.6 billion vs. FY20: $5.5 billion), General Fund revenues (FY19: $410 million vs. FY20: $340 million), and out of state visitors (FY19: 24.6 million vs. FY20: 20 million). Nonetheless, the travel and tourism category retained its position as the state's "fourth largest private-sector employer."[15]

Although Mississippi's tourism industry, like the rest of the nation, had not fully recovered by the spring of 2021, signs of progress were evident. In March of that year, Mississippi House Speaker Philip Gunn, Lieutenant Governor Delbert Hosemann, and members of the Mississippi Tourism Association addressed an audience at the MMH-MCRM and argued the importance of tourism to Mississippi's economic engine. Speaker Gunn said, "Prior to the pandemic we saw a record year for Mississippi tourism and we will continue to work together to see the industry back to and exceed those levels as recovery continues."[16] During the same month, Marlo Dorsey, executive director and CEO of Visit Hattiesburg, wrote a seemingly self-congratulatory article proclaiming that "Mississippi has emerged as an innovative leader in tourism recovery."[17] Later that spring, the US Department of Commerce's Economic Development Administration awarded a $2 million CARES Act Recovery Assistance Grant to the state's southern coastal region.[18] Perhaps, for all these reasons and more, the state's tourism industry appeared to have stabilized during the summer of 2021. The tourism resurgence was evident in the data, published in MDA's *Fiscal Year 2021 Annual Report*, which saw increases in out-of-state visitors (24 million), visitor expenditures ($6.25 billion), and in revenue (General Fund Revenues: $380 million) over the previous fiscal year.[19] Tourism retained its status as the fourth largest private-sector employer as well as "one of the state's largest export industries."[20] However, the unpredictability of the ongoing pandemic, including the rise of coronavirus variants during the second half of 2021 and into 2022, impacted some of those early gains in 2021. Looking to the future, Mississippi's postpandemic recovery will be intriguing to watch, particularly whether the state *increases* its commitment to promoting its civil rights heritage.

An assessment of civil rights tourism's goal of economic development cannot escape questions of cultural co-optation and exploitation. Some have expressed concern that the state's promotion of its civil rights history will ironically serve as an agent of exploitation, with the state's African American population the least likely to benefit economically from the selling of its cultural experiences and legacy. This concern, albeit anecdotal in nature, is not unique to civil rights tourism, but a long-standing issue when dominant cultures actively promote (or co-opt) elements of a nondominant or subaltern group's history. While noting civil rights tourism's positive benefits, including economic uplift to both white and Black communities as well as teaching "tolerance," Dorit Wagner notes that "it can be argued that this fairly new section of tourism is used to help former slave states make yet another profit of the African American plight."[21] This sentiment is echoed by Rolando Herts, executive director of the MDNHA, who admits that issues of economic development are a "huge challenge" in the state. "Who is really benefiting from it economically?" he asks. "If we really start drawing those lines and digging into that, that becomes a whole other conversation. And is it just the reification of plantation power dynamics and plantation economies?"[22]

Similar concerns abound. Writing for the *New Yorker*, a skeptical Calvin Trillin pronounced the MFT a "tourism scheme," a state-led money-making enterprise designed to transform its ghastly historical record of human rights abuses "into an industry."[23] In *Learning from the Germans: Race and the Memory of Evil*, Susan Neiman was no less charitable. Although she concedes that the MFT and Mississippi Blues Trail generate much-needed revenue for poor communities, she describes them as "awkward and eerie" because both "commodify suffering."[24] Darrell White, director of the Natchez Museum of African American History and Culture, calls civil rights tourism the "new cotton." He observed that "there are many individuals planning to pick at it and develop it in some way."[25] As noted in chapter 3, Johnny B. Thomas, mayor of Glendora and founder of the Emmett Till Historic Intrepid Center, remains suspicious of the motives of some whites who are participating in Emmett Till memory work.[26] Perhaps one way to ensure this cultural appropriation does not take place is by balancing a preoccupation with the past with attention to the present and future. Rather than simply serving as a medium to remember the "safe" past, hopefully civil rights tourism can deepen Mississippi's commitment to its third goal: social justice and the twin concerns of reconciliation and social activism. It is certainly in a unique position to do so.

Social Justice: Where Do We Go from Here?

Indeed, as the final gallery in the MCRM asks us, where do we go? Should Mississippi's civil rights tourism industry be confined to the past—to the important work of remembering people, places, and events where resistance to white supremacy and its assault on Black bodies resulted in the expansion of democracy? Or, should Mississippi's civil rights tourism industry also play some sort of social justice role in the present?

For Patricia G. Davis, the answer to these questions is clear: An important element of museums' missions "includes the promotion of critical analyses of the connections between the past and contemporary concerns."[27] As noted earlier, the exclusive focus on safe, less controversial aspects of the past is a central critique of civil rights tourism, irrespective of place and state. While acknowledging the truth-telling function of memory, as previously unmarked lynching sites get unearthed and the biographies of lesser-known leaders such as Reverend George Lee and Amzie Moore transcend their gravesites, civil rights tourism could end up, regrettably, being nothing more than a backward journey through the hazy lens of cultural nostalgia. In this discourse of wistfulness, the "good" movement of the past is remembered, as opposed to its more "radical" branches in the present, for its ability to overcome and for activists' tenacity, courage, and bravery. In some quarters, memories of the Mississippi Movement have been repurposed to reimagine contemporary Mississippi as wholly displaced from its ugly past, where evidence of Black political power must signify tangible racial progress, even healing. In a worse case, civil rights tourism closes off contemporary critique and debate on Mississippi's seemingly interminable and intractable racial, class, and gender inequities and injustices. The blood-soaked battles are over, the movement "won." Of course, the relevance of civil rights tourism to present-day concerns of social justice has probably less to do with the experiences of many out-of-state civil rights tourists who, like all tourists, occupy a temporary and transient role. As the *U.S. Civil Rights Trail* guide makes clear, Mississippi is just one of many southern states with a civil rights trail and tourism infrastructure, offering these temporary consumer-bound travelers a constellation of memory places to experience.[28]

No doubt, out-of-state tourists will be affected, some deeply and profoundly, by their experiences touring the MMH-MCRM, visiting the Medgar and Myrlie Evers Home National Monument, or reading MFT markers. We certainly were. Preconceptions and stereotypes will be both affirmed and challenged. Word of mouth, personal testimonies, and other first-person narratives will circulate among family and friends. In addition, first-person accounts can be found in blogs and travel websites such as Tripadvisor and on influencers' social media accounts. The immediate and most easily quantifiable impact of the out-of-state civil rights tourist is obviously economic, but it is also intricately connected to image management and Mississippi's public face.

That part of the story belongs to the people of Mississippi. Its citizenry—politicians, tourism officials, culture brokers, tour guides, museum curators and docents, educators, ordinary citizens, and others—will collectively decide the extent to which the memories of the Mississippi Movement will serve as an instrument of social good, a vehicle for social justice. The people of Mississippi will determine whether civil rights tourism can transcend its preoccupation with the past and the state's immediate economic and image management goals. In what ways can Mississippi's civil rights tourism industry speak to contemporary issues of race and rights in our current moment? How can civil rights tourism serve as a form of social activism, a subelement of social justice, and meaningful racial reconciliation? When past sins are acknowledged, is there hope for absolution and forgiveness?

The William Winter Institute for Racial Reconciliation (now known as the Alluvial Collective) has been wrestling with these questions since its founding in 1999 as a response to President Bill Clinton's national initiative on race.[29] While the Winter Institute is not a part of the state's civil rights tourism industry, it has partnered with segments of the industry, including the MMH-MCRM. This is not surprising given that former governor William Winter was an early supporter of a state museum dedicated to civil rights. The institute increased its commitment to the museum when it announced in 2018 that it was moving from its base in Oxford on the University of Mississippi campus to Jackson to "form a partnership with the Mississippi Civil Rights Museum and introduce more programs in the capital city."[30] Other like-minded organizations in Mississippi, including the Philadelphia Coalition, share common ground with reconciliation elements of civil rights tourism.[31] Racial reconciliation is also relevant to other forms of heritage tourism, including plantation tourism.[32] We take it as a positive sign that so many organizations dedicated to racial reconciliation intersect with the state's civil rights tourism industry.

While racial reconciliation is certainly a commendable goal, and its relevance to civil rights tourism is undeniable, the journey—as discussed in the opening chapter of this book—is often long, difficult, and fraught with disagreements about process and misperceptions about its function and goals. Reconciliation requires individuals and groups to engage in challenging forms of communication: active listening, empathy, truth telling, personal accountability, forgiveness, and some meaningful form of redress and compensation. In many ways, Mississippi—like the nation—has *only just started* on the path towards reconciliation. For example, although we commonly associate Truth Commissions and other forms of large-scale national reconciliation efforts with *other* countries such as South Africa, Rwanda, and Liberia, the same processes are arguably needed in Mississippi and, indeed, the nation. Even these large-scale efforts are not immune to critique, as communication scholar Courtney Cole recognized when she attended the public hearings of the Truth and Reconciliation Commission of Liberia Diaspora Project in 2008. Although victims of the Liberian Civil Wars engaged in truth telling by narrating their harrowing first-person experiences in a public forum, the hearings were marred by both logistical challenges (location and time) and efforts by former members of the Liberian government to co-opt the event.[33]

In addition to the structural and rhetorical demands of racial reconciliation, such efforts are complicated by the rhetoric of progress that pervades civil rights public memory sites, particularly in the MCRM. If overemphasized, this progressive framing can dilute and delegitimize the power of social critique and activism. Rhetorical scholar Victoria J. Gallagher discovered a similar rhetoric of progress in her analysis of Alabama's Birmingham Civil Rights Institute. She notes that the institute's exhibits reinforce the ideology of progress over any failures of the present, a tactic designed to privilege and uphold the current political system: "Discourse suggesting that failure outweighs progress or that there is a key flaw within the very fabric of the culture is considered radical, extremist."[34] Gallagher concluded, as we do in this book, that "individuals who represent positions differing from current political reality (for instance, socialism, communism, fascism, and revolution) are often ignored, rebuked, and discounted."[35] Pushed to its extreme, the rhetoric of progress ultimately denies the relevance and importance of racial reconciliation and the steps communities must take to actually achieve it. According to this logic, why try to resolve what has already been ameliorated through time, reflective insight, and "progress"?

Although the ground-level realities of remembering a movement dedicated to racial justice within a larger political and social context that continues to uphold white privilege is inherently complex and problematic, current reconciliation efforts through heritage tourism should not be dismissed. For example, Herts describes "connecting the past with the present" as "a philosophical underpinning" of the Delta Center and the MDNHA's civil rights programming, where workshop facilitators are encouraged to explore "how privilege and oppression and power dynamics shape the past and present."[36] As noted in chapter 3, the ETIC's decision to harness Emmett Till's memory through the enactment of "The Apology" is perhaps the most ambitious example in Mississippi of how civil rights tourism can serve as a medium (or at least a starting point) for the reconciliation process. However, according to ETIC executive director Patrick Weems, the overall reception to this quasi-public-private ritual of atonement has been a "mix[ed] bag."[37] In a 2019 interview, Weems described various skeptical responses to "The Apology," noting that some visitors to the center are "morally outraged" when they read it: "This is not enough. How do you expect this to be enough?" He recalled one site visit by representatives from the W. K. Kellogg Foundation, noting "they were very skeptical that this was all a sham" and implied that "The Apology" was created "for tourism."[38] The argument that "The Apology" does not adequately address the crimes committed may also be shared, according to Weems, by some members of the local African American community, including Johnny B. Thomas. Other members of the local community, including two former members of the Emmett Till Memorial Commission, Reverend Willie Williams and John Wilchie, have responded more favorably. In comparing both in-state and out-of-state responses, Weems concluded that "generally people from in-state are more receptive to the apology narrative than out of state."[39]

While "The Apology" has its skeptics, it should be acknowledged that the few public apologies that have transpired in the state have been essentially one-off events. "The Apology" that lives on through the ETIC is different in that acknowledgment and contrition are repeated symbolic rites that occur whenever visitors enter the psycho-physical space of Emmett Till's lynching memory landscape. Memory is never allowed to permanently slide into silence. "The Apology" also makes it clear that civil rights tourism can play *a* role in the state's efforts at racial reconciliation, but the economic and leisure elements of tourism, along with the significant work that still needs to be accomplished, make reconciliation—as noted earlier—a long, difficult, and multidimensional phenomenon. Nan Elizabeth Woodruff is correct when she asserts that "there can be no 'harmony' or 'reconciliation' until communities fully acknowledge their tragic history," especially white Mississippians "who have chosen to ignore the horrendous crimes that occurred within their communities." Indeed, "perpetrators and their descendants must acknowledge the still open wounds of African Americans who have lived side by side with the murderers—and for forty or fifty years."[40]

As a step forward, "The Apology" serves as a key element of truth telling, an important rhetorical signifier of the center's mission as reinforced on the organization's website in all-caps: "RACIAL RECONCILIATION BEGINS BY TELLING THE TRUTH."[41] As a public memory project, the center's mission harnesses collective memories of the past to ameliorate racial animus in the present: "Today, the Emmett Till Interpretive Center exists to tell the story of the Emmett Till tragedy and to point a way towards racial healing. Specifically, the center uses arts and storytelling to help process past pain and to imagine new ways of moving forward."[42] In Glendora, the final display in the ETHIC encourages visitors to become a "warrior for human rights," as "educational healing agents for peace, unity and reconciliation." Although Emmett Till's tragic lynching has also been rhetorically repositioned to serve economic needs, just as the state has doubled down on various birthplace claims and accompanying circular tropes of authenticity, both the ETIC and ETHIC provide bold responses to that question, "Where do we go from here?"

To answer this question, let us return, for a moment, to the MCRM. Walking down the hallway that connects gallery 7 to gallery 8, one begins to experience a gradual ascent from the appalling cruelties of white supremacy and human depravity to new, more affirming sociopolitical terrain. At the same time, displays such as "Challenges of Our Time" make it plain the struggle is far from over. Paralleling the dialectic between racial progress and the work that remains to be done that permeates gallery 8, visitors are encouraged to become social activists. Located above an electronic display titled "What Will Your Light Stand For?" visitors are offered cards, each the size of a small postcard, listing questions organized by category: "Where do we go from here?"; "What would you take a stand for?"; "How can we improve our relationships with others?"; and "How can we make it easier to talk about race?" Visitors may write in responses and submit their cards. Visitor responses are continually projected onto four large panels for all to see. One visitor dreamed that "All races, or backgrounds can unite as one," while another, in an almost pleading tone, called for an end to violence: "I want people two [sic] be friends and not kill or fight." Colorful quotations displayed on mirrors from a variety of inspirational sources, including civil rights leaders (Harriet Tubman, Medgar Evers, Fannie Lou Hamer, Coretta Scott King), writers (Maya Angelou), politicians (Robert F. Kennedy), and a local benefactor (Oseola McCarty) encourage visitors to make a compact with the social good. As a Hamer quotation reminds visitors, "There is one thing you have got to learn about our movement, three people are better than no people." In the nearby Smith Robertson Museum and Cultural Center, a similar interactive experience that solicits visitor comments can also be found in the permanent exhibit. It was created by Pamela Junior, who worked there for seventeen years (part of that time as the museum's manager) before becoming the director of the MCRM (and later, in addition, the MMH). On the second floor, in the center of the Medgar Evers exhibit, visitors confront a similar question: "What are you willing to fight for?" In this space, unlike gallery 8 of the MCRM, visitors are encouraged to select socially themed cards and "place them in the order of their importance to you" in slots numbered 1 to 4. Six cards are available, ranging from policy reform ("The right to a quality education," "The right to have affordable housing," "The right to a steady job") to the Constitution ("The right to free speech") to the dream of a postracial society ("The right to equality for all races"). In another parallel with the MCRM, a second interactive opportunity encourages visitors to respond to a similar social justice question: "Tell us in your own words... How would you make Mississippi better?" Many of the responses on display, from children and adults alike, focus on similar themes found in the MCRM's gallery 8 and range from improving educational opportunities for Mississippians to racial harmony. Twelve-year-old Kayla Williams wrote, "I would like to make a law that bans being unkind to someone because of their skin color." In this room dedicated to the heroism of Medgar Evers, the past is intimately connected to the present as visitors are reminded that Evers "did not die in vain." The theme of social justice/social activism is amplified by associating Evers's civil rights activities and campaigns and his general sense of fearlessness and self-sacrifice with questions directed at visitors: "How much would you give up to support a boycott?" and "How much are you willing to risk for what you believe?" In a 2019 interview, Junior underscored the important role activism plays in how she shapes memories of the Mississippi Movement as director of one of the state's most important public memory sites:

> I attended... Unita Blackwell's funeral service. And the minister, who's from Virginia, her subject was, "What are you going to do? She's dead. Now what are you going to do?" And so that always resonates with me in regards to how I talk to students, how we work with students. It's the next movement, it's the movement, it's the next level, is where do we go from here, as Martin [Luther King Jr.] said in his last book.... And, so I live by that.[43]

While most vernacular representations of civil rights tourism focus on memorializing a person (e.g., Fannie Lou Hamer) or place (e.g., Canton Freedom House), there are glimpses of how work at the grassroots level can do more than retell the past. As noted in chapter 2, Helen Sims's oral performances stretch the span of time from antiquity to present-day realities of police brutality and the murder of unarmed African Americans. In

Jackson, the once abandoned COFO state headquarters at 1017 John R. Lynch St. reopened in 2011 as the "COFO Civil Rights Education Center." This new education center's mission is to "honor the past, *deal with issues of the present, and offer hope for the future* in the same building as the original Council of Federated Organizations."[44] The headquarters is marked by an MFT marker ("COFO Central Offices") and is promoted, among other attractions, in a Visit Jackson brochure.[45] The naming and renaming of organizations and businesses that help remedy African American inequality signifies the relationship between civil rights memory work and the social good: the Aaron Henry Head Start Center in Clarksdale and the Fannie Lou Hamer Cancer Foundation, which promotes awareness and provides access to cancer screening, are some examples. At the same time, while naming and renaming are powerful rhetorical signifiers of equity and inclusivity, simply renaming a hospital, library, or overpass after civil rights leaders can just as easily be used politically by those in power to avoid tackling present-day systemic racism in more substantive ways.

Perhaps the intersection of civil rights tourism and Mississippi's education curriculum may lead to the most productive, and arguably a longer-lasting, engagement with issues of social justice and social activism. Paralleling the state's long-standing tradition of silencing dissent, until relatively recently civil rights movement history was rarely incorporated into the public school system. In July 2006, Governor Haley Barbour signed a law facilitating civil rights and human rights instruction, although schools were not required to do so.[46] Of course, this effort to incorporate civil rights movement instruction in the classroom is overshadowed by the civil rights education that occurred decades earlier in Freedom Schools, the brainchild of Charlie Cobb, a SNCC field secretary, in 1963.[47] The bill paved the way for Mississippi's Board of Education to "make civil rights and human rights education a part of the K–12 curriculum instruction" in Mississippi's public schools.[48] As this landmark legislation makes clear, the state's civil rights memory landscape would serve as an instructional resource for students that would:

> (a) provide assistance and advice to K–12 schools with respect to the Civil Rights Movement and human rights education and awareness programs; (b) survey and catalog the extent to which civil rights and human rights education exists in state curricula; (c) inventory civil rights memorials, exhibits and resources that could be used in classrooms and other educational programs; (d) compile a list of volunteers who are willing to share their knowledge and experiences concerning

the struggle for civil rights; (e) prepare reports for the Governor and the State Legislature on the inclusion of civil rights studies into the educational systems of the state.[49]

Still, by 2017, critics claimed that such efforts were being undercut by the use of outdated textbooks that continue to obfuscate the civil rights movement.[50] It is important to note that this legislation only impacts Mississippi's public schools. White private schools, sometimes called "segregation academies," still dot the Delta region, Jackson, and other parts of the state and are exempt from this legislation. Additionally, in June 2021, Mississippi governor Tate Reeves, while acknowledging that state school districts are not teaching Critical Race Theory (CRT), lambasted the *idea* of allowing these districts to incorporate CRT into the curriculum. "I believe we ought to pass legislation and pass a law to make these school districts unable to teach CRT in our classrooms," he declared.[51] That same year, the Mississippi Center for Public Policy released a report, *Combating Critical Race Theory in Mississippi*, claiming just the opposite: "Within K–12 public education, there is evidence that suggests critical race theory and the ideas behind it *are* being taught."[52] Asserting that CRT is "profoundly harmful" and promoted by theorists who "seek to overturn the existing order," the report strategically *mis-reads* CRT by exploiting Martin Luther King Jr.'s oft-quoted "color-blind" reference in his "I Have a Dream" speech:

> Rather than viewing America as an exceptional republic, established as an experiment in self-government, critical race theory encourages us to see the United States as a conspiracy against people of color. Martin Luther King dreamt of an America in which every individual was judged by the content of their character and not the color of their skin. Instead of celebrating the enormous achievements made since the Civil Rights Movement, critical race theory specifically rejects King's color blind ideal and seeks to racialize every aspect of culture, sport, and public discourse.[53]

Yet, according to the state's superintendent of education, Mississippi public schools are *not* teaching CRT.[54] Unfortunately, this reality did not stop the Mississippi State Senate in January 2022 from advancing Senate Bill 2113, which would effectively ban public educators at all levels—including state supported institutions of higher education—from teaching CRT.[55] African American lawmakers protested the legislation by walking out of the Senate chambers and refusing to vote. Before leaving the chambers, Senator Barbara Blackmon condemned the legislation: "This bill is not morally right."[56] Two months later, the House passed the bill.[57] On March 14, 2022, Governor Tate Reeves signed Senate Bill 2113 into law. On the day of the bill's passage, Reeves provided a rationale for supporting it: "In too many schools around the country, Critical Race Theory is running amok. It threatens the integrity of our kids' education and aims only to humiliate and indoctrinate. In Mississippi, we're taking a strong stand against this progressive fundamentalism. That's why today I was proud to sign legislation that will help keep Critical Race Theory where it belongs—out of Mississippi classrooms."[58]

Notwithstanding the erroneous conclusions about CRT's "infiltration" into Mississippi's school districts, civil rights leaders of the past and present would support many of the basic premises of CRT, namely, that in the United States, racism is the norm and is systemic in nature, language serves to both oppress nondominant groups and operate as a form of counter-hegemonic discourse, and the ideology of racism is promoted by white supremacists and accepted by people of color.[59] Indeed, it is ironic that while the Mississippi Center for Public Policy report co-opts King's words and image to support its own partisan interests, CRT pioneer Kimberlé Crenshaw notes that King was, in reality, "a critical race theorist before there was a name for it."[60]

Beyond the co-optation of King's vision and mission, what is more troubling are accusations that CRT is rolling back efforts to teach civil rights history. For example, in January 2022, *Mississippi Today* reported that the Mississippi Department of Education covertly recommended content changes to its social studies curriculum a month earlier. According to critics of this change, the curricular revisions obscure the past by eliminating specific references to civil rights leaders, white supremacist organizations, and Jim Crow laws.[61] After news of the proposed changes went viral, public outcry led the Department of Education to hold a public hearing.[62] The Mississippi Center for Justice was among the voices fervently opposing the changes, arguing, "History done right helps us to reflect who we are as a community and who we want to be moving forward.... If we want to move forward as Mississippians, we have to reckon accurately and intentionally with our racial history."[63]

Meanwhile, civil rights tourism sites play a critical educational role, particularly as culture wars over CRT are leading to a national retrenchment in telling the story about the civil rights movement. In her analysis of four civil rights memory sites, including the Martin Luther King Jr. Memorial and Center for Nonviolent Social Change (Atlanta) and the NCRM (Memphis), Victoria J. Gallagher found they share the common rhetorical goal of promoting social action. "The educational function of these memory sites," she argued, "is considered particularly important by both staff and visitors because of the comparatively limited availability of information about civil rights history and the role of African Americans and people of color in American history."[64]

Indeed, the MMH-MCRM and other segments of Mississippi's civil rights tourism infrastructure identify education as central to their mission. With a special section on their websites, "Educators," the MMH-MCRM museums are marketed as a site of experiential learning and actively encourage teachers to plan field trips, in-person or virtually. While the museums are a popular site for K–12 field trips, another type of education occurs when multiple generations of family members tour the museum. As MDAH director Katie Blount noted, "One of the most gratifying [experiences] is seeing the multigenerational groups going through the museum together, grandparents explaining the exhibits to younger family members."[65] Reflecting its historical mission, the Smith Robertson Museum and Cultural Center also makes educational materials available, designed largely for children and adolescents, in the form of handouts titled, "Slavery and the Making of America," "What Was Jim Crow," "Black History Trivia," and "The 50 Most Important Figures in Black American History."

In another example, Fannie Lou Hamer's memory has translated into educational opportunities in the Mississippi Delta and beyond. In her letter to K–12 educators, Maegan Parker Brooks—Hamer scholar and a member of the Fannie Lou Hamer Statue Committee—describes how the Fannie Lou Hamer Statue dedication ceremony was an unexpected catalyst for addressing local educational needs as well as showcasing the relationship between memory and social justice:

> The committee members and I publicized the unveiling by reaching out to local and national media organizations, political representatives, and well-known supporters of Fannie Lou Hamer. We also invited local public school teachers, hoping they would bring students to this truly monumental celebration. . . . The teachers' responses to our outreach really surprised me. I knew that Mississippi was one of the first states in the nation to require that the Civil Rights Movement be taught in public schools and I was aware that their state standards explicitly mention Fannie Lou Hamer by name. So, when the teachers told us that they had no materials to teach about Hamer and that students had only a vague idea of who she was or why she was significant. I was, indeed, shocked.[66]

A collaborative partnership between university and local K–12 educators formed to develop the Find Your Voice K–12 Curriculum. Freely accessible through an online resource center, the curriculum's eighteen units "carry forth Fannie Lou Hamer's spirit by encouraging students to reflect on injustices that surround them and to speak out through the creation of their own speeches, film sketches, opinion editorials, debates, narrative poems, and much more."[67] With titles such as "Shining Lights," "Let Your Voice Be Heard," and "Freedom Farm," each lesson plan is carefully crafted for specific grade levels (e.g., grades K–3, 3–5, 6–8) with learning objectives, instructional materials, and step-by-step directions for facilitating classroom exercises.[68] In addition to writing a children's book on Hamer, Brooks also worked directly with the education company BrainPOP to create a Hamer lesson and video for its popular platform, further expanding these educational outreach efforts nationwide.[69]

This partnership also led to the creation of the successful Sunflower County Film Academy (SCFA). Founded in 2018 by filmmaker Joy Elaine Davenport and featuring instructors including filmmakers Dr. Pablo Correa (a collaborator on the Emmett Till Memory Project) and Robert "RJ" Fitzpatrick, the SCFA sponsors an annual summer workshop that trains Delta-area high school students to tell the story of Fannie Lou Hamer's legacy through digital storytelling. It inspires them "to examine the racial barriers that still exist and impact young people today and to look for positive solutions through reflective conversations."[70] In 2020, the MDNHA awarded the program a $22,680 grant, thus deepening the connection between civil rights tourism and education.[71] The 2021 summer workshop was held at the ETIC in Sumner, which is no surprise given their shared goals. The Find Your Voice K–12 Curriculum, SCFA, and other Hamer-related initiatives are part of the larger Fannie Lou Hamer's America project, "a multimodal project aimed at preserving the life and legacy of civil rights icon Fannie Lou Hamer."[72] While the Fannie Lou Hamer Project certainly looks to the past to the late civil rights leader's life and legacy, the project is firmly rooted in affecting social change in the present and the future.

All of the people we interviewed for this book—whether intimately or tangentially connected to civil rights tourism—agreed that civil rights tourism should address contemporary social issues. Rickey Thigpen offered a forceful argument for the state to promote its civil rights history and heritage with an eye to addressing concerns of the present:

> I think the overarching [concern] is that we have to, if we are going to pay homage and make the Civil Rights Museum even worth the

money and the effort and the tears that it took to create it, we have to be dedicated to fostering continued communication, growth, development, you know. We can't take our foot off the pedal. We've come an extraordinarily long way from that museum, but we've got some work to do, i.e., the flag issue and the emotions around that as a state. And how we express ourselves and our differences. We still have, again, people destroying the Emmett Till [historical markers], or a Confederate monument—I think that there's a way to express disagreement without being disrespectful. And until we get there, I think that we've got some growth to do. So that all of that work continues.[73]

It may be that the murder of George Floyd on May 25, 2020, and the massive protests for civil and human rights that followed will do more to accelerate civil rights tourism's ability to speak to issues of social justice than any one individual or organization. Perhaps, the 2020 protests for social justice, as well as the elevation and ascending legitimation of the Black Lives Matter movement, had an impact on the Mississippi legislature's approval of a bill in June 2020 to finally retire its deeply controversial state flag, the last state flag to fly Confederate symbols.[74] As reported in the *Clarion-Ledger* before the passage of the landmark legislation, state senator and chair of the Legislative Black Caucus, Angela Turner-Ford, told reporters: "We need to adopt a flag that is unifying and inclusive. The emotional distress that the current flag perpetuates on people of color extends throughout the United States, casting us and having people to claim we are backwater and retrograde. We need a new brand, we need a new symbol."[75] Mississippi got a new symbol, a new brand. The old state flag was retired to the MDAH, and the new state flag was introduced in a public ceremony in January 2021.[76] The removal of the Confederate flag and Confederate statues is an important step in dismantling the memory (and celebration) of white supremacy as well as moving the state closer to the Mississippi Movement's goal of inclusion, equity, and participation in the democratic system.

While civil rights tourism can and should focus on social justice in the present, this goal is admittedly restrained by a civil rights landscape that is predominately entrenched in the past, from the markers that comprise the MFT to the Fannie Lou Hamer Memorial Garden to the Amzie Moore House Museum and Interpretive Center. However, an alternate reading may render a different verdict. Rather than interpret each gravesite, memorial, statue, or museum display as distinct and a closed text, perhaps we should see Mississippi's civil rights tourism industry as a constellation of interdependent and overlapping texts. Start with the most obscure vernacular space (where tourism has not yet left its mark), move through the ramshackle Mississippi Heritage Consortium in Belzoni to the Medgar and Myrlie Evers Home National Monument in Jackson, traverse the MFT and into the MCRM and its final gallery's call, "Where Do We Go From Here?," and return to the world, rife with present-day injustices. Read in this way, Mississippi's civil rights tourism industry may, indeed, transform into something radical: cultural tourism and public memory as sites for social justice, reconciliation, and redemption.

A Return to Money

Once again, driving east on Highway 8 through early morning fog in late December 2021. Drifting slowly across the dry fields, the fog shrouds this part of the Delta in an otherworldly haze, confirming tourist expectations of the region's haunting, almost supernatural qualities. Past Dockery Farms, through Fannie Lou Hamer's hometown of Ruleville, over Emmett Till's death waters, the Tallahatchie River, and then on to Money Road, that two-lane north-south road that snakes past homes, fields, churches, and trees, parallel to railroad tracks. The fog had dissipated to the west and was replaced by clearing blues skies long before we pulled onto Money Road. Nonetheless, it can be difficult to locate it without GPS—if there was ever a road sign, it's gone now. Whether a metaphor for concealment and silence or evidence of tourism officials' efforts to rebrand this stretch of road as something else—the birthplace of the civil rights movement—the lack of signage remains a mystery.

Since our visit in 2016, little has *appeared* to have changed in Money. Look closer, however, and change is the one constant. A small plastic sign, pitched askew on the ground, sits where the "Bryant's Grocery" MFT marker once stood. The marker was reported missing in early September 2021. "This marker is temporarily down for repair," the sign reads, echoing an all-too-familiar narrative concerning Emmett Till historical markers in the Delta.

Nearly a decade since the renovation of Ben Roy's Service Station was completed in 2013, the building is showing signs of age once again. Gazing through its dirty windows, its interior is a chaotic jumble of artifacts and still devoid of interpretive signage—giving the impression of an abandoned memory project in stasis. Although an "open" sign advertising Mission Beverages hangs from the front window, the door is locked, and the renovated building has never been open to the public. The Bryant's Grocery building has, of course, changed, too. Some of the green vines that once engulfed the

Temporary Sign in Place of "Bryant's Grocery" Mississippi Freedom Trail Marker. Photo by Stephen A. King.

building have either been hacked away or gone dormant during the winter, further revealing the structure's continued deterioration as well as a sign deterring would-be trespassers with an ominous threat: "PRIVATE PROPERTY. No one allowed on property. Violators will be prosecuted." Presumably, the owners of the building and surrounding property want to keep visitors from venturing too close to the space where Emmett Till and Carolyn Bryant met so many years ago. Gazing at the building's ruins, it is easy to question whether civil rights tourism can realistically achieve social justice. If ever there was a metaphor for our collective, deliberate will to forget some aspects of our history and to actively discourage their memory, this place is clearly it. And yet that history is not forgotten.

Thanks to the efforts of local people and the state and federal government, memory persists. It persists in Sumner every time a visitor to the Emmett Till Interpretive Center reads "The Apology" aloud. It persists in Glendora at the Emmett Till Historic Intrepid Center when tourists gaze upon the recreation of Bryant's Grocery and Till's open casket. It persists in Jackson, where the actual front door of the Bryant's Grocery building sits on display in the MCRM. And, yes, it even persists here in Money. As we revisited Money during this final trip in 2021, two tourists in a car with North Carolina plates parked in front of the missing MFT marker. Both appeared to fit the profile of a civil rights tourist (white, Baby Boomers). Like others we encountered during our fieldwork, they briefly toured the grounds, took a few photos, and left, driving north on Money Road to their next destination. The white cyclist we met here five years ago, the man who rejected the constructive and healing properties of memory and denied Emmett Till's humanity, did *not* reappear. Soon, the "Bryant's Grocery" MFT marker will be repaired and reinstalled, allowing it to once again speak truth to terror. Faced with what has at times been deliberate and willful acts of forgetting, memory persists.

How memory persists, both in Mississippi and beyond, will shape our perceptions of the movement and civil rights tourism's transformative potential in the years to come. What forms will future memorialization efforts take? As always, cultural flashpoints abound. During the summer of 2021, Juneteenth became a federal holiday when President Joseph Biden signed the Juneteenth National Independence Day Act. Despite support from a bipartisan majority in Congress, Montana representative Matt Rosendale joined a handful of Republicans in the House who voted against the measure. "This legislation is the culmination of decades of efforts by the Left to prevent unashamed celebrations of our national story, heritage, and history," he tweeted.[77] Arguing that the new holiday would displace July 4th celebrations with "one that will inevitably focus on America's darkest moments," Rosendale articulated a position that mirrors what once was Mississippi's response to civil rights memory work, as well as that of the cyclist we spoke with in Money five years earlier: to cast aside, to ignore, to move on.[78] "America is good," Rosendale asserted, "and efforts to cast the country as otherwise should be opposed."[79] As Rosendale's public response to the Juneteenth legislation illustrates, there is still a deep desire by many in this country to forget anything from the past that might bring shame to those in the present.

Even as the perpetual *apologia* ritual at the Emmett Till Interpretive Center suggests that the wound left from Till's lynching may never fully close, "The Apology" achieves some measure of healing as it is repeated with each visit there. And perhaps the same is true for Money. The shell of the building that once housed Bryant's Grocery continues to crumble. And, at some point in the not-too-distant future, it will be reduced to little more than a pile of rubble on an overgrown lot. Even then, however, its affective power will be evidenced in the flow of tourists who will inevitably continue to travel there. Memory persists.

If there is anything to learn from Congressman Rosendale's missive, it is that the recalcitrance and racism that once prevented Mississippi from embracing its own movement history are not confined to the state's borders. Both are *pervasive* nationwide. In a broader national context, Mississippi's efforts to market its history in a way that is faithful to that past—however imperfect those efforts may be—can serve as an example for how to embrace truth telling in the spirit of social justice. And now, tourists who visit the Magnolia State will have the benefit of a broader infrastructure—museums, monuments, interpretive centers, roadside markers, and more—to learn about the Mississippi Movement, the racist system that tried (and failed) to thwart it, and, perhaps, how that movement continues, or *can* continue, to achieve social justice in the present.

NOTES

Preface

1. Isabel Wilkerson, *Caste: The Origins of Our Discontents* (New York: Random House, 2020), 24.

Introduction

1. Vanessa McCray, "Mississippi Town Feels the Weight of History," *The Blade*, February 19, 2017, https://www.toledoblade.com/Toledo-Magazine/2017/02/19/Weight-of-history-Crumbling-Mississippi-sites-were-the-backdrop-to-the-infamous-slaying-of-Emmett-Till.html.

2. Mississippi Tourism Association, *Mississippi Official Tour Guide*, 2020, 60.

3. Dave Tell, "Homesite of J. W. Milam: The Site of an Influential Fiction," *Emmett Till Memory Project*, n.d., accessed February 4, 2023, https://tillapp.emmett-till.org/items/show/15. For more on the birthplace myth, see also Dave Tell, *Remembering Emmett Till* (Chicago: University of Chicago Press, 2019), 121–60.

4. Tell, *Remembering Emmett Till*, 164–65.

5. Tell, *Remembering Emmett Till*, 174.

6. Tell, *Remembering Emmett Till*, 178.

7. Tell, *Remembering Emmett Till*, 164.

8. Tell, *Remembering Emmett Till*, 185.

9. Peter Holley, "An Emmett Till Historical Marker in Mississippi was Destroyed by Vandals—Again," *Washington Post*, June 26, 2017, https://www.washingtonpost.com/news/post-nation/wp/2017/06/26/an-emmett-till-historical-marker-in-mississippi-was-destroyed-by-vandals-again/.

10. "The Verdict at Sumner," *Jackson Daily News*, September 25, 1955, quoted in Davis W. Houck and Matthew A. Grindy, *Emmett Till and the Mississippi Press* (Jackson: University Press of Mississippi, 2008), 109.

11. David Zarefsky, "Four Senses of Rhetorical History," in *Doing Rhetorical History: Concepts and Cases*, ed. Kathleen J. Turner (Tuscaloosa: University of Alabama Press, 1998), 21.

12. Michael Calvin McGee, "Text, Context, and the Fragmentation of Contemporary Culture," *Western Journal of Speech Communication* 54, no. 3 (1990): 279, https://doi.org/10.1080/10570319009374343. For more on how McGee's notion of textual fragments has been used in public memory scholarship, see Roger C. Aden, Min Wha Han, Stephanie Norander, Michael E. Pfahl, Timothy P. Pollack, and Stephanie L. Young, "Re-Collection:

A Proposal for Refining the Study of Collective Memory and Its Places," *Communication Theory* 19, no. 3 (2009): 311–36, doi: 10.1111/j.1468-2885.2009.01345.x.

13. Bruce E. Gronbeck, "The Rhetorics of the Past: History, Argument, and Collective Memory," in *Doing Rhetorical History: Concepts and Cases*, ed. Kathleen J. Turner (Tuscaloosa: University of Alabama Press, 1998), 49.

14. Carole Blair, Greg Dickinson, and Brian L. Ott, "Introduction: Rhetoric/Memory/Place," in *Places of Public Memory: The Rhetoric of Museums and Memorials*, ed. Greg Dickinson, Carole Blair, and Brian L. Ott (Tuscaloosa: University of Alabama Press, 2010), 29.

15. Blair, Dickinson, and Ott, "Introduction: Rhetoric/Memory/Place," 29.

16. Kendall R. Phillips, introduction to *Framing Public Memory*, ed. Kendall R. Phillips (Tuscaloosa: University of Alabama Press, 2004), 7; Sara R. Kitsch, "Minting Public Memory: Substitution Logics and Gendered Commemoration in the First Spouse Coin," *Women's Studies in Communication* 40, no. 4 (2017): 420, https://doi.org/10.1080/07491409.2017.1373717.

17. Blair, Dickinson, and Ott, "Introduction: Rhetoric/Memory/Place," 6.

18. John Dittmer, telephone interview by Roger Davis Gatchet and Stephen A. King, June 16, 2021.

19. See, for example, Charles Reagan Wilson, ed., *The New Encyclopedia of Southern Culture*, vol. 4, *Myth, Manners, and Memory* (Chapel Hill: University of North Carolina Press, 2006). See individual chapters by George B. Tindall ("Mythic South"), Wayne Mixon ("New South Myth"), and Darden A. Pyron ("Plantation Myth").

20. Owen J. Dwyer and Derek H. Alderman, *Civil Rights Memorials and the Geography of Memory* (Chicago: Center for American Places at Columbia College Chicago, 2008), 48.

21. Owen J. Dwyer, "Interpreting the Civil Rights Movement: Place, Memory, and Conflict," *Professional Geographer* 52, no. 4 (2000): 662, doi: 10.1111/0033-0124.00255.

22. Dwyer and Alderman, *Civil Rights Memorials*, 8.

23. Owen J. Dwyer, "Interpreting the Civil Rights Movement: Contradiction, Confirmation, and the Cultural Landscape," in *The Civil Rights Movement in American Memory*, ed. Renee C. Romano and Leigh Raiford (Athens: University of Georgia Press, 2006), 6.

24. Glenn Eskew, "The Birmingham Civil Rights Institute and the New Ideology of Tolerance," in *The Civil Rights Movement in American Memory*, ed. Renee C. Romano and Leigh Raiford (Athens: University of Georgia Press, 2006), 33.

25. Dwyer and Alderman, *Civil Rights Memorials*, 8.

26. Glenn T. Eskew, "From Civil War to Civil Rights: Selling Alabama as Heritage Tourism," *International Journal of Hospitality and Tourism Administration* 2, no. 3–4 (2001): 205, https://doi.org/10.1300/J149v02n03_09.

27. Derek H. Alderman, "Street Names and the Scaling of Memory: The Politics of Commemorating Martin Luther King, Jr. within the African American Community," *Area* 35, no. 2 (2003): 163–73, https://doi.org/10.1111/1475-4762.00250.

28. Eskew, "From Civil War to Civil Rights," 209.

29. Edward P. Morgan, "The Good, the Bad, and the Forgotten: Media Culture and Public Memory of the Civil Rights Movement," in *The Civil Rights Movement in American Memory*, ed. Renee C. Romano and Leigh Raiford (Athens: University of Georgia Press, 2006), 141.

30. Morgan, "The Good, the Bad, and the Forgotten," 141.

31. "The Continuing Struggle for a National King Holiday," *Ebony*, January 1988, 28, 30.

32. "The Continuing Struggle," 30.

33. Derek H. Alderman, "Street Names as Memorial Arenas: The Reputational Politics of Commemorating Martin Luther King Jr. in a Georgia County," in *The Civil Rights Movement in American Memory*, ed. Renee C. Romano and Leigh Raiford (Athens: University of Georgia Press, 2006), 69.

34. Alderman, "Street Names and the Scaling of Memory," 164.

35. Bernard J. Armada, "Memorial Agon: An Interpretive Tour of the National Civil Rights Museum," *Southern Communication Journal* 63, no. 3 (1998): 237–38, http://dx.doi.org/10.1080/10417949809373096.

36. Michael Honey, "Doing Public History at the National Civil Rights Museum: A Conversation with Juanita Moore," *The Public Historian* 17, no. 1 (1995): 77, https://doi.org/10.2307/3378352.

37. Owen J. Dwyer, "Location, Politics, and the Production of Civil Rights Memorial Landscapes," *Urban Geography* 23, no. 1 (2002): 33–42, https://doi.org/10.2747/0272-3638.23.1.31.

38. Associated Press, "Black Tourism Power," *Marketing News*, June 22, 1998, 1.

39. Eskew, "From Civil War to Civil Rights," 202.

40. Eskew, "From Civil War to Civil Rights," 206.

41. Eskew, "From Civil War to Civil Rights," 205–8.

42. Shaila K. Dewan, "Civil Rights Battlegrounds Enter World of Tourism," *New York Times*, August 10, 2004, https://www.nytimes.com/2004/08/10/us/civil-rights-battlegrounds-enter-world-of-tourism.html?smid=url-share.

43. Sandhya Somashekhar, "Black History Becoming a Star Tourist Attraction," *Washington Post*, August 15, 2005, https://www.washingtonpost.com/wp-dyn/content/article/2005/08/14/AR2005081401031.html.

44. Jim Carrier, *A Traveler's Guide to the Civil Rights Movement* (Orlando: Harcourt, 2004); Charles E. Cobb Jr., *On the Road to Freedom: A Guided Tour of the Civil Rights Trail* (Chapel Hill: Algonquin, 2008); Townsend Davis, *Weary Feet, Rested Souls: A Guided History of the Civil Rights Movement* (New York: W. W. Norton, 1998); and Frye Gaillard, *Alabama's Civil Rights Trail: An Illustrated Guide to the Cradle of Freedom*, with Jennifer Lindsay and Jane DeNeefe (Tuscaloosa: University of Alabama Press, 2010).

45. Karen Fields, "What One Cannot Remember Mistakenly," in *History and Memory in African-American Culture*, ed. Geneviève Fabre and Robert O'Meally (New York: Oxford University Press, 1994), 150.

46. Robert O'Meally and Geneviève Fabre, Introduction to *History and Memory in African-American Culture*, ed. Geneviève Fabre and Robert O'Meally (New York: Oxford University Press, 1994), 5.

47. O'Meally and Fabre, Introduction to *History and Memory*, 7.

48. O'Meally and Fabre, Introduction to *History and Memory*, 11.

49. Patricia G. Davis, *Laying Claim: African American Cultural Memory and Southern Identity* (Tuscaloosa: University of Alabama Press, 2016), 7.

50. Davis, *Laying Claim*, 8.

51. Davis, *Laying Claim*, 17 (original emphasis).

52. Karlos K. Hill, *Beyond the Rope: The Impact of Lynching on Black Culture and Memory* (Cambridge: Cambridge University Press, 2016), 4, 5.

53. Hill, *Beyond the Rope*, 39.

54. Hill, *Beyond the Rope*, 58.

55. Leigh Raiford, *Imprisoned in a Luminous Glare: Photography and the African American Freedom Struggle* (Chapel Hill: University of North Carolina Press, 2011), 40.

56. Raiford, *Imprisoned in a Luminous Glare*, 88.

57. Hill, *Beyond the Rope*, 69–103.

58. Davis, *Laying Claim*, 72.

59. Susan Neiman, *Learning from the Germans: Race and the Memory of Evil* (New York: Farrar, Straus and Giroux, 2019), 210. Mississippi Department of Archives and History director, Katie Blount, emphasizes that the state never intervened in the construction or rhetorical framing of either museum's exhibit. The MDAH's interactions with the state legislature were limited to securing funding for the museums (see Katie Blount, Zoom interview by Roger Davis Gatchet and Stephen A. King, August 26, 2020). Neiman's conversations with Rachel Myers, now the Deputy Director of the MMH-MCRM, also reveal that "there wasn't much oversight" from the state, which "had too much to do to examine the content of the museum they'd demanded." See Neiman, *Learning from the Germans*, 209–10.

60. Leigh Raiford and Renee C. Romano, "Introduction: The Struggle Over Memory," in *The Civil Rights Movement in American Memory*, ed. Renee C. Romano and Leigh Raiford (Athens: University of Georgia Press, 2006), xii. Emphasis in original.

61. See, for example, Derek H. Alderman, "'History by the Spoonful' in North Carolina: The Textual Politics of State Highway Historical Markers," *Southeastern Geographer* 52, no. 4 (2012): 355–73, doi: 10.1353/sgo.2012.0035; Alderman, "Street Names and the Scaling of Memory"; Kevin Bruyneel, "The King's Body: The Martin Luther King Jr. Memorial and the Politics of Collective Memory," *History and Memory* 26, no. 1 (2014): 75–108, doi: 10.2979/histmemo.26.1.75; Dwyer, "Interpreting the Civil Rights Movement"; Dwyer and Alderman, *Civil Rights Memorials and the Geography of Memory*; Owen Dwyer, David Butler, and Perry Carter, "Commemorative Surrogation and the American South's Changing Heritage Landscape," *Tourism Geographies* 15, no. 3 (2013): 424–43, https://doi.org/10.1080/14616688.2012.699091; Jennifer Fuller, "Debating the Present through the Past: Representations of the Civil Rights Movement in the 1990s," in *The Civil Rights Movement in American Memory*, ed. Renee C. Romano and Leigh Raiford (Athens: University of Georgia Press, 2006), 167–96; Larry J. Griffin and Kenneth A. Bollen, "What Do These Memories Do?: Civil Rights Remembrance and Racial Attitudes," *American Sociological Review* 74, no. 4 (2009): 594–614, https://doi.org/10.1177%2F000312240907400405; Larry J. Griffin and Peggy G. Hargis, "Surveying Memory: The Past in Black and White," *Southern Literary Journal* 40, no. 2 (2008): 42–69, doi: 10.1353/slj.0.0017; Leigh Raiford, "Restaging Revolution: Black Power, *Vibe* Magazine, and Photographic Memory," in *The Civil Rights Movement in American Memory*, ed. Renee C. Romano and Leigh Raiford (Athens: University of Georgia Press, 2006), 220–49; and Renee Romano, "Moving beyond 'The Movement That Changed the World': Bringing the History of the Cold War into Civil Rights Museums," *Public Historian* 31, no. 2 (2009): 32–51, https://doi.org/10.1525/tph.2009.31.2.32.

62. Steve Estes, "Engendering Movement Memories: Remembering Race and Gender in the Mississippi Movement," in *The Civil Rights Movement in American Memory*, ed. Renee C. Romano and Leigh Raiford (Athens: University of Georgia Press, 2006), 307.

63. Dwyer, "Interpreting the Civil Rights Movement," 664.

64. Dwyer, "Interpreting the Civil Rights Movement," 667.

65. Dwyer, "Interpreting the Civil Rights Movement," 667.

66. For example, see Dwyer, "Location, Politics, and the Production of Civil Rights Memorial Landscapes," 43.

67. The three goals are generally reflective of the literature on civil rights tourism. See, for example, Eskew, "From Civil War to Civil Rights"; Ronald Loewe, "Civil Rights Tourism in Mississippi: Openings, Closures, Redemption and Remuneration," *Sociology Mind* 4, no. 1 (2014): 84–92, http://dx.doi.org/10.4236/sm.2014.41011; Dorit Wagner, "The American South: From Civil Rights Struggle to Civil Rights Tourism," *American Studies Journal*, 56 (2012), doi: 10.18422/56-05. For blues tourism goals, see Stephen A. King, *I'm Feeling the Blues Right Now: Blues Tourism and the Mississippi Delta* (Jackson: University Press of Mississippi, 2011).

68. "Civil Rights Music Commemoration," *Bolivar Bullet*, March 12, 2018.

69. Loewe, "Civil Rights Tourism in Mississippi," 87.

70. John E. Fleming, "Introduction," in *Telling Our Stories: Museum of Mississippi History and Mississippi Civil Rights Museum*, Mississippi Department of Archives and History (Jackson: University Press of Mississippi, 2017), 99.

71. Tell, *Remembering Emmett Till*, 195–239.

72. Mississippi Development Authority, "Mississippi Freedom Trail," *Visit Mississippi* (blog), accessed June 23, 2021, http://visitmississippi.org/mississippi-freedom-trail/.

73. Mississippi Development Authority, "Civil Rights," *Visit Mississippi*, accessed June 23, 2021, https://visitmississippi.org/things-to-do/point-of-interest/type/civil-rights/.

74. King, *I'm Feeling the Blues Right Now*, 9–11.

75. Patryk Labuda, "Racial Reconciliation in Mississippi: An Evaluation of the Proposal to Establish a Mississippi Truth and Reconciliation Commission," *Harvard Journal on Racial and Ethnic Justice* 27 (2011): 47.

76. Douglas A. Foster, "Reclaiming Reconciliation: The Corruption of 'Racial Reconciliation' and How It Might Be Reclaimed for Racial Justice and Unity," *Journal of Ecumenical Studies* 55, no. 1 (2020): 66, doi: 10.1353/ecu.2020.0015.

77. Ronald W. Walters, *The Price of Racial Reconciliation* (Ann Arbor: University of Michigan Press, 2008), 2.

78. Charles J. Ogletree and Austin Sarat, "Introduction: Bridging the Black-White Divide," in *Racial Reconciliation and the Healing of a Nation: Beyond Law and Rights*, ed. Charles J. Ogletree Jr. and Austin Sarat (New York: New York University Press, 2017), 3.

79. Mississippi Development Authority, *Fiscal Year 2021 Annual Report*, 2021, 17, https://mississippi.org/news/reports/; Mississippi Development Authority, *Fiscal Year 2020 Annual Report*, 2020, 8, https://mississippi.org/news/reports/; Mississippi Development Authority, *Fiscal Year 2019 Annual Report*, 2019, 12, https://mississippi.org/news/reports/.

80. Mississippi Development Authority, *Fiscal Year 2022 Annual Report*, 2022, 17, https://mississippi.org/news/reports/.

81. Mississippi Development Authority, *Mississippi Development Guide*, 2021, 14, https://mississippi.org/news/reports/.

82. King, *I'm Feeling the Blues Right Now*, 12.

83. King, *I'm Feeling the Blues Right Now*, 14.

84. Rickey Thigpen, interview by Roger Davis Gatchet and Stephen A. King, Jackson, Mississippi, May 21, 2019.

85. Davis, *Laying Claim*, 83.

86. Danielle Morgan, Zoom interview by Roger Davis Gatchet and Stephen A. King, November 12, 2020; Thigpen, interview.

87. Thigpen, interview.

88. Pamela Junior, interview by Roger Davis Gatchet and Stephen A. King, Jackson, Mississippi, May 24, 2019.

89. Mandala Research, *The African American Traveler, 2011 Edition: Final Report*, (Alexandria: Mandala Research, 2011), 10.

90. See Armada, "Memorial Agon"; Jason Edward Black, "Here Is a Strange and Bitter Crop: Emmett Till and the Rhetorical Complications of Treescape Memory," *Argumentation and Advocacy* 55, no. 1 (2019): 24–41, https://doi.org/10.1080/10511431.2018.1491769; Courtney E. Cole, "Commemorating Mass Violence: Truth Commission Hearings as a Genre of Public Memory," *Southern Communication Journal* 83, no. 3 (2018): 149–66, https://doi.org/10.1080/1041794X.2018.1432067; Greg Dickinson, Brian L. Ott, and Eric Aoki, "Spaces of Remembering and Forgetting: The Reverent Eye/I at the Plains Indian Museum," *Communication and Critical/Cultural Studies* 3, no. 1 (2006): 27–47, https://doi.org/10.1080/14791420500505619; Marouf Hasian Jr., "Remembering and Forgetting the 'Final Solution': A Rhetorical Pilgrimage through the U.S. Holocaust Memorial Museum," *Critical Studies in Media Communication* 21, no. 1 (2004): 64–92; https://doi.org/10.1080/0739318042000184352; J. David Maxson, "Second Line to Bury White Supremacy: Take 'Em Down Nola, Monument Removal, and Residual Memory," *Quarterly Journal of Speech* 106, no. 1 (2020): 48–71, https://doi.org/10.1080/00335630.2019.1704428; Nicholas S. Paliewicz and Marouf Hasian Jr., "Mourning Absences, Melancholic Commemoration, and the Contested Public Memories of the National September 11 Memorial and Museum," *Western Journal of Communication* 80, no. 2 (2016): 140–62, https://doi.org/10.1080/10570314.2015.1128559; Deborah Paredez, *Selenidad: Selena, Latinos, and the Performance of Memory* (Durham: Duke University Press, 2009); Carly S. Woods, Joshua P. Ewalt, and Sara J. Baker, "A Matter of Regionalism: Remembering Brandon Teena and Willa Cather at the Nebraska History Museum," *Quarterly Journal of Speech* 99, no. 3 (2013): 341–63, https://doi.org/10.1080/00335630.2013.806818.

91. Susan Neiman, *Learning from the Germans: Race and the Memory of Evil* (New York: Farrar, Straus and Giroux, 2019), 227–28.

92. Dave Tell, "Delta Inn: Did a Lawyer Steal a Sign?," *Emmett Till Memory Project*, n.d., accessed February 4, 2023, https://tillapp.emmett-till.org/items/show/16.

93. Dwight Conquergood, *Cultural Struggles: Performance, Ethnography, Praxis*, ed. E. Patrick Johnson (Ann Arbor: University of Michigan Press, 2013), 48, ProQuest Ebook Central.

94. Conquergood, *Cultural Struggles*. See also Sara L. McKinnon, Robert Asen, Karma R. Chávez, and Robert Glenn Howard, eds., *Text + Field: Innovations in Rhetorical Method* (University Park: Pennsylvania State University Press, 2016); Samantha Senda-Cook, Aaron Hess, Michael K. Middleton, and Danielle Endress, eds., *Readings in Rhetorical Fieldwork* (New York: Routledge, 2019).

95. Sherisoo, "Small, but Powerful, Displays Await," *Tripadvisor*, April 1, 2019, https://www.tripadvisor.com/Attraction_Review-g43833-d105886-Reviews-Smith_Robertson_Museum_and_Cultural_Center-Jackson_Mississippi.html.

96. Joshua P. Ewalt, Jessy J. Ohl, and Damien Smith Pfister, "Rhetorical Field Methods in the Tradition of *Imitatio*," in *Text + Field: Innovations in Rhetorical Method*, ed. Sara L. McKinnon, Robert Asen, Karma R. Chávez, and Robert Glenn Howard (University Park: Pennsylvania State University Press, 2016), 53.

97. Sara L. McKinnon, Robert Asen, Karma R. Chávez, and Robert Glenn Howard, "Introduction: Articulating Text and Field in the Nodes of Rhetorical Scholarship," in *Text + Field: Innovations in Rhetorical Method*, ed. Sara L. McKinnon, Robert Asen, Karma R. Chávez, and Robert Glenn Howard (University Park: Pennsylvania State University Press, 2016), 4.

98. John Van Maanen, *Tales of the Field: On Writing Ethnography* (Chicago: University of Chicago Press, 1988), 1.

99. Van Maanen, *Tales of the Field*, 4–5.

100. Thigpen, interview.

101. Jamie Landau, "Feeling Rhetorical Critics: Another Affective-Emotional Field Method for Rhetorical Studies," in *Text + Field: Innovations in Rhetorical Method*, ed. Sara L. McKinnon, Robert Asen, Karma R. Chávez, and Robert Glenn Howard (University Park: Pennsylvania State University Press, 2016), 74.

102. Jacqueline Jones Royster, "When the First Voice You Hear Is Not Your Own," *College Composition and Communication* 47, no. 1 (1996): 32.

103. Mississippi Tourism Association, *Mississippi Official Tour Guide*, 2021.

CHAPTER ONE. From Movement to Memory: A Rhetorical History of Civil Rights Tourism in Mississippi

1. Deborah D. Douglas, *U.S. Civil Rights Trail: A Traveler's Guide to the People, Places, and Events That Made the Movement* (Berkeley: Moon, 2021), 216.

2. Paul Hendrickson, "Mississippi Haunting," *Washington Post*, February 27, 2000, https://www.washingtonpost.com/archive/lifestyle/magazine/2000/02/27/mississippi-haunting/52da6813-c1c7-410f-b834-f01a7e20cad3/.

3. Mississippi Development Authority, "Music," n.d., accessed June 24, 2021, https://visitmississippi.org/things-to-do/point-of-interest/type/music/. See also Stephen A. King, *I'm Feeling the Blues Right Now: Blues Tourism and the Mississippi Delta* (Jackson: University Press of Mississippi, 2011), 78–91.

4. Douglas, *U.S. Civil Rights Trail*, vii, 227, 479. A fourth reference to the birthplace myth can be found in a fold-out map included with the book, where a historical timeline references Till's lynching, calling it "a catalyst for the modern civil rights movement."

5. Dorit Wagner, "The American South: From Civil Rights Struggle to Civil Rights Tourism," *American Studies Journal* 56 (2012), doi: 10.18422/56-05.

6. Dave Tell, *Remembering Emmett Till* (Chicago: University of Chicago Press, 2019), 121–60.

7. John Dittmer, *Local People: The Struggle for Civil Rights in Mississippi* (Urbana: University of Illinois Press, 1994), 57.

8. Dittmer, *Local People*, 423.

9. Nan Elizabeth Woodruff, *American Congo: The African American Freedom Struggle in the Delta* (Cambridge: Harvard University Press, 2003), 191.

10. James C. Cobb, *The Most Southern Place on Earth: The Mississippi Delta and the Roots of Regional Identity* (New York: Oxford University Press, 1992), 211.

11. Woodruff, *American Congo*, 192.

12. Dittmer, *Local People*, 19.

13. Michael Vinson Williams, "The Struggle for Black Citizenship: Medgar Wiley Evers and the Fight for Civil Rights in Mississippi," in *The Civil Rights Movement in Mississippi*, ed. Ted Ownby (Jackson: University Press of Mississippi, 2013), 63. Emphasis in original.

14. Glenda Elizabeth Gilmore, *Defying Dixie: The Radical Roots of Civil Rights, 1919–1950* (New York: W. W. Norton, 2008), 404.

15. Dernoral Davis, "When Youth Protest: The Mississippi Civil Rights Movement, 1955–1970," *Mississippi History Now*, August 2001, https://www.mshistorynow.mdah.ms.gov/articles/60/the-mississippi-civil-rights-movement-1955-1970-when-youth-protest.

16. Dittmer, *Local People*, 1–2.

17. Dennis J. Mitchell, *A New History of Mississippi* (Jackson: University Press of Mississippi, 2014), 396.

18. Mitchell, *A New History of Mississippi*, 396–97.

19. Françoise N. Hamlin, *Crossroads at Clarksdale: The Black Freedom Struggle in the Mississippi Delta after World War II* (Chapel Hill: University of North Carolina Press, 2012), 30.

20. Charles M. Payne, *I've Got the Light of Freedom: The Organizing Tradition and the Mississippi Freedom Struggle* (Berkeley: University of California Press, 1995), 31–32; Davis, "When Youth Protest."

21. David T. Beito and Linda Royster Beito, *T. R. M. Howard: Doctor, Entrepreneur, Civil Rights Pioneer* (Oakland, CA: Independent Institute, 2018), xix.

22. Davis, "When Youth Protest."

23. Davis, "When Youth Protest."

24. Payne, *I've Got the Light of Freedom*, 29.

25. Amzie Moore, interview by Michael Garvey, Cleveland, Mississippi, March 29 and April 13, 1977, transcript, University of Southern Mississippi Center for Oral History and Cultural Heritage, 5–10, https://usm.access.preservica.com/uncategorized/IO_24fe894d-6bfc-4c1e-a8d9-ac4a26046155/.

26. Moore, interview, 6.

27. Moore, interview, 11.

28. Quoted in C. Gerald Fraser, "Amzie Moore, 1960's Leader for Voting Registration, Dies," *New York Times*, February 7, 1982, https://nyti.ms/2P6pcDg.

29. Charles McLaurin, phone interview by Roger Davis Gatchet and Stephen A. King, December 4, 2021.

30. Payne, *I've Got the Light of Freedom*, 33; Hamlin, *Crossroads at Clarksdale*, 16.

31. Laura Visser-Maessen, *Robert Parris Moses: A Life in Civil Rights and Leadership at the Grassroots* (Chapel Hill: University of North Carolina Press, 2016), 3, 4.

32. Visser-Maessen, *Robert Parris Moses*, 1.

33. Hamlin, *Crossroads at Clarksdale*, 16.

34. Hodding Carter III, "Citadel of the Citizens Council," *New York Times Magazine*, November 12, 1961, 23.

35. The Citizens' Council, "Birth of an Idea," n.d., Walter Sillers Jr. Papers (Box 133), Delta State University Archives and Museums, Cleveland, Mississippi.

36. Dittmer, *Local People*, 102–3; Payne, *I've Got the Light of Freedom*, 105–6, 111–12.

37. Moore, interview, 32–36, 27–28.

38. Moore, interview, 46.

39. Moore, interview, 6–7.

40. Payne, *I've Got the Light of Freedom*, 47.

41. Michael Vinson Williams, *Medgar Evers: Mississippi Martyr* (Fayetteville: University of Arkansas Press, 2011), 14.

42. Myrlie Evers, interview by Orlando Bagwell, November 27, 1985, transcript, Washington University in St. Louis, 1, http://repository.wustl.edu/concern/videos/gq67jt04b.

43. Evers, interview, 3–4.

44. Williams, *Medgar Evers*, 28.

45. Williams, *Medgar Evers*, 33, 37.

46. Evers, interview, 6.

47. Dittmer, *Local People*, 49.

48. Dittmer, *Local People*, 49.

49. Dittmer, *Local People*, 49; Jim Carrier, *A Traveler's Guide to the Civil Rights Movement* (Orlando: Harcourt, 2004), 275.

50. Myrlie Evers with William Peters, *For Us, the Living* (Garden City, NY: Doubleday, 1967), 5.

51. Janet Dewart Bell, *Lighting the Fires of Freedom: African American Women in the Civil Rights Movement* (New York: New Press, 2018), 197–98.

52. Dittmer, *Local People*, 120.

53. Stephanie R. Rolph, *Resisting Equality: The Citizens' Council, 1954–1989* (Baton Rouge: Louisiana State University Press, 2018), 94.

54. Dernoral Davis, "Medgar Evers and the Origin of the Civil Rights Movement in Mississippi," *Mississippi History Now*, October 2003, https://www.mshistorynow.mdah.ms.gov/issue/medgar-evers-and-the-origin-of-the-civil-rights-movement-in-mississippi.

55. Evers, interview, 26–27.

56. Evers with William Peters, *For Us, the Living*, 374.

57. Bell, *Lighting the Fires of Freedom*, 194.

58. Bell, *Lighting the Fires of Freedom*, 194.

59. Davis, "When Youth Protest."

60. Cobb, *The Most Southern Place on Earth*, 232.

61. Wesley Hogan, "Grassroots Organizing in Mississippi that Changed National Politics," in *The Civil Rights Movement in Mississippi*, ed. Ted Ownby (Jackson: University Press of Mississippi, 2013), 8.

62. Council of Federated Organizations, "What Is COFO?," Ed King Collection, Box 2 (Folder 6), Department of Archives and Special Collections, University of Mississippi, Oxford, Mississippi, 1.

63. Dittmer, *Local People*, 89.

64. Cobb, *The Most Southern Place on Earth*, 231.

65. Payne, *I've Got the Light of Freedom*, 107.

66. "T. W. A. K. Confederate Mother's Day—1961," n.d., Ku Klux Klan Collection, Box 1 (Folder 6), Department of Archives and Special Collections, University of Mississippi, Oxford, Mississippi, n.p.

67. Hezekiah Watkins, Zoom interview by Roger Davis Gatchet and Stephen A. King, January 12, 2021.

68. Watkins, Zoom interview.

69. Helen Singleton, interview, November 8, 2001, transcript, Freedom Riders 40th Anniversary Oral History Project, Department of Archives and Special Collections, University of Mississippi, Oxford, Mississippi, 1.

70. Singleton, interview, 3.

71. "Parchman Penitentiary" was intended to be the second roadside marker on the Mississippi Freedom Trail. The marker was nowhere to be found outside the prison grounds when the authors visited the site in July 2016. For a time after that, the marker was listed as being "under repair" on the MDA's Visit Mississippi website, but all references to it have since been removed. Another marker located near the prison's main entrance, "Parchman Farm Blues," is part of the Mississippi Blues Trail. One state employee we spoke with speculated the MFT marker may actually be located within the prison grounds, but another later confirmed it was never installed.

72. Tiyi M. Morris, *Womanpower Unlimited and the Black Freedom Struggle in Mississippi* (Athens: University of Georgia Press, 2015), 20.

73. Aram Goudsouzian, *Down to the Crossroads: Civil Rights, Black Power, and the Meredith March Against Fear* (New York: Farrar, Straus and Giroux, 2014), 13.

74. Mitchell, *A New History of Mississippi*, 450.

75. Dittmer, *Local People*, 201.

76. Dittmer, *Local People*, 201–5.

77. Jon N. Hale, *The Freedom Schools: Student Activists in the Mississippi Civil Rights Movement* (New York: Columbia University Press, 2016), 5. See also Dittmer, *Local People*, 258–59.

78. "Prospectus for the Mississippi Freedom Summer," Spring 1964, Ed King Collection (Mississippi Freedom Project), Box 2 (Folder 6), Archives and Special Collections, University of Mississippi, Oxford, Mississippi, 1.

79. Davis, "When Youth Protest."

80. Dittmer, *Local People*, 251.

81. Dittmer, *Local People*, 247.

82. Quoted in Dudley Lehew, "CR Workers React after Finding of Three Bodies," *Jackson Daily News*, August 1964, Ed King Collection (Mississippi Freedom Project), Box 2 (Folder 6), Archives and Special Collections, University of Mississippi, Oxford, Mississippi, n.p.

83. Mitchell, *A New History of Mississippi*, 454–55.

84. Dittmer, *Local People*, 271.

85. Dittmer, *Local People*, 285.

86. Fannie Lou Hamer, "Testimony before the Credentials Committee, Democratic National Convention," August 22, 1964, *American Rhetoric*, https://www.americanrhetoric.com/speeches/fannielouhamercredentialscommittee.htm; Chris Myers Asch, *The Senator and the Sharecropper: The Freedom Struggles of James O. Eastland and Fannie Lou Hamer* (Chapel Hill: University of North Carolina Press, 2008), 210–13.

87. Dittmer, *Local People*, 392.

88. Goudsouzian, *Down to the Crossroads*, 246.

89. Peniel E. Joseph, *Waiting 'Til the Midnight Hour: A Narrative History of Black Power in America* (New York: Henry Holt, 2006), 28, 53.

90. Dittmer, *Local People*, 423.

91. Hamlin, *Crossroads at Clarksdale*, 262.

92. Kevin Sack, "Mississippi Reveals Dark Secrets of a Racist Time," *New York Times*, March 18, 1998, http://www.nytimes.com/1998/03/18/us/mississippi-reveals-dark-secrets-of-a-racist-time.html. As Sarah Rowe-Sims notes, several years passed before the Sovereignty Commission was finally disbanded: "Although the commission ceased to function in 1973,

the agency was not officially dissolved until 1977. In January 1977, Mississippi legislators introduced bills to abolish the commission and dispose of its records and equipment. After much heated debate, the legislature approved an act which abolished the commission and authorized its records be sealed at the Mississippi Department of Archives and History until July 1, 2027." See Sarah Rowe-Sims, "The Mississippi State Sovereignty Commission: An Agency History," *Mississippi History Now*, September 2002, https://mshistorynow.mdah.ms .gov/issue/mississippi-sovereignty-commission-an-agency-history. The MFT "Parchman Penitentiary" marker briefly mentions the Mississippi State Sovereignty Commission; however, as noted earlier, this marker is not available for public viewing.

93. Mitchell, *A New History of Mississippi*, 468–70; Stephen A. Berrey, *The Jim Crow Routine: Everyday Performances of Race, Civil Rights, and Segregation in Mississippi* (Chapel Hill: University of North Carolina Press, 2015), 142–44.

94. Dittmer, *Local People*, 429, 430.

95. Payne, *I've Got the Light of Freedom*, 410–11.

96. Burt Buchanan, "Magnolias and Manufacturing: Southern Imagery in Mississippi's Promotional Publications, 1945–1955," in *Mediated Images of the South: The Portrayal of Dixie in Popular Culture*, ed. Alison F. Slade, Dedria Givens-Carroll, and Amber J. Narro (Lanham, MD: Lexington Books, 2012), 90. For a detailed historical study of the BAWI program, see James C. Cobb, *The Selling of the South: The Southern Crusade for Industrial Development, 1936–1990*, 2nd ed. (Urbana: University of Illinois Press, 1993).

97. Buchanan, "Magnolias and Manufacturing," 90.

98. Buchanan, "Magnolias and Manufacturing," 90.

99. Mississippi Advertising Commission, "For the First Time, a Great State Offers Planned Cooperation to Industry," advertisement, Series 552, 1937, Mississippi Department of Archives and History, Jackson, Mississippi, https://da.mdah.ms.gov/series/sac/552/detail/190658.

100. "In Mississippi It's a Real . . . Thanksgiving," advertisement, Series 552, 1936, Mississippi Department of Archives and History, Jackson, Mississippi, https://da.mdah.ms.gov/series /sac/552/detail/190652.

101. Buchanan, "Magnolias and Manufacturing," 92.

102. Mississippi State Board of Development, *Mississippi Tourist Guide 1941*, 1941, Mississippi Department of Archives and History, Jackson, Mississippi, 7, 41, 60.

103. Ted Ownby, "Nobody Knows the Troubles I've Seen, but Does Anybody Want to Hear about Them When They're on Vacation?," in *Southern Journeys: Tourism, History, and Culture in the Modern South*, ed. Richard D. Starnes (Tuscaloosa: University of Alabama Press, 2003), 245–46.

104. Tourism and Public Affairs Department, Mississippi Agricultural and Industrial Board, *Mississippi: Your Guide to Travel*, n.d., ca. 1975. The Mississippi Department of Archives and History chronicles a total of twenty-one indigenous tribes that lived on the land which would eventually become part of the territory of Mississippi between 1500 and 1800. The Mississippi Territory was created in 1798, and Mississippi became a state in 1817. The Choctaw, Chickasaw, and Natchez were some of the region's most prominent indigenous peoples. The authors acknowledge the lands of these nations and groups, both past and present, where we conducted fieldwork for this book. See Mississippi Department of Archives and History, "Mississippi Archeology Trails: Indian Tribes of Mississippi," accessed February 14, 2022, http://trails.mdah.ms.gov/education/tribes.htm. For a history of the Mississippi Territories, see Mitchell, *A New History of Mississippi*, 50–81. Another state cultural heritage

trail, the Mississippi Mound Trail, features a total of thirty-three markers located in Mississippi. See Mississippi Department of Archives and History, "Mississippi Mound Trail," n.d., accessed March 6, 2022, http://trails.mdah.ms.gov/mmt/index.html.

105. Tourism and Public Affairs Department, *Mississippi*, 35.

106. Sylvia Higginbotham and Lisa Monti, *The Insiders' Guide to Mississippi* (Manteo, NC: The Insiders' Guides, 1994), v.

107. Higginbotham and Monti, *The Insiders' Guide to Mississippi*, v.

108. Katie Blount, Zoom interview by Roger Davis Gatchet and Stephen A. King, August 26, 2020.

109. Blount, Zoom interview.

110. Blount, Zoom interview.

111. Amanda Lyons, "Giving Shape and Substance to Our Society: William F. Winter, Leadership, and the Mississippi Department of Archives and History," *Southern Quarterly* 54, no. 1 (2016): 130; William E. Schmidt, "Mississippi Collects Memories of Rights Struggle in a Museum," *New York Times*, December 7, 1984.

112. Blount, Zoom interview.

113. Neil R. McMillen, "Reconstruction and Its Aftermath: Mississippi History, 1865–1890," *Journal of American History* 77, no. 1 (1990): 240, https://doi.org/10.2307/2078658.

114. "Patti Carr Black," Mississippi Writers and Musicians, accessed June 18, 2021, https://www.mswritersandmusicians.com/mississippi-writers/patti-carr-black.

115. Center for the Study of Southern Culture, "About," n.d., accessed February 5, 2023, https://southernstudies.olemiss.edu/about/. The center's mission is to "investigate, document, interpret, and teach about the American South." In 2019, the center articulated a new "aspirational" vision statement that includes the following sentence relevant to civil rights and racial reconciliation: "The Center's curriculum teaches about a new South, *honestly confronts troubling histories*, and attracts innovative leaders and thinkers for faculty, staff, and student positions" (emphasis added). See Center for the Study of Southern Culture, "Vision Statement for Spring 2029," n.d., accessed June 18, 2021, https://southernstudies.olemiss.edu/media/CSSC-Vision-2029-finalPDF.pdf.

116. King, *I'm Feeling the Blues Right Now*, 60.

117. Blount, Zoom interview.

118. *Ole Miss Plans Commemoration of Meredith's 25th Anniversary*, September 24, 1987, Civil Rights Commemoration Initiative Collection, Box 1 (Folder 4), Department of Archives and Special Collections, University of Mississippi, Oxford, Mississippi, n.p.; *Integration Commemoration Continues with Programs on Oct. 9, Oct. 12*, September 30, 1987, Civil Rights Commemoration Initiative Collection, Box 1 (Folder 4), Department of Archives and Special Collections, University of Mississippi, Oxford, Mississippi, n.p.

119. Nash Molpus, "Civil Rights Memorial Design Selected," *The Southern Register*, Fall 2002, 1.

120. Molpus, "Civil Rights Memorial Design Selected," 4.

121. Ronald Bailey, *Remembering Medgar Evers . . . for a New Generation* (Oxford: Heritage Publications, 1988), Franklin E. Moak Collection, Series 2, Subseries 8, Department of Archives and Special Collections, University of Mississippi, Oxford, Mississippi, 20.

122. Mississippi Department of Economic and Community Development, *African-American Heritage Guide*, ca. 1990, Department of Archives and Special Collections, University of Mississippi, Oxford, Mississippi, 1.

123. Mississippi Department of Economic and Community Development, *African-American Heritage Guide*, 1.

124. Rickey Thigpen, interview by Roger Davis Gatchet and Stephen A. King, Jackson, Mississippi, May 21, 2019.

125. Quoted in "Statue of Medgar Evers Unveiled in Jackson, Ms.," *Jet*, July 20, 1992, 6.

126. Wayne F. Timmer and Anne Marie Decker, "Medgar Evers Home Renovation," 1995. Mississippi Department of Archives and History, Jackson, Mississippi, n.p.

127. Claire Whitlinger, *Between Remembrance and Repair: Commemorating Racial Violence in Philadelphia, Mississippi* (Chapel Hill: University of North Carolina Press, 2020), 47–49. Despite Philadelphia's moral awakening, white resentment and backlash ensued after the first commentative event. According to Whitlinger, "when employees of the local newspaper arrived at work the day after the commemoration, they were confronted by an ominous message. The white columns flanking the entry to their downtown office had been defaced with red spray paint spelling 'K-K-K,' the lettering large and hurried." Within seventy-two hours after the event, Dick Molpus, Mississippi's then secretary of state who helped organize the event, "received twenty-six death threats" (48).

128. Whitlinger, *Between Remembrance and Repair*, 60.

129. Ronald Loewe, "Civil Rights Tourism in Mississippi: Openings, Closures, Redemption and Remuneration," *Sociology Mind* 4, no. 1 (2014): 85.

130. Whitlinger, *Between Remembrance and Repair*, 36.

131. Helen Sims, performance, Belzoni, Mississippi, July 18, 2016.

132. *Aaron E. Henry Federal Building and United States Post Office*, HR 1279, 106th Cong., 2d sess., *Congressional Record* 146, no. 36, daily ed. (March 28, 2000): H1428–30, https://www.congress.gov/106/crec/2000/03/28/CREC-2000-03-28.pdf.

133. Minion K. C. Morrison, *Aaron Henry of Mississippi: Inside Agitator* (Fayetteville: University of Arkansas Press, 2015), 19, 32, 37.

134. Morrison, *Aaron Henry of Mississippi*, 42–43, 123.

135. Morrison, *Aaron Henry of Mississippi*, 61–64.

136. Carrier, *A Traveler's Guide*, 257–58.

137. King, *I'm Feeling the Blues Right Now*, 76–77.

138. King, *I'm Feeling the Blues Right Now*, 145.

139. Mississippi Delta National Heritage Area, "Our Mission, Vision, and Goals," accessed February 5, 2023, https://www.msdeltaheritage.com/mission-vision-goals.

140. Quoted in "Delta Center Director Receives Service Award," Delta State University, June 13, 2014, https://www.deltastate.edu/news-and-events/2014/06/delta-center-director-receives-service-award/.

141. Rolando Herts, Zoom interview by Roger Davis Gatchet and Stephen A. King, November 12, 2021.

142. Mississippi Development Authority, *Fiscal Year 2021 Annual Report*, 2021, 16, https://mississippi.org/news/reports/.

143. Jerry Mitchell, "Civil Rights Landmarks Disappearing from Landscape," *Clarion-Ledger*, June 23, 2014, https://www.clarionledger.com/story/opinion/2014/06/23/civil-rights-landmarks-disappearing-landscape/11270899/.

144. Quoted in Mitchell, "Civil Rights Landmarks Disappearing from Landscape."

CHAPTER TWO. Breaking Ground: Vernacular Efforts in Mississippi Civil Rights Tourism

1. Rolando Herts, Zoom interview by Roger Davis Gatchet and Stephen A. King, November 12, 2021.

2. Mississippi Delta National Heritage Area, "Civil Rights Sites of the Mississippi Delta and the National Parks Service's African American Civil Rights Grant Program," October 27, 2021, webinar, 1:25:40, https://www.msdeltaheritage.com/civil-rights.

3. Maja Mikula, "Vernacular Museum: Communal Bonding and Ritual Memory Transfer among Displaced Communities," *International Journal of Heritage Studies* 21, no. 8 (2015): 757–58, 768–70, https://doi.org/10.1080/13527258.2015.1020961.

4. Patricia G. Davis, *Laying Claim: African American Cultural Memory and Southern Identity* (Tuscaloosa: University of Alabama Press, 2016), 100.

5. Bernard J. Armada, "Memorial Agon: An Interpretive Tour of the National Civil Rights Museum," *Southern Communication Journal* 63, no. 3 (1998): 237, http://dx.doi.org/10.1080/10417949809373096.

6. Karen De Bres, "Defining Vernacular Tourism," *Annals of Tourism Research* 23, no. 4 (1996): 945–47, https://doi.org/10.1016/0160-7383(96)00024-2.

7. John M. Sloop and Kent A. Ono, "Out-law Discourse: The Critical Politics of Material Judgment," *Philosophy and Rhetoric* 30, no. 1 (1997): 51.

8. Sarah Hagedorn VanSlette and Josh Boyd, "Lawbreaking Jokers: Tricksters Using Outlaw Discourse," *Communication Quarterly* 59, no. 5 (2011): 592, https://doi.org/10.1080/01463373.2011.614214.

9. Helen Sims, oral performance, Belzoni, Mississippi, July 18, 2016.

10. John Dittmer, *Local People: The Struggle for Civil Rights in Mississippi* (Urbana: University of Illinois Press, 1994), 187.

11. Glen Cotton, telephone interview by Roger Davis Gatchet and Stephen A. King, August 28, 2020.

12. Cotton, telephone interview.

13. Congress of Racial Equality, "In Perspective: A Story of Mississippi Heroism," n.d., ca. 1964, Micro 793 (Reel 2, Segment 35), Freedom Summer Digital Collection, Wisconsin Historical Society, https://content.wisconsinhistory.org/digital/collection/p15932coll2/id/41985.

14. Nell Luter Floyd, "It Is in Their Honor," *Clarion-Ledger*, February 23, 2017, https://www.clarionledger.com/story/news/local/madison/2017/02/23/honor/98332202/.

15. Cotton, telephone interview.

16. Cotton, telephone interview.

17. "CORE Office Is Shaken by Blast in Canton, Miss.," *New York Times*, June 9, 1964, https://nyti.ms/2TGIbM2; James P. Marshall, *Student Activism and Civil Rights in Mississippi: Protest Politics and the Struggle for Racial Justice, 1960–1965* (Baton Rouge: Louisiana State University Press, 2013), 108.

18. Cotton, telephone interview.

19. Cotton, telephone interview.

20. Barbara Blackmon sponsored bills in the state senate in 2016 and 2017 that would have issued a $2,000,000 bond for the museum. Similarly, Edward Blackmon Jr., sponsored bills in the state house for bonds ranging from $500,000 to $2,000,000 every year between

2016 and 2020. None of these proposed bills made it out of committee. He renewed his efforts with another sponsored bill in the 2023 session that is currently in committee, as of this writing.

21. Cotton, telephone interview.
22. Cotton, telephone interview.
23. Cotton, telephone interview.
24. Michael Jones, Google Review of Canton Freedom House, 2021, https://g.co/kgs/SAqi3K.
25. Cotton, telephone interview.
26. Dittmer, *Local People*, 53; Charles M. Payne, *I've Got the Light of Freedom: The Organizing Tradition and the Mississippi Freedom Struggle* (Berkeley: University of California Press, 1995), 36–37.
27. "The Reverend George Lee" MFT marker is the eleventh marker in the series and is located at the intersection of Church Street and First Street in Belzoni. The marker is located adjacent to Green Grove Baptist Church where Lee's funeral was held. After Lee's brutal murder, Courts continued his civil rights activities until he, too, was shot. He recovered from his wounds and left Mississippi for Chicago. He died in 1969. After nearly seventy years, Lee's murder is still a cold case.
28. Sims, oral performance.
29. Helen Sims, interview by Paul Ortiz, September 20, 2012, MFP-110, transcript, Samuel Proctor Oral History Program, University of Florida, 10–11, https://ufdc.ufl.edu/AA00021048/00001.
30. Sims, interview, 1.
31. "The Mississippi Heritage Consortium," n.d., accessed January 8, 2022, http://www.thefannielouhamercivilrightsmuseum.com/the-mississippi-heritage-consortium.html.
32. "Heritage Village," n.d., accessed June 24, 2021, http://www.thereverandgeorgeleemuseumsofafricanamericanhistoryandheritage.com/heritage-village.html.
33. "The Re-Enactment Society," n.d., accessed June 24, 2021, http://www.thefannielouhamercivilrightsmuseum.com/the-re-enactment-society.html; "The Mississippi Lynch and Civil Rights Memorial Project Inc.," n.d., accessed June 24, 2021, http://www.thefannielouhamercivilrightsmuseum.com/the-mississippi-lynch-and-civil-rights-memorial-project-inc.html.
34. Sims, interview, 17.
35. Sims, oral performance.
36. James C. Scott, *Domination and the Arts of Resistance: Hidden Transcripts* (New Haven: Yale University Press, 1990), 19.
37. Ken Hudson, Google Review of Fannie Lou Hamer Civil Rights Museum, 2018, https://goo.gl/maps/Um7WKfJ5uL8HxoiG8.
38. L. C. Dorsey, "A Prophet Who Believed," *Sojourners*, December 1982, Box 1 (Folder 8), Ed King Collection, Department of Archives and Special Collections, University of Mississippi, Oxford, Mississippi.
39. Kay Mills, *This Little Light of Mine: The Life of Fannie Lou Hamer* (Lexington: University Press of Kentucky, 2007), 7.
40. Maegan Parker Brooks, "Oppositional Ethos: Fannie Lou Hamer and the Vernacular Persona," *Rhetoric and Public Affairs* 14, no. 3 (2011): 521, doi: 10.1353/rap.2011.0024.
41. Chris Myers Asch, *The Senator and the Sharecropper: The Freedom Struggles of James O. Eastland and Fannie Lou Hamer* (Chapel Hill: University of North Carolina Press, 2008), 176.

42. *Fannie Lou Hamer: Courage and Faith*, produced by Linda L. Coles, aired February 20, 2006, Mississippi Public Broadcasting.

43. Mississippi Freedom Democratic Party, "By Laws of the Mississippi Freedom Democratic Party," March 12, 1969, 1, Box 2 (Folder 3), Fannie Lou Hamer Collection, Department of Archives and Special Collections, University of Mississippi, Oxford, Mississippi.

44. "The Mississippi Freedom Democratic Party," n.d., Box 2 (Folder 3), Fannie Lou Hamer Collection, Department of Archives and Special Collections, University of Mississippi, Oxford, Mississippi, 2.

45. WGBH-TV, "Charles McLaurin: 'The Foot Soldier,'" *American Experience*, n.d., accessed March 17, 2022, video, 7:48, https://www.pbs.org/wgbh/americanexperience/features/freedomsummer-at50-charles-mclaurin-foot-soldier/.

46. Mills, *This Little Light of Mine*, 38–39.

47. Mills, *This Little Light of Mine*, 57–58.

48. Asch, *The Senator and the Sharecropper*, 194.

49. Maegan Parker Brooks, *A Voice That Could Stir an Army: Fannie Lou Hamer and the Rhetoric of the Black Freedom Movement* (Jackson: University Press of Mississippi, 2014), 59.

50. Brooks, "Oppositional Ethos," 530–31.

51. Asch, *The Senator and the Sharecropper*, 209, 214.

52. Asch, *The Senator and the Sharecropper*, 255.

53. Mills, *This Little Light of Mine*, 308.

54. Brooks, *A Voice That Could Stir an Army*, 11.

55. Van Arnold, "Fannie Lou Hamer Cancer Foundation to Host Groundbreaking for State-of-the-Art Headquarters in Ruleville Oct. 31," University of Southern Mississippi, October 22, 2019, https://www.usm.edu/news/2019/release/fannie-lou-hamer-cancer-foundation-opening-headquarters.php; "Fannie Lou Hamer Cancer Foundation to Get New Site," *The Mississippi Link*, May 23–29, 2013, 10, https://themississippilink.com/wp-content/uploads/2012/01/May-23-2013.pdf.

56. Brooks, *A Voice That Could Stir an Army*, 11.

57. Asch, *The Senator and the Sharecropper*, 291.

58. "Head Start Timeline," *Head Start/ECLKC*, last updated February 16, 2019, https://eclkc.ohs.acf.hhs.gov/about-us/article/head-start-timeline.

59. Hattie Jordan, interview by Sarah Blanc and Khama Weatherspoon, September 24, 2010, MFP-060, transcript, Samuel Proctor Oral History Program, University of Florida, 1, https://ufdc.ufl.edu/AA00020253/00001.

60. Kaitara Baker, *Courage to Lead*, Vimeo, June 20, 2018, video, 4:27, https://vimeo.com/275965279.

61. Jordan, interview, 1–2.

62. Jordan, interview, 17.

63. Jordan, interview, 2.

64. Jordan, interview, 3–4.

65. Maegan Parker Brooks, *Fannie Lou Hamer: America's Freedom Fighting Woman* (Lanham, MD: Rowman and Littlefield, 2020), 188.

66. Baker, *Courage to Lead*.

67. A Facebook page for the FLH Memorial Garden and Museum Foundation suggests that this organization played a central role in raising funds to create the Ruleville museum

and renovate the Memorial Garden, but historical details are sparse, and the page has been largely inactive since 2019. See https://www.facebook.com/FLHfoundation.

68. Brooks, *A Voice*, 239.

69. "Fannie Lou Hamer Park and Multi-Purpose Complex, Ruleville, MS," Fannie Lou Hamer's America, n.d., accessed March 17, 2022, https://www.fannielouhamersamerica.com/driving-tour/fannie-lou-hamer-memorial-center.

70. Stephen A. King, "People Get Ready: The Civil Rights Movement, Protest Music, and the Rhetoric of Resistance," in *Social Controversy and Public Address in the 1960s and Early 1970s: A Rhetorical History of the United States*, vol. 9, ed. Richard J. Jensen (East Lansing: Michigan State University Press, 2017), 273.

71. Charles McLaurin, telephone interview by Roger Davis Gatchet and Stephen A. King, December 4, 2021.

72. Roger Davis Gatchet and Stephen A. King, "'I Call Him Father of Us All': Vicarious Transcendence at the B. B. King Museum and Delta Interpretive Center," *Communication and Critical/Cultural Studies* 15, no. 1 (2018): 53–69, https://doi.org/10.1080/14791420.2018.1434315.

73. McLaurin, telephone interview.

74. McLaurin, telephone interview.

75. Charles McLaurin, interview by Emilye Crosby, December 5, 2016, AFC 2010/039: CRHP0121, transcript, Southern Oral History Program, National Museum of African American History and Culture, 96, https://tile.loc.gov/storage-services/service/afc/afc2010039/afc2010039_crhp0121/afc2010039_crhp0121_ms01.pdf.

76. Brooks, *Fannie Lou Hamer*, 185.

77. McLaurin, telephone interview.

78. McLaurin, interview by Emilye Crosby, 99.

79. Brooks, *Fannie Lou Hamer*, 185.

80. McLaurin, interview by Emilye Crosby, 99.

81. Brooks, *Fannie Lou Hamer*, 186.

82. Brooks, *Fannie Lou Hamer*, 186.

83. McLaurin, telephone interview.

84. Brooks, *Fannie Lou Hamer*, 186; see also 187–88.

85. ROAR Foundation, "Repaying Our Ancestors Respectfully," April 2006, last updated October 2010, http://www.fannielouhamer.info/roar.html. See also McLaurin, interview by Emilye Crosby, 99.

86. ROAR Foundation, "Repaying Our Ancestors Respectfully."

87. ROAR Foundation, "Fannie Lou Hamer Statue Donors," last updated September 16, 2012, http://www.fannielouhamer.info/donors.html.

88. McLaurin, telephone interview.

89. Brooks, *Fannie Lou Hamer*, 190; ROAR Foundation, "Fannie Lou Hamer Statue Drive," March 2009, last updated April 2012, http://www.fannielouhamer.info/hamer_statue.html.

90. Hattie Jordan, interview by Sarah Blanc and Khama Weatherspoon, 5.

91. Mr. Kinetik, Google Review of Fannie Lou Hamer Memorial Garden, 2019, https://g.co/kgs/Ro85jT.

92. Fannie Lou Hamer Statue Committee, "Fannie Lou Hamer Statue Unveiling Set for October 5, 2012," news release, August 20, 2012, https://www.crmvet.org/anc/1210flh.pdf.

93. Mills, *This Little Light of Mine*, n.p.

94. McLaurin, telephone interview.

95. Brooks, *Fannie Lou Hamer*, 192 (original emphasis).

96. Gerard Edic, "Marker Honors Hamer," *Greenwood Commonwealth*, October 7, 2020, https://www.gwcommonwealth.com/news-top-stories/marker-honors-hamer#sthash.H1SzMxPI.dpbs.

97. McLaurin, telephone interview.

98. Sims, interview, 11–12.

99. "MHC Awards Over $450,000 to Help Mississippi Cultural Organizations Recover from COVID," Mississippi Humanities Council, September 1, 2021, http://mshumanities.org/mhc-awards-over-450000-to-help-mississippi-cultural-organizations-recover-from-covid/.

100. Lici Beveridge, "This Mississippi Museum Received a Grant for $50,000. Find Out Why," *Clarion-Ledger*, January 11, 2022, https://www.clarionledger.com/story/news/local/2022/01/11/fannie-lou-hamer-museum-awarded-grant-southern-poverty-law-center/9162050002/.

101. Cotton, telephone interview.

CHAPTER THREE. Remembering the Lynching of Emmett Till: From Experiential to "Dark" Tourism

1. Carole Blair, Greg Dickinson, and Brian L. Ott, "Introduction: Rhetoric/Memory/Place," in *Places of Public Memory: The Rhetoric of Museums and Memorials*, ed. Greg Dickinson, Carole Blair, and Brian L. Ott (Tuscaloosa: University of Alabama Press, 2010), 6–8.

2. Debbie Elliott, "'Why Don't Y'all Let That Die?' Telling The Emmett Till Story in Mississippi," *National Public Radio*, August 28, 2019, https://www.npr.org/2019/08/28/755024458/why-don-t-y-all-let-that-die-telling-the-emmett-till-story-in-mississippi.

3. Dave Tell, *Remembering Emmett Till* (Chicago: University of Chicago Press, 2019), 22. The Emmett Till Memorial Highway is marked with a blue metal sign located on the outskirts of Greenwood at the intersection of Highway 49W and Highway 82.

4. Dave Tell, "Commentary: Protecting the Memory of Emmett Till from the Scourge of Vandals," *Chicago Tribune*, July 26, 2019, https://www.chicagotribune.com/opinion/commentary/ct-opinion-emmett-till-sign-vandalism-20190726-7kjjvedmzvhgxpvxspvsf5fg4u-story.

5. Tell, *Remembering Emmett Till*, 242.

6. Andreas Preuss, "Emmett Till Memorial Sign Scarred by Bullet Holes," *CNN*, October 22, 2016, http://www.cnn.com/2016/10/22/us/mississippi-emmett-till-sign-bullets/index.html.

7. The second sign went on display at the Smithsonian National Museum of American History in 2021. See Derrick Ward and Andrea Swalec, "Bullet-Riddled Emmett Till Sign on Display in U.S. History Museum," NBC4 Washington, September 3, 2021, https://www.nbcwashington.com/news/local/bullet-riddled-emmett-till-sign-smithsonian-national-museum-american-history/2791174/.

8. Kayla Epstein, "This Emmett Till Memorial Was Vandalized Again. And Again. And Again. Now, It's Bulletproof," *Washington Post*, October 20, 2019, https://www.washingtonpost.com/history/2019/10/20/this-emmett-till-memorial-was-vandalized-again-again-again-now-its-bulletproof/.

9. Quoted in Elliott, "'Why Don't Y'all Let That Die?'"

10. Neil Vigdor, "Emmett Till Sign Photo Leads Ole Miss Fraternity to Suspend Members," *New York Times*, July 25, 2019, https://www.nytimes.com/2019/07/25/us/emmett-till-ole-miss-students-fraternity.html.

11. Epstein, "This Emmett Till Memorial." Standing before the new bullet-proof marker, Tell told a group of onlookers that the bullet-proof sign's fine print remembers the marker's history of vandalism: "The fine print does something that no other sign has ever done. It acknowledges the vandalism. It records the theft and the gunshots because that's part of the story, too. And if there's a chance now to move forward, we not only have to reckon with what happened in 1955, we also have to reckon with the ongoing story that's been happening since 1955." See Kazi Mehedi Hasan, "Prof Dave Tell Talks about Emmett Till Memorial Marker Repeatedly Vandalized," YouTube, November 20, 2019, video, 1:25, https://youtu.be/FoDiSPgxWho.

12. Hannah Knowles, "White Supremacists Gathered at Emmett Till's Bulletproof Memorial to Shoot a Video," *Washington Post*, November 4, 2019, https://www.washingtonpost.com/history/2019/11/04/emmett-tills-cousin-white-nationalists-memorial-more-they-do-we-can-do-more/. Ironically, the League of the South's publicity stunt led to an outpouring of donations to the Emmett Till Memorial Commission. ETIC's executive director, Patrick Weems, reported the commission received $10,000 in donations in less than forty-eight hours after the incident: "This group came out there to divide us . . . but they only made our effort stronger"; "We have had support from all around the country of people helping us out. Every time something like this happens, we get another $10,000 to help us." See Jimmie E. Gates, "Donations to Emmett Till Memorial Pour in Following White Nationalist Group's Filming," *Clarion-Ledger*, November 4, 2019, https://www.clarionledger.com/story/news/local/2019/11/04/emmett-till-memorial-gets-donations-after-white-nationalists-film/4154831002/.

13. Quoted in Peter Holley, "An Emmett Till Historical Marker in Mississippi Was Destroyed by Vandals—Again," *Washington Post*, June 26, 2017, https://www.washingtonpost.com/news/post-nation/wp/2017/06/26/an-emmett-till-historical-marker-in-mississippi-was-destroyed-by-vandals-again/. See also Kayla Epstein, "When a Memorial to Emmett Till Was Vandalized, These High School Students Stepped Up," *Washington Post*, June 30, 2017, http://wapo.st/2uoN1eS?tid=ss_mail&utm_term=.aa2f398aff09.

14. Hammons and Associates, "Mississippi Freedom Trail," n.d., accessed December 15, 2021, https://hammons.com/portfolio-archive/mississippi-freedom-trail/.

15. Emily Wagster Pettus, "Emmett Till Marker in Mississippi Toppled but Not Vandalized," *Associated Press*, September 3, 2021, https://apnews.com/article/mississippi-emmett-till-6e707514564ab9a155b772cc98bd6312.

16. Isabella Grullón Paz, "Questions Swirl after Yet Another Emmett Till Sign Comes Down," *New York Times*, September 4, 2021, https://www.nytimes.com/2021/09/04/us/emmett-till-sign-missing.html.

17. Gabriela Szymanowska, "'Hard to Understand': Emmett Till Marker Broken Days After 66th Anniversary of His Death," *Clarion-Ledger*, September 3, 2021, https://www.clarionledger.com/story/news/local/2021/09/03/emmett-till-marker-near-bryants-grocery-money-mississippi-missing/5713864001/.

18. Paz, "Questions Swirl."

19. J. David Maxson, "'Second Line to Bury White Supremacy': Take 'Em Down Nola, Monument Removal, and Residual Memory," *Quarterly Journal of Speech* 106, no. 1 (2020): 51, https://doi.org/10.1080/00335630.2019.1704428.

20. Susan Svrluga, "Former Ole Miss Student Pleads Guilty to Hanging Noose around Statue Honoring the First Black Student," *Washington Post*, March 24, 2016, https://www.washingtonpost.com/news/grade-point/wp/2016/03/24/former-ole-miss-student-pleads-guilty-to-hanging-noose-around-statue-honoring-the-first-black-student/.

21. Svrluga, "Former Ole Miss Student Pleads Guilty."

22. For example, see Davis W. Houck and Matthew A. Grindy, *Emmett Till and the Mississippi Press* (Jackson: University Press of Mississippi, 2008); Mamie Till-Mobley and Christopher Benson, *Death of Innocence: The Story of the Hate Crime that Changed America* (New York: One World, 2003); Timothy B. Tyson, *The Blood of Emmett Till* (New York: Simon and Schuster, 2017); Stephen J. Whitfield, *A Death in the Delta: The Story of Emmett Till* (New York: Free Press, 1988); and Darryl Mace, *In Remembrance of Emmett Till: Regional Stories and Media Responses to the Black Freedom Struggle* (Lexington: University Press of Kentucky, 2014).

23. *The Murder of Emmett Till*, DVD, directed and produced by Stanley Nelson (Alexandria, VA: PBS Home Video, 2004); *The Untold Story of Emmett Till*, DVD, directed by Keith A. Beauchamp (New York: Thinkfilm, 2005).

24. UPM Staff, "*Women of the Movement* to Premier on ABC," University Press of Mississippi, January 4, 2022, https://www.upress.state.ms.us/News/2022/WOMEN-OF-THE-MOVEMENT-to-premiere-on-ABC.

25. Michael Andor Brodeur, "Whose Song Is This to Sing? A New Opera about Emmett Till Faces Scrutiny and Protest," *Washington Post*, March 22, 2022, https://www.washingtonpost.com/music/2022/03/22/emmett-till-opera-protest/.

26. "Senate Passes Bill to Give Congressional Gold Medal to Emmett Till and His Mother," *PBS News Hour*, January 12, 2022, https://www.pbs.org/newshour/nation/senate-passes-bill-to-give-congressional-gold-medal-to-emmett-till-and-his-mother.

27. Amy B. Wang and Felicia Sonmez, "Biden Signs Bill Making Lynching a Federal Hate Crime," *Washington Post*, March 29, 2022, https://www.washingtonpost.com/politics/2022/03/29/biden-signs-bill-lynching-hate-crime/.

28. Dave Tell, "The 'Shocking Story' of Emmett Till and the Politics of Public Confession," *Quarterly Journal of Speech* 94, no. 2 (2008): 157, https://doi.org/10.1080/00335630801975426.

29. Emmett Till Memory Project, "About the Emmett Till Memory Project," n.d., accessed February 9, 2023, https://tillapp.emmett-till.org/about/.

30. Dave Tell, "Remembering Emmett Till: Reflections on Geography, Race, and Memory," *Advances in the History of Rhetoric* 20, no. 2 (2017): 133, https://doi.org/10.1080/15362426.2017.1325414.

31. Emmett Till Memory Project, "About."

32. Tell, "Remembering Emmett Till: Reflections," 135.

33. Emmett Till Memory Project, "Tours," n.d., accessed June 21, 2021, https://tillapp.emmett-till.org/tours/browse/.

34. Quoted in Elliott, "'Why Don't Y'all Let That Die?'"

35. Till-Mobley, *Death of Innocence*, 19.

36. Till-Mobley, *Death of Innocence*, 14, 16–17.

37. Till-Mobley, *Death of Innocence*, 37–39.

38. Till-Mobley, *Death of Innocence*, 19–21, 99.
39. Till-Mobley, *Death of Innocence*, 98–100.
40. Till-Mobley, *Death of Innocence*, 100–101.
41. Devery S. Anderson, *Emmett Till: The Murder That Shocked the World and Propelled the Civil Rights Movement* (Jackson: University Press of Mississippi, 2015), 22–23.
42. Anderson, *Emmett Till*, 26–27. Because Maurice did not possess a driver's license, he and the group were instructed not to drive beyond a nearby country store. The group ignored their instructions and drove an additional three miles to downtown Money.
43. Anderson, *Emmett Till*, 27.
44. Elliott J. Gorn, *Let the People See: The Story of Emmett Till* (New York: Oxford University Press, 2018), 26.
45. Anderson, *Emmett Till*, 28–29. See also Whitfield, *A Death in the Delta*, 17.
46. Tyson, *The Blood of Emmett Till*, 53.
47. Tyson, *The Blood of Emmett Till*, 53; Anderson, *Emmett Till*, 29.
48. Tyson, *The Blood of Emmett Till*, 54; Anderson, *Emmett Till*, 31.
49. Tyson, *The Blood of Emmett Till*, 54.
50. Gorn, *Let the People See*, 27–28; Tyson, *The Blood of Emmett Till*, 54.
51. Quoted in Tyson, *The Blood of Emmett Till*, 54.
52. Anderson, *Emmett Till*, 33; Till-Mobley, *Death of Innocence*, 122. Anderson argues that Mamie Till's explanation is historical revisionism—her public comments in the months after the lynching and trial did not tie the whistle to a speech impediment. According to Anderson, Emmett's mother "rarely mentioned the whistle at all." See Anderson, 394–95 (note 84).
53. Tyson, *Blood of Emmett Till*, 166–67.
54. Tyson, *Blood of Emmett Till*, 6–7. After the publication of Tyson's book in 2017 revealing Bryant's (now Carolyn Bryant Donham) explosive confession, the Civil Rights Division of the Justice Department reopened an investigation of the Till murder. Four years later, the same agency decided to close the case because it could not "prove the woman lied to federal investigators about her story." Laura Jarrett, "Justice Department Closes Investigation into Emmett Till Killing after Failing to Prove Key Witness Lied," *CNN*, December 7, 2021, https://www.cnn.com/2021/12/06/politics/emmett-till-case-closed/index.html. See also Marouf A. Hasian Jr. and Nicholas S. Paliewicz, *Racial Terrorism: A Rhetorical Investigation of Lynching* (Jackson: University Press of Mississippi, 2021), 97. In March 2022, Till's relatives pushed for the Justice Department to reverse its earlier decision and bring the case before a grand jury. See Julia James, "Emmett Till's Family Wants Carolyn Bryant Donham Brought to Justice," *Mississippi Today*, March 11, 2022, https://mississippitoday.org/2022/03/11/emmett-tills-family-wants-carolyn-bryant-donham-brought-to-justice/. Later that summer, researchers discovered an arrest warrant dated August 29, 1955, charging Carolyn Bryant with kidnapping. It was never served, which led to a grand jury investigation that ultimately resulted in no indictments. As of this writing (February 2023), the case remains closed. See Alex Traub, "1955 Arrest Warrant in Emmett Till Case Is Found in Court Basement," *New York Times*, June 30, 2022, https://www.nytimes.com/2022/06/30/us/emmett-till-carolyn-bryant-arrest-warrant.html?smid=url-share; Rick Rojas, "Mississippi Grand Jury Declines to Indict Woman in Emmett Till Murder Case," *New York Times*, August 9, 2022, https://www.nytimes.com/2022/08/09/us/emmett-till-murder-grand-jury.html?smid=url-share.
55. Whitfield, *A Death*, 22.
56. Quoted in Tyson, *Blood of Emmett Till*, 10, 11.

57. Tyson, *Blood of Emmett Till*, 8–12.

58. Tell, "Remembering Emmett Till: Reflections," 121–22.

59. Tell, "Remembering Emmett Till: Reflections," 122.

60. Tell, "Remembering Emmett Till: Reflections," 131.

61. Tyson, *Blood of Emmett Till*, 130.

62. Tyson, *Blood of Emmett Till*, 173.

63. Afterward, both men were arrested on separate kidnapping charges. They were eventually acquitted. Since they could not be charged again for the same crime, Bryant and Milam later sat down with journalist William Bradford Huie for a piece that would later be published in *Look* magazine, and were paid (as well as their lawyers) an estimated $4,419 for their recollections of the murder. See Tell, "Remembering Emmett Till: Reflections," 124.

64. "Legal Processes Continue," *Commercial Appeal*, September 24, 1955, 6; "The Verdict at Sumner," editorial, *Clarion-Ledger/Jackson Daily News*, September 25, 1955, 8.

65. Houck and Grindy, *Emmett Till and the Mississippi Press*, 154. Also, see Hutto's reporting on posttrial Sumner, described as returning to a stage of slumber, a metaphor for forgetting. Ralph Hutto, "Now Sumner Is Just Another Sleepy Delta Town," *Jackson State Times*, September 24, 1955.

66. "What You Can Do about the Disgrace in Sumner," editorial, *Chicago Defender*, October 1, 1955, in *The Lynching of Emmett Till: A Documentary Narrative*, ed. Christopher Metress (Charlottesville: University of Virginia Press, 2002), 127.

67. "Death in Mississippi," *Commonweal*, September 23, 1955, 603–4.

68. "The Shame of Our Nation," editorial, *Daily Worker*, September 26, 1955, in *The Lynching of Emmett Till: A Documentary Narrative*, ed. Christopher Metress (Charlottesville: University of Virginia Press, 2002), 118–19.

69. "Another Negro," letter to the editor, *Norfolk Virginia Pilot*, September 27, 1955.

70. Anderson, *Emmett Till*, 61.

71. Anderson, *Emmett Till*, 56. See also Leigh Raiford, *Imprisoned in a Luminous Glare: Photography and the African American Freedom Struggle* (Chapel Hill: University of North Carolina Press, 2011), 87–89.

72. Julie Buckner Armstrong, *Mary Turner and the Memory of Lynching* (Athens: University of Georgia Press, 2011), 112.

73. Anderson, *Emmett Till*, 169–73.

74. Karlos K. Hill, *Beyond the Rope: The Impact of Lynching on Black Culture and Memory* (Cambridge: Cambridge University Press, 2016), 4–5.

75. For more on the subject of cultural narratives of lynching in the United States, see Hill, *Beyond the Rope*.

76. Armstrong, *Mary Turner*, 16.

77. Pablo Correa, *Restoration and Reconciliation*, Vimeo, November 11, 2017, video, 3:01, https://vimeo.com/242383672.

78. See Paul Hendrickson, "Mississippi Haunting," *Rhetoric and Public Affairs* 8, no. 2 (2005): 178, doi: 10.1353/rap.2005.0074; and Davis W. Houck, "Killing Emmett," *Rhetoric and Public Affairs* 8, no. 2 (2005): 255, doi: 10.1353/rap.2005.0078.

79. Tell, "Remembering Emmett Till: Reflections," 124, 127.

80. Danielle Morgan, Zoom interview by Roger Davis Gatchet and Stephen A. King, November 12, 2020.

81. Morgan, Zoom interview.

82. "Discover Money Road," advertisement, *Living Blues*, December 2015, 58.

83. "Discover Money Road," advertisement.

84. Michel-Rolph Trouillot, *Silencing the Past: Power and the Production of History* (Boston: Beacon, 1995), 48.

85. Bruce Conforth and Gayle Dean Wardlow, *Up Jumped the Devil: The Real Life of Robert Johnson* (Chicago: Chicago Review, 2019), 252–53.

86. Conforth and Wardlow, *Up Jumped the Devil*, 253.

87. Conforth and Wardlow, *Up Jumped the Devil*, 253–54.

88. "Find America's Soul Laid Bare on Money Road," advertisement, *Living Blues*, June 2015, 68.

89. "Find America's Soul Laid Bare on Money Road," advertisement.

90. "Find America's Soul Laid Bare on Money Road," advertisement.

91. Conforth and Wardlow, *Up Jumped the Devil*, 248–50.

92. James C. Cobb, *The Most Southern Place on Earth: The Mississippi Delta and the Roots of Regional Identity* (New York: Oxford University Press, 1992), 237.

93. Kenneth Burke, *A Grammar of Motives* (Berkeley: University of California Press, 1969), xv.

94. Burke, *A Grammar of Motives*, xv.

95. See, for example, a Mississippi Tourism Association brochure where "Till's kidnapping and murder" are "widely considered the catalyst for the modern Civil Rights Movement" (Mississippi Tourism Association, *Mississippi Freedom Trail*, brochure, revised July 2020, n.p.).

96. Greenwood Convention and Visitors Bureau, "Greenwood: Epicenter for Civil Rights Movement," n.d., accessed June 22, 2021, https://www.visitgreenwood.com/news/epicenter-for-civil-rights/.

97. Greenwood Convention and Visitors Bureau, *Remembering the Struggle for Civil Rights: The Greenwood Sites*, brochure, n.d.

98. Greenwood Convention and Visitors Bureau, *Remembering the Struggle for Civil Rights*.

99. Anderson, *Emmett Till*, 355.

100. Greenwood Convention and Visitors Bureau, "Money Road," n.d., accessed December 22, 2020, https://www.visitgreenwood.com/experience/.

101. Greenwood Convention and Visitors Bureau, "History, Culture and Architecture," n.d., accessed December 22, 2020, https://www.visitgreenwood.com/history/. Emphasis added. The same itinerary includes a two-sentence description of "Civil Rights" and directions for visitors to find two Mississippi Freedom Markers ("Bryant's Grocery," "'Black Power' Speech").

102. Mississippi Tourism Association, "Pivotal Civil Rights Sites: A 3-Day Itinerary," n.d., accessed December 22, 2020, https://visitmississippi.org/blog/pivotal-mississippi-civil-rights-sites-a-3-day-itinerary/.

103. Christine Harold and Kevin Michael DeLuca, "Behold the Corpse: Violent Images and the Case of Emmett Till," *Rhetoric & Public Affairs* 8, no. 2 (2005): 271, doi: 10.1353/rap.2005.0075. Emphasis in original.

104. Quoted in Joe Atkins and Tom Brennan, "Bryant Wants the Past to 'Stay Dead,'" *Clarion-Ledger*, August 25, 1985. Emphasis added.

105. Greenwood Convention and Visitors Bureau, *Unique Delta Experiences*, brochure, June 1, 2019.

106. Morgan, Zoom interview.

107. Bryn Stole, "Confronting Past, Mississippi Town Erects Emmett Till Museum," Reuters, March 21, 2015, http://www.reuters.com/article/usa-emmetttill-museum-idUSKBN0 MH0EV20150321. The ETIC is housed in the space that was previously a grocery store, Wong's Grocery. See Tell, *Remembering Emmett Till*, 110.

108. Tell, *Remembering Emmett Till*, 19.

109. Tell, *Remembering Emmett Till*, 104.

110. "Preserving Emmett Till's Memory," C-SPAN, September 2, 2021, video, 1:21:22, https://www.c-span.org/video/?514412-1/work-preserving-emmett-tills-memory.

111. Emmett Till Interpretive Center, "History of the Center," n.d., accessed February 9, 2023, https://www.emmett-till.org/history.

112. Tell, *Remembering Emmett Till*, 104; "Preserving Emmett Till's Memory."

113. Tell, *Remembering Emmett Till*, 104–5.

114. Tell, *Remembering Emmett Till*, 105.

115. Sustainable Equity, LLC, n.d., accessed February 9, 2023, https://www.sustainableequity.net/.

116. Tell, *Remembering Emmett Till*, 106–7.

117. Emmett Till Interpretive Center, "History of the Center."

118. Quoted in Maya Miller, "Till Interpretive Center Seeks to Rewrite Civil Rights Narrative," *Jackson Free Press*, August 26, 2015, https://www.jacksonfreepress.com/news/2015/aug/26/till-interpretive-center-seeks-rewrite-civil-right/.

119. Ian M. Borton, "Effects of Race, Sex, and Victims' Reasons for Victim-Offender Dialogue," *Conflict Resolution Quarterly* 27, no. 2 (2009): 216, doi: 10.1002/crq.256.

120. Tell, "Remembering Emmett Till: Reflections," 126.

121. Emmett Till Interpretive Center, "The Apology," n.d., accessed March 24, 2020, http://www.emmett-till.org/new-apology.

122. Emmett Till Interpretive Center, "The Apology."

123. Patrick Weems, interview by Roger Davis Gatchet and Stephen A. King, Oxford, Mississippi, May 23, 2019.

124. Dallen J. Timothy, *Cultural Heritage and Tourism: An Introduction* (Bristol, England: Channel View, 2011), 443.

125. Timothy, *Cultural Heritage and Tourism*, 447–65.

126. The exhibit developed out of an oral history project at Delta State University (DSU) and was funded in part by a grant from the Mississippi Humanities Council. The impetus for the project developed from the work of Dr. Henry Outlaw, emeritus chairperson and faculty member in DSU's Department of Physical Sciences and program associate at DSU's Delta Center for Culture and Learning. In our 2019 interview with DSU archivist Emily Jones, she remembers the genesis of the Emmett Till traveling exhibit: "Dr. Outlaw asked me if I would help him build an exhibit based on the oral histories that he had collected from some of the folks that had participated in the trial or were simply witnesses to the trial. . . . [T]hat exhibit was only in-house created. We had more students and teachers bring their classes through for that exhibit than anything I have seen since. And that spurred us to create the traveling exhibit, the Emmett Till traveling exhibit. We just took all that information and turned it

into something that can go out to different places" (Emily Jones, interview by Stephen A. King, Cleveland, Mississippi, August 5, 2019).

127. Walter R. Fisher, "Narration as a Human Communication Paradigm: The Case of Public Moral Argument," *Communication Monographs* 51, no. 1 (1984): 1–22, https://doi.org/10.1080/03637758409390180.

128. Susan Neiman, *Learning from the Germans: Race and the Memory of Evil* (New York: Farrar, Straus and Giroux, 2019), 211.

129. US Census Bureau, "Annual Estimates of the Resident Population for Incorporated Places: April 1, 2010 to July 1, 2019," *City and Town Population Totals, 2010–2019*, accessed June 15, 2021, https://www2.census.gov/programs-surveys/popest/tables/2010-2019/cities/totals/SUB-IP-EST2019-ANNRES-28.xlsx.

130. Tell, *Remembering Emmett Till*, 197.

131. Johnny B. Thomas and Thomas J. Durant Jr., *A Stone of Hope: Rising above Slavery, Jim Crow, and Poverty in Glendora, Mississippi* (Bloomington, IN: Xlibris, 2017), 131–33.

132. Tell, *Remembering Emmett Till*, 195–96, 214–16.

133. Tell, *Remembering Emmett Till*, 214–15.

134. Tell, *Remembering Emmett Till*, 233.

135. Tell, *Remembering Emmett Till*, 235.

136. Tell, *Remembering Emmett Till*, 199.

137. Johnny B. Thomas, interview by Roger Davis Gatchet and Stephen A. King, Glendora, Mississippi, May 23, 2019.

138. See also, Tell, *Remembering Emmett Till*, 196.

139. Tell, *Remembering Emmett Till*, 208.

140. Thomas, interview. See also, Thomas and Durant, *A Stone of Hope*, 121.

141. Thomas and Durant, *A Stone of Hope*, 41.

142. Patrick Weems, interview.

143. The ETHIC's complete mission and vision statements are on display in the museum itself.

144. Tell, *Remembering Emmett Till*, 236–37.

145. Quoted in Neiman, *Learning from the Germans*, 235.

146. Thomas, interview.

147. Tell, "Remembering Emmett Till: Reflections," 130–33. For an in-depth analysis of Glendora's role in memorializing Till and the means by which Mayor Thomas finally secured funds to create and renovate the ETHIC, see chapter 5 in Tell's 2019 book, *Remembering Emmett Till*.

148. Stephen A. King, *I'm Feeling the Blues Right Now: Blues Tourism in the Mississippi Delta* (Jackson: University Press of Mississippi, 2011), 69.

149. Thomas and Durant, *A Stone of Hope*, 112.

150. Thomas and Durant, *A Stone of Hope*, 112.

151. Quoted in Aallyah Wright, Kelsey Davis Betz, and Bobby Harrison, "For Some in the Delta, Revisiting Emmett Till's Murder about Appeasing Mississippi's Conscience," *Mississippi Today*, July 14, 2018, https://mississippitoday.org/2018/07/14/for-some-in-the-delta-revisiting-emmett-tills-murder-is-about-appeasing-mississippis-conscious/.

152. Thomas, interview.

153. Weems, interview.

154. "Preserving Emmett Till's Memory."

155. Kate Siber, "Mississippi Reckoning," *National Parks*, Winter 2019, https://www.npca.org/articles/2020-mississippi-reckoning.

156. Siber, "Mississippi Reckoning."

157. Quoted in Allie Northcutt, "Civil Rights Immersion Trip's Impact on Students," Wabash College, December 10, 2021, https://www.wabash.edu/news/story/11841.

CHAPTER FOUR. Private Spaces, Public Memories: Mississippi's Civil Rights Historic House Museums

1. Mingo Tingle, "Historic Resources Inventory Fact Sheet," Mississippi Department of Archives and History, October 29, 2008, https://www.apps.mdah.ms.gov/Public/prop.aspx?id=101848&view=facts&y=812.

2. Charles E. Cobb, *This Nonviolent Stuff'll Get You Killed: How Guns Made the Civil Rights Movement Possible* (New York: Basic, 2014), 63, ProQuest Ebook Central.

3. Charles E. Cobb Jr. *On the Road to Freedom: A Guided Tour of the Civil Rights Trail* (Chapel Hill: Algonquin, 2008), 294.

4. John Dittmer, *Local People: The Struggle for Civil Rights in Mississippi* (Urbana: University of Illinois Press, 1994), 166.

5. Jennifer Baughn, "Historic Resources Inventory Fact Sheet," Mississippi Department of Archives and History, September 7, 2008, https://www.apps.mdah.ms.gov/Public/prop.aspx?id=32997&view=facts&y=1011; Jennifer V. O. Baughn, "Medgar and Myrlie Evers House National Historic Landmark Nomination," National Park Service, August 20, 2018, 4, https://www.apps.mdah.ms.gov/nom/prop/32997.pdf.

6. Baughn, "Medgar and Myrlie Evers House," 4, 23.

7. Baughn, "Medgar and Myrlie Evers House," 25.

8. National Park Service, "List of NHLs By State," *National Historic Landmarks*, accessed June 25, 2021, https://www.nps.gov/subjects/nationalhistoriclandmarks/list-of-nhls-by-state.htm.

9. National Park Service, "Secretary Zinke Designates Medgar and Myrlie Evers Home as African American Civil Rights Network Site," news release, August 3, 2018, https://www.nps.gov/orgs/1207/secretary-zinke-designates-medgar-and-myrlie-evers-home-as-african-american-civil-rights-network-site.htm.

10. "Medgar and Myrlie Evers Home Officially Established as National Monument," *Delta Democrat-Times*, December 10, 2020, https://www.ddtonline.com/medgar-and-myrlie-evers-home-officially-established-national-monument#sthash.D50T9Rrh.fC7HkjXc.dpbs.

11. US Department of the Interior, "Trump Administration Establishes Medgar and Myrlie Evers Home National Monument," press release, December 10, 2020, last edited March 12, 2021, https://www.doi.gov/pressreleases/trump-administration-establishes-medgar-and-myrlie-evers-home-national-monument.

12. Dorothy C. Barck, "The First Historic House Museum," *Journal of the Society of Architectural Historians* 14, no. 2 (1955): 30–32, https://doi.org/10.2307/987787; Linda Young, *Historic House Museums in the United States and the United Kingdom: A History* (Lanham, MD: Rowman and Littlefield, 2017), 45.

13. Patrick H. Butler, "Past, Present, and Future: The Place of the House Museum in the Museum Community," in *Interpreting Historic House Museums*, ed. Jessica Foy Donnelly (Walnut Creek, CA: AltaMira, 2002), 28–29.

14. Young, *Historic House Museums*, 2.

15. Young, *Historic House Museums*, 1.

16. Susan T. Falck, *Remembering Dixie: The Battle to Control Historical Memory in Natchez, Mississippi, 1865–1941* (Jackson: University Press of Mississippi, 2019), 3.

17. Mississippi Advertising Commission, "Historical Mississippi," advertisement, Series 552, 1937, Mississippi Department of Archives and History, Jackson, Mississippi, https://da.mdah.ms.gov/series/sac/552/detail/190656.

18. Tourism and Public Affairs Department, Mississippi Agricultural and Industrial Board, *Mississippi: Your Guide to Travel*, n.d., ca. 1975, 61.

19. "10 Most Updates: Mississippi's Freedom Houses" and "2021 10 Most Endangered Historic Places in Mississippi," *Elevation: The Journal of the Mississippi Heritage Trust* (Fall 2021): 14, 47.

20. Young, *Historic House Museums*, 10–12.

21. Young, *Historic House Museums*, 31.

22. Young, *Historic House Museums*, 32.

23. Jim Carrier, *A Traveler's Guide to the Civil Rights Movement* (Orlando: Harcourt, 2004), 264.

24. Carrier, *A Traveler's Guide*, 264.

25. Belinda Stewart Architects, "Amzie Moore House Restoration," n.d., https://belindastewartarchitects.com/portfolio/amzie-moore-house/; Angela Quezada, "Amzie Moore Home Ribbon Cutting," YouTube, March 28, 2016, video, 2:56, https://youtu.be/ZUqWBOO2UM4.

26. "The Amzie Moore Home Restoration and Preservation Project: Project Narrative" (Application for Mississippi Civil Rights Historical Sites Grant), 2011, Mississippi Department of Archives and History, Jackson, Mississippi, 26.

27. Angela Quezada, "Amzie Moore Home Ribbon Cutting."

28. Cleveland Tourism, *Cleveland Mississippi Tourism*, brochure, n.d.; Cleveland Tourism, *Visit Cleveland Mississippi*, brochure, n.d.

29. "The Amzie Moore Home," *2021 Welcome Guide Cleveland & Bolivar County*, issue 9, 2021, 159.

30. Mississippi Tourism Association, *Mississippi Official Tour Guide*, 2021, 44, 52, 64, 79.

31. The house originally had a single bathroom. A second bathroom was added during its restoration to bring the Moore House up to code (Emily Jones, interview by Stephen A. King, Cleveland, Mississippi, August 5, 2019).

32. Young, *Historic House Museums*, 21.

33. Kenneth Burke, *A Grammar of Motives* (Berkeley: University of California Press, 1969), 506.

34. Barry Brummett, *Rhetorical Dimensions of Popular Culture* (Tuscaloosa: University of Alabama Press, 1991), 27, EBSCOhost eBook Academic Collection.

35. Victoria J. Gallagher and Margaret R. LaWare, "Sparring with Public Memory: The Rhetorical Embodiment of Race, Power, and Conflict in the *Monument to Joe Louis*," in

Places of Public Memory: The Rhetoric of Museums and Memorials, ed. Greg Dickinson, Carole Blair, and Brian L. Ott (Tuscaloosa: University of Alabama Press, 2010), 92.

36. Claire Sisco King, "Hitching Wagons to Stars: Celebrity, Metonymy, Hegemony, and the Case of Will Smith," *Communication and Critical/Cultural Studies* 14, no. 1 (2017): 85, https://doi.org/10.1080/14791420.2016.1202422.

37. Claire Sisco King, "American Queerer: Norman Rockwell and the Art of Queer Feminist Critique," *Women's Studies in Communication* 39, no. 2 (2016): 167, https://doi.org/10.1080/07491409.2016.1165778.

38. Saul D. Alinsky, *Rules for Radicals: A Pragmatic Primer for Realistic Radicals* (New York: Vintage, 1971).

39. Charles M. Payne, *I've Got the Light of Freedom: The Organizing Tradition and the Mississippi Freedom Struggle* (Berkeley: University of California Press, 1995), 44.

40. Charles McLaurin, phone interview by Roger Davis Gatchet and Stephen A. King, December 4, 2021.

41. Wesley C. Hogan, *Many Minds, One Heart: SNCC's Dream for a New America* (Chapel Hill: University of North Carolina Press, 2007), 37.

42. During our visit to the museum, we were accompanied by Will Hooker and Emily Jones—both of whom were instrumental in the development of the museum and its displays. They provided additional insight into the house and its history while we toured the space.

43. Carrier, *A Traveler's Guide*, 264.

44. Stephen A. King, *I'm Feeling the Blues Right Now: Blues Tourism and the Mississippi Delta* (Jackson: University Press of Mississippi, 2011).

45. Owen J. Dwyer, "Interpreting the Civil Rights Movement: Place, Memory, and Conflict," *Professional Geographer* 52, no. 4 (2000): 667, doi: 10.1111/0033-0124.00255.

46. Carrier, *A Traveler's Guide*, 272.

47. Baughn, "Historic Resources Inventory Fact Sheet."

48. Wayne F. Timmer and Anne Marie Decker, "Medgar Evers Home Renovation," 1995, Mississippi Department of Archives and History, Jackson, Mississippi, n.p.

49. Timmer and Decker, n.p.

50. Timmer and Decker, n.p.

51. Willie Morris, *The Ghosts of Medgar Evers: A Tale of Race, Murder, Mississippi, and Hollywood* (New York: Random House, 1998), 186.

52. Ashley F. G. Norwood, "Rural Civil Rights Sites Crave Collaboration with New Jackson Museum," *Mississippi Today*, December 16, 2017, https://mississippitoday.org/2017/12/16/rural-civil-rights-sites-fear-eclipse-by-new-jackson-museum/.

53. Deborah Barfield Berry, "Bill Would Order Study on Medgar Evers' Home," *Clarion-Ledger*, March 24, 2016, https://www.clarionledger.com/story/news/2016/03/24/bill-would-order-study-medgar-evers-home/82219336/.

54. Berry, "Bill Would Order Study."

55. Cobb, *On the Road to Freedom*, 276.

56. Stephen A. King, "Memory, Mythmaking, and Museums: Constructive Authenticity and the Primitive Blues Subject," *Southern Communication Journal* 71, no. 3 (2006): 237, https://doi.org/10.1080/10417940600846029.

57. King, "Memory, Mythmaking, and Museums," 241.

58. Cobb, *On the Road to Freedom*, 276.

59. Cobb, *On the Road to Freedom*, 276.

60. Myrlie B. Evers with William Peters, *For Us, the Living* (Garden City: Doubleday, 1967), 279.

61. Baughn, "Medgar and Myrlie Evers House," 5; Therese Apel, "Mississippi Marks 50th Anniversary of Medgar Evers' Death," *Chicago Tribune*, June 12, 2013, https://www.chicagotribune.com/news/ct-xpm-2013-06-12-sns-rt-us-usa-race-eversbre95b190-20130612-story.html.

62. Rickey Thigpen, interview by Roger Davis Gatchet and Stephen A. King, Jackson, MS, May 21, 2019.

63. Janet Dewart Bell, *Lighting the Fires of Freedom: African American Women in the Civil Rights Movement* (New York: New Press, 2018), 1.

64. *Medgar and Myrlie Evers Home National Monument Act*, S. Report 115–370, 115th Cong., 2d sess., November 15, 2018, https://www.congress.gov/congressional-report/115th-congress/senate-report/370/1.

CHAPTER FIVE. Marking the Past: The Mississippi Freedom Trail and Signs of Racial Truth

1. Mamie Till Mobley, "Emmett Till Civil Rights Marker at Bryant's Store in Money Mississippi," YouTube, September 14, 2012, video, 1:49, https://youtu.be/wA5oeXLVS54.

2. Mobley, "Emmett Till Civil Rights Marker."

3. Interestingly, the website for the Jackson Convention and Visitors Bureau (or Visit Jackson) identifies some civil rights–themed state markers as if they are part of the Mississippi Freedom Trail, even though the sign series are distinct. The website includes a green state marker for the Smith Robertson School in a list of MFT markers located in Jackson. See "Mississippi Blues, Freedom & Writer Trails," Visit Jackson, n.d., accessed March 18, 2022, https://www.visitjackson.com/mississippi-blues-trail/.

4. Jim Carrier, "Traveling the Civil Rights Trail," *Washington Post*, August 26, 2011, https://www.washingtonpost.com/opinions/traveling-the-civil-rights-trail/2011/08/26/gIQAaVL7gJ_story.html.

5. Phil McCausland, "Tamales, Catfish and Meringue Pie: Delicacies of the Mississippi Delta," *New York Times*, May 4, 2016, https://www.nytimes.com/2016/05/08/travel/tamales-catfish-pie-delicacies-of-the-mississippi-delta.html?smid=url-share.

6. Richard Rubin, "The Freedom Trail in Mississippi Is a Chronicle of Outrage and Courage," *New York Times*, September 10, 2018, https://www.nytimes.com/2018/09/10/travel/mississippi-freedom-trail.html.

7. "The United States Civil Rights Trail Podcast," n.d., accessed March 24, 2022, https://civilrightstrail.com/podcast/.

8. Mississippi Development Authority, *Annual Report 2012*, 26, https://da.mdah.ms.gov/series-files/mda/mda-ar/pdf/mda-annual-report2012.pdf.

9. Mississippi Development Authority, *Annual Report 2012*, 26.

10. Based on the location of our fieldwork, which took place largely in the Delta region, Jackson, and Oxford, we used convenience sampling to select the markers for analysis. During our first field research trip in 2016, we visited ten markers in the following order: Fannie Lou Hamer (Ruleville), William Chapel (Ruleville), The Reverend George Lee (Belzoni),

"Black Power" Speech (Greenwood), Bryant's Grocery (Money), Marks Mule Train and Poor People's Campaign (Marks), Amzie Moore (Cleveland), University of Mississippi (Oxford), T. R. M. Howard (Mound Bayou), and Aaron Henry (Clarksdale). Three years later, in 2019, we visited thirteen additional markers in the following order: Greyhound Bus Station (Jackson), Capitol Rally (Jackson), Jackson Municipal Library Sit-In (Jackson), Woolworth's Sit-In (Jackson), WLBT-TV (Jackson), Jackson State Tragedy (Jackson), COFO Central Offices (Jackson), Medgar Evers House (Jackson), Madison County Movement (Canton), Bombings in Jewish Community (Jackson), Tougaloo College (Tougaloo), C. C. Bryant (McComb), and Clyde Kennard (Hattiesburg).

11. It should be noted that the rear panel of some of the markers we visited—especially "'Black Power' Speech," "Woolworth's Sit-In," "Tougaloo College," and "Aaron Henry,"—were nearly indecipherable at the time due to the effects of weather erosion, sun damage, and heat.

12. Michael S. Bowman, "Looking for Stonewall's Arm: Tourist Performance as Research Method," in *Opening Acts: Performance in/as Communication and Cultural Studies*, ed. Judith Hamera (Thousand Oaks, CA: Sage, 2006), 116.

13. A number of memory scholars have addressed the relationship between memory objects and their location or context. For example, see Bernard J. Armada, "Memorial Agon: An Interpretive Tour of the National Civil Rights Museum," *Southern Communication Journal* 63, no. 3 (1998): 235–43, https://doi.org/10.1080/10417949809373096; Deborah F. Atwater and Sandra L. Herndon, "Cultural Space and Race: The National Civil Rights Museum and MuseumAfrica," *Howard Journal of Communications* 14, no. 1 (2003): 15–28, https://doi.org/10.1080/10646170304273; Gregory Clark, "Rhetorical Experience and the National Jazz Museum in Harlem," in *Places of Public Memory: The Rhetoric of Museums and Memorials*, ed. Greg Dickinson, Carole Blair, and Brian L. Ott (Tuscaloosa: University of Alabama Press, 2010), 113–35; Dave Tell, "Remembering Emmett Till: Reflections on Geography, Race, and Memory," *Advances in the History of Rhetoric* 20, no. 2 (2017): 121–38, https://doi.org/10.1080/15362426.2017.1325414; and Bowman, "Looking for Stonewall's Arm."

14. Stephen A. King, *I'm Feeling the Blues Right Now: Blues Tourism and the Mississippi Delta* (Jackson: University Press of Mississippi, 2011), 145.

15. Samuel M. Otterstrom and James A. Davis, "Historical Markers in the Western United States: Regional and Cultural Contrasts," *Journal of Heritage Tourism* 15, no. 5 (2020): 536, https://doi.org/10.1080/1743873X.2019.1695804.

16. Derek H. Alderman, "'History by the Spoonful' in North Carolina: The Textual Politics of State Highway Historical Markers," *Southeastern Geographer* 52, no. 4 (2012): 357.

17. Alderman, "'History by the Spoonful,'" 358.

18. Alderman, "'History by the Spoonful,'" 360; Michael Hill, "North Carolina's History on a Stick: Historical Markers and Public Commemoration," *Commemorative Landscapes of North Carolina*, 2012, http://docsouth.unc.edu/commland/features/essays/hill/.

19. Bob Brinkman, "Invisible Texans: Seeking Minorities in 100 Years of Texas Historical Markers," *Touchstone* 29 (2010): 58.

20. Otterstrom and Davis, "Historical Markers," 534.

21. Stephen P. Hanna and E. Fariss Hodder, "Reading the Signs: Using a Qualitative Geographic Information System to Examine the Commemoration of Slavery and Emancipation on Historical Markers in Fredericksburg, Virginia," *Cultural Geographies* 22, no. 3 (2015): 526.

22. Alderman, "'History by the Spoonful,'" 365; see also 367.

23. Otterstrom and Davis, "Historical Markers," 534.

24. Hill, "North Carolina's History on a Stick."

25. Otterstrom and Davis, "Historical Markers," 535.

26. Oddly, when the authors visited the "Jackson State Tragedy" MFT, the detailed rear text (see photo at https://www.mississippimarkers.com/civil-rights.html) had been replaced by a duplicate of the same twelve lines of text that appear on the front side.

27. The "Madison County Movement" MFT marker in Canton notes cross burnings but does not explicitly name the Klan.

28. Interestingly, the "Wharlest Jackson Sr." green marker in Natchez—funded by the local Masonic lodge and not part of the of the state's green marker series—references the Klan as responsible for the murder of Jackson in 1967. As the marker notes, "Members of the Ku Klux Klan targeted Jackson, because he was treasurer of the Natchez Chapter of the NAACP and had received a promotion at Armstrong Tire and Rubber Company that would otherwise have gone to a white employee."

29. *Fannie Lou Hamer: Courage and Faith*, produced by Linda L. Coles, aired February 20, 2006, Mississippi Public Broadcasting.

30. For more on solidification as a rhetorical process in social movements, see John W. Bowers, Donovan J. Ochs, Richard J. Jensen, and David P. Schulz, *The Rhetoric of Agitation and Control*, 3rd ed. (Long Grove, IL: Waveland, 2010), 29–40.

31. Bowers, Ochs, Jensen, and Schulz, *The Rhetoric of Agitation and Control*, 7.

32. Bowers, Ochs, Jensen, and Schulz, *The Rhetoric of Agitation and Control*, 7–8.

33. Waldo Martin, "Civil Rights, African American," in *The New Encyclopedia of Southern Culture*, vol. 24, *Race*, ed. Thomas C. Holt and Laurie B. Green (Chapel Hill: University of North Carolina Press, 2013), 44.

34. Aram Goudsouzian, *Down to the Crossroads: Civil Rights, Black Power, and the Meredith March against Fear* (New York: Farrar, Straus and Giroux, 2014), 251.

35. Lance Hill, *The Deacons for Defense: Armed Resistance and the Civil Rights Movement* (Chapel Hill: University of North Carolina Press, 2004), 46, 189–91, 206. For a detailed analysis of the Deacons for Defense's presence in Mississippi, see chapter 11; Peniel E. Joseph, *Stokely: A Life* (New York: Basic Civitas, 2014), 107.

36. Akinyele Umoja, "'It's Time for Black Men . . .': The Deacons for Defense and the Mississippi Movement," in *The Civil Rights Movement in Mississippi*, ed. Ted Ownby (Jackson: University Press of Mississippi, 2013), 204–5.

37. John Dittmer, *Local People: The Struggle for Civil Rights in Mississippi* (Urbana: University of Illinois Press, 1994), 411.

38. Donna Ladd, "Jackson Tragedy: The RNA, Revisited," *Jackson Free Press*, March 5, 2014, https://www.jacksonfreepress.com/news/2014/mar/05/jackson-tragedy-rna-revisited/.

39. Ladd, "Jackson Tragedy."

40. Ladd, "Jackson Tragedy."

41. Dittmer, *Local People*, 408–9.

42. Dittmer, *Local People*, 411.

43. Dana L. Cloud, "Hegemony or Concordance?: The Rhetoric of Tokenism in 'Oprah' Winfrey's Rags-to-Riches Biography," *Critical Studies in Mass Communication* 13, no. 2 (1996): 116, https://doi.org/10.1080/15295039609366967 (original emphasis).

44. Peniel E. Joseph, "Introduction: Toward a Historiography of the Black Power Movement," in *The Black Power Movement: Rethinking the Civil Rights-Black Power Era*, ed. Peniel E. Joseph (New York: Routledge, 2006), 2.

45. Rolando Herts, Zoom interview by Roger Davis Gatchet and Stephen A. King, November 12, 2021.

46. Herts, Zoom interview.

47. John Dougherty, Google Review of Canton Freedom House, 2021, https://g.co/kgs/H4Noyj.

48. Tourists interested in "recreating" the March Against Fear trek can first visit the "March Against Fear" marker in Hernando (near Memphis), followed by "'Black Power' Speech" in Greenwood before arriving at the "Capitol Rally" site in Jackson.

CHAPTER SIX. "This Little Light of Mine": Truth Telling at the Mississippi Civil Rights Museum

1. Campbell Robertson and Ellen Ann Fentress, "For Opening of Civil Rights Museum, Some Division," *New York Times*, December 6, 2017.

2. See Richard Gonzales, "African-American Congressmen Will Skip Mississippi Civil Rights Event to Avoid Trump," *National Public Radio*, December 7, 2017, https://www.npr.org/sections/thetwo-way/2017/12/07/569282666/african-american-congressmen-will-skip-mississippi-civil-rights-event-to-avoid-t; Michael D. Shear and Ellen Ann Fentress, "Trump, Rejecting Calls to Stay Away, Speaks at Civil Rights Museum," *New York Times*, December 9, 2017, https://www.nytimes.com/2017/12/09/us/politics/trump-mississippi-civil-rights-museum.html?smid=url-share.

3. Pamela Junior, interview by Roger Davis Gatchet and Stephen A. King, Jackson, Mississippi, May 24, 2019.

4. Robertson and Fentress, "For Opening of Civil Rights Museum."

5. Conceived and constructed as distinct museums, the Museum of Mississippi History and Mississippi Civil Rights Museum are located in the same complex and opened on the same day. Our analysis in this chapter focuses on the Mississippi Civil Rights Museum.

6. Mississippi Department of Archives and History, letter to museum members, October 8, 2019.

7. "Mississippi Civil Rights Museum Sees Almost 3,000 Visitors in Eight Hours," *WJTV*, January 20, 2020, https://www.wjtv.com/news/mississippi-civil-rights-museum-sees-almost-3000-visitors-in-eight-hours/.

8. Holland Cotter, "The New Mississippi Civil Rights Museum Refuses to Sugarcoat History," *New York Times*, December 18, 2017, https://nyti.ms/2kJDWtX.

9. "Purpose of the Law," editorial, *Daily Clarion-Ledger*, October 2, 1902, 2; Jackson Citizens Council, "Keep the Pools Closed," editorial/advertisement, *Clarion-Ledger*, May 5, 1968, 8F; Sarah Fowler, "5 Things to Know About the New Mississippi Civil Rights Museum," *Clarion-Ledger*, November 7, 2017, https://www.clarionledger.com/story/news/local/2017/11/07/5-things-know-new-mississippi-civil-rights-museum/839305001/.

10. Jerry Mitchell, "Mississippi Civil Rights Museum 'Best One Yet,'" *Clarion-Ledger*, December 12, 2017, https://www.clarionledger.com/story/news/local/journeytojustice/2017/12/12/mississippi-civil-rights-museum-best-one-yet/942282001/.

11. John Dittmer, telephone interview by Roger Davis Gatchet and Stephen A. King, June 16, 2021.

12. The authors visited the MCRM together on multiple occasions during a ten-day trip in May 2019. Each museum visit lasted approximately six hours. Because the museum

permits both photography and video, the authors took approximately three thousand photographs documenting every display, artifact, and line of text in the entire exhibit. They also captured digital video recordings of all audiovisual and interactive displays. In addition to writing fieldnotes that served as the starting point for developing this chapter's rhetorical themes, the authors also interviewed Pamela Junior, the MMH-MCRM director, Hezekiah Watkins, an MCRM docent and Mississippi Movement activist, and historian John Dittmer, who consulted on the exhibit.

13. For example, see Greg Dickinson, Carole Blair, and Brian L. Ott, eds., *Places of Public Memory: The Rhetoric of Museums and Memorials* (Tuscaloosa: University of Alabama Press, 2010); Greg Dickinson, Brian L. Ott, and Eric Aoki, "Spaces of Remembering and Forgetting: The Reverent Eye/I at the Plains Indian Museum," *Communication and Critical/Cultural Studies* 3, no. 1 (2006): 27–47, https://doi.org/10.1080/14791420500505619; and Nicholas S. Paliewicz and Marouf Hasian Jr., "Mourning Absences, Melancholic Commemoration, and the Contested Public Memories of the National September 11 Memorial and Museum," *Western Journal of Communication* 80, no. 2 (2016): 140–62, https://doi.org/10.1080/10570314.2015.1128559.

14. Stephen A. King, "Memory, Mythmaking, and Museums: Constructive Authenticity and the Primitive Blues Subject," *Southern Communication Journal* 71, no. 3 (2006): 238–39, https://doi.org/10.1080/10417940600846029.

15. Bernard J. Armada, "Memorial Agon: An Interpretive Tour of the National Civil Rights Museum," *Southern Communication Journal* 63, no. 3 (1998): 235–43, https://doi.org/10.1080/10417949809373096; Roger Davis Gatchet and Stephen A. King, "'I Call Him Father of Us All': Vicarious Transcendence at the B. B. King Museum and Delta Interpretive Center," *Communication and Critical/Cultural Studies* 15, no. 1 (2018): 53–69, https://doi.org/10.1080/14791420.2018.1434315; King, "Memory, Mythmaking, and Museums"; Carly S. Woods, Joshua P. Ewalt, and Sara J. Baker, "A Matter of Regionalism: Remembering Brandon Teena and Willa Cather at the Nebraska History Museum," *Quarterly Journal of Speech* 99, no. 3 (2013): 341–63, https://doi.org/10.1080/00335630.2013.806818.

16. Nicholas S. Paliewicz, "Bent but Not Broken: Remembering Vulnerability and Resiliency at the National September 11 Memorial Museum," *Southern Communication Journal* 82, no. 1 (2017): 11, https://doi.org/10.1080/1041794X.2016.1252422.

17. M. Elizabeth Weiser, *Museum Rhetoric: Building Civic Identity in National Spaces* (University Park: Pennsylvania State University Press, 2017), 42.

18. Weiser, *Museum Rhetoric*, 42.

19. Mississippi Department of Archives and History, *Telling Our Stories: Museum of Mississippi History and Mississippi Civil Rights Museum* (Jackson: University Press of Mississippi, 2017).

20. Susan Mancino, "A Communicative Review of Museums," *Review of Communication* 15, no. 3 (2015): 269, https://doi.org/10.1080/15358593.2015.1077988.

21. Mancino, "A Communicative Review of Museums," 266.

22. Marouf Hasian Jr., "Remembering and Forgetting the 'Final Solution': A Rhetorical Pilgrimage through the U.S. Holocaust Memorial Museum," *Critical Studies in Media Communication* 21, no. 1 (2004): 65, https://doi.org/10.1080/0739318042000184352.

23. Hasian, "Remembering and Forgetting the 'Final Solution,'" 65–66.

24. Armada, "Memorial Agon"; Deborah F. Atwater and Sandra L. Herndon, "Cultural Space and Race: The National Civil Rights Museum and MuseumAfrica," *Howard Journal*

of Communications 14, no. 1 (2003): 15–28, https://doi.org/10.1080/10646170304273; Marouf Hasian Jr., and Nicholas S. Paliewicz, "Taking the Reparatory Turn at the National Memorial for Peace and Justice," *International Journal of Communication* 14 (2020): 2227–45, https://ijoc.org/index.php/ijoc/article/view/12312/3055. See also Julie D. Nelson, "Memorializing the Civil Rights Movement: African American Rhetorics and the International Civil Rights Center and Museum," *Rhetoric Review* 40, no. 1 (2021): 46–58, https://doi.org/10.1080/07350198.2020.1841504.

25. Amanda Lyons, "Giving Shape and Substance to Our Society: William F. Winter, Leadership, and the Mississippi Department of Archives and History," *Southern Quarterly* 54, no. 1 (2016): 130; "Museum Exhibits Relive U.S.' Civil Rights Era," *Jet*, December 31–January 7, 1985, 19.

26. Glenn T. Eskew, "Two Mississippi Museums: Museum of Mississippi History; Mississippi Civil Rights Museum," *American Historical Review* 123, no. 4 (2018): 1273, https://doi.org/10.1093/ahr/rhy185.

27. In a 2010 interview with the *Weekly Standard*, Barbour appeared to praise the Citizens' Council's role in preventing the KKK from establishing a foothold in his hometown of Yazoo City. After his remarks made headlines, Barbour responded: "My point was my town rejected the Ku Klux Klan, but nobody should construe that to mean I think the town leadership were saints, either. Their vehicle, called the 'Citizens [sic] Council,' is totally indefensible, as is segregation. It was a difficult and painful era for Mississippi, the rest of the country, and especially African Americans who were persecuted in that time." See Frank James, "Haley Barbour Explains He Wasn't Praising Racist Group," *National Public Radio*, December 21, 2010, https://www.npr.org/sections/itsallpolitics/2010/12/21/132232306/haley-barbour-explains-he-wasnt-praising-racist-group.

28. Haley Barbour, "Barbour Outlines Purpose of Civil Rights Museum Commission," *Madison County Journal*, October 12, 2006.

29. Laura Hipp, "Museum Receives Panel's Support," *Clarion-Ledger*, December 21, 2006; Haley Barbour, "State of the State," *WLBT*, January 16, 2007, https://www.wlbt.com/story/5946343/state-of-the-state-complete-text/.

30. Christianna Jackson, "Civil Rights Museum Underway," *Jackson Free Press*, July 12, 2012, https://www.jacksonfreepress.com/news/2012/jul/12/civil-rights-museum-underway/.

31. Earnest McBride, "Split in Choosing Funding Over Location for Civil Rights Museum," *Jackson Advocate*, March 3, 2011.

32. Emily Wagster Pettus, "Civil Rights Museum Not Yet a Done Deal," *Clarion-Ledger*, February 4, 2007.

33. Hipp, "Museum Receives."

34. "Museum: Downtown Jackson Appropriate," editorial, *Clarion-Ledger*, February 16, 2008.

35. Ronnie Agnew, editorial, "Civil Rights Museum Belongs in Capital City," *Clarion-Ledger*, February 17, 2008.

36. Hipp, "Museum Receives."

37. Haley Barbour, "Barbour Outlines."

38. Haley Barbour, "State of the State."

39. "No Civil Rights Museum in Miss. Despite Pivotal Role," *Clarion-Ledger*, November 28, 2010.

40. "No Civil Rights Museum in Miss. Despite Pivotal Role."

41. "No Civil Rights Museum in Miss. Despite Pivotal Role."

42. Kim Severson, "New Museums to Shine a Spotlight on Civil Rights Era," *New York Times*, February 19, 2012, https://nyti.ms/2FvN2WK.

43. Haley Barbour and Reuben V. Anderson, foreword to *Telling Our Stories: Museum of Mississippi History and Mississippi Civil Rights Museum*, Mississippi Department of Archives and History (Jackson: University Press of Mississippi, 2017), ix.

44. Barbour and Anderson, *Telling Our Stories*, ix–x.

45. Sarah Richardson and Lily Kleppertknoop, "Mississippi Plans Dual Museums," *American History*, October 2013, 8; Jerry Mitchell, "Historic Museums Planned," *Clarion-Ledger*, June 2, 2013.

46. Mitchell, "Historic Museums Planned."

47. Associated Press, "Miss. Lawmakers Agree to Borrow $250M in Bonds," *The Dispatch*, April 19, 2016, https://cdispatch.com/news/article.asp?aid=49602.

48. Barbour and Anderson, *Telling Our Stories*, x.

49. Anthony Warren, "Museums to Pump Millions into Jackson's Economy," *Northside Sun*, October 3, 2013.

50. Warren, "Museums to Pump Millions."

51. Junior, interview.

52. Mississippi Civil Rights Museum, "Galleries," n.d., accessed March 24, 2022, http://mcrm.mdah.ms.gov/galleries/galleries. See brief descriptions of each gallery, some of which reference the words of civil rights leaders (e.g., King, Hamer).

53. Rickey Thigpen, interview by Roger Davis Gatchet and Stephen A. King, Jackson, Mississippi, May 21, 2019. Original emphasis.

54. Dittmer, telephone interview.

55. maapar, "Worthwhile visit!," *Tripadvisor*, March 17, 2019, https://www.tripadvisor.com/ShowUserReviews-g43833-d13382408-r659120872-Mississippi_Civil_Rights_Museum-Jackson_Mississippi.html.

56. drwalterw, "Amazing Place," *Tripadvisor*, February 11, 2020, https://www.tripadvisor.com/ShowUserReviews-g43833-d13382408-r744428565-Mississippi_Civil_Rights_Museum-Jackson_Mississippi.html.

57. Mississippi Tourism Association, advertisement, *Mississippi Official Tour Guide*, 2022, 45.

58. Mississippi Civil Rights Museum, "Galleries."

59. John W. Bowers, Donovan J. Ochs, Richard J. Jensen, and David P. Schulz, *The Rhetoric of Agitation and Control*, 3rd ed. (Long Grove, IL: Waveland, 2010), 7–8.

60. Akinyele Omowale Umoja, *We Will Shoot Back: Armed Resistance in the Mississippi Freedom Movement* (New York: New York University Press, 2013), 183.

61. Umoja, *We Will Shoot Back*, 185.

62. Edward Onaci, *Free the Land: The Republic of New Afrika and the Pursuit of a Black Nation-State* (Chapel Hill: University of North Carolina Press, 2020), 1, 4.

Conclusion

1. Helen Sims, oral performance, Belzoni, Mississippi, July 18, 2016.

2. Stephen A. King, *I'm Feeling the Blues Right Now: Blues Tourism and the Mississippi Delta* (Jackson: University Press of Mississippi, 2011), 90.

3. Quoted in "Civil Rights on Display," *New York Times Upfront*, February 19, 2018, 4.

4. Myrlie Evers and William F. Winter, introduction to *Telling Our Stories: Museum of Mississippi History and Mississippi Civil Rights Museum*, Mississippi Department of Archives and History (Jackson: University Press of Mississippi, 2017), xii.

5. For consistency purposes, the authors reference both museums because they are marketed as "twin museums" or "two Mississippi Museums." The MCRM is the focus, and is praised, in the majority of journalistic accounts.

6. Liz Willen, "Never Mind Trump's Visit—Mississippi's New Civil Rights Museum Is a Real Game Changer for Education," *The Hechinger Report*, December 11, 2017, https://hechingerreport.org/never-mind-trumps-visit-mississippis-new-civil-rights-museum-real-game-changer-education/.

7. Associated Press, "Attendance Beats Expectations at Mississippi History Museums," *Clarion-Ledger*, July 10, 2018, https://www.clarionledger.com/story/news/2018/07/10/mississippi-new-history-museums-attendance-expectations-civil-rights/773248002/.

8. "Civil Rights Museum Attendance Earns Jackson State Recognition," WJTV, September 26, 2018, https://www.wjtv.com/news/metro/civil-rights-museum-attendance-earns-jackson-state-recognition/.

9. Roslyn Anderson, "Two Mississippi Museums Project Celebrates One Year, Exceeds Expectations," WDAM, December 10, 2018, https://www.wdam.com/2018/12/11/two-mississippi-museums-project-celebrates-one-year-exceeds-expectations/.

10. Amber Helsel and Dustin Cardon, "Pamela Junior Named Director of Two Mississippi Museums," *Jackson Free Press*, July 5, 2019, https://www.jacksonfreepress.com/news/2019/jul/05/pamela-junior-named-director-two-mississippi-museu/.

11. "Mississippi Civil Rights Museum Sees Almost 3,000 Visitors in Eight Hours," WJTV, January 20, 2020, https://www.wjtv.com/news/mississippi-civil-rights-museum-sees-almost-3000-visitors-in-eight-hours/.

12. Jacob Gallant and Reggi Marion, "Two Museums Reopen After 4 Months," WLBT, July 7, 2020, https://www.wlbt.com/2020/07/07/two-museums-reopen-after-months/.

13. Mississippi Department of Archives and History, "MDAH To Reopen Museums & Library in July," press release, July 4, 2020, https://www.mdah.ms.gov/news/mdah-to-reopen-museums-library-in-july.

14. HB 1791, Mississippi Legislature, 2020 Regular Session, http://billstatus.ls.state.ms.us/documents/2020/html/HB/1700-1799/HB1791PS.htm.

15. Mississippi Development Authority, *Fiscal Year 2020 Annual Report*, 2020, 8, https://mississippi.org/news/reports/; Mississippi Development Authority, *Fiscal Year 2019 Annual Report*, 2019, 12, https://mississippi.org/news/reports/.

16. "Visit Mississippi: Officials Tout the Importance [*sic*] State's Tourism Industry, *Vicksburg Post*, March 24, 2021, https://www.vicksburgpost.com/2021/03/24/visit-mississippi-officials-tout-the-importance-states-tourism-industry/.

17. Marlo Dorsey, "How Mississippi Emerged as a Leader in Tourism Recovery," *Travel Pulse*, March 17, 2021, https://www.travelpulse.com/news/destinations/how-mississippi-emerged-as-a-leader-in-tourism-recovery.html.

18. Chet Landry, "U.S. Department of Commerce Investing $2,000,000 in South Mississippi Tourism," WLOX, April 12, 2021, https://www.wlox.com/2021/04/13/us-department-commerce-investing-south-mississippi-tourism/.

19. Mississippi Development Authority, *Fiscal Year 2021 Annual Report*, 2021, 17, https://mississippi.org/news/reports/.

20. Mississippi Development Authority, *Fiscal Year 2021 Annual Report*.

21. Dorit Wagner, "The American South: From Civil Rights Struggle to Civil Rights Tourism," *America Studies Journal* 56 (2012), doi: 10.18422/56-05.

22. Rolando Herts, Zoom interview by Roger Davis Gatchet and Stephen A. King, November 12, 2021.

23. Calvin Trillin, "Back on the Bus," *New Yorker*, July 25, 2011, 36.

24. Susan Neiman, *Learning from the Germans: Race and the Memory of Evil* (New York: Farrar, Straus and Giroux, 2019), 220–21.

25. Quoted in Mia Taylor, "The Rise of Civil Rights Tourism in America's Deep South," *TheStreet*, October 23, 2016, https://www.thestreet.com/personal-finance/education/the-rise-of-civil-rights-tourism-in-america-s-deep-south-13859635.

26. Aallyah Wright, Kelsey Davis Betz, and Bobby Harrison, "For Some in the Delta, Revisiting Emmett Till's Murder about Appeasing Mississippi's Conscience," *Mississippi Today*, July 14, 2018, https://mississippitoday.org/2018/07/14/for-some-in-the-delta-revisiting-emmett-tills-murder-is-about-appeasing-mississippis-conscious/.

27. Patricia A. Davis, *Laying Claim: African American Cultural Memory and Southern Identity* (Tuscaloosa: University of Alabama Press, 2016), 87.

28. Deborah D. Douglas, *U.S. Civil Rights Trail: A Traveler's Guide to the People, Places, and Events that Made the Movement* (New York: Moon, 2021).

29. King, *I'm Feeling the Blues*, 170.

30. Taylor Vance, "William Winter Institute Relocates to Jackson after 19 years at Ole Miss," *Daily Mississippian*, January 31, 2018, https://thedmonline.com/william-winter-institute-relocates-jackson-19-years-ole-miss/.

31. Ronald Loewe, "Civil Rights Tourism in Mississippi: Openings, Closures, Redemption and Remuneration," *Sociology Mind* 4, no. 1 (2014): 85, http://dx.doi.org/10.4236/sm.2014.41011.

32. Jodi Skipper, "Community Development through Reconciliation Tourism: The Behind the Big House Program in Holly Springs, Mississippi," *Community Development* 47, no. 4 (2016): 525–26, doi: 10.1080/15575330.2016.1146783.

33. Courtney E. Cole, "Commemorating Mass Violence: Truth Commission Hearings as a Genre of Public Memory," *Southern Communication Journal* 83, no. 3 (2018): 161–63, https://doi.org/10.1080/1041794X.2018.1432067.

34. Victoria J. Gallagher, "Memory and Reconciliation in the Birmingham Civil Rights Institute," *Rhetoric and Public Affairs* 2, no. 2 (1999): 316, https://doi.org/10.1353/rap.2010.0067.

35. Gallagher, "Memory and Reconciliation," 316.

36. Herts, Zoom interview.

37. Patrick Weems, personal communication, May 11, 2021.

38. Patrick Weems, interview by Roger Davis Gatchet and Stephen A. King, Oxford, Mississippi, May 23, 2019.

39. Weems, personal communication.

40. Nan Elizabeth Woodruff, "The Contested Terrain of Historical Memory in Contemporary Mississippi," *Revue Électronique D'études Sur Le Monde Anglophone* 8, no. 3 (2011), https://doi.org/10.4000/erea.1811.

41. Emmett Till Interpretive Center, n.d., accessed April 18, 2021, https://www.emmett-till.org/.

42. Emmett Till Interpretive Center, "History of the Center," n.d., February 9, 2023, https://www.emmett-till.org/history.

43. Pamela Junior, interview by Roger Davis Gatchet and Stephen A. King, Jackson, Mississippi, May 24, 2019.

44. National Park Service, "Mississippi: COFO Civil Rights Education Center," last updated February 23, 2021, accessed April 30, 2021, https://www.nps.gov/articles/000/mississippi-cofo-civil-rights-education-center.htm. Emphasis added.

45. Visit Jackson! Mississippi, Attraction Guides, brochure, n.d.

46. Linda Jacobson, "History Lessons," *Education Week*, April 4, 2006, https://www.edweek.org/leadership/history-lessons/2006/04.

47. John Dittmer, *Local People: The Struggle for Civil Rights in Mississippi* (Urbana: University of Illinois Press, 1994), 258.

48. SB 2718, Mississippi Legislature, 2006 Regular Session, http://billstatus.ls.state.ms.us/documents/2006/html/SB/2700-2799/SB2718SG.htm.

49. SB 2718, Mississippi Legislature.

50. Sierra Mannie, "Mississippi Textbooks Gloss Over Civil Rights Struggle," *Education Week*, October 4, 2017, https://www.edweek.org/leadership/mississippi-textbooks-gloss-over-civil-rights-struggle/2017/10.

51. Quoted in Josh Carter, "Gov. Reeves Says He Would Support Legislation That Bans Critical Race Theory in Miss. Classrooms," WLBT, June 14, 2021, https://www.wlbt.com/2021/06/14/gov-reeves-says-he-would-support-legislation-that-bans-critical-race-theory-miss-classrooms/.

52. Mississippi Center for Public Policy, *Combating Critical Race Theory in Mississippi*, n.d., accessed January 13, 2022, 2, https://mspolicy.org/wp-content/uploads/2021/10/Combating-Critical-Race-Theory-FINAL.pdf (emphasis added).

53. Mississippi Center for Public Policy, *Combating Critical Race Theory*, 5.

54. Steven Gagliano, "State Superintendent Says Critical Race Theory Isn't in Mississippi Schools," *SuperTalk Mississippi Media*, June 22, 2021, https://www.supertalk.fm/state-superintendent-says-critical-race-theory-isnt-in-mississippi-schools/.

55. Thao Ta and Kaitlin Howell, "Mississippi Senate Passes Bill to Ban Critical Race Theory," WJTV, January 21, 2022, https://www.wjtv.com/news/politics/focused-on-politics/mississippi-senate-passes-bill-to-ban-critical-race-theory/.

56. Ta and Howell, "Mississippi Senate Passes Bill."

57. Jamiel Lynch and Jeremy Grisham, "Mississippi Governor Signs into Law Prohibition on Schools Teaching Critical Race Theory," CNN, March 14, 2022, https://www.cnn.com/2022/03/14/politics/mississippi-critical-race-theory-law/index.html.

58. Tate Reeves, "Governor Reeves Takes Action against Critical Race Theory," *Facebook*, March 14, 2022, https://www.facebook.com/tatereeves/videos/771428113837269/.

59. See, for example, Olmsted's articulation of Critical Race Theory as a rhetorical phenomenon in Audrey P. Olmsted, "Words Are Acts: Critical Race Theory as a Rhetorical Construct," *Howard Journal of Communications* 9, no. 4 (1998): 325, https://doi.org/10.1080/106461798246934.

60. Kimberlé Crenshaw, interview by KK Ottesen, "An Architect of Critical Race Theory: 'We Cannot Allow All of the Lessons from the Civil Rights Movement Forward to Be Packed Up and Put Away For Storage,'" *Washington Post*, January 19, 2022, https://www.washingtonpost.com/lifestyle/magazine/an-architect-of-critical-race-theory-we-cannot-allow-all-of-the-lessons-from-the-civil-rights-movement-forward-to-be-packed-up-and-put-away-for-storage/2022/01/14/24bb31de-627e-11ec-a7e8-3a8455b71fad_story.html.

61. Kayleigh Skinner, "Is Mississippi Really Removing Civil Rights History from Its Teaching Standards?," *Mississippi Today*, January 5, 2022, https://mississippitoday.org/2022/01/05/mississippi-civil-rights-history-social-studies/.

62. Skinner, "Is Mississippi Really Removing Civil Rights History."

63. Quoted in Mac Gordon, "State's Racial History Up for Discussion—Again," *Clarion-Ledger*, January 13, 2022, https://www.clarionledger.com/story/opinion/2022/01/14/mississippi-history-could-taught-without-mlk-kkk-jim-crow-impact/9161835002/.

64. Victoria J. Gallagher, "Memory as Social Action: Cultural Projection and Generic Form in Civil Rights Memorials," in *New Approaches to Rhetoric*, ed. Patricia A. Sullivan and Steven R. Goldzwig (Thousand Oaks, CA: Sage, 2004), 162–63.

65. Jerry Mitchell, "Mississippi Civil Rights, History Museums Set to Surpass Attendance Projections," *Clarion-Ledger*, February 22, 2018, https://www.clarionledger.com/story/news/2018/02/22/mississippi-civil-rights-history-museums-set-surpass-attendance-projections/351167002/.

66. Maegan Parker Brooks, letter, "Editor's Introduction," Fannie Lou Hamer's America, n.d., accessed March 30, 2022, https://www.fannielouhamersamerica.com/find-your-voice/curricular-units. Find Your Voice: The Online Resource for Fannie Lou Hamer Studies is funded through grants from the W. K. Kellogg Foundation and the MDNHA.

67. "Curricular Units," Fannie Lou Hamer's America, n.d., accessed March 30, 2022, https://www.fannielouhamersamerica.com/find-your-voice/curricular-units.

68. "Curricular Units."

69. "BrainPOP and Willamette Professor Partner on New Fannie Lou Hamer Animated Movie," Fannie Lou Hamer's America, August 21, 2019, https://www.fannielouhamersamerica.com/press/brainpop-and-willamette-professor-partner-on-new-fannie-lou-hamer-animated-movie.

70. "Sunflower County Film Academy," Fannie Lou Hamer's America, n.d., accessed March 30, 2022, https://www.fannielouhamersamerica.com/sunflower-county-film-academy.

71. "Sunflower County Film Academy Awarded $22k MDNHA Grant," Fannie Lou Hamer's America, September 5, 2020, https://www.fannielouhamersamerica.com/press/sunflower-county-film-academy-awarded-22k-mdnha-grant.

72. "Fannie Lou Hamer's America Project to Receive Humanities Award," Fannie Lou Hamer's America, December 7, 2021, https://www.fannielouhamersamerica.com/press/fannie-lou-hamers-america-project-to-receive-humanities-award.

73. Rickey Thigpen, interview by Roger Davis Gatchet and Stephen A. King, Jackson, Mississippi, May 21, 2019.

74. Paul LeBlanc, "Mississippi State Legislature Passes Bill to Remove Confederate Symbol from State Flag In Historic Vote," CNN, June 29, 2020, https://www.cnn.com/2020/06/28/politics/mississippi-flag-confederate-emblem/index.html.

75. Keisha Rowe and Lici Beveridge, "Mississippi's State Flag Controversy over the Confederate Emblem: What You Should Know," *Clarion-Ledger*, June 24, 2020, https://www.clarionledger.com/story/news/2020/06/24/mississippi-state-flag-confederate-flag-ms-controversy/3243712001/.

76. Veronica Stracqualursi, "Mississippi Ratifies and Raises Its New State Flag Over the State Capitol for the First Time," CNN, January 13, 2021, https://www.cnn.com/2021/01/12/politics/mississippi-new-state-flag-flown/index.html.

77. Matt Rosendale (@RepRosendale), "I voted against a bill that would make Juneteenth National Independence Day a federal holiday . . . ," Twitter, June 16, 2021, https://twitter.com/RepRosendale/status/1405307496894451717.

78. Matt Rosendale (@RepRosendale), "Their intent is to replace the Fourth of July . . . ," Twitter, June 16, 2021, https://twitter.com/RepRosendale/status/1405307656642912256.

79. Matt Rosendale, "Rep. Rosendale Statement on Juneteenth Vote," June 16, 2021, https://rosendale.house.gov/news/documentsingle.aspx?DocumentID=191.

BIBLIOGRAPHY

Books

Alderman, Derek H. "Street Names as Memorial Arenas: The Reputational Politics of Commemorating Martin Luther King Jr. in a Georgia County." In *The Civil Rights Movement in American Memory*, edited by Renee C. Romano and Leigh Raiford, 67–95. Athens: University of Georgia Press, 2006.

Alinsky, Saul D. *Rules for Radicals: A Pragmatic Primer for Realistic Radicals*. New York: Vintage, 1971.

Anderson, Devery S. *Emmett Till: The Murder That Shocked the World and Propelled the Civil Rights Movement*. Jackson: University Press of Mississippi, 2015.

Armstrong, Julie Buckner. *Mary Turner and the Memory of Lynching*. Athens: University of Georgia Press, 2011.

Asch, Chris Myers. *The Senator and the Sharecropper: The Freedom Struggles of James O. Eastland and Fannie Lou Hamer*. Chapel Hill: University of North Carolina Press, 2008.

Barbour, Haley, and Reuben V. Anderson. Forward to *Telling Our Stories: Museum of Mississippi History and Mississippi Civil Rights Museum*, Mississippi Department of Archives and History, ix–x. Jackson: University Press of Mississippi, 2017.

Beito, David T., and Linda Royster Beito. *T. R. M. Howard: Doctor, Entrepreneur, Civil Rights Pioneer*. Oakland, CA: Independent Institute, 2018.

Bell, Janet Dewart. *Lighting the Fires of Freedom: African American Women in the Civil Rights Movement*. New York: New Press, 2018.

Berrey, Stephen A. *The Jim Crow Routine: Everyday Performances of Race, Civil Rights, and Segregation in Mississippi*. Chapel Hill: University of North Carolina Press, 2015.

Blair, Carole, Greg Dickinson, and Brian L. Ott. "Introduction: Rhetoric/Memory/Place." In *Places of Public Memory: The Rhetoric of Museums and Memorials*, edited by Greg Dickinson, Carole Blair, and Brian L. Ott, 1–54. Tuscaloosa: University of Alabama Press, 2010.

Bowers, John W., Donovan J. Ochs, Richard J. Jensen, and David P. Schulz. *The Rhetoric of Agitation and Control*. 3rd ed. Long Grove, IL: Waveland, 2010.

Bowman, Michael S. "Looking for Stonewall's Arm: Tourist Performance as Research Method." In *Opening Acts: Performance in/as Communication and Cultural Studies*, edited by Judith Hamera, 102–33. Thousand Oaks, CA: Sage, 2006.

Brooks, Maegan Parker. *Fannie Lou Hamer: America's Freedom Fighting Woman*. Lanham, MD: Rowman and Littlefield, 2020.

Brooks, Maegan Parker. *A Voice that Could Stir an Army: Fannie Lou Hamer and the Rhetoric of the Black Freedom Movement*. Jackson: University Press of Mississippi, 2014.

Brummett, Barry. *Rhetorical Dimensions of Popular Culture*. Tuscaloosa: University of Alabama Press, 1991. EBSCOhost eBook Academic Collection.

Buchanan, Burt. "Magnolias and Manufacturing: Southern Imagery in Mississippi's Promotional Publications, 1945–1955." In *Mediated Images of the South: The Portrayal of Dixie in Popular Culture*, edited by Alison F. Slade, Dedria Givens-Carroll, and Amber J. Narro, 89–105. Lanham: Lexington Books, 2012.

Burke, Kenneth. *A Grammar of Motives*. Berkeley: University of California Press, 1969.

Butler, Patrick H. "Past, Present, and Future: The Place of the House Museum in the Museum Community." In *Interpreting Historic House Museums*, edited by Jessica Foy Donnelly, 18–42. Walnut Creek, CA: AltaMira, 2002.

Carrier, Jim. *A Traveler's Guide to the Civil Rights Movement*. Orlando: Harcourt, 2004.

Clark, Gregory. "Rhetorical Experience and the National Jazz Museum in Harlem." In *Places of Public Memory: The Rhetoric of Museums and Memorials*, edited by Greg Dickinson, Carole Blair, and Brian L. Ott, 113–35. Tuscaloosa: University of Alabama Press, 2010.

Cobb, Charles E. Jr. *On the Road to Freedom: A Guided Tour of the Civil Rights Trail*. Chapel Hill: Algonquin, 2008.

Cobb, Charles E. Jr. *This Nonviolent Stuff'll Get You Killed: How Guns Made the Civil Rights Movement Possible*. New York: Basic, 2014. ProQuest Ebook Central.

Cobb, James C. *The Most Southern Place on Earth: The Mississippi Delta and the Roots of Regional Identity*. New York: Oxford University Press, 1992.

Cobb, James C. *The Selling of the South: The Southern Crusade for Industrial Development, 1936–1990*, 2nd ed. Urbana: University of Illinois Press, 1993.

Conforth, Bruce, and Gayle Dean Wardlow. *Up Jumped the Devil: The Real Life of Robert Johnson*. Chicago: Chicago Review, 2019.

Conquergood, Dwight. *Cultural Struggles: Performance, Ethnography, Praxis*. Edited by Patrick Johnson. Ann Arbor: University of Michigan Press, 2013. ProQuest Ebook Central.

Davis, Patricia G. *Laying Claim: African American Cultural Memory and Southern Identity*. Tuscaloosa: University of Alabama Press, 2016.

Davis, Townsend. *Weary Feet, Rested Souls: A Guided History of the Civil Rights Movement*. New York: W. W. Norton, 1998.

Dittmer, John. *Local People: The Struggle for Civil Rights in Mississippi*. Urbana: University of Illinois Press, 1994.

Douglas, Deborah D. *U.S. Civil Rights Trail: A Traveler's Guide to the People, Places, and Events That Made the Movement*. Berkeley: Moon, 2021.

Dwyer, Owen J. "Interpreting the Civil Rights Movement: Contradiction, Confirmation, and the Cultural Landscape." In *The Civil Rights Movement in American Memory*, edited by Renee C. Romano and Leigh Raiford, 5–27. Athens: University of Georgia Press, 2006.

Dwyer, Owen J., and Derek H. Alderman. *Civil Rights Memorials and the Geography of Memory*. Chicago: The Center for American Places at Columbia College Chicago, 2008.

Eskew, Glenn. "The Birmingham Civil Rights Institute and the New Ideology of Tolerance." In *The Civil Rights Movement in American Memory*, edited by Renee C. Romano and Leigh Raiford, 28–66. Athens: University of Georgia Press, 2006.

Estes, Steve. "Engendering Movement Memories: Remembering Race and Gender in the Mississippi Movement." In *The Civil Rights Movement in American Memory*, edited by Renee C. Romano and Leigh Raiford, 290–312. Athens: University of Georgia Press, 2006.

Evers, Myrlie, with William Peters. *For Us, the Living*. Garden City, NY: Doubleday, 1967.

Evers, Myrlie, and William F. Winter. "Introduction." In *Telling Our Stories: Museum of Mississippi History and Mississippi Civil Rights Museum*, Mississippi Department of Archives and History, xi–xii. Jackson: University Press of Mississippi, 2017.

Ewalt, Joshua P., Jessy J. Ohl, and Damien Smith Pfister. "Rhetorical Field Methods in the Tradition of *Imitatio*." In *Text + Field: Innovations in Rhetorical Method*, edited by Sara L. McKinnon, Robert Asen, Karma R. Chávez, and Robert Glenn Howard, 40–55. University Park: Pennsylvania State University Press, 2016.

Falck, Susan T. *Remembering Dixie: The Battle to Control Historical Memory in Natchez, Mississippi, 1865–1941*. Jackson: University Press of Mississippi, 2019.

Fields, Karen. "What One Cannot Remember Mistakenly." In *History and Memory in African-American Culture*, edited by Geneviève Fabre and Robert O'Meally, 150–63. New York: Oxford University Press, 1994.

Fleming, John E. "Introduction." In *Telling Our Stories: Museum of Mississippi History and Mississippi Civil Rights Museum*, Mississippi Department of Archives and History, 99–101. Jackson: University Press of Mississippi, 2017.

Fuller, Jennifer. "Debating the Present through the Past: Representations of the Civil Rights Movement in the 1990s." In *The Civil Rights Movement in American Memory*, edited by Renee C. Romano and Leigh Raiford, 167–96. Athens: University of Georgia Press, 2006.

Gaillard, Frye. *Alabama's Civil Rights Trail: An Illustrated Guide to the Cradle of Freedom*. With Jennifer Lindsay and Jane DeNeefe. Tuscaloosa: University of Alabama Press, 2010.

Gallagher, Victoria J. "Memory as Social Action: Cultural Projection and Generic Form in Civil Rights Memorials." In *New Approaches to Rhetoric*, edited by Patricia A. Sullivan and Steven R. Goldzwig, 149–71. Thousand Oaks, CA: Sage, 2004.

Gallagher, Victoria J., and Margaret R. LaWare. "Sparring with Public Memory: The Rhetorical Embodiment of Race, Power, and Conflict in the *Monument to Joe Louis*." In *Places of Public Memory: The Rhetoric of Museums and Memorials*, edited by Greg Dickinson, Carole Blair, and Brian L. Ott, 87–112. Tuscaloosa: University of Alabama Press, 2010.

Gilmore, Glenda Elizabeth. *Defying Dixie: The Radical Roots of Civil Rights 1919–1950*. New York: W. W. Norton, 2008.

Gorn, Elliott J. *Let the People See: The Story of Emmett Till*. New York: Oxford University Press, 2018.

Goudsouzian, Aram. *Down to the Crossroads: Civil Rights, Black Power, and the Meredith March Against Fear*. New York: Farrar, Straus and Giroux, 2014.

Gronbeck, Bruce E. "The Rhetorics of the Past: History, Argument, and Collective Memory." In *Doing Rhetorical History: Concepts and Cases*, edited by Kathleen J. Turner, 47–60. Tuscaloosa: University of Alabama Press, 1998.

Hale, Jon N. *The Freedom Schools: Student Activists in the Mississippi Civil Rights Movement*. New York: Columbia University Press, 2016.

Hamlin, Françoise N. *Crossroads at Clarksdale: The Black Freedom Struggle in the Mississippi Delta after World War II*. Chapel Hill: University of North Carolina Press, 2012.

Higginbotham, Sylvia, and Lisa Monti. *The Insiders' Guide to Mississippi*. Manteo, NC: The Insiders' Guides, 1994.

Hill, Karlos K. *Beyond the Rope: The Impact of Lynching on Black Culture and Memory*. Cambridge: Cambridge University Press, 2016.

Hill, Lance. *The Deacons for Defense: Armed Resistance and the Civil Rights Movement*. Chapel Hill: University of North Carolina Press, 2004.

Hogan, Wesley. "Grassroots Organizing in Mississippi that Changed National Politics." In *The Civil Rights Movement in Mississippi*, edited by Ted Ownby, 3–34. Jackson: University Press of Mississippi, 2013.

Hogan, Wesley. *Many Minds, One Heart: SNCC's Dream for a New America*. Chapel Hill: University of North Carolina Press, 2007.

Houck, Davis W., and Matthew A. Grindy. *Emmett Till and the Mississippi Press*. Jackson: University Press of Mississippi, 2008.

Joseph, Peniel E. "Introduction: Toward a Historiography of the Black Power Movement." In *The Black Power Movement: Rethinking the Civil Rights-Black Power Era*, edited by Peniel E. Joseph, 1–25. New York: Routledge, 2006.

Joseph, Peniel E. *Stokely: A Life*. New York: Basic Civitas, 2014.

Joseph, Peniel E. *Waiting 'Til the Midnight Hour: A Narrative History of Black Power in America*. New York: Henry Holt, 2006.

King, Stephen A. *I'm Feeling the Blues Right Now: Blues Tourism and the Mississippi Delta*. Jackson: University Press of Mississippi, 2011.

King, Stephen A. "People Get Ready: The Civil Rights Movement, Protest Music, and the Rhetoric of Resistance." In *Social Controversy and Public Address in the 1960s and Early 1970s: A Rhetorical History of the United States*, vol. 9, edited by Richard J. Jensen, 251–89. East Lansing: Michigan State University Press, 2017.

Landau, Jamie. "Feeling Rhetorical Critics: Another Affective-Emotional Field Method for Rhetorical Studies." In *Text + Field: Innovations in Rhetorical Method*, edited by Sara L. McKinnon, Robert Asen, Karma R. Chávez, and Robert Glenn Howard, 72–85. University Park: Pennsylvania State University Press, 2016.

Mace, Darryl. *In Remembrance of Emmett Till: Regional Stories and Media Responses to the Black Freedom Struggle*. Lexington: University Press of Kentucky, 2014.

Mandala Research. *The African American Traveler, 2011 Edition: Final Report*. Alexandria, VA: Mandala Research, 2011.

Marshall, James P. *Student Activism and Civil Rights in Mississippi: Protest Politics and the Struggle for Racial Justice, 1960–1965*. Baton Rouge: Louisiana State University Press, 2013.

Martin, Waldo. "Civil Rights, African American." In *The New Encyclopedia of Southern Culture*, vol. 24, *Race*, edited by Thomas C. Holt and Laurie B. Green, 39–44. Chapel Hill: University of North Carolina Press, 2013.

McKinnon, Sara L., Robert Asen, Karma R. Chávez, and Robert Glenn Howard. "Introduction: Articulating Text and Field in the Nodes of Rhetorical Scholarship." In *Text + Field: Innovations in Rhetorical Method*, edited by Sara L. McKinnon, Robert Asen, Karma R. Chávez, and Robert Glenn Howard, 1–21. University Park: Pennsylvania State University Press, 2016.

McKinnon, Sara L., Robert Asen, Karma R. Chávez, and Robert Glenn Howard, eds. *Text + Field: Innovations in Rhetorical Method*. University Park: Pennsylvania State University Press, 2016.

Mills, Kay. *This Little Light of Mine: The Life of Fannie Lou Hamer*. Lexington: University Press of Kentucky, 2007.

Mississippi Department of Archives and History. *Telling Our Stories: Museum of Mississippi History and Mississippi Civil Rights Museum*. Jackson: University Press of Mississippi, 2017.

Mitchell, Dennis J. *A New History of Mississippi*. Jackson: University Press of Mississippi, 2014.

Morgan, Edward P. "The Good, the Bad, and the Forgotten: Media Culture and Public Memory of the Civil Rights Movement." In *The Civil Rights Movement in American Memory*, edited by Renee C. Romano and Leigh Raiford, 137–66. Athens: University of Georgia Press, 2006.

Morris, Tiyi M. *Womanpower Unlimited and the Black Freedom Struggle in Mississippi*. Athens: University of Georgia Press, 2015.

Morris, Willie. *The Ghosts of Medgar Evers: A Tale of Race, Murder, Mississippi, and Hollywood*. New York: Random House, 1998.

Morrison, Minion K. C. *Aaron Henry of Mississippi: Inside Agitator*. Fayetteville: University of Arkansas Press, 2015.

Neiman, Susan. *Learning from the Germans: Race and the Memory of Evil*. New York: Farrar, Straus and Giroux, 2019.

Newman, Bob. *Shadows of Emmett Till*. Heidelberg, Germany: Kehrer, 2022.

Ogletree, Charles J., and Austin Sarat. "Introduction: Bridging the Black-White Divide." In *Racial Reconciliation and the Healing of a Nation: Beyond Law and Rights*, edited by Charles J. Ogletree and Austin Sarat, 1–24. New York: New York University Press, 2017.

O'Meally, Robert, and Geneviève Fabre. Introduction to *History and Memory in African-American Culture*, edited by Geneviève Fabre and Robert O'Meally (3–17). New York: Oxford University Press, 1994.

Onaci, Edward. *Free the Land: The Republic of New Afrika and the Pursuit of a Black Nation-State*. Chapel Hill: University of North Carolina Press, 2020.

Ownby, Ted. "Nobody Knows the Troubles I've Seen, but Does Anybody Want to Hear about Them When They're on Vacation?" In *Southern Journeys: Tourism, History, and Culture in the Modern South*, edited by Richard D. Starnes, 240–49. Tuscaloosa: University of Alabama Press, 2003.

Paredez, Deborah. *Selenidad: Selena, Latinos, and the Performance of Memory*. Durham: Duke University Press, 2009.

Payne, Charles M. *I've Got the Light of Freedom: The Organizing Tradition and the Mississippi Freedom Struggle*. Berkeley: University of California Press, 1995.

Phillips, Kendall R. Introduction to *Framing Public Memory*, 1–14. Edited by Kendall R. Phillips. Tuscaloosa: University of Alabama Press, 2004.

Raiford, Leigh. *Imprisoned in a Luminous Glare: Photography and the African American Freedom Struggle*. Chapel Hill: University of North Carolina Press, 2011.

Raiford, Leigh. "Restaging Revolution: Black Power, *Vibe* Magazine, and Photographic Memory." In *The Civil Rights Movement in American Memory*, edited by Renee C. Romano and Leigh Raiford, 220–49. Athens: University of Georgia Press, 2006.

Raiford, Leigh, and Renee C. Romano. "Introduction: The Struggle Over Memory." In *The Civil Rights Movement in American Memory*, edited by Renee C. Romano and Leigh Raiford, xi–xxiv. Athens: University of Georgia Press, 2006.

Rolph, Stephanie R. *Resisting Equality: The Citizens' Council, 1954–1989*. Baton Rouge: Louisiana State University Press, 2018.

Scott, James C. *Domination and the Arts of Resistance: Hidden Transcripts*. New Haven: Yale University Press, 1990.

Senda-Cook, Samantha, Aaron Hess, Michael K. Middleton, and Danielle Endress, eds. *Readings in Rhetorical Fieldwork*. New York: Routledge, 2019.

"The Shame of Our Nation." Editorial. *Daily Worker*. September 26, 1955. In *The Lynching of Emmett Till: A Documentary Narrative*, edited by Christopher Metress, 118–19. Charlottesville: University of Virginia Press, 2002.

Sharpe, Christina. *In the Wake: On Blackness and Being*. Durham: Duke University Press, 2016.

Tell, Dave. *Remembering Emmett Till*. Chicago: University of Chicago Press, 2019.

Thomas, Johnny B., and Thomas J. Durant Jr. *A Stone of Hope: Rising above Slavery, Jim Crow, and Poverty in Glendora, Mississippi*. Bloomington, IN: Xlibris, 2017.

Till-Mobley, Mamie, and Christopher Benson. *Death of Innocence: The Story of the Hate Crime That Changed America*. New York: One World, 2003.

Timothy, Dallen J. *Cultural Heritage and Tourism: An Introduction*. Bristol, England: Channel View, 2011.

Trouillot, Michel-Rolph. *Silencing the Past: Power and the Production of History*. Boston: Beacon, 1995.

Tyson, Timothy B. *The Blood of Emmett Till*. New York: Simon and Schuster, 2017.

Umoja, Akinyele. "'It's Time for Black Men . . .': The Deacons for Defense and the Mississippi Movement." In *The Civil Rights Movement in Mississippi*, edited by Ted Ownby, 204–29. Jackson: University Press of Mississippi, 2013.

Umoja, Akinyele. *We Will Shoot Back: Armed Resistance in the Mississippi Freedom Movement*. New York: New York University Press, 2013.

Van Maanen, John. *Tales of the Field: On Writing Ethnography*. Chicago: University of Chicago Press, 1988.

Visser-Maessen, Laura. *Robert Parris Moses: A Life in Civil Rights and Leadership at the Grassroots*. Chapel Hill: University of North Carolina Press, 2016.

Walters, Ronald W. *The Price of Racial Reconciliation*. Ann Arbor: University of Michigan Press, 2008.

Weiser, M. Elizabeth. *Museum Rhetoric: Building Civic Identity in National Spaces*. University Park: Pennsylvania State University Press, 2017.

"What You Can Do about the Disgrace in Sumner." Editorial. *Chicago Defender*. October 1, 1955. In *The Lynching of Emmett Till: A Documentary Narrative*, edited by Christopher Metress, 127–28. Charlottesville: University of Virginia Press, 2002.

Whitfield, Stephen J. *A Death in the Delta: The Story of Emmett Till*. Baltimore: John Hopkins University Press, 1988.

Whitlinger, Claire. *Between Remembrance and Repair: Commemorating Racial Violence in Philadelphia, Mississippi*. Chapel Hill: University of North Carolina Press, 2020.

Wilkerson, Isabel. *Caste: The Origins of Our Discontents*. New York: Random House, 2020.

Williams, Michael Vinson. *Medgar Evers: Mississippi Martyr*. Fayetteville: University of Arkansas Press, 2011.

Williams, Michael Vinson. "The Struggle for Black Citizenship: Medgar Wiley Evers and the Fight for Civil Rights in Mississippi." In *The Civil Rights Movement in Mississippi*, edited by Ted Ownby, 59–89. Jackson: University Press of Mississippi, 2013.

Wilson, Charles Reagan, ed. *The New Encyclopedia of Southern Culture*, vol. 4, *Myth, Manners, and Memory*. Chapel Hill: University of North Carolina Press, 2006.

Woodruff, Nan Elizabeth. *American Congo: The African American Freedom Struggle in the Delta*. Cambridge: Harvard University Press, 2003.

Young, Linda. *Historic House Museums in the United States and the United Kingdom: A History*. Lanham, MD: Rowman and Littlefield, 2017.

Zarefsky, David. "Four Senses of Rhetorical History." In *Doing Rhetorical History: Concepts and Cases*, edited by Kathleen J. Turner, 19–32. Tuscaloosa: University of Alabama Press, 1998.

Journals

Aden, Roger C., Min Wha Han, Stephanie Norander, Michael E. Pfahl, Timothy P. Pollack, and Stephanie L. Young. "Re-Collection: A Proposal for Refining the Study of Collective Memory and Its Places." *Communication Theory* 19, no. 3 (2009): 311–36. doi: 10.1111/j.1468-2885.2009.01345.x.

Alderman, Derek H. "'History by the Spoonful' in North Carolina: The Textual Politics of State Highway Historical Markers." *Southeastern Geographer* 52, no. 4 (2012): 355–73. doi: 10.1353/sgo.2012.0035.

Alderman, Derek H. "Street Names and the Scaling of Memory: The Politics of Commemorating Martin Luther King, Jr. within the African American Community." *Area* 35, no. 2 (2003): 163–73. https://doi.org/10.1111/1475-4762.00250.

Armada, Bernard J. "Memorial Agon: An Interpretive Tour of the National Civil Rights Museum." *Southern Communication Journal* 63, no. 3 (1998): 235–43. http://dx.doi.org/10.1080/10417949809373096.

Atwater Deborah F., and Sandra L. Herndon. "Cultural Space and Race: The National Civil Rights Museum and MuseumAfrica," *Howard Journal of Communications* 14, no. 1 (2003): 15–28. https://doi.org/10.1080/10646170304273.

Barck, Dorothy C. "The First Historic House Museum." *Journal of the Society of Architectural Historians* 14, no. 2 (1955): 30–32. https://doi.org/10.2307/987787.

Black, Jason Edward. "Here Is a Strange and Bitter Crop: Emmett Till and the Rhetorical Complications of Treescape Memory." *Argumentation and Advocacy* 55, no. 1 (2019): 24–41. https://doi.org/10.1080/10511431.2018.1491769.

Borton, Ian M. "Effects of Race, Sex, and Victims' Reasons for Victim-Offender Dialogue." *Conflict Resolution Quarterly* 27, no. 2 (2009): 215–35. doi: 10.1002/crq.256.

Brinkman, Bob. "Invisible Texans: Seeking Minorities in 100 Years of Texas Historical Markers." *Touchstone* 29 (2010): 58–65.

Brooks, Maegan Parker. "Oppositional Ethos: Fannie Lou Hamer and the Vernacular Persona." *Rhetoric and Public Affairs* 14, no. 3 (2011): 511–48. doi: 10.1353/rap.2011.0024.

Bruyneel, Kevin. "The King's Body: The Martin Luther King Jr. Memorial and the Politics of Collective Memory." *History and Memory* 26, no. 1 (2014): 75–108. doi: 10.2979/histmemo.26.1.75.

Cloud, Dana L. "Hegemony or Concordance?: The Rhetoric of Tokenism in 'Oprah' Winfrey's Rags-to-Riches Biography." *Critical Studies in Mass Communication* 13, no. 2 (1996): 115–37. https://doi.org/10.1080/15295039609366967.

Cole, Courtney E. "Commemorating Mass Violence: Truth Commission Hearings as a Genre of Public Memory." *Southern Communication Journal* 83, no. 3 (2018): 149–66. https://doi.org/10.1080/1041794X.2018.1432067.

De Bres, Karen. "Defining Vernacular Tourism." *Annals of Tourism Research* 23, no. 4 (1996): 945–48. https://doi.org/10.1016/0160-7383(96)00024-2.

Dickinson, Greg, Brian L. Ott, and Eric Aoki. "Spaces of Remembering and Forgetting: The Reverent Eye/I at the Plains Indian Museum." *Communication and Critical/Cultural Studies* 3, no. 1 (2006): 27–47. https://doi.org/10.1080/14791420500505619.

Dwyer, Owen J. "Interpreting the Civil Rights Movement: Place, Memory, and Conflict." *Professional Geographer* 52, no. 4 (2000): 660–71. doi: 10.1111/0033-0124.00255.

Dwyer, Owen J. "Location, Politics, and the Production of Civil Rights Memorial Landscapes." *Urban Geography* 23, no. 1 (2002): 31–56. https://doi.org/10.2747/0272-3638.23.1.31.

Dwyer, Owen, David Butler, and Perry Carter. "Commemorative Surrogation and the American South's Changing Heritage Landscape." *Tourism Geographies* 15, no. 3 (2013): 424–43. https://doi.org/10.1080/14616688.2012.699091.

Eskew, Glenn T. "From Civil War to Civil Rights: Selling Alabama as Heritage Tourism." *International Journal of Hospitality and Tourism Administration* 2, no. 3–4 (2001): 201–14. https://doi.org/10.1300/J149v02n03_09.

Eskew, Glenn T. "Two Mississippi Museums: Museum of Mississippi History; Mississippi Civil Rights Museum." *American Historical Review* 123, no. 4 (2018): 1272–75. https://doi.org/10.1093/ahr/rhy185.

Fisher, Walter R. "Narration as a Human Communication Paradigm: The Case of Public Moral Argument." *Communication Monographs* 51, no. 1 (1984): 1–22. https://doi.org/10.1080/03637758409390180.

Foster, Douglas A. "Reclaiming Reconciliation: The Corruption of 'Racial Reconciliation' and How It Might Be Reclaimed for Racial Justice and Unity." *Journal of Ecumenical Studies* 55, no. 1 (2020): 63–81. doi: 10.1353/ecu.2020.0015.

Gallagher, Victoria J. "Memory and Reconciliation in the Birmingham Civil Rights Institute." *Rhetoric and Public Affairs* 2, no. 2 (1999): 303–20. https://doi.org/10.1353/rap.2010.0067.

Gatchet, Roger Davis, and Stephen A. King. "'I Call Him Father of Us All': Vicarious Transcendence at the B. B. King Museum and Delta Interpretive Center." *Communication and Critical/Cultural Studies* 15, no. 1 (2018): 53–69. https://doi.org/10.1080/14791420.2018.1434315.

Griffin, Larry J., and Kenneth A. Bollen. "What Do These Memories Do?: Civil Rights Remembrance and Racial Attitudes." *American Sociological Review* 74, no. 4 (2009): 594–614. https://doi.org/10.1177%2F000312240907400405.

Griffin, Larry J., and Peggy G. Hargis. "Surveying Memory: The Past in Black and White." *Southern Literary Journal* 40, no. 2 (2008): 42–69. doi: 10.1353/slj.0.0017.

Hanna, Stephen P., and E. Fariss Hodder. "Reading the Signs: Using a Qualitative Geographic Information System to Examine the Commemoration of Slavery and Emancipation on Historical Markers in Fredericksburg, Virginia." *Cultural Geographies* 22, no. 3 (2015): 509–29.

Harold, Christine, and Kevin Michael DeLuca. "Behold the Corpse: Violent Images and the Case of Emmett Till," *Rhetoric & Public Affairs* 8, no. 2 (2005): 263–86. doi: 10.1353/rap.2005.0075.

Hasian, Marouf, Jr. "Remembering and Forgetting the 'Final Solution': A Rhetorical Pilgrimage through the U.S. Holocaust Memorial Museum." *Critical Studies in Media Communication*, 21, no. 1 (2004): 64–92. https://doi.org/10.1080/0739318042000184352.

Hasian, Marouf, Jr., and Nicholas S. Paliewicz. "Taking the Reparatory Turn at the National Memorial for Peace and Justice." *International Journal of Communication* 14 (2020): 2227–45. https://ijoc.org/index.php/ijoc/article/view/12312/3055.

Hendrickson, Paul. "Mississippi Haunting." *Rhetoric and Public Affairs* 8, no. 2 (2005): 177–88. doi: 10.1353/rap.2005.0074.

Honey, Michael. "Doing Public History at the National Civil Rights Museum: A Conversation with Juanita Moore." *The Public Historian* 17, no. 1 (1995): 71–84. https://doi.org/10.2307/3378352.

Houck, Davis W. "Killing Emmett." *Rhetoric and Public Affairs* 8, no. 2 (2005): 225–62. doi: 10.1353/rap.2005.0078.

King, Claire Sisco. "American Queerer: Norman Rockwell and the Art of Queer Feminist Critique." *Women's Studies in Communication* 39, no. 2 (2016): 157–76. https://doi.org/10.1080/07491409.2016.1165778.

King, Claire Sisco. "Hitching Wagons to Stars: Celebrity, Metonymy, Hegemony, and the Case of Will Smith." *Communication and Critical/Cultural Studies* 14, no. 1 (2017): 83–102. https://doi.org/10.1080/14791420.2016.1202422.

King, Stephen A. "Memory, Mythmaking, and Museums: Constructive Authenticity and the Primitive Blues Subject." *Southern Communication Journal* 71, no. 3 (2006): 235–50. https://doi.org/10.1080/10417940600846029.

Kitsch, Sara R. "Minting Public Memory: Substitution Logics and Gendered Commemoration in the First Spouse Coin." *Women's Studies in Communication* 40, no. 4 (2017): 419–39. https://doi.org/10.1080/07491409.2017.1373717.

Labuda, Patryk. "Racial Reconciliation in Mississippi: An Evaluation of the Proposal to Establish a Mississippi Truth and Reconciliation Commission." *Harvard Journal on Racial and Ethnic Justice* 27 (2011): 1–48.

Loewe, Ronald. "Civil Rights Tourism in Mississippi: Openings, Closures, Redemption and Remuneration." *Sociology Mind* 4, no. 1 (2014): 84–92. http://dx.doi.org/10.4236/sm.2014.41011.

Lyons, Amanda. "Giving Shape and Substance to Our Society: William F. Winter, Leadership, and the Mississippi Department of Archives and History." *Southern Quarterly* 54, no. 1 (2016): 116–38.

Mancino, Susan. "A Communicative Review of Museums." *Review of Communication* 15, no. 3 (2015): 258–73. https://doi.org/10.1080/15358593.2015.1077988.

Maxson, J. David. "Second Line to Bury White Supremacy: Take 'Em Down Nola, Monument Removal, and Residual Memory." *Quarterly Journal of Speech* 106, no. 1 (2020): 48–71. https://doi.org/10.1080/00335630.2019.1704428.

McGee, Michael Calvin. "Text, Context, and the Fragmentation of Contemporary Culture." *Western Journal of Speech Communication* 54, no. 3 (1990): 274–89. https://doi.org/10.1080/10570319009374343.

McMillen, Neil R. "Reconstruction and Its Aftermath: Mississippi History, 1865–1890." *Journal of American History* 77, no. 1 (1990): 239–46. https://doi.org/10.2307/2078658.

Mikula, Maja. "Vernacular Museum: Communal Bonding and Ritual Memory Transfer among Displaced Communities." *International Journal of Heritage Studies* 21, no. 8 (2015): 757–72. https://doi.org/10.1080/13527258.2015.1020961.

Nelson, Julie D. "Memorializing the Civil Rights Movement: African American Rhetorics and the International Civil Rights Center and Museum." *Rhetoric Review* 40, no. 1 (2021): 46–58. https://doi.org/10.1080/07350198.2020.1841504.

Olmsted, Audrey P. "Words Are Acts: Critical Race Theory as a Rhetorical Construct." *Howard Journal of Communications* 9, no. 4 (1998): 323–31. https://doi.org/10.1080/106461798246934.

Otterstrom, Samuel M., and James A. Davis. "Historical Markers in the Western United States: Regional and Cultural Contrasts." *Journal of Heritage Tourism* 15, no. 5 (2020): 533–53. https://doi.org/10.1080/1743873X.2019.1695804.
Paliewicz, Nicholas S. "Bent but Not Broken: Remembering Vulnerability and Resiliency at the National September 11 Memorial Museum." *Southern Communication Journal* 82, no. 1 (2017): 1–14. https://doi.org/10.1080/1041794X.2016.1252422.
Paliewicz, Nicholas S., and Marouf Hasian, Jr. "Mourning Absences, Melancholic Commemoration, and the Contested Public Memories of the National September 11 Memorial and Museum." *Western Journal of Communication* 80, no. 2 (2016): 140–62. https://doi.org/10.1080/10570314.2015.1128559.
Romano, Renee. "Moving beyond 'The Movement That Changed the World': Bringing the History of the Cold War into Civil Rights Museums." *Public Historian* 31, no. 2 (2009): 32–51. https://doi.org/10.1525/tph.2009.31.2.32.
Royster, Jacqueline Jones. "When the First Voice You Hear Is Not Your Own." *College Composition and Communication* 47, no. 1 (1996): 29–40.
Skipper, Jodi. "Community Development through Reconciliation Tourism: The Behind the Big House Program in Holly Springs, Mississippi." *Community Development* 47, no. 4 (2016): 514–29. doi: 10.1080/15575330.2016.1146783.
Sloop, John M., and Kent A. Ono. "Out-law Discourse: The Critical Politics of Material Judgment." *Philosophy and Rhetoric* 30, no. 1 (1997): 50–69.
Tell, Dave. "Remembering Emmett Till: Reflections on Geography, Race, and Memory." *Advances in the History of Rhetoric* 20, no. 2 (2017): 121–38. https://doi.org/10.1080/15362426.2017.1325414.
Tell, Dave. "The 'Shocking Story' of Emmett Till and the Politics of Public Confession." *Quarterly Journal of Speech* 94, no. 2 (2008): 156–78. https://doi.org/10.1080/00335630801975426.
VanSlette, Sarah Hagedorn, and Josh Boyd. "Lawbreaking Jokers: Tricksters Using Outlaw Discourse." *Communication Quarterly* 59, no. 5 (2011): 591–602. https://doi.org/10.1080/01463373.2011.614214.
Wagner, Dorit. "The American South: From Civil Rights Struggle to Civil Rights Tourism." *American Studies Journal* 56 (2012). doi: 10.18422/56-05.
Woodruff, Nan Elizabeth. "The Contested Terrain of Historical Memory in Contemporary Mississippi." *Revue Électronique D'études Sur Le Monde Anglophone* 8, no. 3 (2011). https://doi.org/10.4000/erea.1811.
Woods, Carly S., Joshua P. Ewalt, and Sara J. Baker. "A Matter of Regionalism: Remembering Brandon Teena and Willa Cather at the Nebraska History Museum." *Quarterly Journal of Speech* 99, no. 3 (2013): 341–63. https://doi.org/10.1080/00335630.2013.806818.

Magazines

Associated Press. "Black Tourism Power." *Marketing News*, June 22, 1998.
Carter, Hodding III. "Citadel of the Citizens Council." *New York Times Magazine*, November 12, 1961.
"Civil Rights on Display." *New York Times Upfront*, February 19, 2018.
"The Continuing Struggle for a National King Holiday." *Ebony*, January 1988.

"Death in Mississippi." *Commonweal*, September 23, 1955.
"Discover Money Road." Advertisement. *Living Blues*, December 2015.
"Find America's Soul Laid Bare on Money Road." Advertisement. *Living Blues*, June 2015.
Levin, Kevin M. "Where It Comes to Historical Markers, Every Word Matters." *Smithsonian Magazine*, July 6, 2017. https://www.smithsonianmag.com/history/when-it-comes-historical-markers-every-word-matters-180963973/.
Massie, Robert K. "Mississippi, The Old South Besieged." *USA*1*, July 1962.
Molpus, Nash. "Civil Rights Memorial Design Selected." *Southern Register*, Fall 2002.
"Museum Exhibits Relive U.S.' Civil Rights Era." *Jet*, December 31-January 7, 1985.
Richardson, Sarah, and Lily Kleppertknoop. "Mississippi Plans Dual Museums." *American History*, October 2013.
"Statue of Medgar Evers Unveiled in Jackson, Ms." *Jet*, July 20, 1992.
"10 Most Updates: Mississippi's Freedom Houses." *Elevation: The Journal of the Mississippi Heritage Trust*, Fall 2021.
Trillin, Calvin. "Back on the Bus." *New Yorker*, July 25, 2011.
"2021 10 Most Endangered Historic Places in Mississippi." *Elevation: The Journal of the Mississippi Heritage Trust*, Fall 2021.

Newspapers and Newsletters

Agnew, Ronnie. Editorial. "Civil Rights Museum Belongs in Capital City." *Clarion-Ledger*, February 17, 2008.
Another Negro. Letter to the editor. *Norfolk Virginia Pilot*, September 27, 1955.
Apel, Therese. "Mississippi Marks 50th Anniversary of Medgar Evers' Death." *Chicago Tribune*, June 12, 2013. https://www.chicagotribune.com/news/ct-xpm-2013-06-12-sns-rt-us-usa-race-eversbre95b190-20130612-story.html.
Associated Press. "Attendance Beats Expectations at Mississippi History Museums." *Clarion-Ledger*, July 10, 2018. https://www.clarionledger.com/story/news/2018/07/10/mississippi-new-history-museums-attendance-expectations-civil-rights/773248002/.
Associated Press. "Miss. Lawmakers Agree to Borrow $250M in Bonds." *The Dispatch*, April 19, 2016. https://cdispatch.com/news/article.asp?aid=49602.
Atkins, Joe, and Tom Brennan. "Bryant Wants the Past to 'Stay Dead.'" *Clarion-Ledger*, August 25, 1985.
Barbour, Haley. "Barbour Outlines Purpose of Civil Rights Museum Commission." *Madison County Journal*, October 12, 2006.
Berry, Deborah Barfield. "Bill Would Order Study on Medgar Evers' Home." *Clarion-Ledger*, March 24, 2016. https://www.clarionledger.com/story/news/2016/03/24/bill-would-order-study-medgar-evers-home/82219336/.
Beveridge, Lici. "This Mississippi Museum Received a Grant for $50,000. Find Out Why." *Clarion-Ledger*, January 11, 2022. https://www.clarionledger.com/story/news/local/2022/01/11/fannie-lou-hamer-museum-awarded-grant-southern-poverty-law-center/9162050002/.
Brodeur, Michael Andor. "Whose Song Is This to Sing? A New Opera about Emmett Till Faces Scrutiny and Protest." *Washington Post*, March 22, 2022. https://www.washingtonpost.com/music/2022/03/22/emmett-till-opera-protest/.

Carrier, Jim. "Traveling the Civil Rights Trail." *Washington Post*, August 26, 2011. https://www.washingtonpost.com/opinions/traveling-the-civil-rights-trail/2011/08/26/gIQAaVL7gJ_story.html.

"Civil Rights Music Commemoration." *Bolivar Bullet*, March 12, 2018.

"CORE Office Is Shaken by Blast in Canton, Miss." *New York Times*, June 9, 1964. https://nyti.ms/2TGIbM2.

Cotter, Holland. "The New Mississippi Civil Rights Museum Refuses to Sugarcoat History." *New York Times*, December 18, 2017. https://nyti.ms/2kJDWtX.

Crenshaw, Kimberlé. "An Architect of Critical Race Theory: 'We Cannot Allow All of the Lessons from the Civil Rights Movement Forward to Be Packed Up and Put Away for Storage.'" By KK Ottesen. *Washington Post*, January 19, 2022. https://www.washingtonpost.com/lifestyle/magazine/an-architect-of-critical-race-theory-we-cannot-allow-all-of-the-lessons-from-the-civil-rights-movement-forward-to-be-packed-up-and-put-away-for-storage/2022/01/14/24bb31de-627e-11ec-a7e8-3a8455b71fad_story.html.

Dewan, Shalia K. "Civil Rights Battlegrounds Enter World of Tourism." *New York Times*, August 10, 2004. https://www.nytimes.com/2004/08/10/us/civil-rights-battlegrounds-enter-world-of-tourism.html?smid=url-share.

Edic, Gerard. "Marker Honors Hamer." *Greenwood Commonwealth*, October 7, 2020. https://www.gwcommonwealth.com/news-top-stories/marker-honors-hamer#sthash.H1SzMxPI.dpbs.

Epstein, Kayla. "This Emmett Till Memorial Was Vandalized Again. And Again. And Again. Now, It's bulletproof." *Washington Post*, October 20, 2019. https://www.washingtonpost.com/history/2019/10/20/this-emmett-till-memorial-was-vandalized-again-again-again-now-its-bulletproof/.

Epstein, Kayla. "When a Memorial to Emmett Till Was Vandalized, These High School Students Stepped Up." *Washington Post*, June 30, 2017. http://wapo.st/2u0N1eS?tid=ss_mail&utm_term=.aa2f398aff09.

Floyd, Nell Luter. "It Is in Their Honor." *Clarion-Ledger*, February 23, 2017. https://www.clarionledger.com/story/news/local/madison/2017/02/23/honor/98332202/.

Fowler, Sarah. "5 Things to Know about the New Mississippi Civil Rights Museum." *Clarion-Ledger*, November 7, 2017. https://www.clarionledger.com/story/news/local/2017/11/07/5-things-know-new-mississippi-civil-rights-museum/839305001/.

Fraser, C. Gerald. "Amzie Moore, 1960's Leader for Voting Registration, Dies." *New York Times*, February 7, 1982. https://nyti.ms/2P6pcDg.

Gates, Jimmie E. "Donations to Emmett Till Memorial Pour in Following White Nationalist Group's Filming." *Clarion-Ledger*, November 4, 2019. https://www.clarionledger.com/story/news/local/2019/11/04/emmett-till-memorial-gets-donations-after-white-nationalists-film/4154831002/.

Gordon, Mac. "State's Racial History Up for Discussion—Again." *Clarion-Ledger*, January 13, 2022. https://www.clarionledger.com/story/opinion/2022/01/14/mississippi-history-could-taught-without-mlk-kkk-jim-crow-impact/9161835002/.

Helsel, Amber, and Dustin Cardon. "Pamela Junior Named Director of Two Mississippi Museums." *Jackson Free Press*, July 5, 2019. https://www.jacksonfreepress.com/news/2019/jul/05/pamela-junior-named-director-two-mississippi-museu/.

Hendrickson, Paul. "Mississippi Haunting." *Washington Post*, February 27, 2000. https://www.washingtonpost.com/archive/lifestyle/magazine/2000/02/27/mississippi-haunting/52da6813-c1c7-410f-b834-f01a7e20cad3/.

Hipp, Laura. "Museum Receives Panel's Support." *Clarion-Ledger*, December 21, 2006.
Holley, Peter. "An Emmett Till Historical Marker in Mississippi Was Destroyed by Vandals—Again." *Washington Post*, June 26, 2017. https://www.washingtonpost.com/news/post-nation/wp/2017/06/26/an-emmett-till-historical-marker-in-mississippi-was-destroyed-by-vandals-again/.
Hutto, Ralph. "Now Sumner Is Just Another Sleepy Delta Town." *Jackson State Times*, September 24, 1955.
Jackson, Christianna. "Civil Rights Museum Underway." *Jackson Free Press*, July 12, 2012. https://www.jacksonfreepress.com/news/2012/jul/12/civil-rights-museum-underway/.
Jackson Citizens Council. "Keep the Pools Closed." Editorial/advertisement. *Clarion-Ledger*, May 5, 1968.
James, Julia. "Emmett Till's Family Wants Carolyn Bryant Donham Brought to Justice." *Mississippi Today*, March 11, 2022. https://mississippitoday.org/2022/03/11/emmett-tills-family-wants-carolyn-bryant-donham-brought-to-justice/.
Knowles, Hannah. "White Supremacists Gathered at Emmett Till's Bulletproof Memorial to Shoot a Video." *Washington Post*, November 4, 2019. https://www.washingtonpost.com/history/2019/11/04/emmett-tills-cousin-white-nationalists-memorial-more-they-do-we-can-do-more/.
Ladd, Donna. "Jackson Tragedy: The RNA, Revisited." *Jackson Free Press*, March 5, 2014. https://www.jacksonfreepress.com/news/2014/mar/05/jackson-tragedy-rna-revisited/.
"Legal Processes Continue." *Commercial Appeal*, September 24, 1955.
McBride, Earnest. "Split in Choosing Funding over Location for Civil Rights Museum." *Jackson Advocate*, March 3, 2011.
McCausland, Phil. "Tamales, Catfish and Meringue Pie: Delicacies of the Mississippi Delta." *New York Times*, May 4, 2016. https://www.nytimes.com/2016/05/08/travel/tamales-catfish-pie-delicacies-of-the-mississippi-delta.html?smid=url-share.
McCray, Vanessa. "Mississippi Town Feels the Weight of History." *The Blade*, February 19, 2017. https://www.toledoblade.com/Toledo-Magazine/2017/02/19/Weight-of-history-Crumbling-Mississippi-sites-were-the-backdrop-to-the-infamous-slaying-of-Emmett-Till.html.
"Medgar and Myrlie Evers Home Officially Established as National Monument." *Delta Democrat-Times*, December 10, 2020. https://www.ddtonline.com/medgar-and-myrlie-evers-home-officially-established-national-monument#sthash.D50T9Rrh.fC7HkjXc.dpbs.
Miller, Maya. "Till Interpretive Center Seeks to Rewrite Civil Rights Narrative." *Jackson Free Press*, August 26, 2015. https://www.jacksonfreepress.com/news/2015/aug/26/till-interpretive-center-seeks-rewrite-civil-right.
Mitchell, Jerry. "Civil Rights Landmarks Disappearing from Landscape." *Clarion-Ledger*, June 23, 2014, https://www.clarionledger.com/story/opinion/2014/06/23/civil-rights-landmarks-disappearing-landscape/11270899/.
Mitchell, Jerry. "Historic Museums Planned." *Clarion-Ledger*, June 2, 2013.
Mitchell, Jerry. "Mississippi Civil Rights, History Museums Set to Surpass Attendance Projections." *Clarion-Ledger*, February 22, 2018. https://www.clarionledger.com/story/news/2018/02/22/mississippi-civil-rights-history-museums-set-surpass-attendance-projections/351167002/.
Mitchell, Jerry. "Mississippi Civil Rights Museum 'Best One Yet.'" *Clarion-Ledger*, December 12, 2017. https://www.clarionledger.com/story/news/local/journeytojustice/2017/12/12/mississippi-civil-rights-museum-best-one-yet/942282001/.

Mitchell, Jerry. "'They Just Want History to Die': Owners Demand $4 Million for Crumbling Emmett Till Store," *Clarion-Ledger*, August 29, 2018. https://www.clarionledger.com/story/news/2018/08/29/emmett-till-owners-crumbling-store-where-saga-began-demand-4-m/943941002/.

"Museum: Downtown Jackson Appropriate." Editorial. *Clarion-Ledger*, February 16, 2008.

"No Civil Rights Museum in Miss. Despite Pivotal Role." *Clarion-Ledger*, November 28, 2010.

Norwood, Ashley F. G. "Rural Civil Rights Sites Crave Collaboration with New Jackson Museum." *Mississippi Today*, December 16, 2017. https://mississippitoday.org/2017/12/16/rural-civil-rights-sites-fear-eclipse-by-new-jackson-museum/.

Paz, Isabella Grullón. "Questions Swirl after Yet Another Emmett Till Sign Comes Down." *New York Times*, September 4, 2021. https://www.nytimes.com/2021/09/04/us/emmett-till-sign-missing.html.

Pettus, Emily Wagster. "Civil Rights Museum Not Yet a Done Deal." *Clarion-Ledger*, February 4, 2007.

Pettus, Emily Wagster. "Emmett Till Marker in Mississippi Toppled but Not Vandalized." *Associated Press*, September 3, 2021. https://apnews.com/article/mississippi-emmett-till-6e707514564ab9a155b772cc98bd6312.

"Purpose of the Law." Editorial. *Daily Clarion-Ledger*, October 2, 1902.

Robertson, Campbell, and Ellen Ann Fentress. "For Opening of Civil Rights Museum, Some Division." *New York Times*, December 6, 2017.

Rojas, Rick. "Mississippi Grand Jury Declines to Indict Woman in Emmett Till Murder Case." *New York Times*, August 9, 2022. https://www.nytimes.com/2022/08/09/us/emmett-till-murder-grand-jury.html?smid=url-share.

Rowe, Keisha, and Lici Beveridge. "Mississippi's State Flag Controversy over the Confederate Emblem: What You Should Know." *Clarion-Ledger*, June 24, 2020. https://www.clarionledger.com/story/news/2020/06/24/mississippi-state-flag-confederate-flag-ms-controversy/3243712001/.

Rubin, Richard. "The Freedom Trail in Mississippi Is a Chronicle of Outrage and Courage." *New York Times*, September 10, 2018. https://www.nytimes.com/2018/09/10/travel/mississippi-freedom-trail.html.

Sack, Kevin. "Mississippi Reveals Dark Secrets of a Racist Time." *New York Times*, March 18, 1998. http://www.nytimes.com/1998/03/18/us/mississippi-reveals-dark-secrets-of-a-racist-time.html.

Schmidt, William E. "Mississippi Collects Memories of Rights Struggle in a Museum." *New York Times*, December 7, 1984.

Severson, Kim. "New Museums to Shine a Spotlight on Civil Rights Era." *New York Times*, February 19, 2012. https://nyti.ms/2FvN2WK.

Shear, Michael D., and Ellen Ann Fentress. "Trump, Rejecting Calls to Stay Away, Speaks at Civil Rights Museum." *New York Times*, December 9, 2017. https://www.nytimes.com/2017/12/09/us/politics/trump-mississippi-civil-rights-museum.html?smid=url-share.

Skinner, Kayleigh. "Is Mississippi Really Removing Civil Rights History from Its Teaching Standards?" *Mississippi Today*. January 5, 2022. https://mississippitoday.org/2022/01/05/mississippi-civil-rights-history-social-studies/.

Somashekhar, Sandhya. "Black History Becoming a Star Tourist Attraction." *Washington Post*, August 15, 2005. https://www.washingtonpost.com/wp-dyn/content/article/2005/08/14/AR2005081401031.html.

Svrluga, Susan. "Former Ole Miss Student Pleads Guilty to Hanging Noose around Statue Honoring the First Black Student." *Washington Post*, March 24, 2016. https://www.washingtonpost.com/news/grade-point/wp/2016/03/24/former-ole-miss-student-pleads-guilty-to-hanging-noose-around-statue-honoring-the-first-black-student/.

Szymanowska, Gabriela. "'Hard to Understand': Emmett Till Marker Broken Days after 66th Anniversary of His Death." *Clarion-Ledger*, September 3, 2021. https://www.clarionledger.com/story/news/local/2021/09/03/emmett-till-marker-near-bryants-grocery-money-mississippi-missing/5713864001/.

Tell, Dave. "Commentary: Protecting the Memory of Emmett Till from the Scourge of Vandals." *Chicago Tribune*, July 26, 2019. https://www.chicagotribune.com/opinion/commentary/ct-opinion-emmett-till-sign-vandalism-20190726-7kjjvedmzvhgxpvxspvsf5fg4u-story.html.

Traub, Alex. "1955 Arrest Warrant in Emmett Till Case Is Found in Court Basement." *New York Times*, June 30, 2022. https://www.nytimes.com/2022/06/30/us/emmett-till-carolyn-bryant-arrest-warrant.html?smid=url-share.

Vance, Taylor. "William Winter Institute Relocates to Jackson after 19 years at Ole Miss." *Daily Mississippian*, January 31, 2018. https://thedmonline.com/william-winter-institute-relocates-jackson-19-years-ole-miss/.

"The Verdict at Sumner." Editorial. *Clarion-Ledger/Jackson Daily News*, September 25, 1955.

Vigdor, Neil. "Emmett Till Sign Photo Leads Ole Miss Fraternity to Suspend Members." *New York Times*, July 25, 2019. https://www.nytimes.com/2019/07/25/us/emmett-till-ole-miss-students-fraternity.html.

"Visit Mississippi: Officials Tout the Importance [sic] State's Tourism Industry. *Vicksburg Post*, March 24, 2021. https://www.vicksburgpost.com/2021/03/24/visit-mississippi-officials-tout-the-importance-states-tourism-industry/.

Wang, Amy B., and Felicia Sonmez. "Biden Signs Bill Making Lynching a Federal Hate Crime." *Washington Post*, March 29, 2022. https://www.washingtonpost.com/politics/2022/03/29/biden-signs-bill-lynching-hate-crime/.

Warren, Anthony. "Museums to Pump Millions into Jackson's Economy." *Northside Sun*, October 3, 2013.

Wright, Aallyah, Kelsey Davis Betz, and Bobby Harrison. "For Some in the Delta, Revisiting Emmett Till's Murder about Appeasing Mississippi's Conscience." *Mississippi Today*, July 14, 2018. https://mississippitoday.org/2018/07/14/for-some-in-the-delta-revisiting-emmett-tills-murder-is-about-appeasing-mississippis-conscious/.

Special Collection Documents

"The Amzie Moore Home Restoration and Preservation Project: Project Narrative" (Application for Mississippi Civil Rights Historical Sites Grant). 2011. Mississippi Department of Archives and History, Jackson, Mississippi.

Bailey, Ronald. *Remembering Medgar Evers . . . for a New Generation*. Oxford: Heritage Publications, 1988. Series 2, Subseries 8. Franklin E. Moak Collection. Department of Archives and Special Collections. University of Mississippi, Oxford, Mississippi.

The Citizens' Council. "Birth of an Idea." Walter Sillers Jr. Papers (Box 133). Delta State University Archives and Museums, Cleveland, Mississippi.

Congress of Racial Equality. "In Perspective: A Story of Mississippi Heroism." N.d., ca. 1964. Micro 793 (Reel 2, Segment 35). Freedom Summer Digital Collection. Wisconsin Historical Society. https://content.wisconsinhistory.org/digital/collection/p15932coll2/id/41985.

Council of Federated Organizations. "What Is COFO?" Box 2 (Folder 6). Ed King Collection. Department of Archives and Special Collections. University of Mississippi, Oxford, Mississippi.

Dorsey, L. C. "A Prophet Who Believed." *Sojourners*. December 1982. Box 1 (Folder 8). Ed King Collection. Department of Archives and Special Collections. University of Mississippi, Oxford, Mississippi.

Gray, Victoria J. "Black Politics in Mississippi." National Conference for New Politics Convention. September 2, 1967. Box 2 (Folder 3). Fannie Lou Hamer Collection. Department of Archives and Special Collections. University of Mississippi, Oxford, Mississippi.

Lehew, Dudley. "CR Workers React after Finding of Three Bodies." *Jackson Daily News*. August 1964. Box 2 (Folder 6). Ed King Collection (Mississippi Freedom Project). Department of Archives and Special Collections. University of Mississippi, Oxford, Mississippi.

Mississippi Advertising Commission. "For the First Time, a Great State Offers Planned Cooperation to Industry." Advertisement. Series 552. 1937. Mississippi Department of Archives and History, Jackson, Mississippi. https://da.mdah.ms.gov/series/sac/552/detail/190658.

Mississippi Advertising Commission. "Historical Mississippi." Advertisement. Series 552. 1937. Mississippi Department of Archives and History, Jackson, Mississippi. https://da.mdah.ms.gov/series/sac/552/detail/190656.

Mississippi Advertising Commission. "In Mississippi It's a Real . . . Thanksgiving." Advertisement. Series 552, 1936. Mississippi Department of Archives and History, Jackson, Mississippi. https://da.mdah.ms.gov/series/sac/552/detail/190652.

Mississippi Department of Economic and Community Development. *African-American Heritage Guide*. N.d., ca. 1990. Department of Archives and Special Collections. University of Mississippi, Oxford, Mississippi.

Mississippi Freedom Democratic Party. "By Laws of the Mississippi Freedom Democratic Party." March 12, 1969. Box 2 (Folder 3). Fannie Lou Hamer Collection. Department of Archives and Special Collections. University of Mississippi, Oxford, Mississippi.

Mississippi Freedom Democratic Party. "The Mississippi Freedom Democratic Party." N.d. Box 2 (Folder 3). Fannie Lou Hamer Collection. Department of Archives and Special Collections. University of Mississippi, Oxford, Mississippi.

Mississippi State Board of Development. *Mississippi Tourist Guide 1941*. 1941. Mississippi Department of Archives and History, Jackson, Mississippi.

"Prospectus for the Mississippi Freedom Summer." Spring 1964. Box 2 (Folder 6). Ed King Collection. Department of Archives and Special Collections. University of Mississippi, Oxford, Mississippi.

Singleton, Helen. Interview. November 8, 2001. Transcript. Freedom Riders 40th Anniversary Oral History Project. Department of Archives and Special Collections. University of Mississippi, Oxford, Mississippi.

Timmer, Wayne F., and Anne Marie Decker. "Medgar Evers Home Renovation." 1995. Mississippi Department of Archives and History, Jackson, Mississippi.

"T. W. A. K. Confederate Mother's Day—1961." N.d. Box 1 (Folder 6). Ku Klux Klan Collection. Department of Archives and Special Collections. University of Mississippi, Oxford, Mississippi.

University of Mississippi. *Integration Commemoration Continues with Programs on Oct. 9, Oct. 12.* September 30, 1987. Box 1 (Folder 4). Civil Rights Commemoration Initiative Collection. Department of Archives and Special Collections. University of Mississippi, Oxford, Mississippi.

University of Mississippi. *Ole Miss Plans Commemoration of Meredith's 25th Anniversary.* September 24, 1987. Box 1 (Folder 4). Civil Rights Commemoration Initiative Collection. Department of Archives and Special Collections. University of Mississippi, Oxford, Mississippi.

Internet Sources

Anderson, Roslyn. "Two Mississippi Museums Project Celebrates One Year, Exceeds Expectations." *WDAM*. December 10, 2018. https://www.wdam.com/2018/12/11/two-mississippi-museums-project-celebrates-one-year-exceeds-expectations/.

Arnold, Van. "Fannie Lou Hamer Cancer Foundation to Host Groundbreaking for State-of-the-Art Headquarters in Ruleville Oct. 31." University of Southern Mississippi. October 22, 2019. https://www.usm.edu/news/2019/release/fannie-lou-hamer-cancer-foundation-opening-headquarters.php.

Barbour, Haley. "State of the State." *WLBT*. January 16, 2007. https://www.wlbt.com/story/5946343/state-of-the-state-complete-text/.

Baughn, Jennifer. "Historic Resources Inventory Fact Sheet." Mississippi Department of Archives and History. September 7, 2008. https://www.apps.mdah.ms.gov/Public/prop.aspx?id=32997&view=facts&y=1011.

Baughn, Jennifer V. O. "Medgar and Myrlie Evers House National Historic Landmark Nomination." National Park Service. August 20, 2018. https://www.apps.mdah.ms.gov/nom/prop/32997.pdf.

Belinda Stewart Architects. "Amzie Moore House Restoration." N.d. https://belindastewartarchitects.com/portfolio/amzie-moore-house/.

"BrainPOP and Willamette Professor Partner on New Fannie Lou Hamer Animated Movie." Fannie Lou Hamer's America. August 21, 2019. https://www.fannielouhamersamerica.com/press/brainpop-and-willamette-professor-partner-on-new-fannie-lou-hamer-animated-movie.

Brooks, Maegan Parker. Letter. "Editor's Introduction." Fannie Lou Hamer's America. N.d. Accessed March 30, 2022. https://www.fannielouhamersamerica.com/find-your-voice/curricular-units.

Carter, Josh. "Gov. Reeves Says He Would Support Legislation That Bans Critical Race Theory in Miss. Classrooms." *WLBT*. June 14, 2021. https://www.wlbt.com/2021/06/14/gov-reeves-says-he-would-support-legislation-that-bans-critical-race-theory-miss-classrooms/.

Center for the Study of Southern Culture. "About." N.d. Accessed February 5, 2023. https://southernstudies.olemiss.edu/about/.

Center for the Study of Southern Culture. "Vision Statement for Spring 2029." N.d. Accessed June 18, 2021. https://southernstudies.olemiss.edu/media/CSSC-Vision-2029-finalPDF.pdf.

"Civil Rights Museum Attendance Earns Jackson State Recognition." *WJTV*. September 26, 2018. https://www.wjtv.com/news/metro/civil-rights-museum-attendance-earns-jackson-state-recognition/.

"Curricular Units." Fannie Lou Hamer's America. N.d. Accessed March 30, 2022. https://www.fannielouhamersamerica.com/find-your-voice/curricular-units.

Davis, Dernoral. "Medgar Evers and the Origin of the Civil Rights Movement in Mississippi." *Mississippi History Now*. October 2003. https://www.mshistorynow.mdah.ms.gov/issue/medgar-evers-and-the-origin-of-the-civil-rights-movement-in-mississippi.

Davis, Dernoral. "When Youth Protest: The Mississippi Civil Rights Movement, 1955–1970." *Mississippi History Now*. August 2001. https://www.mshistorynow.mdah.ms.gov/issue/the-mississippi-civil-rights-movement-1955-1970-when-youth-protest.

"Delta Center Director Receives Service Award." Delta State University. June 13, 2014. https://www.deltastate.edu/news-and-events/2014/06/delta-center-director-receives-service-award/.

Dorsey, Marlo. "How Mississippi Emerged as a Leader in Tourism Recovery." *Travel Pulse*. March 17, 2021. https://www.travelpulse.com/news/destinations/how-mississippi-emerged-as-a-leader-in-tourism-recovery.html.

Dougherty, John. Google Review of Canton Freedom House. 2021. https://g.co/kgs/H4Noyj.

drwalterw. "Amazing Place." *Tripadvisor*. February 11, 2020. https://www.tripadvisor.com/ShowUserReviews-g43833-d13382408-r744428565-Mississippi_Civil_Rights_Museum-Jackson_Mississippi.html.

Elliott, Debbie. "'Why Don't Y'all Let That Die?' Telling The Emmett Till Story in Mississippi." *National Public Radio*. August 28, 2019. https://www.npr.org/2019/08/28/755024458/why-don-t-y-all-let-that-die-telling-the-emmett-till-story-in-mississippi.

Emmett Till Interpretive Center. N.d. Accessed April 18, 2021. https://www.emmett-till.org/.

Emmett Till Interpretive Center. "The Apology." N.d. Accessed March 24, 2020. http://www.emmett-till.org/new-apology.

Emmett Till Interpretive Center. "History of the Center." N.d. Accessed February 9, 2023. https://www.emmett-till.org/history.

Emmett Till Memory Project. "About the Emmett Till Memory Project." N.d. Accessed February 9, 2023. https://tillapp.emmett-till.org/about/.

Emmett Till Memory Project. "Tours." N.d. Accessed June 21, 2021. https://tillapp.emmett-till.org/tours/browse/.

Evers, Myrlie. Interview by Orlando Bagwell. November 27, 1985. Transcript. Washington University in St. Louis. http://repository.wustl.edu/concern/videos/gq67jto4b.

Fannie Lou Hamer. "Testimony before the Credentials Committee, Democratic National Convention." August 22, 1964. *American Rhetoric*. https://www.americanrhetoric.com/speeches/fannielouhamercredentialscommittee.htm.

"Fannie Lou Hamer Cancer Foundation to Get New Site." *The Mississippi Link*. May 23–29, 2013. https://themississippilink.com/wp-content/uploads/2012/01/May-23-2013.pdf.

"Fannie Lou Hamer Park and Multi-Purpose Complex, Ruleville, MS." Fannie Lou Hamer's America. N.d. Accessed March 17, 2022. https://www.fannielouhamersamerica.com/driving-tour/fannie-lou-hamer-memorial-center.

Fannie Lou Hamer Statue Committee. "Fannie Lou Hamer Statue Unveiling Set for October 5, 2012." News release. August 20, 2012. https://www.crmvet.org/anc/1210flh.pdf.

"Fannie Lou Hamer's America Project to Receive Humanities Award." Fannie Lou Hamer's America. December 7, 2021. https://www.fannielouhamersamerica.com/press/fannie-lou-hamers-america-project-to-receive-humanities-award.

Gagliano, Steven. "State Superintendent Says Critical Race Theory Isn't in Mississippi Schools." *SuperTalk Mississippi Media*. June 22, 2021. https://www.supertalk.fm/state-superintendent-says-critical-race-theory-isnt-in-mississippi-schools/.

Gallant, Jacob, and Reggi Marion. "Two Museums Reopen after 4 Months." *WLBT*. July 7, 2020. https://www.wlbt.com/2020/07/07/two-museums-reopen-after-months/.

Gonzales, Richard. "African-American Congressmen Will Skip Mississippi Civil Rights Event to Avoid Trump." *National Public Radio*. December 7, 2017. https://www.npr.org/sections/thetwo-way/2017/12/07/569282666/african-american-congressmen-will-skip-mississippi-civil-rights-event-to-avoid-t.

Greenwood Convention and Visitors Bureau. "Change Began Here." N.d. Accessed June 22, 2021. https://www.visitgreenwood.com/wp-content/uploads/2021/02/Civil_Rights_Brochure.pdf.

Greenwood Convention and Visitors Bureau. "Greenwood: Epicenter for Civil Rights Movement." N.d. Accessed June 22, 2021. https://www.visitgreenwood.com/news/epicenter-for-civil- rights/.

Greenwood Convention and Visitors Bureau. "History, Culture and Architecture." N.d. Accessed December 22, 2020. https://www.visitgreenwood.com/history.

Greenwood Convention and Visitors Bureau. "Money Road." N.d. Accessed December 22, 2020. https://www.visitgreenwood.com/experience/.

Hammons and Associates. "Mississippi Freedom Trail." N.d. Accessed December 15, 2021. https://hammons.com/portfolio-archive/mississippi-freedom-trail/.

"Head Start Timeline." *Head Start/ECLKC*. Last updated February 16, 2019. https://eclkc.ohs.acf.hhs.gov/about-us/article/head-start-timeline.

"Heritage Village." N.d. Accessed June 24, 2021. http://www.thereverandgeorgeleemuseumsofafricanamericanhistoryandheritage.com/heritage-village.html.

Hill, Michael. "North Carolina's History on a Stick: Historical Markers and Public Commemoration." *Commemorative Landscapes of North Carolina*. 2012. http://docsouth.unc.edu/commland/features/essays/hill/.

Hudson, Ken. Google Review of Fannie Lou Hamer Civil Rights Museum. 2018. https://goo.gl/maps/Um7WKfJ5uL8HxoiG8.

Jacobson, Linda. "History Lessons." *Education Week*. April 4, 2006. https://www.edweek.org/leadership/history-lessons/2006/04.

James, Frank. "Haley Barbour Explains He Wasn't Praising Racist Group." *National Public Radio*. December 21, 2010. https://www.npr.org/sections/itsallpolitics/2010/12/21/132232306/haley-barbour-explains-he-wasnt-praising-racist-group.

Jarrett, Laura. "Justice Department Closes Investigation into Emmett Till Killing after Failing to Prove Key Witness Lied." *CNN*. December 7, 2021. https://www.cnn.com/2021/12/06/politics/emmett-till-case-closed/index.html.

Jones, Michael. Google Review of Canton Freedom House. 2021. https://g.co/kgs/SAqi3K.

Jordan, Hattie. Interview by Sarah Blanc and Khama Weatherspoon. September 24, 2010. MFP-060. Transcript. Samuel Proctor Oral History Program. University of Florida. https://ufdc.ufl.edu/AA00020253/00001.

Landry, Chet. "U.S. Department of Commerce Investing $2,000,000 in South Mississippi Tourism." *WLOX*. April 12, 2021. https://www.wlox.com/2021/04/13/us-department-commerce-investing-south-mississippi-tourism/.

LeBlanc, Paul. "Mississippi State Legislature Passes Bill to Remove Confederate Symbol from State Flag in Historic Vote." *CNN*. June 29, 2020. https://www.cnn.com/2020/06/28/politics/mississippi-flag-confederate-emblem/index.html.

Levenson, Eric. "How Minneapolis Police First Described the Murder of George Floyd, and What We Know Now." *CNN*. April 21, 2021. https://www.cnn.com/2021/04/21/us/minneapolis-police-george-floyd-death.

Lynch, Jamiel, and Jeremy Grisham. "Mississippi Governor Signs into Law Prohibition on Schools Teaching Critical Race Theory." *CNN*. March 14, 2022. https://www.cnn.com/2022/03/14/politics/mississippi-critical-race-theory-law/index.html.

maapar. "Worthwhile visit!" *Tripadvisor*. March 17, 2019. https://www.tripadvisor.com/ShowUserReviews-g43833-d13382408-r659120872-Mississippi_Civil_Rights_Museum-Jackson_Mississippi.html.

Mannie, Sierra. "Mississippi Textbooks Gloss Over Civil Rights Struggle." *Education Week*. October 4, 2017. https://www.edweek.org/leadership/mississippi-textbooks-gloss-over-civil-rights-struggle/2017/10.

McLaurin, Charles. Interview by Emilye Crosby. December 5, 2016. AFC 2010/039: CRHP0121. Transcript. Southern Oral History Program. National Museum of African American History and Culture. https://tile.loc.gov/storage-services/service/afc/afc2010039/afc2010039_crhp0121/afc2010039_crhp0121_ms01.pdf.

"Medgar Evers' Home Established as a National Monument in Jackson." *NBC News*. March 13, 2019. https://www.nbcnews.com/news/nbcblk/medgar-evers-home-established-national-monument-jackson-n982936.

"MHC Awards Over $450,000 to Help Mississippi Cultural Organizations Recover from COVID." Mississippi Humanities Council. September 1, 2021. http://mshumanities.org/mhc-awards-over-450000-to-help-mississippi-cultural-organizations-recover-from-covid/.

"Mississippi Blues, Freedom & Writer Trails." Visit Jackson. N.d. Accessed March 18, 2022. https://www.visitjackson.com /mississippi-blues-trail/.

Mississippi Center for Public Policy. *Combating Critical Race Theory in Mississippi*. N.d. Accessed January 13, 2022. https://mspolicy.org/wp-content/uploads/2021/10/Combating-Critical-Race-Theory-FINAL.pdf.

Mississippi Civil Rights Museum. "Galleries." N.d. Accessed March 24, 2022. http://mcrm.mdah.ms.gov/galleries/galleries.

"Mississippi Civil Rights Museum Sees Almost 3,000 Visitors in Eight Hours." *WJTV*. January 20, 2020. https://www.wjtv.com/news/mississippi-civil-rights-museum-sees-almost-3000-visitors-in-eight-hours/.

Mississippi Delta National Heritage Area. "Our Mission, Vision, and Goals." Accessed February 5, 2023. https://www.msdeltaheritage.com/mission-vision-goals.

Mississippi Department of Archives and History. "Mississippi Archeology Trails: Indian Tribes of Mississippi." Accessed February 14, 2022. http://trails.mdah.ms.gov/education/tribes.htm.

Mississippi Department of Archives and History. "Mississippi Mound Trail." N.d. Accessed March 6, 2022. http://trails.mdah.ms.gov/mmt/index.html.

Mississippi Department of Archives and History. "MDAH to Reopen Museums & Library in July." Press release. July 4, 2020. https://www.mdah.ms.gov/news/mdah-to-reopen-museums-library-in-july.

Mississippi Development Authority. *Annual Report 2012*. https://da.mdah.ms.gov/series-files/mda/mda-ar/pdf/mda-annual-report2012.pdf.

Mississippi Development Authority. "Civil Rights." *Visit Mississippi*. Accessed June 23, 2021. https://visitmississippi.org/things-to-do/point-of-interest/type/civil-rights/.

Mississippi Development Authority. *Fiscal Year 2022 Annual Report*. 2022. https://mississippi.org/news/reports/.

Mississippi Development Authority. *Fiscal Year 2021 Annual Report*. 2021. https://mississippi.org/news/reports/.

Mississippi Development Authority. *Fiscal Year 2020 Annual Report*. 2020. https://mississippi.org/news/reports/.

Mississippi Development Authority. *Fiscal Year 2019 Annual Report*. 2019. https://mississippi.org/news/reports/.

Mississippi Development Authority. *Mississippi Development Guide*. 2021. https://mississippi.org/news/reports/.

Mississippi Development Authority. "Mississippi Freedom Trail." *Visit Mississippi* (blog). Accessed June 23, 2021. http://visitmississippi.org/mississippi-freedom-trail/.

Mississippi Development Authority. "Music." *Visit Mississippi*. Accessed June 24, 2021. https://visitmississippi.org/things-to-do/point-of-interest/type/music/.

"The Mississippi Heritage Consortium." N.d. Accessed January 8, 2022. http://www.thefannielouhamercivilrightsmuseum.com/the-mississippi-heritage-consortium.html.

Mississippi Legislature. House. HB 1791. 2020 Regular Session. http://billstatus.ls.state.ms.us/documents/2020/html/HB/1700-1799/HB1791PS.htm.

Mississippi Legislature. Senate. SB 2718. 2006 Regular Session. http://billstatus.ls.state.ms.us/documents/2006/html/SB/2700-2799/SB2718SG.htm.

"The Mississippi Lynch and Civil Rights Memorial Project Inc." N.d. Accessed June 24, 2021. http://www.thefannielouhamercivilrightsmuseum.com/the-mississippi-lynch-and-civil-rights-memorial-project-inc.html.

Mississippi Tourism Association. "Greenwood." Accessed December 22, 2020. http://www.visitthedelta.com/greenwood.

Mississippi Tourism Association. "Pivotal Civil Rights Sites: A 3-Day Itinerary." N.d. Accessed December 22, 2020. https://visitmississippi.org/blog/pivotal-mississippi-civil-rights-sites-a-3-day-itinerary/.

Moore, Amzie. Interview by Michael Garvey. Cleveland, Mississippi. March 29 and April 13, 1977. Transcript. Center for Oral History and Cultural Heritage. University of Southern Mississippi. https://usm.access.preservica.com/uncategorized/IO_24fe894d-6bfc-4c1e-a8d9-ac4a26046155/.

Mr. Kinetik. Google Review of Fannie Lou Hamer Memorial Garden. 2019. https://g.co/kgs/Ro85jT.

Museum of Mississippi History. "Educators." N.d. Accessed April 30, 2021. http://mmh.mdah.ms.gov/learn/educators.

National Park Service. "List of NHLs By State." *National Historic Landmarks*. Accessed June 25, 2021. https://www.nps.gov/subjects/nationalhistoriclandmarks/list-of-nhls-by-state.htm.

National Park Service. "Mississippi: COFO Civil Rights Education Center." Last updated February 23, 2021. Accessed April 30, 2021. https://www.nps.gov/articles/000/mississippi-cofo-civil-rights-education-center.htm.

National Park Service. "Secretary Zinke Designates Medgar and Myrlie Evers Home as African American Civil Rights Network Site." News release. August 3, 2018. https://www.nps.gov/orgs/1207/secretary-zinke-designates-medgar-and-myrlie-evers-home-as-african-american-civil-rights-network-site.htm.

Northcutt, Allie. "Civil Rights Immersion Trip's Impact on Students." Wabash College. December 10, 2021. https://www.wabash.edu/news/story/11841.

"Patti Carr Black." Mississippi Writers and Musicians. Accessed June 18, 2021. https://www.mswritersandmusicians.com/mississippi-writers/patti-carr-black.

Preuss, Andreas. "Emmett Till Memorial Sign Scarred by Bullet Holes." *CNN*. October 22, 2016. http://www.cnn.com/2016/10/22/us/mississippi-emmett-till-sign-bullets/index.html.

"The Re-Enactment Society." N.d. Accessed June 24, 2021. http://www.thefannielouhamercivilrightsmuseum.com/the-re-enactment-society.html.

Reeves, Tate. "Governor Reeves Takes Action against Critical Race Theory." *Facebook*. March 14, 2022. https://www.facebook.com/tatereeves/videos/771428113837269/.

"Remembering Emmett Till." US Civil Rights Trail. N.d. Accessed June 30, 2021. https://civilrightstrail.com/experience/sumner/.

ROAR Foundation. "Fannie Lou Hamer Statue Donors." Last updated September 16, 2012. http://www.fannielouhamer.info/donors.html.

ROAR Foundation. "Fannie Lou Hamer Statue Drive." March 2009, last updated April 2012. http://www.fannielouhamer.info/hamer_statue.html.

ROAR Foundation. "Repaying Our Ancestors Respectfully." April 2006, last updated October 2010. http://www.fannielouhamer.info/roar.html.

Rosendale, Matt (@RepRosendale). "I voted against a bill that would make Juneteenth National Independence Day a federal holiday. . . ." Twitter. June 16, 2021. https://twitter.com/RepRosendale/status/1405307496894451717.

Rosendale, Matt (@RepRosendale). "Rep. Rosendale Statement on Juneteenth Vote." June 16, 2021. https://rosendale.house.gov/news/documentsingle.aspx?DocumentID=191.

Rosendale, Matt (@RepRosendale). "Their intent is to replace the Fourth of July. . . ." Twitter. June 16, 2021. https://twitter.com/RepRosendale/status/1405307656642912256.

Rowe-Sims, Sarah. "The Mississippi State Sovereignty Commission: An Agency History." *Mississippi History Now*. September 2002. https://mshistorynow.mdah.ms.gov/issue/mississippi-sovereignty-commission-an-agency-history.

Royer, David, and Shay Arthur. "Casting Call Goes Out as Filming Set to Start in Memphis and Mississippi for Series on Emmett Till Family." *WREG*. January 21, 2021. https://wreg.com/news/abc-series-puts-out-casting-call-as-filming-set-to-start-in-memphis-mississippi/.

"Senate Passes Bill to Give Congressional Gold Medal to Emmett Till and His Mother." *PBS News Hour*. January 12, 2022. https://www.pbs.org/newshour/nation/senate-passes-bill-to-give-congressional-gold-medal-to-emmett-till-and-his-mother.

Sherisoo. "Small, but Powerful, Displays Await." *Tripadvisor*. April 1, 2019. https://www.tripadvisor.com/Attraction_Review-g43833-d105886-Reviews-Smith_Robertson_Museum_and_Cultural_Center-Jackson_Mississippi.html.

Siber, Kate. "Mississippi Reckoning." *National Parks*. Winter 2019. https://www.npca.org/articles/2020-mississippi-reckoning.

Sims, Helen. Interview by Paul Ortiz. September 20, 2012. MFP-110. Transcript. Samuel Proctor Oral History Program. University of Florida. https://ufdc.ufl.edu/AA00021048/00001.

Stole, Bryn. "Confronting Past, Mississippi Town Erects Emmett Till Museum." Reuters. March 21, 2015. http://www.reuters.com/article/usa-emmetttill-museum-idUSKBN0MH0EV20150321.

Stracqualursi, Veronica. "Mississippi Ratifies and Raises Its New State Flag over the State Capitol for the First Time." *CNN*. January 13, 2021. https://www.cnn.com/2021/01/12/politics/mississippi-new-state-flag-flown/index.html.

"Sunflower County Film Academy." Fannie Lou Hamer's America. N.d. Accessed March 30, 2022. https://www.fannielouhamersamerica.com/sunflower-county-film-academy.

"Sunflower County Film Academy Awarded $22k MDNHA Grant." Fannie Lou Hamer's America. September 5, 2020. https://www.fannielouhamersamerica.com/press/sunflower-county-film-academy-awarded-22k-mdnha-grant.

Sustainable Equity, LLC. N.d. Accessed February 9, 2023. https://www.sustainableequity.net/.

Ta, Thao, and Kaitlin Howell. "Mississippi Senate Passes Bill to Ban Critical Race Theory." *WJTV*. January 21, 2022. https://www.wjtv.com/news/politics/focused-on-politics/mississippi-senate-passes-bill-to-ban-critical-race-theory/.

Taylor, Mia. "The Rise of Civil Rights Tourism in America's Deep South." *TheStreet*. October 23, 2016. https://www.thestreet.com/personal-finance/education/the-rise-of-civil-rights-tourism-in-america-s-deep-south-13859635.

Tell, Dave. "Delta Inn: Did a Lawyer Steal a Sign?" *Emmett Till Memory Project*. N.d. Accessed February 4, 2023. https://tillapp.emmett-till.org/items/show/16.

Tell, Dave. "Homesite of J. W. Milam: The Site of an Influential Fiction." *Emmett Till Memory Project*. N.d. Accessed February 4, 2023. https://tillapp.emmett-till.org/items/show/15.

Tingle, Mingo. "Historic Resources Inventory Fact Sheet." Mississippi Department of Archives and History. October 29, 2008. https://www.apps.mdah.ms.gov/Public/prop.aspx?id=101848&view=facts&y=812.

"The United States Civil Rights Trail Podcast." N.d. Accessed March 24, 2022. https://civilrightstrail.com/podcast/.

UPM Staff. "*Women of the Movement* to Premier on ABC." University Press of Mississippi. January 4, 2022. https://www.upress.state.ms.us/News/2022/WOMEN-OF-THE-MOVEMENT-to-premiere-on-ABC.

US Census Bureau. "Annual Estimates of the Resident Population for Incorporated Places: April 1, 2010 to July 1, 2019." *City and Town Population Totals, 2010–2019*. Accessed June 15, 2021. https://www2.census.gov/programs-surveys/popest/tables/2010-2019/cities/totals/SUB-IP-EST2019-ANNRES-28.xlsx.

US Congress. House. *Aaron E. Henry Federal Building and United States Post Office*. HR 1279. 106th Cong., 2d sess. *Congressional Record* 146, no. 36, daily ed. (March 28, 2000): H1428–30. https://www.congress.gov/106/crec/2000/03/28/CREC-2000-03-28.pdf.

US Congress. House. *Medgar and Myrlie Evers Home National Monument Act*. S. Report 115-370. 115th Cong., 2d sess. November 15, 2018. https://www.congress.gov/congressional-report/115th-congress/senate-report/370/1.

US Department of the Interior. "Trump Administration Establishes Medgar and Myrlie Evers Home National Monument." Press release. December 10, 2020, last edited March 12, 2021. https://www.doi.gov/pressreleases/trump-administration-establishes-medgar-and-myrlie-evers-home-national-monument.

Ward, Derrick, and Andrea Swalec. "Bullet-Riddled Emmett Till Sign on Display in U.S. History Museum." NBC4 Washington. September 3, 2021. https://www.nbcwashington.com/news/local/bullet-riddled-emmett-till-smithsonian-national-museum-american-history/2791174/.

Willen, Liz. "Never Mind Trump's Visit. Mississippi's New Civil Rights Museum Is a Real Game Changer for Education." *The Hechinger Report*. December 11, 2017. https://hechingerreport.org/never-mind-trumps-visit-mississippis-new-civil-rights-museum-real-game-changer-education/.

Brochures, Flyers, Tourism Guides, and Other Miscellaneous Material

"The Amzie Moore Home." *2021 Welcome Guide Cleveland & Bolivar County*. Issue 9. 2021.

Cleveland Tourism. *Cleveland Mississippi Tourism*. Brochure. N.d.

Cleveland Tourism. *Visit Cleveland Mississippi*. Brochure. N.d.

Greenwood Convention and Visitors Bureau. *Remembering the Struggle for Civil Rights: The Greenwood Sites*. Brochure. N.d.

Greenwood Convention and Visitors Bureau. *Unique Delta Experiences*. Brochure. June 1, 2019.

Mississippi Department of Archives and History. Letter to museum members. October 8, 2019.

Mississippi Tourism Association. *Mississippi Freedom Trail*. Brochure. Revised July 2020.

Mississippi Tourism Association. *Mississippi Official Tour Guide*. 2022.

Mississippi Tourism Association. *Mississippi Official Tour Guide*. 2021.

Mississippi Tourism Association. *Mississippi Official Tour Guide*. 2020.

Tourism and Public Affairs Department, Mississippi Agricultural and Industrial Board. *Mississippi: Your Guide to Travel*. N.d., ca. 1975.

Visit Jackson! Mississippi. *Attraction Guides*. Brochure. N.d.

Audio and Video Media

Baker, Kaitara. Courage to Lead. Vimeo. June 20, 2018. Video, 4:27. https://vimeo.com/275965279.

Correa, Pablo. *Restoration and Reconciliation*. Vimeo. November 11, 2017. Video, 3:01. https://vimeo.com/242383672.

Fannie Lou Hamer: Courage and Faith. Produced by Linda L. Coles. Aired February 20, 2006. Mississippi Public Broadcasting.

Hasan, Kazi Mehedi. "Prof Dave Tell Talks about Emmett Till Memorial Marker Repeatedly Vandalized." YouTube. November 20, 2019. Video, 1:25. https://youtu.be/FoDiSPgxWho.

Mamie Till Mobley. "Emmett Till Civil Rights Marker at Bryant's Store in Money Mississippi." YouTube. September 13, 2012. Video, 1:49. https://youtu.be/wA5oeXLVS54.

Mississippi Delta National Heritage Area. "Civil Rights Sites of the Mississippi Delta and the National Parks Service's African American Civil Rights Grant Program." October 27, 2021. Webinar, 1:25:40. https://www.msdeltaheritage.com/civil-rights.

Mississippi Today. "Fannie Lou Hamer Memorial Garden." YouTube. October 5, 2017. Video, 3:18. https://www.youtube.com/watch?v=dCshm1-pZVo.

The Murder of Emmett Till. DVD. Directed and produced by Stanley Nelson. Alexandria, VA: PBS Home Video, 2004.

Quezada, Angela. "Amzie Moore Home Ribbon Cutting." YouTube. March 28, 2016. Video, 2:56. https://youtu.be/ZUqWBOO2UM4.

The Untold Story of Emmett Till. DVD. Directed by Keith A. Beauchamp. New York: Thinkfilm, 2005.

Till. DVD. Directed by Chinonye Chukwu. Universal City: Orion, 2022.

WGBH-TV. "Charles McLaurin: 'The Foot Soldier.'" *American Experience*. N.d. Accessed March 17, 2022. Video, 7:48. https://www.pbs.org/wgbh/americanexperience/features/freedomsummer-at50-charles-mclaurin-foot-soldier/.

"Preserving Emmett Till's Memory." C-SPAN. September 2, 2021. Video, 1:21:22. https://www.c-span.org/video/?514412-1/work-preserving-emmett-tills-memory.

Performances

Sims, Helen. Oral performance. Belzoni, Mississippi. July 18, 2016.

Author Interviews

Blount, Katie. Zoom interview by Roger Davis Gatchet and Stephen A. King. August 26, 2020.

Cotton, Glen. Telephone interview by Roger Davis Gatchet and Stephen A. King. August 28, 2020.

Dittmer, John. Telephone interview by Roger Davis Gatchet and Stephen A. King. June 16, 2021.

Herts, Rolando. Zoom interview by Roger Davis Gatchet and Stephen A. King. November 12, 2021.

Jones, Emily. Interview by Stephen A. King. Cleveland, Mississippi. August 5, 2019.

Junior, Pamela. Interview by Roger Davis Gatchet and Stephen A. King. Jackson, Mississippi. May 24, 2019.

McLaurin, Charles. Telephone interview by Roger Davis Gatchet and Stephen A. King. December 4, 2021.

Morgan, Danielle. Zoom interview by Roger Davis Gatchet and Stephen A. King. November 12, 2020.

Thigpen, Rickey. Interview by Roger Davis Gatchet and Stephen A. King. Jackson, Mississippi. May 21, 2019.

Thomas, Johnny B. Interview by Roger Davis Gatchet and Stephen A. King. Glendora, Mississippi. May 23, 2019.

Watkins, Hezekiah. Zoom interview by Roger Davis Gatchet and Stephen A. King. January 12, 2021.

Weems, Patrick. Interview by Roger Davis Gatchet and Stephen A. King. Oxford, Mississippi. May 23, 2019.

INDEX

African-American Heritage Guide, 50
Alluvial Collective. *See* William Winter Institute for Racial Reconciliation
Amzie Moore House Museum and Interpretive Center. *See* Moore House
authenticity, 22, 32–33, 60, 65, 67, 78, 85, 97, 119, 120, 130, 131–34, 165, 191

Balance Agriculture with Industry program (BAWI), 44–47, 120
Barbour, Haley, 167, 168, 169, 170, 193, 236n27
Beckwith, Byron De La, 39, 41, 118, 130, 131–32, 135, 148
Belzoni, MS, 66, 148, 160
Ben Roy's Service Station, 4–5, 199
Black, Patti Carr, 48–49
Black Bayou, 94, 109–10
Black Panther Party, 151, 179–80
Black Power, 10, 43, 151–53, 156, 160, 179–81
Black United Front, 180
Blackmon, Barbara, 63, 195, 216–17n20
Blackmon, Edward, Jr., 63, 216–17n20
blues tourism, 18–19, 20, 22, 27, 53, 54, 97–98, 112, 121–22, 139
Broad Street Park, 43
Brown v. Board of Education of Topeka, 34, 43–44, 178
Bryant, C. C., 40, 121, 146, 153
Bryant, Carolyn, 4, 14, 93, 96, 223n54
Bryant, Roy, 4, 5, 93, 94, 96, 100, 101, 104, 106, 149, 224n63
Bryant's Grocery and Meat Market, 3–4, 5, 6, 54, 55, 93, 94, 96, 97, 100, 110, 199–200, 201
Burke, Kenneth, 98–99

Canton, MS, 58, 61, 62, 64, 144
Canton Freedom House Civil Rights Museum, 61–65, 85, 121, 158, 216–17n20
Carmichael, Stokely, 41, 43, 151, 156, 180–81
Center for the Study of Southern Culture, 28, 49, 214n115
Chaney, James, 42, 51, 171
Citizens' Council, 35, 37, 39, 42, 118, 127, 148, 167, 236n27
Civil Rights Commemoration Initiative, 49
civil rights movement, 3–4, 9, 10, 17, 20, 33, 35–36, 39, 41, 44, 69, 73, 83, 87, 99, 101, 109, 123–25, 127–29, 134, 146, 149, 151–52, 179, 193–95
Civil Rights Research and Documentation Project, 49–50
civil rights tourism, 8–9, 16, 102, 130, 139–40, 183, 186; in Alabama, 11, 13, 14, 183; birthplace myth, 9, 33, 99, 109, 209n4; COVID-19 pandemic impact on, 185; and economic development goals, 18–19, 122, 140, 184–86, 190; focus on past and present, 10, 18, 69, 84, 86, 104–5, 138, 150, 155–58, 186–87, 189, 192; grassroots promotion of, 59, 61–86, 112; history of, 10–14, 44–55; and image management goals, 19–20, 184; Martin Luther King Jr. holiday, 11, 12, 184; MDAH role in, 48–49, 139–40; relationship with blues tourism, 25; resistance towards, 183; rhetoric of progress, 189; and social justice goals, 20–22, 71, 103, 104, 111–12, 114, 138, 186–99, 200; truth telling, 9, 19–20, 21, 65, 147, 171, 181

civil rights tourists, 14, 22–23, 31, 55, 187, 200
Clarksdale, MS, 25, 52, 55, 153
Cleveland, MS, 28, 35, 36, 37, 117, 121–22, 124, 125–26, 127
collective memory. *See* public memory
Confederate monuments, 8–9, 11, 15, 32, 53, 60, 89, 107, 198
Congress of Racial Equality (CORE), 40, 42, 61–62, 65, 124, 146, 152
Cotton, Glen, 58, 61–65, 85–86
Council of Federated Organizations (COFO), 40, 42, 57, 124, 152–53, 178, 193
Courts, Gus, 66, 217n27
Critical Race Theory, 194–95

dark tourism, 105
Deacons for Defense and Justice, 152

Emmett Till Historic Intrepid Center (ETHIC), 20, 107–12, 191, 200
Emmett Till Interpretive Center (ETIC), 21, 89, 91, 102–7, 111, 112–13, 189–91, 197, 200, 201, 226–27n126
Emmett Till Memorial Commission (ETMC), 21, 88, 91, 102–3, 104, 108, 112–13, 114, 139, 190, 221n12
Emmett Till Memorial Highway, 88
Emmett Till Memorial Park and Interpretive Nature Trail, 109
Emmett Till Memory Project, 91–92, 197
Equal Justice Initiative, 150, 161
Evers, Charles, 34
Evers, Medgar, 50, 51, 134–38, 146, 147, 192; assassination, 39, 41, 118, 130, 131–33, 148, 171; birth of, 37; early career, 34, 35, 38; military service, 37–38; as NAACP field secretary, 38–39
Evers, Myrlie, 37, 38, 39, 118, 119–20, 121, 130, 132, 133, 134, 135–38
Evers House, 120; attacks on, 131; authenticity, 130, 131–34; design, 132; focus on Evers's assassination, 131–33; gendered representation of exhibit, 134–37; as hero house, 121, 137–38; as historic site, 118–19, 131, 135; ownership of, 131, 134; restoration, 51, 130
experiential tourism, 97, 101–2

Fannie Lou Hamer Civil Rights Museum (Belzoni). *See* Sims Museum
Fannie Lou Hamer Memorial Garden (Ruleville). *See* Memorial Garden
Fannie Lou Hamer Museum (Ruleville). *See* Hamer Museum
Fannie Lou Hamer's America (project), 196–97
Ferris, William R., 49
fieldwork, 23–29, 92, 141, 213n104, 231–32n10, 234–35n12
Freedom Farm Cooperative, 73, 74, 78, 83, 154
Freedom Rides, 40–41, 140

Ghosts of Mississippi (film), 130–31, 133
Glendora, MS, 20, 92, 107–9, 110, 112, 113, 200
Glisson, Susan, 103
Goodman, Andrew, 42, 51, 171
Greenwood, MS, 19, 24, 53, 61, 94, 97–99, 112, 156–57, 168
Greenwood Convention and Visitors Bureau (CVB), 90, 97–102, 112

Hamer, Fannie Lou, 36, 42–43, 59, 69, 70, 71–73, 74, 76, 77–84, 146, 147, 150, 154, 155, 159, 191, 196–97
Hamer Museum, 71, 73–78, 80, 84, 85, 184–85, 218–19n67
Hammons, Allan, 89
Hattiesburg, MS, 50, 52, 53, 168
Head Start, 37, 52, 73, 128, 154, 155, 179, 193
Henry, Aaron, 36, 38, 52, 55, 146, 153, 154–55, 172, 193
historic houses, 16, 119, 120–21, 123, 138
history, "Great Man" version of, 10, 12, 17–18, 121, 154–55
Howard, T. R. M., 35, 36, 38, 151, 153

infrapolitics, 70

Jackson, MS, 3, 6, 8, 22–23, 26, 29, 31, 38–39, 40–42, 50–51, 53, 130, 131, 141, 147, 148, 152, 158, 160–61, 164, 165, 168–69, 180, 184, 194, 231n3
Jaynes-Diming, Jessie, 88, 103, 114
Jet (magazine), 95, 106, 111, 149

Jim Crow, 20, 34, 128–29, 173
Johnson, Robert, 25, 97–98
Jordan, David L., 24, 168, 169
Jordan, Hattie Robinson, 73–74, 76, 79, 80
Juneteenth, 201
Junior, Pamela, 23, 163, 191, 192

Kennedy, Robert F., 128
King, Martin Luther, Jr., 11, 12, 18, 19, 43, 73, 76, 128, 159, 160, 170, 192, 194, 195
Ku Klux Klan, 40–41, 42, 117, 118, 150, 175, 176, 233n28, 236n27

lateral deviance, 151, 177, 178, 179, 180
League of the South, 88, 221n12
Lee, Rev. George W., 66, 69, 70, 148, 153, 187, 217n27
Little, Jerome G., 102, 139
Living Blues (magazine), 28, 97–99
Lost Cause movement, 11, 15, 48, 107
lynching, 8, 16, 19, 27, 38, 61, 68, 69, 91, 96, 100, 105, 143, 150, 161, 164, 170, 173, 175

Magnolia Mutual Life Insurance Company, 38
Malcolm X, 43, 151, 179
Marks, MS, 159
McComb, MS, 40, 50, 53, 121, 128, 153
McLaurin, Charles, 36, 72, 76, 78–80, 84, 85–86, 126
MCRM. *See* Mississippi Civil Rights Museum
Medgar and Myrlie Evers Home National Monument. *See* Evers House
Memorial Garden, 60, 71, 73, 78–84, 198, 218–19n67
Meredith, James, 41, 43, 49, 73, 89, 155, 160, 234n48
metonymy, 123–26, 128, 129, 137–38, 150, 173
MFT. *See* Mississippi Freedom Trail
Milam, J. W., 4, 5, 94, 96, 100, 101, 104, 106, 109, 149, 224n63
Milam Plantation, 4, 94, 114
Mississippi, 5–6, 8–10, 14, 15, 20, 29, 31–32, 44–48, 120–21, 184–85, 188, 193–95, 198
Mississippi Advertising Commission, 44–47, 120

Mississippi Blues Trail, 41, 53, 139, 140, 143, 186, 212n71
Mississippi Civil Rights Historical Sites grant, 5, 122
Mississippi Civil Rights Movement. *See* Mississippi Movement
Mississippi Civil Rights Museum (MCRM), 6, 16–17, 55, 61, 182, 206n59, 234–35n12; attendance, 19, 23, 164, 184; Black resistance theme, 174–76; COVID-19 pandemic impact on, 184–85; critical reception, 32, 164, 183–84; economic impact of, 169, 184, 185; educational function of, 196; emphasis on vertical deviance, 177–81; history of, 55, 167–69; layout, 170–71; location, 164, 165, 167–68, 170; opening, 163; and social justice, 186, 188, 189, 191–92, 199; and truth telling, 9, 19–20, 173, 181; white violence theme, 61, 171–76, 181
Mississippi Delta National Heritage Area (MDNHA), 53–54, 57, 157, 189, 197
Mississippi Department of Archives and History (MDAH), 5, 48–49, 57, 63, 108, 110, 122, 140, 167, 168, 198, 206n59
Mississippi Development Authority (MDA), 20, 22, 55, 79, 140, 169
Mississippi Freedom Democratic Party (MFDP), 37, 42–43, 52, 72, 155
Mississippi Freedom Trail (MFT), 14, 20, 32, 41, 54–55, 61, 139–41, 161, 198, 231n3; "Aaron Henry" marker, 31, 52, 153, 154–55, 160; agitating and organizing theme, 150–55; American Dream theme, 153–54; "Amzie Moore" marker, 37, 118, 122, 125–26, 147, 155, 160; "'Black Power' Speech" marker, 43, 61, 151, 156; "Bombings in Jewish Community" marker, 160; "Bryant's Grocery" marker, 5, 6, 33, 88–89, 139, 141, 148–49, 199, 200, 201; "C. C. Bryant" marker, 153; "Capitol Rally" marker, 61, 151, 160; "COFO Central Offices" marker, 40, 193; and contrast with MCRM, 164–65, 176; critical reception, 140, 186; depictions of violence, 146–50; "Fannie Lou Hamer" marker, 60, 80, 81, 83, 148, 150, 154; "Greyhound Bus Station" marker,

160–61; "Jackson Municipal Library Sit-In" marker, 40; "Jackson State Tragedy" marker, 148, 233n26; "Madison County Movement" marker, 144, 233n27; marker design, 143–46, 155, 157; marker locations, 158–59; "Marks Mule Train and Poor People's Campaign" marker, 159; "Medgar Evers Home" marker, 131, 135, 148, 155; "Parchman Penitentiary" marker, 212n71, 212–13n92; preoccupation with past, 155–58; political participation theme, 154–55; "The Reverend George Lee" marker, 66, 145, 148, 217n27; sacred and secular spaces, 158–61; "T. R. M. Howard" marker, 35, 151, 153; tokenist biography, 154; "Tougaloo College" marker, 147, 150; "University of Mississippi" marker, 155; "William Chapel" marker, 145, 147, 156, 159–60; "Woolworth's Sit-In" marker, 148
Mississippi Heritage Consortium. *See* Sims Museum
Mississippi Movement, 10, 17, 48–49, 57, 124–25, 127–29, 152; birthplace myth, 33, 209n4; during 1960–1968, 39–44; forms of agitation, 146, 151, 160–61, 177–81; Freedom Summer, 42; Freedom Vote, 42; impact of, 43; influence on Amzie Moore Sr., 35–37; influence on Medgar and Myrlie Evers, 37–39; influence on national civil rights movement, 127–29; Mississippi Freedom Democratic Party, 42–43; premovement period, 33–35
Mississippi State Sovereignty Commission, 42, 43, 150, 212–13n92
MMH. *See* Museum of Mississippi History
Money, MS, 3–4, 6, 33, 93, 96, 139, 199–201
Money Road, 90, 97–98, 100, 199
Moore, Amzie, II, 122
Moore, Amzie, Sr., 9, 30, 35, 52, 61, 76, 146, 187; birth of, 35; Citizens' Council, 37, 127; and Head Start, 37; impact of Great Depression on, 35; military experience (WWII), 36; Mississippi Department of Archives and History historical marker (green series), 125; and Mississippi Freedom Democratic Party, 37; Mississippi Freedom Trail marker, 37, 122, 125–26; as NAACP chapter president, 36; Pan-Am Change and Service station, 36, 127; postal employee, 35; and Regional Council of Negro Leadership, 36; significance to the Mississippi Movement, 35–36; and Student Nonviolent Coordinating Committee, 37, 117
Moore House, 24, 147, 160, 198; architecture, 122; and Cleveland, MS tourism, 121–22; as "command center," 117, 124, 137; exhibit space, 119, 123–25; as hero house, 121; layout, 123; location of, 117; metonymy, 119, 123, 129; mission statement, 117; restoration of, 122; as "safe house," 117, 122, 124, 137; themes, 119, 125–28, 137
Moses, Robert (Bob), 36–37, 40
Mound Bayou, MS, 38, 153, 178
Museum of Mississippi History (MMH), 164, 170

National Association for the Advancement of Colored People (NAACP), 25, 35, 40, 95, 127–28, 151–52
National Civil Rights Museum (NCRM), 13, 166

official culture, 59–61, 66, 183, 196
official tourism, 32, 47, 60–61
Ole Miss. *See* University of Mississippi
out-law discourse, 60

Parchman Farm (prison), 24, 41
Parker, Wheeler, Jr., 92–93, 139
Parks, Rosa, 12, 95, 170
Philadelphia Coalition, 51, 103, 188, 215n127
Po' Monkey's, 25, 70
public memory: and African American identity, 14–17; definition of, 6–8; and historical markers, 142–43, 157, 161; and history dialectic, 7; and museums, 165–67; relationship between history and criticism, 6; residual memory, 89; scholarship of civil rights, 17–18; as textual fragments, 7

racial reconciliation. *See* civil rights tourism: and social justice goals

Reeves, Tate, 194, 195
Regional Council of Negro Leadership (RCNL), 35, 36, 127
Repaying Our Ancestors Respectfully (ROAR), 79
Republic of New Afrika (RNA), 152, 180
Ruleville, MS, 73, 78–80, 159

Schwerner, Michael, 42, 51, 171
Shield, Rudy, 180
Sims, Helen, 24, 52, 59, 60, 66, 78, 85, 192; as Lula, the Old Storyteller, 68–71
Sims Museum, 59, 60, 66–71, 85
Singleton, Helen, 41
Smith Robertson Museum and Cultural Center, 26, 35, 191–92, 196
social activism. *See* civil rights tourism: and social justice goals
Southern Christian Leadership Conference (SCLC), 71, 151, 159
"Struggle for Equal Rights, The" (exhibit), 49, 167
Student Nonviolent Coordinating Committee (SNCC), 17, 37, 40, 71, 151–52, 159
Sumner, MS, 24–25, 102–3, 107, 113
Sumner courthouse, 103–4, 107, 113
Sunflower County Film Academy, 197

Tallahatchie River, 88, 94, 100, 115, 149, 159, 199
Thomas, Johnny B., 107, 108, 109, 112–14, 186
Thompson, Bennie G., 85, 108, 163
Till, Emmett: birthplace of, 92; Congressional Gold Medal, 91; criticism of Till tourism, 5; early childhood, 92; funeral of, 95; influence on civil rights movement, 3, 10, 33, 95, 99, 101; interaction with Carolyn Bryant, 14, 93, 200; lynching, 87, 94; in popular culture, 90–91; "River Site" historical marker, 88, 221n11; and Robert Johnson, 19; scholarship of, 91; Till Trial, 5, 94–95; trip to Money, MS, 93, 223n42; "wolf whistle," 14, 93, 223n52
Till, Louis, 92
Till Trail of Terror Tour, 107

Till-Mobley, Mamie, 91, 92, 95, 223n52
Tougaloo College, 40, 118, 119, 130, 140, 147, 167–68
Tribble, Ray, 5
Tutwiler, MS, 24

vernacular tourism, 9, 58–61, 84–86, 192
vertical deviance, 151, 177–79, 181

University of Mississippi, 38, 41, 49–50, 88, 89, 136, 155, 188
US Civil Rights Trail, 32, 33, 61, 140, 187

Wallace, George, 13
Watkins, Hezekiah, 41, 171
Watson, Minnie White, 26, 130, 131, 133
Weems, Patrick, 89, 96, 102, 103, 104, 105, 107, 110, 113–14, 190, 221n12
"Wharlest Jackson Sr." marker, 233n28
Whitten, John W., Jr., 25, 95
Whitten, John W., III, 25, 87–88
William Chapel Missionary Baptist Church, 71–72, 77, 145, 147, 156, 159–60
William Winter Institute for Racial Reconciliation (Alluvial Collective), 50, 103, 188
Womanpower Unlimited, 41
Woolworth's, 8, 148
Wright, Moses "Mose," 92–93, 95
Wright, Simeon, 93

ABOUT THE AUTHORS

Photo by P. Renee Foster

STEPHEN A. KING is chairperson and professor of communication at St. Edward's University in Austin, Texas. King has written extensively about rhetoric, public memory, and cultural tourism. He is the author of *Reggae, Rastafari, and the Rhetoric of Social Control* and *I'm Feeling the Blues Right Now: Blues Tourism and the Mississippi Delta*.

Photo by Amanda Davis Gatchet

ROGER DAVIS GATCHET is an associate professor in the Department of Communication and Media at West Chester University of Pennsylvania. His research focuses on the rhetoric of public memory and popular culture, as well as oral history.

www.ingramcontent.com/pod-product-compliance
Lightning Source LLC
Chambersburg PA
CBHW030611230426
43661CB00053B/1935